D1566304

MEDIEVAL ENGLISH
RELIGIOUS AND ETHICAL LITERATURE

George Russell

MEDIEVAL ENGLISH RELIGIOUS AND ETHICAL LITERATURE

Essays in Honour of
G. H. Russell

Edited by
Gregory Kratzmann and James Simpson

D .S .BREWER

© Contributors 1986

First published 1986 by D. S. Brewer
240 Hills Road, Cambridge
an imprint of Boydell & Brewer Ltd
PO Box 9, Woodbridge, Suffolk IP12 3DF
and Wolfeboro, New Hampshire, USA

ISBN 0 85991 220 5

British Library Cataloguing in Publication Data

Medieval English religious and ethical literature:
  essays in honour of G. H. Russell.
  1. English literature — Middle English, 1100–1500
  — History and criticism
  I. Kratzmann, Gregory   II. Simpson, James
  III. Russell, G. H.
  820.9001   PR255
ISBN 0-85991-220-5

Library of Congress Cataloging in Publication Data

Medieval English religious and ethical literature.
  Includes index.
  1. English literature — Middle English, 1100–1500
—
History and criticism.   2. Christian literature, English
— History and criticism.   3. Theology in litera-
ture.   4. Ethics in literature.   5. Russell, G. Hugh
(George Hugh), 1927–   .   I. Russell, G. Hugh
(George Hugh), 1927–   .   II. Kratzmann, G. C.,
1949–   .   III. Simpson, James, 1954–   .
PR251.M34   1986   820'.9'382   86-6837
ISBN 0-85991-220-5

Printed in Great Britain by
St Edmundsbury Press, Bury St Edmunds, Suffolk

CONTENTS

Editors' note

The publication of this book has been made possible by subsidies granted by the Publications Committee of La Trobe University, the Office of Research and Graduate Studies at The University of Melbourne, and the English Department of The University of Melbourne. This assistance is gratefully acknowledged.

GEORGE RUSSELL AS A TOPIC IN HIS OWN RIGHT

Vincent Buckley

I first met George Russell in Sydney, in the early Fifties. He must have been not long returned from Cambridge, to which I was yet to go. I had not heard of him before, and found him an intriguing presence. We were to some extent in the same scholarly field and, as his own recollections were later to define it, his background was in some ways similar to my own: Catholic, rural, colonial, Irish-Antipodean, provincial, poor and highminded. I did not learn any of this at the time, because he has always been a man of great reticence which, combined with an extraordinary modesty, forbids him to talk about himself if he can talk about anything else. Thus, for the time, it was other features of his personality which struck me. I did not think of him as a New Zealander; he seemed distinctively a Sydney man, member of a group of Sydney Catholic intellectuals which flourished at various stages of the Fifties and early Sixties, and which included the poet and editor James McAuley, the sculptor Tom Bass, the composer and broadcasting executive Richard Connolly, the scholar Henry Strakosch, and the historian Patrick O'Farrell.

Even in this company, George Russell had a shine about him. It came, I think, not from his seeming an achiever (I, for one, was not sure just what he 'did', as compared with McAuley or Bass), but rather from a stance, a deliberateness of exchange, a readiness for laughter, an attentiveness to whatever discourse should arise, and a basic friendliness. It was a physical quality as much as anything. He and his friends struck me as both scholarly and spiritually confident, in a way which was dashing but not disreputable. He was at that time a Lecturer in English at the University of Sydney, to which he was later to return as Reader and where he would, later still, accept a chair. He had not begun there, but Sydney was and is a great magnet for New Zealanders. On the other hand, George Russell's movement from and towards had been rather unusual.

He did his primary schooling at 'a small Catholic convent school at Wellington, a two-teacher school, with two formidable but in their way intensely dedicated nuns running the whole school.' From there, he went to the College of the Marist Fathers in Wellington, but after 1½ years, when his parents moved to a farm at Palmerston North, 100 miles north of Wellington, they found that the Marists could not board him, so he did the rest of his secondary schooling at Palmerston North Boys High School, 'a very good school indeed', where he took his Matriculation and post-Matriculation years.

At Victoria University College, Wellington, 'then a small university college, part of the federal system of New Zealand', he undertook an Arts Honours Course:

Again I was fortunate; it was not a distinguished place, but good, very Scottish in origin and nature. It had a good intellectual tradition. I doubled English with Classics. In English studies I was taught by Ian Gordon, who was a protege of Grierson, one of Grierson's students from Edinburgh; he was by no means a reject, he was a man who nowadays would hold down a job in England, or indeed anywhere, with ease. He was a very, very good teacher of literature. The course was a most orthodox course of literary history, but Gordon's training with Grierson enabled him to inject into it a reasonably rigorous critical component, so that we read widely across the whole range of English literature. We were also encouraged to read critically, and to read for ourselves, so that I ended up with a pretty fair coverage of literature from all periods. Old English of course was compulsory, but we came up to Yeats and Eliot, who were difficult, new, very much the voice of contemporary European culture. I was lucky enough to get a post-graduate travelling scholarship.

Many other people had done the same kind of thing, so that there had been set up from New Zealand an orthodox *cursus honorum* whereby one took out an undergraduate degree in New Zealand, and went on to Oxford, where one took on the Schools, the undergraduate examin-ation, over again. This was held, I assume, to be a kind of correction, a kind of deepening, a kind (I suspect) of what some might call Pommising. Several people who had done this had remained to be pretty influential in Oxford. It was for many the end of a journey begun in New Zealand.

Well, whether perversely or not, I didn't like this. I never liked being in a herd; and in the course of my studies I had come across the work of Basil Willey, whose work, though novel to me, appealed very much: the direction of his thought, the linking of literature with the thought of the time. It was fresher, newer, than anything I had done before. I had no contacts so I did the sort of thing that I suppose a country lad does – I sat down and wrote a letter to Basil Willey ...

The letter was successful, and Russell was at Cambridge, at Willey's college, Pembroke, from 1946 to 1948. There he wrote his still unpublished dissertation, *The Prose of the English Recusants 1558–1603*, which was supervised first by Cecil Bald of Clare and later by Enid Welsford of Newnham, and examined by Muriel Bradbrook and C.J.Sisson, 'father of Rosemary Anne Sisson, who was a contemporary of mine at Cambridge'. But the chief influences on him were two others, Basil Willey who had helped his arrival, and David Knowles. He was being pulled irresistibly away from sterile index-scholarship and sterile evaluation towards medieval civilisation, a concern with large intellectual constructs and broad movements in thought, and the value of meditation as work, as process, and as a means to understanding:

So my beginnings go back to Basil Willey. It was no doubt under the influence of his way of thinking that I sought out the lectures I did. I was

2

not very attracted to the prevailing Leavisitism, for, although I am not anti-Leavisite in any partisan sense (I think a great deal of what Leavis and his collaborators have done, and have always been attracted by their insistence on values), I was much more historically minded. I stumbled across some lectures advertised in the History school, by Dom David Knowles.

Knowles was a Benedictine monk, who was at the same time the Professor of Medieval History. I did two courses with him, in successive years. One was on St Francis and his times, and the second was on St Dunstan and his times, that is, it was a study in the history and polity of the state and church in late Anglo-Saxon England. It wasn't really the courses that were of prime importance to me, so much as what I absorbed from him (osmotically, of course, because he wasn't a proselytiser) on the nature of the Benedictine ideal and Benedictine life. I think that this is something which (no doubt in a vastly diminished form) has stayed with me ever since. When I think back to those days – Catholic Action, 'engagement of Catholics in the world', making sense of one's vocation in eschatological terms, the Benedictine notion of work and prayer (work which is a kind of prayer), and a working out of one's destiny in the world in terms of the humdrum, the everyday, the fortunate and unfortunate aspects of work … all of this made a deep impression, and work has ever since been a very sacred thing to me: never just a workaday thing. So that I never really separate work from relaxation, I never really close up at the end of the week, or even of a day; it's all really one continuum for me, it's human activity in some sense, sanctified and hence open to be profaned. And one's failures, of course, are the failures of profanation. That's the kind of legacy Knowles gave to me.

After Cambridge, he 'had a choice of whether to stay in England or go back to the Antipodes'. He took a lectureship at Kings College at the University of London for a year, then chose to go home to Wellington where, after a further year, he took an appointment at the University of Sydney in 1950. There he stayed for three years, first as Lecturer then as Senior Lecturer, before becoming the Darnell Professor of English Literature and Language at the University of Queensland in Brisbane, where he remained until 1957. Then he returned to Sydney as Reader.

Such mobility within a regional university system has not been unusual in modern times (indeed, I was advised thirty years ago never to stay more than three years in the one place); yet it is certainly noteworthy, and I have asked George Russell about it. The answer seems to be that it was a university system in formation, with certain distinctive or crucial features still to be established, and with special strains in each place which told against the life of a scholar-teacher, even one willing to work very hard at pioneering a school or a faculty. Sometimes the strains came from old habit, sometimes from new crassness. The newcomer walked straight into maladministration, or vendetta, or entrenched self-interest, and there was very little he could do about any of them. Sydney, for example, in this early period, was 'a very tough training ground, ruinously tough in some ways, though it did give me many of the techniques which I have followed ever since. It taught me how to lecture, for example; we used to lecture to vast crowds of students, often unruly, and you had to learn to engage them.'

But he found a 'set of most unpleasant personal conflicts among certain members of the English Department', which provided one pressure for him to move to Queensland. His stint there was 'quite ill-starred, and obviously premature'. It was a constant struggle totally to rebuild the university; many of the staff were 'poorly qualified, most with tenured jobs, and some of them within my own department.' There he taught medieval courses and general ones, and gave lecture courses in the sixteenth and seventeenth centuries; he also offered a first year course in drama. He had some very fine students including David Malouf, Judith Green, James and Marie Tulip, John Hardy and Elaine Barry; but he had to leave, otherwise he would have ended up as a fulltime remedial administrator just as he was getting into his stride as a scholar. One may guess that he was also too innocent and inexperienced to survive a very long ordeal by administration.

He returned to Sydney, to a Readership from 1957 to 1961, and the McCaughey Professorship of Early English Language and Literature until the end of 1965. At that point he was invited to Canberra; there, although he took a large share in the planning not merely to reform the university administration but also to set up the Academy of the Humanities, the earlier trials recurrred in a new form. His comments take him from Sydney to Canberra (1966–1971), and from there to Melbourne, where he accepted an invitation to submit his name for the Chair of English Language and Literature; he held this chair from 1971 to 1983.

I returned to Sydney and did most of my senior, responsible, exacting academic work there. Then came the disastrous confrontation between the incumbents of the Challis Chair of English Literature and the Chair of Australian Literature. It was a nasty situation from the beginning, but I was abroad in 1964, and when I came back in late 1964, I found that it had become so horrendous that, despite what I tried to do to heal wounds and bring parties together, the terrible virus of divisiveness had entered the bloodstream of the Department. In the midst of all this, I had an approach from Canberra, from the A.N.U., who had a vacant chair. I said Yes, and went there with high hopes.

I left Sydney with great relief, but Canberra was in many ways a great disappointment to me. The Institute didn't work very well; it was a very closed academic society, and I felt there were many things about it that I could never square with my principles.

But I worked hard there, I threw myself into it, and did far more administrative work in the faculty, the deparment, and the University than I've done anywhere else. It absorbed a great deal of time; the new

4

Vice-Chancellor, Sir John Crawford, asked me if I would participate in some forums which he had in mind. I was in fact brought into a think-tank which also included P.H.Partridge, (C.A.) Gibb, and (Noel) Dunbar. I didn't finally think I was getting far, though I stuck with it.

There was a distinct shortage of good students, too. The Canberra students in those days were not good. So, when the Melbourne offer came through, I knew what was in prospect, but I thought I would come down to face what I knew was the going situation.

You may ask, Why did you come? Well, I thought, granted the Sydney experience, things could improve. As you know, I was wrong in that. But I've never regretted my coming to Melbourne, for the real reason for my deciding to take the risk was that I had a sense of the essential fertility of the department, yourself, Peter (Steele), Chris (Wallace-Crabbe) and Evan (Jones) were there, and I thought the Department has those people who do those sorts of things, this must be a department of potential. By and large, I thought it worked out moderately well.

I'm pretty much of a loner, however, and apart from a few pretty close and dear personal friends, I never found myself able to engage in the broader society of Melbourne. I saw myself to be something of an outsider there, someone who was tolerated rather than incorporated; I wouldn't say I was ever unhappy there, though I was often exhausted, or disappointed, or exasperated. But this is a story I shall have to tell some day in my own terms.

It is in those terms that a working life, combined with a certain movement (generally southward) and repeated disappointment, *can* be understood, even 'explained'. In the interviews he did with or for me, George Russell did not mention his research work, for which of course he is famous among medievalists and among all who are aware of the 'Matter of Piers'. He spoke, rather, about his general working conditions, which were disorienting. The reason seems to be that he was invited to each successive appointment for an ostensible reason (that he was a distinguished scholar) but also with an undeclared one (that he was an experienced administrator and consultant, deeply trustworthy, hard-working and wise); the situation into which he came was in each case either defective or troubled; he was used as a troubleshooter and elected to high administrative or consultative office; his teaching thus became fragmented if plentiful, and his opportunities for research shrank slightly year by year.

If this is so, (and it rings all too plausibly to me) it is a grave reflection on the Australian university system, with its tendency to accumulate routine duties while deconcentrating intellectual activity. The only way for a distinguished scholar to break through this wire fence of requirements and taboos is to refuse to do anything but his 'own' work; but, then, he would probably be too ruthless and uncaring to be a scholar of much distinction for very long. George Russell, in any case, would never do that; the qualities

5

which helped him to give strength to so many colleagues in so many difficulties proved a broken crutch to him in his own need.

Nevertheless, his reputation throughout Australia as an exemplary colleague, scholar and executive continued to grow, even though his scholarly work is of a deeply specialised kind, and he has never had an executive post of wide power. People could see his force in certain qualities of demeanour, indeed of presence, coming from the values which he espouses. He worked, too, at his central scholarly task, an edition of the C-Text of *Piers Plowman*, producing as by-products a number of essays on monasticism (and a book, still being written, on what is shown about the creative process by Langland's reworkings of his own text). At the height of this activity, he was more than once Head or elected Chairman of our department; and his health began to decline.

Even in bad health, he was by all accounts a teacher of unusual authority flowing from unusual control of a broad array of facts and issues. If in one place he tells how Sydney University, with its mass lecture classes, taught him how to lecture, in other places he ascribes to Dom David Knowles his inwardness with teaching methods, and speaks of his preference for small classes.

Knowles, he says, was as able to engage the most intelligent student in a seminar as to elicit the strengths of weaker students. Of these there were quite a number in the postwar years. It was an untypical Cambridge, with many older students almost all of whom had seen war service, and who had gained a high sense of authority from their horrendous experiences. 'It was not at all the world of *Brideshead Revisited*, it was utterly different'. In this atmosphere, Knowles taught him how to listen, to attend: a Benedictine virtue:

> (Teaching is) really the attempt to get the students to face a system of values as these are expressed in, or as these *are* the creative writing of any particular period or time.
> The important thing is not so much *what* you teach as *how* you teach. It doesn't seem to matter *what* they are engaged with, it is *how* they are engaging themselves. I made a choice for medieval teaching ...

And as a 'medieval' teacher he elicited a strong response from many generations of students; the more closely they were his personal pupils, the less they saw him as he saw himself, as problematic or unsuccessful or unconvincing. For them, it is the sense of presence that is so important. Stephanie Trigg became his student in her first year and several years later did her doctorate with him; from the most remote to the closest form of attention, she found him greatly impressive – almost an institution in himself, as her prose suggests:

> My first encounter with George's teaching was as an over-enthusiastic first-year student attending a series of optional lectures on medieval

literature. From the top of the lecture theatre, it seemed as if the lecturer was standing in a kind of pit. The theatre was cold and dark, and as I sat with about thirty other students, I felt I had finally arrived at University. For about six or more weeks, George read and translated part of Chaucer's *Nun's Priest's Tale*. I remember being vaguely aware that there was something slightly incongruous or indeed, mysterious, about this tall, grave man, dressed soberly in a dark suit and tie, reading with great dignity, patience and humour, what seemed a very strange story about a couple of garrulous chickens and a thieving fox.

Through my years as an undergraduate, I learned to slow down my habit of rapid reading, although I can distinctly remember chafing at the bit at the slowness of George's reading. Wanting to make Middle English easy for myself, I also resented being told that I couldn't rely on its apparent semantic similarities with Modern English, and that I had to look up the most 'obvious' words in my glossary. One of George's most frequent ways of introducing new material to his students was to say, 'As you know ...', and then to mention a medieval philosopher or make some linguistic point of which we had no idea. At first we found this flattering and then it had the effect of suggesting how little we did know and quite often the presumably desired effect of sending us off to the dictionaries or commentaries to make sure that the next time we *did* know. It raised our self-image and the standards we set ourselves: as did his way of addressing a lecture theatre filled with raggedy students with 'Ladies and Gentlemen'. We were never sure if George was being ironic or not.

Through my friendship with his daughter Margaret, I began to see George not only as a teacher but also as a friend, and as a terrific host and raconteur. He was no longer drinking any wine when I knew him, but others have corroborated my stories of being invited up to Docker Street for dinner and being treated to a generous flow of delicious and irresistible wines. George has a reputation for the blackness of his sense of humour, and it's true that I've heard some savagely funny stories from him, but he is also the man who is deeply engaged with birds and animals and who has a penchant for pigs and pig stories: I think he must have a small menagerie, or piggery, at least, of porkers given him by friends and associates who know of his delight in the porcine. I stayed in George's house one year when he and Isabel were in America and the one firm injunction they left was to make sure that the bird-bath in the back garden was always full. Last year he arrived in Melbourne after driving down from Mildura with a white face and looking shaken. It turned out that he had hit a kangaroo on the road. Since then I think he travels by bus or train.

Notwithstanding my great affection and respect for George, it was my experience with him as my doctoral supervisor that made me realise why he is such a great scholar and teacher. For my first interview with him, I'd prepared an elaborate plan for the entire thesis, and an ambitious schedule for its completion. George looked it over carefully, and then commented, 'Well, these things are made to be disregarded'. We went on pretty well from there. For my thesis, I was editing *Wynnere and Wastoure* (whose opening lines George had given us as an unseen in my third year!). It is written in the same metre as *Piers Plowman*, and some of my most precious memories of those years are of the days when I'd confess myself stumped as to whether to emend my manuscript or not at a given point, and when George would give me a comparable example from *Piers* and say how he was putting off making a full decision about it.

He also had the knack of making one's work seem important, partly in his ready condemnation of much of the Middle English scholarship I was working with, but also by drawing connections between my work and his own. My drafts would come back covered with scrupulous annotations, and I still have the detailed suggestions he made about the punctuation of my text. He had gone through the whole poem, offering a consistent and logical pointing. Although I don't see George very often now, I still find myself using him as a standard by which to measure my own work.

Venetia Nelson was his pupil from an earlier generation and a different place, Sydney in the 1960s; but she was also his research assistant, and her relationship with him as a postgraduate student lasted for several years. She was, in short, a friend of his in the years when his vitality so impressed me on our first acquaintance. She knew him most closely in the years of his greatest hopefulness about the institutions which he graced; and her central view of him is of his own central vision, his religious humanism:

Reverence is a daring word to give to any person, and yet I do not hesitate to use it about George Russell. Some sense of depth came out of him, something in keeping with the sheer size of the man; more than this, some high seriousness, in his person, in his beliefs and in all that he dealt with. As students we sensed that he did not hold a position lightly, that he did not say something for the sake of its political value, that he did not teach some extra course because it was a way of securing his own position or keeping some other academic in his place. Perhaps in the days when I was a student academics were not so likely to teach in accordance with some fashionable conceptual framework as they are now, but certainly there was no suggestion of any such thing with him, nor would he have had any truck with it. He taught what he knew about and what he believed in, and those things he held strongly came from his own depths.

He was as serious and uncompromising on things that mattered as the man who became his life's work, William Langland; and yet in innocent, joyful things he had a boundless sense of humour and enthusiasm. Like Langland he took his stand on two things: his real and profound religious faith and his ultimate respect for the unique human person. Like Langland he had a passionate contempt for the phoney and the unjust, and as passionate an affirmation of the humble, the unpretentious and the faithful – his favourite word about people he liked was 'unassuming'. Perhaps because we knew he could be savage about what he saw as wrongheaded – as savage as Langland on the friars – his patient, even elaborate courtesy to his students stood out as memorable.

When he gave us a special course of lectures on early Middle English literature – a subject not much studied in those days – we felt we were in the presence of something rare and authentic. If I were to use one word to describe what came out of his teaching I would say that he spoke with authority. First, his field was textual criticism, the fundamental discipline for reading texts at any distance from our own time, so his knowledge was not only *about* a text but concerned the text directly in its intrinsic shape, evolution and origin; second, there was no gap between what he was, what he believed, and what he taught. We knew that in his teaching he was giving out a great part of himself – which I believe every authentic teacher does – and though some of us did not share his religious beliefs, or his high seriousness, or his love of the Middle Ages, yet we saw what it was that came out of him and revered him for it.

Somewhat later than Venetia Nelson, Penelope Curtis came to be George Russell's postgraduate student after having been his colleague, and friend, during the first half of the 1970s. Her comments treat one of his traits which the others do not mention: his image of self-doubt; but she makes explicit another quality which is present implicitly throughout Venetia's remarks: the manner in which his spiritual and moral virtues are there as a form of physicality. She also stresses the deeply contemplative nature of his speech:

When I first saw George, I forgot anything I had imagined about him and was held simply by the scuplture of his head: its mass, the unpredictability of its angles, the originality of the whole. Talking to him soon afterwards, about whatever two or three topics were then occupying me (one was Russian dissident literature), I found him deeply and precisely informed on each, and easy, warm, unselfimportant. The next time I met him, I was so moved by the qualities I sensed in him (or was it by his voice?), that I found myself volunteering, at once, and forever, that trust in him which we give to our dearest friends.

One of George's trials is that everyone wants to be close to him and experience his warmth, and many sense that a quick and effective means to this end is to make him anxious about something. He has been much oppressed in this way (it may even be at the root of that self-doubt which so dismays his friends). But to say that he strives in the most private and profound ways for goodness and truth *is* to praise his scholarship and teaching: for there is no gap.

George is extremely experienced in committee work, trusted by everyone, and well-known for his punctilious fulfilment of all kinds of obligation: yet one feels him to be, first, a man with a mysterious and even guarded inner life, a man who has denied himself many opportunities for enjoying that inner life, but who has lived it nevertheless. As a teacher, he opens this life, he shares it.

His teaching is meditative, musical and radical. To break into his thought is like breaking fictional decorum: you lose the illumination. To hear him talk about Langland is to see something growing underground in the dark. It is George's own originality, even more than his patience, his learning, or his radically spiritual inner life, which gives him the affinity with Langland: so that, in discovering to a class the uniqueness of Langland's mind, or of his sense of process, George opens to it similar qualities of his own. I think of him as a creative writer not so much lost as re-cast.

These testimonies span more than two decades which, in George's own account, were for him decades of disturbance and at least partial failure. What is interesting is that he and his former pupils are talking about utterly different matters and, in a sense, two different persons. They see him as colleague, mentor, teacher, thinker, man of feeling, and presence; he is concerned with himself as administrator, and non-achiever. The image he presents of an academic executive is of someone committed to a task which is salvific: there are places, institutions, communities, ventures to be saved, he is invited to save them, and finds that, in the end, he simply cannot.

Once again, this is in itself a commentary on the academic world, in that it cannot fully use a man of great talents who is driven both by his conscience and that world's need. But, clearly, saving administrative outfits is not a central vocation of most scholars and critics. While George thinks he was failing at that, his ex-students respond to him as, in effect, a success on whom they can depend from stage to stage of their own development (Stephanie Trigg), or in whose succeeding they are collaborative (Venetia Nelson), or as a friend-mentor to be admired in an almost aesthetic way (Penelope Curtis). Significantly, all three came to be his friends (Penelope in fact taught with him), and the aesthetic factor looms large in what all three responded to. Yeats might have called this *style*, although from another angle it is an attribute of what I may call *personing*. I too respond to him in this way, conscious (as the others are) that the stylish combines with, expresses, the moral and the emotional. Individual style, as distinct from institutional confidence, is rare in modern universities; it is the younger sibling of eccentricity.

In him it goes with a shyness so deep that it would be impossible for him to like large ventures or large crowds; he is a 'small group man'; and, when he was discussing this predisposition, he associated it not only with the small group world of his childhood but also with his decision not to stay in England, or anywhere in Europe, at the time when that opportunity first opened up for him, but to come home to a world which still kept some innocence and hence some communal possibility. I see in this logical transition a further reference to his love of small groups:

10

I've always been a small group man, in all the things I've done. Such political activity as I've been involved in, such activities engaged by the life and work of the church, have all been small groups affairs; and I believe this is consistent with a whole concept of how one responds to the world. I don't deny the efficacy of larger, more aggressive, more exhilarating movements of a much more public kind – I'm sure many people are best employed in those contexts. I've never felt that I am, so I've always, in teaching, and in all enterprises, tended to work in small groups: I feel this is perhaps the result of my background, my experiences as a boy in a small country town, in particular, in the New Zealand Catholic tradition, which was that of a tiny insignificant minority, primarily Irish, not very highly educated Irish immigrants, who didn't step out of line very much, who kept their counsels and their values, kept their integrity I think, but perhaps at a very high cost. It is gone now, but it left an indelible mark on me. The other marks are the scars I have got from my academic experience, in Sydney in particular. I've always as a result tried to be a conciliator rather than an aggressor; I always tried to avoid conflict, without sacrificing principle.

You asked me why I elected to return to this part of the world. Well, I went to a Europe that was just emerging from the cataclysm of the Second World War. I found an enormous amount that was rivettingly exciting and engaging in England and on the Continent. But I came to feel that this was a culture in ruins, a ruin that the war had only accelerated, a ruin that had clearly been concealed for a long time, maybe a century, and that the catastrophes had simply speeded the whole process up in a horrifying way.

Now I looked to this part of the world (Australasia) as being still innocent, and as being capable of keeping itself free from the diseases that infected the mother lode; a society that was necessarily unsophisticated, even crude, but nevertheless innocent, and in innocence evil was not triumphant; and therefore there was the potential for doing things quite other than had been done in the European tradition. I came to think that I would come back to a culture that was not only personally safe, and therefore not disturbing, but also potentially richer. I would now say something very different; for the potentialities were not realised, the opportunities were not taken, we fell for Panderism, for a kind of spurious internationalism, which as one could predict gave us the bad and left us very little of the good. So far as I'm concerned I now see a chance passed up, gone, perhaps not finally. I'm not pessimistic, I'm still optimistic, but that optimism is pretty sadly dented.

Whatever I did was done in dedication to a principle: work and pray, pray and work; the Benedictine ideal; and the notion of consensus, the notion of the avoidance of extremes, the notion of the danger of conflict, the attempt at the cultivation of the simple and innocent: all Benedictine propositions. This is not so much the *rationale* as the *spirituale* of the matter.

11

It is worth following this passage just as it comes off the tape to be transcribed; for it shows very clearly George Russell's way of associating and situating things which constantly concern him, so that a methodological issue, or preference, will end in a metaphysical insistence or religious insight. I had indeed asked him whether he was aware of there being a strong national tone to many of his judgements, and whether I was correct in thinking that, whenever there was a savage conflict in his immediate environment of work, shock and surprise were among his first reactions. The reflections which I have recorded above are part of his reply to these questions. It is clear that he is preoccupied with contemplative community as an ethical and psychological norm, and that he has not been able to find such a community in university English departments.

It is ironic that the communities in risk of breakdown should have existed for George Russell in Australia, for the Australia of his youth and mine was in some ways a world of naive consumerism, of simple rather than obsessive pleasures reached for in a ruling atmosphere of duty and mutuality; it was the world which Barry Humphries was preparing to leave, and from which artists like Sidney Nolan and Leonard French had had to undergo their healing absences. As Humphries was to show, nostalgia for such a society often explodes in resentment and scorn. Why would a medievalist come back to it? Perhaps from a feeling that this was the place to which his temperament was equal, even if his talents far outstripped it.

George Russell's answer was more complex than that; but temperament also has to be taken into account. And if temperament launched him into this cultural cycle, history bound him in it. The world which it dominated was one where the Protestant sense of purpose and responsibility was weakening. Russell possessed in fine measure the virtues which the Protestants were unobtrusively losing, and he also possessed an anxiety about their continuance; but he had been *trained* in them; from early boyhood on, he had found Cambridge and Europe a little slummish because they had failed such virtues, and his sense of duty was thereby expanded. What is a contemplative scholar, a Benedictine spirit, a person of communal bent, to do with a situation like this, or with his own anxiety about it? It seems only last week that he emerged from the constrictions of his place and class to enjoy the possibility of contemplation or of scholarship; now he has to turn away from these to undertake and undergo committees which are necessary to save the institution itself.

George Russell could never resolve the conflicts created, in him more than in others in whom nevertheless conflict arose, by selection committees. He found it hard to say Yes because it was in a sense impossible for him to say No. He hated to choose *finally*; his spirit rejected finality. Once, after we had appointed the only possible candidate, he murmured to me, 'I hope we've done the right thing.' We had not, as it happened.

He was always at his best as an adviser when he did not have to give the deciding vote on an appointment, or to lead the process of grading; in fact, he had to take part in far too many rush decisions, and he knew from long experience that there are no sure ways of spotting candidates whose defects do not appear on that raddled and careful mask, the dossier. Even old and trusted consultants will often advise you badly, since they do not always have adequate evidence about the things which reassuring rumour persuades them they know. Faced with all this George Russell could have wihdrawn to his texts, leaving *praxis* to professional committeemen (or even, sometimes, women) who do not really care whom they appoint so long as it looks right, and there is no comeback. But, the more such people choose the committee table, the more George Russell felt obliged to sit over against them.

When he *was* convinced about the worth of a candidate, he would speak with unrivalled authority, with a courtly simplicity which carried its own rhetorical and evidential force. Where others might judge in terms of clubbability, he knew that being a colleague involves serious and delicate moral qualities. The first is easy to identify in an interview, the second almost impossible. When George asked 'Do you think he/she is all right?', he did not mean 'clubbable' or 'like us', but 'trustworthy'.

Despite his expertness in a rather specialised field, he is also what Americans call a 'generalist', as one would expect from a study of his reseach record. His deep subject, his abiding sub-text, is a history of the spirit. Perhaps he would be best suited by an inter-disciplinary structure; but such a thing has not been available to us in the older Australian universities, especially in Melbourne. When he came to that university, the English department was not merely experiencing some disquiet, but was losing by stages its more experienced teachers of Old and Middle English; and there was some feeling that 'the language side' was not justifying its privileged position in Pure School courses. This may be merely a variant of the old semi-truth that things get smaller as they shrink. In any case, George Russell was given no chance to rectify the effects of shrinkage in the part before he was called on to find a way of re-constituting the whole. It was the case of Brisbane and Canberra over again.

His declared view of how medieval studies have developed and how they may now go would be in line either with an inter-disciplinary approach or with one which saw such studies as the nucleus of a larger study, whether historical or critical. Like many others, he does not favour 'an elitist, mandarin-like training of a very small number of language specialists', and he feels that Medieval Studies 'can no longer demand to be made compulsory in English courses'. Literature is 'one of the manifestations of human culture', linked in time and space and logic with other manifestations; 'so there is no need for the field to shrink; it can expand in all sorts of ways. My own guess is that Chaucer for the modern undergraduate is less difficult than Milton is – about then the difficulties begin'.

This interesting remark is that of a man who has gladly taught Modern Drama and for years conducted a Senior Honours seminar in the Novel. It argues an interest both in general issues and in a variety of texts. But in the circumstances of Australian universities the first of these has always been hard to follow out. It could be argued that both at Canberra and Melbourne

13

circumstances prevented George Russell integrating the medieval field as he would have wished to do; at the same time, they did not allow him to develop intra- or inter-disciplinary studies in the ways in which his talents as a 'generalist' scholar would have led him. He was far too urgently needed to represent department and faculty interests in university forums, and to give a stabilising presence in what were for much of the time disturbed and self-threatening milieux. There is a moral here, but not one which universities, faculties or departments are likely to heed.

In any case, as a consultant executive, George was unrivalled; and he is still. His advice comes with deep practice, but it is always pondered, and always addressed to the matter in hand; he concentrates on the issue so disinterestedly that he can mobilise even his own fears and self-doubt towards a solution. This quality of deep and broad attentiveness is seen also in his ways of preparing minutes or reports for discussion, and in his forming of lectures and addresses. He is most punctilious in answering correspondence and seeing to enquiries. It is a courtly attitude, and it is what I think of as his 'hostly' spirit. He has always been, in fact, a magnificent host, unendingly thoughtful, and as lavish of conversation as of the German wines which he favoured. Even when his own health made him a teetotaller, he was known to pour unstintingly for others.

Not that he is simply a gregarious man; in the deepest sense he is not gregarious at all. On the contrary, he is a noted solitary, a loner, as he notes himself; and there is about him an air of Walton's melancholic, trailing in the water of his future his long lines of memory. Perhaps melancholy is the spice of the scholar's life, just a readiness for laughter is what makes the scholar apt to be a teacher. Those of his students whom I have known well, including my own wife, speak with reverence of his teaching – its breadth, its address to the matter in hand, its capacity to mobilise discrete evidence, its deep relaxation. At one stage, perhaps in silent commentary on the cult of Old Norse which ruled in our department, he spoke of setting up, with one or two likely spirits, a reading group in Old Irish. I was looking forward to joining it, as a complete tyro; health beat us all to the crossing.

Since his teaching and his chief scholarly work are closed to me, it is as a colleague, a friend, an intellectual and a spiritual epiphany that I value him. These dimensions were visible even in his day-to-day administration. For example, he characteristically said Yes to people's requests, even when he was also perhaps unduly conscious of difficulties which they carried for himself. If he advised in a warning manner, he never threatened, and never abused. It was as though people's rights were established by ancient norms, by some Magna Carta and common law of the clerisy, in which all shared if they did the common work, and not only professors and supposed geniuses deserved favour. Sometimes, to help a colleague, he would waive his own rights in some matter.

This sense of common law is no mere fancy on my part. George has an extraordinary inwardness with what the university tradition *means* for its members: not a mere ability to interpret regulations (although even that skill is rare enough), but an ability to see what is so central to the whole university experience that it is not to be removed or lessened by any fiat. I know nobody so inward, and always consult him if I have the least doubt about the propriety or the justice of any proposal.

As an intellectual, he shows a taste for factuality and a broad ease with facts, and he applies these to a training of the spirit in intellectual history. It is no accident that while, in speaking, he can deliver perfectly formed sentences and paragraphs, in writing he produces a limpid, easy, periodic prose which also has personality stamped upon it. The result is a form of democracy: his interlocutors and readers may be instructed, but they are never overborne. His authority is gently interrogative in mode; it asks for assent, and readily assents to disagreement. It is perhaps not surprising that this eminent man, who in his interviews with me declared himself always conscious, though in no Manichean or pessimistic way, that Evil 'comes to us in our everyday lives and ... has always seemed to lurk very close', has in retirement gone to a country town and there teaches unlettered men how to read and write.

GEORGE RUSSELL: A REMINISCENCE

Clive James

George Russell is a great teacher and I was the worst student he ever had. It could be argued that the opinion of a bad student ought not be allowed to count for much in the assessment of a teacher's quality. But George Russell's eminence as a teacher is not in doubt. Too many star students would willingly give testimony about his influence on their lives. What might perhaps add an extra, unexpected dimension to the encomiastic chorus is the testimony of a student whose biological resistance to being taught was a phenomenon of immunology. If George Russell could influence even me, there must have been something uncanny about him.

Having, to nobody's surprise greater than my own, conned my way into the English Honours school after two undistinguished years of the ordinary pass course, I joined George's high-powered class in Anglo-Saxon, opened my newly-purchased text book for the first time, and sat there as if staring at a cobra. Until that moment I had had no idea that Anglo-Saxon was a foreign language. My petrified gaze must somehow have aroused George's sympathy, not normally a commodity that he made freely available to dolts.

The woman to whom I am now married was at that time a fellow student – the sort of student that every teacher dreams of teaching. Her presence by my side must have made up for the fact that I was the sort of student every teacher dreams of getting rid of, because together we were invited by George and his wife Isabel to dinner at their house in Pennant Hills. George picked us up in his car at Pennant Hills station. The visit became a regular thing; which says a lot for Isabel's tolerance, because for someone who drank George's wine as if it were water I got a great deal of talking done. My companion, needless to say, was the soul of moderation, possessing the judicious self-assessment appropriate to her faultless academic record unblemished by any grade lower than A or honour other than first. She delighted the Russells. But I think it fair to say that it was I who fascinated them. Wide-eyed behind his glasses, George watched enthralled while the contents of his cellar vanished inside me. I think he took a scientific interest in seeing if one of the finer things of life could work its civilising influence even on someone who was throwing it in a high curve over the taste buds so that it didn't touch flesh until it hit the back of the throat. At the end of the evening George drove us all the way back to town, to obviate the possibility of my boarding the electric train and falling out of the opposite door on to the track. Though I am assured that he invariably drove us all the way to Town Hall, today I can't remember us having even once crossed the Harbour Bridge. It must mean that I was unconscious every time.

In class I stayed awake but it didn't make much difference. For the Union revue I adapted an Anglo-Saxon text about the Battle of Maldon into a sketch

16

in which two warriors from each team faced off across a very small river and pronounced incomprehensible war-cries. The sketch was a big hit with those members of the audience who were familiar with Old English texts. This was as close as I came to any kind of rapport with our ancestral tongue. Less forgiveable was how I remained impervious even to George's special seminars in which he touched upon a wider field, the Middle Ages in Europe. Unfortunately I had no Latin and it didn't occur to me at that time to acquire any, busy as I was with such important matters as editing the *Honi Soit* literary page.

But I can remember now being impressed even at the time by George's grave humility as he introduced a discussion of *European Literature and the Latin Middle Ages*, by Ernst Robert Curtius. 'This', said George, his hands poised above the volume as if he were about to break bread, 'is a great book'. Then he opened it. It hardly needs saying that I had neither the preparation nor the spare time to corroborate his opinion, but the moment stayed with me.

George listened tolerantly as I informed him of my plans to spend five years in Europe doing odd jobs while looting the area of its cultural wealth and composing poetic masterpieces by night, before returning to take my rightful place as an Australian man of letters, position and political influence. He heard me out with a patience aided by cold beer. Sipping reflectively, George ventured the suggestion that in the unlikely event of my scheme failing to reach immediate fruition I might drop him a line, because if the necessity ever arose for me to take refuge once more in a university, he had a certain amount of pull at his old Cambridge college. Grandly I let him know that the possibility would never arise. The place of the artist was not in the cloisters, but in the world.

The place of this artist turned out to be in the soup. As I write this note, the second volume of my unreliable memoirs is about to be published, whereupon the full story of how I failed to ignite the Thames will be edifyingly available for any reader still harbouring the delusion that all the Australians who sailed for England in the early Sixties achieved instant success. I, for one, achieved a depth of oblivion from which I could see to climb out only by the light of my lucky stars. George, as ever conscientious beyond the call of duty, or perhaps once again impelled by the self-mortifying requirements of his lay religious order, wrote me fulsome references by airletter so that I might apply for jobs which a glance must have told him had a dead end. Finally, when I had at last concurred with the otherwise universal opinion that I was unemployable, he wrote the letter which secured me a place at Cambridge.

Safe inside the oak doors of his old college, Pembroke, I immediately set about betraying his trust by giving my principal attention to Footlights. What reading I found time for was off the course. On one of George's visits to London I met him for a drink and gave him an account of my progress that was probably the real reason for the sour look which at the time I put down to the unspeakable English beer. My degree was obtained more by turn of phrase than by proof of diligence and I must have been the only graduate in history who got himself registered as a PhD candidate merely so that he might become President of a dramatic society. Mine was scarcely a shining academic record. It was almost a police record. Always I read any book except the one specified. But I never stopped reading. Nor did I ever stop listening to music or looking at paintings. In George's house I had somehow got the idea, more by osmosis than observation, that an education was something you went on acquiring all your life. Perhaps I got the idea too well, and too often postponed what I should have tackled early. But I got the idea.

We would all like to set our minds in order, and that applies most to those of us who are obliged to lead disorderly lives. As I consume, in the TV studio, hundreds of hours that I might have spent making yet another attempt to get somewhere with Greek, my great teachers are with me as an ideal. I think it was while George was holding a seminar about the austere dedication of the Brethren of the Common Life that he first mentioned Rachel. She wasn't a real woman, she was a spirit – the spirit of contemplation. For the monk, to be denied her company was to be left desolate. To forsake her was madness. Expounding this concept, George spoke as both a man of religion and a humanist. At the time I had little idea of what he meant. A quarter of a century later I am still proof against religion of any stamp, and will no doubt remain so until my pagan grave. But humanism, the thirst for concentrated meaning that turns a classic text into a fountain of refreshment, has by now become as vivid for me as the river of light became for Dante. I wish I had good enough Latin to read the *Annals* of Tacitus as I can read his *Histories*, or read his *Histories* as I can read his *Agricola*. But after my first hour of construing those uranium sentences whose density, like that of Shostakovitch's string quartets, is the guarantee of their truth and the truth's private defiance of state terror, I could at last, not lulled but consoled, see the twentieth century for what it was, a time like any other. When I closed the book I held my hands above it as if to touch it might burn them, and only later realised that the gesture had been an echo.

So George Russell has had his influence, beginning with a few words and ending far away, as an important part of his pupil's attitude to life. There are other, better pupils with less erratic tales to tell. But I was the test case, the one sent to try him.

THE WARRIOR CHRIST AND THE UNARMED HERO

Alison Finlay

As a prelude to his account of the crucifixion in Passus XVIII of *Piers Plowman*, Langland uses the metaphor of a young knight in his presentation of Christ:

Oon semblable to the Samaritan, and somdeel to Piers the Plowman,
Barefoot on an asse bak bootles cam prikye,
Withouten spores other spere; spakliche he loked,
As is the kynde of a knyght that cometh to be dubbed,
To geten hym gilte spores on galoches ycouped.
   Thanne was Feith in a fenestre, and cryde '*A! Fili David!*'
As dooth an heraud of armes whan aventrous cometh to justes.
Olde Jewes of Jerusalem for joye thei songen,
Benedictus qui venit in nomine Domini.
   Thanne I frayned at Feith what al that fare bymente,
And who sholde juste in Jerusalem. 'Jesus,' he seide,
'And fecche that the fend claymeth – Piers fruyt the Plowman.'
'Is Piers in this place?' quod I, and he preynte on me.
'This Jesus of his gentries wol juste in Piers armes,
In his helm and in his haubergeon – *humana natura.*
That Crist be noght biknowe here for *consummatus Deus*,
In Piers paltok the Plowman this prikiere shal ryde;
For no dynt shal hym dere as *in deitate Patris.*'
'Who shal juste with Jesus?' quod I, 'Jewes or scrybes?'
'Nay,' quod Feith, 'but the fend and fals doom to deye.'[1]

Langland uses the metaphor of the joust partly to create a sense of urgent and joyful anticipation, which contrasts strikingly with the bleak, literal account of the crucifixion which immediately follows it. But this contrast of modes is not the only paradoxical element in the image presented. The idea of Christ as a young knight 'that cometh to be dubbed', his potentiality as yet untried, contributes to the anticipatory tone, but also to the mystery surrounding his true nature; it also provides a satisfyingly concrete basis for the reference to his being unarmed, 'withouten spores other spere'. Langland borrows a motif from romance in suggesting that Christ is an 'aventrous', a wandering knight who, like Lancelot, conceals his true greatness by preparing to fight in the guise of a lesser man. That Christ assumes the habergeon of Piers Plowman, *humana natura*, alludes to the fact that his divine nature can

[1] William Langland, *The Vision of Piers Plowman*, A critical edition of the B-Text, edited by A.V.C.Schmidt (London, 1978), p.220.

19

only be revealed to men through his assumption of humanity. At the same time, the military connotations of the imagery are contradicted by the equation of Christ's arms with his humanity: this is a conflict in which the weapons of secular warfare are redundant. By introducing references to Christ 'barefoot on an asse bak' and to the homely 'paltok' of Piers Plowman, Langland juxtaposes humility with the formal dignity suggested by his military imagery.

Thus Langland makes use of current literary images of conflict to convey the complexity of significance of Christ and the crucifixion. The image of Christ as a warrior whose weapons, paradoxically, are humility and passivity, is similarly employed in the earliest representation of the crucifixion in English poetry, *The Dream of the Rood*. Like Langland, the poet makes conscious use of the vocabulary and images of the secular poetry available to him. Christ is presented in terms appropriate to a heroic leader of men, 'se geong hæleð' (line 39), his disciples as 'hilderincas' (line 72), and the Cross itself, most strikingly, in personified form as the faithful retainer, and yet simultaneously the slayer, of Christ. The power of the metaphor is cumulative, and resides rather in the sense of relationship implied between lord and follower than in a detailed depiction of either in heroic terms. Thus the inappropriate reference to the disciples as 'hilderincas' is justified, within the context of the poem, because it alludes to their relationship wih Christ, implying its parallelism with that of a secular warrior and his lord. So the image of Christ as a heroic leader is indirectly extended.

The personification of the Cross, which occupies the forefront of the poem, also helps to establish this idea. It is through the personality and emotions superimposed upon the Cross that the poet expresses his paradox, both intellectual and emotional: the faithful retainer obeys his lord, and yet is the instrument of his destruction; Christ is executed as a criminal, and yet ordains his own death. To the extent that Christ's sufferings are transferred to the Cross, the Cross and Christ are one and the same; and this is a further expression of the miraculous complexity of the event. But the result of the poem's concentration on the Cross might seem to be that the presence and power of Christ himself is rather thinly suggested. Is the term 'geong hæleð', applied to Christ, given any more substance than the incongruous designation of the disciples as 'hilderincas'?

By means of the personification of the Cross, Christ's role as commander is suggested, through the emphasis on its duty of absolute obedience:

Þǣr ic þā ne dorste   ofer Dryhtnes word
būgan oððe berstan,   þā ic bifian geseah
eorðan sceatas.   Ealle ic mihte
fēondas gefyllan,   hwæðre ic fæste stōd.

(lines 35–38)[2]

But the direct references to Christ, on the whole, either emphasize his

---

[2] All references to this poem are to the edition of Michael Swanton (Manchester, 1970).

divinity: 'þæt wæs God ælmihtig' (line 39), 'heofona Hlāford' (line 45); or take advantage of terms appropriate to either divine or secular contexts: 'Frēan mancynnes' (line 33), 'Dryhten' (line 35). The only direct depiction of Christ in heroic terms resides in the emphasis on his own volition. He hastens to mount on the Cross, his intention twice signalled by the auxiliary verb 'wolde', the repetition of which links the act of crucifixion and its significance:

Þæt hē mē wolde on gestīgan   (line 34b)
þā hē wolde mancyn lȳsan   (line 41b)

And he removes his own garments, rather than being stripped by his executioners: 'Ongyrede hine þā geong hæleð' (line 39a). This image is an odd one, since as one editor has noted, 'Christ was only very rarely depicted naked at the crucifixion'.[3] According to the Biblical account, Christ was stripped of the fine robe in which he had been mocked, and dressed in his own clothes: 'And after that they had mocked him, they took the robe off from him, and put his own raiment on him, and led him away to crucify him.'[4] In the Old English gloss on this passage, the verb *ongyrwan* is used, with Christ as its passive object: 'Ond æfter ðon bismeredon him ongeredon hine ðyryfte ond gegeredon hine mið his gewedum ond gelæddon hine þæt hia on rode genæglede.' In *The Dream of the Rood*, the same verb, used reflexively, emphasizes Christ's own volition. I wish to suggest that this usage, besides reversing the realistically passive presentation of Christ's role, deliberately calls upon a traditional heroic image, for which there is considerable evidence particularly in later Icelandic poetic and historical texts, of the warrior so pre-eminent that he is able, as a supremely defiant gesture, to renounce the protection of arms or armour.

The Old English verb *(ge)gyrwan* and the almost identical *(ge)gearwian* are very general in their sense. Related to *gearo*, 'ready', they mean primarily 'to prepare', with the specific senses of 'to dress', 'to furnish', 'to adorn'. *Gyrwan*, indeed, is used twice in this last sense in *The Dream of the Rood*: the Cross is 'gegyred mid golde' (line 16), and 'mid since gegyrwed' (line 23). But another specialized sense is 'to arm, prepare for battle':

Þā wearð snelra werod   snūde gegearewod,
cēnra tō campe

(*Judith*, lines 199–200)[5]

gyrede hine georne   mid gæstlicum
wæpnum [7 wædum]

(*Guðlac A*, lines 177–8)[6]

---

[3] Swanton, p.113.
[4] Matthew 27. 31 (King James Version).
[5] *The Anglo-Saxon Poetic Records*, edited by G.P.Krapp and E.V.K.Dobbie, 6 vols (London and New York, 1931–53), IV.
[6] All references to this poem are to *The Guthlac Poems of the Exeter Book*, edited by Jane Roberts (Oxford, 1979).

The verb *gyrwan* is used twice in this sense in *Beowulf*, at the beginning and end of a passage which suggests the kind of context to which the poet of *The Dream of the Rood* may have been alluding. This is the formal, ceremonious account of the arming of Beowulf before his encounter with Grendel's mother (lines 1441–72). The long, elaborately constructed sentences, the description and near-personification of each of the 'mægenfultuma' which are to accompany the hero, may well derive from a traditional technique for setting the scene for a sequence of climactic action. It certainly serves this purpose in *Beowulf*, although the poet, like the poet of *The Dream of the Rood*, repeatedly juxtaposes formal elements with reminders of the exceptional nature of the contest to come:

>scolde herebyrne   hondum gebrōden,
>sīd ond searofāh   sund cunnian

>(lines 1443–4)[7]

It is contrast, too, which rounds off the passage, as Beowulf is compared with Unferð:

>Ne wæs þæm ōðrum swā,
>syððan hē hine tō gūðe   gegyred hæfde.

>(lines 1471–2)

The opening of the passage,

>Gyrede hine Bēowulf
>eorlgewædum

>(lines 1441–2)

is parallel in syntax to the use in *The Dream of the Rood* of the verb's negative form: 'Ongyrede hine þā geong hæleð'. The sense of *gyrwan* is usually particularized by the addition of an adverbial phrase, such as 'mid golde' (*The Dream of the Rood*, line 16), 'tō gūðe' (*Beowulf*, line 1472). The absence of such a qualification in line 39 of *The Dream of the Rood* leaves the verb conveniently ambivalent. The literal meaning, as the biblical account makes clear, must be 'undressed', but the traditional associations of *gyrwan* in conjunction with such a subject as 'geong hæleð' call to mind a variation on the theme of the warrior preparing for battle. The fact that Christ strips off, rather than assuming, his armour, suggests by simple contrast with the expected state of affairs the exceptional nature of the coming conflict.

However, it is my contention that the connotations of *ongyrwan* also call upon more specific parallels with heroic tradition. *Beowulf* furnishes another example of the prelude to a battle, in which the motif of a hero renouncing weapons is used. Before his fight with Grendel, Beowulf announces,

[7] All references to this poem are to the edition of F.Klaeber, third edition (Boston, 1950).

'Nō ic mē an herewæsmun   hnāgran talige
gūþgeweorca,   þonne Grendel hine;
forþan ic hine sweorde   swebban nelle,
aldre benēotan,   þēah ic eal mæge;
nāt hē þāra gōda,   þæt hē mē ongēan slea,
rand gehēawe,   þēah ðe hē rōf sie
nīþgeweorca;   ac wit on niht sculon
secge ofersittan,   gif hē gesēcean dear
wīg ofer wæpen.

(lines 677–85)

It is true that the *Beowulf* poet puts this motif to a purpose which transcends the heroic, since he emphasizes the hero's trust in God to an extent that implies it to be an alternative to weapons:

ond siþðan wītig God
on swā hwæþere hond   hālig Dryhten
mǣrðo dēme,   swā him gemet þince.

(lines 685–7)

The speech is followed by the assertion that success was determined by God: 'Ac him Dryhten forgeaf/ wīgspēda gewiofu' (lines 696–7), and the generalized affirmation of God's power:

Sōð is gecȳþed,
þæt mihtig God   manna cynnes
wēold *w*īdeferhð.

(lines 700–2)

But this conclusion to the preamble to the fight is in direct contrast to its beginning. Beowulf's speech is introduced as 'gylpworda sum', the term commonly applied to a speech of boastful defiance often delivered before the beginning of a combat. Immediately before this speech, however, the poet details the hero's disarming, in patent contrast to the arming to be expected in such a context, and to the one actually described so ceremoniously before the fight with Grendel's mother:

Ða hē him of dyde   īsernbyrnan,
helm of hafelan,   sealde his hyrsted sweord,
īrena cyst   ombihtþegne,
ond gehealdan hēt   hildegeatwe.

(lines 671–4)

The most obvious function of Beowulf's successful fight without weapons is to confirm his reputation for great physical prowess, already rumoured to the Danes in the tall tales of sailors:

Ðonne sægdon þæt   sǣlīþende,
þā ðe gifsceattas   Gēata fyredon
þyder tō þance,   þæt hē þrītiges
manna mægencræft   on his mundgripe
heaþorōf hæbbe.

(lines 377–381)

Similar fights are commonplace in the Icelandic sagas, where they serve the same purpose of magnifying the hero's strength and adding a suggestion of non-human or bestial savagery. In chapter 65 of *Egils saga Skallagrímssonar*, for instance, the hero kills an opponent (like Grendel, capable of rendering weapons useless) by biting through his windpipe.[8] In chapter 19 of *Bjarnar saga hítdœlakappa*, the hero kills a man by throwing him violently to the ground.[9] Both these heroes are associated elsewhere in their sagas with non-human attributes. Egill, in particular, belongs to a family with a long-standing reputation for lycanthropy.

This somewhat primitive heroic device, however, plays a minimal part in *Beowulf*. Whereas Egill and Bjorn are without weapons by accident, Beowulf's volition in setting them aside is emphasized. This serves partly to underline the hero's sagacity, which contrasts with the ignorance of his followers about Grendel's nature and powers:

Þǣr genehost brægd
eorl Bēowulfes   ealde lāfe,
wolde frēadrihtnes   feorh ealgian,
mǣres þēodnes,   ðǣr hīe meahton swā.
Hīe þæt ne wiston   þā hīe gewin drugon,
heardhicgende   hildemecgas,
ond on healf gehwone   hēawan þōhton,
sāwle sēcan: þone synscaðan
ænig ofer eorþan   īrenna cyst,
gūðbilla nān   grētan nolde.

(lines 794–803)

But the most prominent feature of Beowulf's *gylpword* is his insistence on laying aside the advantage of weapons in order to meet his adversary on equal terms: a gesture in the same style as Byrhtnoð's concession to the vikings in *The Battle of Maldon*.

The motif of the unarmed warrior reappears once more in Old English

---

[8] *Íslenzk Fornrit*, Volume II, *Egils saga Skalla-Grímssonar*, edited by Sigurður Nordal (Reykjavík, 1933).
[9] *Íslenzk Fornrit*, Volume III, *Borgfirðinga sǫgur*, edited by Sigurður Nordal and Guðni Jónsson (Reykjavík, 1938).

poetry where Guðlac, in his fight against demonic foes, renounces the use of the sword

> No ic eow sweord ongean
> mid gebolgne hond   oðberan þence,
> worulde wæpen,   ne sceal þes wong Gode
> þurh blodgyte   gebuen weorðan
>
> (*Guðlac A*, lines 302–7)

The poet of *Guðlac A* distances himself from the heroic tradition by his emphasis on the metaphorical nature of his use of its imagery, both in this passage ('worulde wæpen'), and in an earlier phrasing reminiscent of the arming of Beowulf:

> Eadig oretta,   *ond*wiges heard,
> gyrede hine georne   mid gæstlicum
> wæpnum [7 wædum]
>
> (lines 176–8)

In a comprehensive survey of military diction in Old English, in which she assembles impressive evidence that 'the tradition of the soldier of Christ was known in pre-Conquest England and much of the military language in Christian contexts was inspired by that tradition and not by the inherited traditions of the Germanic heroic world', Joyce Hill differentiates the use of this motif in *Guðlac* from that in *Beowulf*.[10] She adds, 'Furthermore, if Guðlac's renunciation reminds us of Beowulf's, we must not forget that Beowulf, in making a similar renunciation, was exceptional within the heroic tradition' (page 68). However, the difficulty of distinguishing between genuine heroic traditions and material derived from the Latin literature of the church is well illustrated by the fact that Norse texts give some support for the motif of the unarmed warrior as an element of the common Germanic heritage.

There are several references in the sagas of the kings of Norway which make up Snorri Sturluson's *Heimskringla*, dating from the early thirteenth century, to kings going unarmed into battle. This comparatively late prose source is, however, based on skaldic stanzas of earlier date, and the references to the abandoning of mail-coats are supported by Snorri's citation of his verse sources. This is hardly surprising if the motif is, as it seems, a literary device representing the grand gesture proper to the heroic demeanour, although it is sometimes possible to deduce a practical justification for the custom. Roberta Frank, referring to the account of King Haraldr harðráði (the Stern) in the battle of Stamford Bridge, suggests: 'A practical reason for leaving coats of mail behind at the ships on a hot September day is indicated

---

[10] Joyce Hill, 'The Soldier of Christ in Old English Prose and Poetry', *Leeds Studies in English*, New Series, 12 (1981), 57–80.

by a scene on the Bayeux Tapestry that depicts the difficult task of carrying burnies – each of which weighed at least thirty pounds – off the boats: a pole is inserted through their sleeves and held by a man at either end.'[11]

King Hákon inn góði (the Good) is said by Snorri to have fought without a coat of mail in his last battle, in which he was killed in 961: 'Segja menn svá, at konungr steypði af sér brynjunni, áðr orrusta tóksk.' (People say that the king threw off his coat of mail before the battle began.)[12] Snorri's source is the *Hákonarmál* (Lay of Hákon) by the poet Eyvindr Skáldaspillir (Plagiarist), which he quotes extensively. Eyvindr was composing during the lifetime of Hákon himself. In the *Hákonarmál*, the king is first displayed impressively armed, awaiting battle; before it begins, however, he defiantly casts off his coat of mail, while retaining his golden helmet:

Hrauzk ór hervóðum,	(The leader of men flung his
hratt á vǫll brynju	war-dress from him; he threw
vísi verðungar,	his coat of mail to the ground
áðr til vígs tœki.	before he entered the battle.
Lék við ljóðmǫgu,	He fought against men; he had
skyldi land verja	to defend his land. The
gramr enn glaðværi,	cheerful prince stood wearing
stóð und gullhjalmi.	his golden helmet.)

King Magnús inn góði (the Good) is represented in similar fashion in a battle against the heathen Wends in 1043. Like Hákon's battle, this too was a contest against enormous odds; unlike Hákon's, it was not the scene of the apocalyptic last stand of a rightful king. Whereas heroic images are used of Hákon to commemorate and aggrandize the king after his fall, the purpose of the impressive treatment of Magnús's fight at Hlýrskógsheiðr is to lend colour to the attribution of his victory to a miracle performed by his (dead) father, Saint Óláfr. The image itself, however, is remarkably similar in its presentation: 'Magnús konungr steypði af sér hringabrynju ok hafði ýzta rauða silkiskyrtu ok tók í hǫnd sér øxina Hel, er átt hafði Óláfr konungr.' (King Magnús threw off his ringed coat of mail, and was wearing a red silk tunic outside his other clothes, and he took in his hand the axe called Hel, which had belonged to King Óláfr).[13] A verse by the contemporary Arnórr jarlaskáld (poet of the jarls) is cited in corroboration:

Óð með øxi breiða	(The king advanced steadily
ódæsinn framm ræsir,	with the broad axe, and cast
varð um hilmi Hǫrða	aside his coat of mail. The din
hjǫdynr, en varp brynju,	of battle raged around the

[11] Roberta Frank, *Old Norse Court Poetry*, Islandica 42 (Ithaca and London, 1978), p.152.

[12] *Íslenzk Fornrit*, Volume XXVI, *Heimskringla I*, edited by Bjarni Aðalbjarnarson (Reykjavík, 1941), pp.186–7.

[13] *Íslenzk Fornrit*, Volume XXVIII, *Heimskringla III*, edited by Bjarni Aðalbjarnarson (Reykjavík, 1951), pp.43–4.

þás of skapt, en skipti
skapvǫrðr himins jǫrðu,
Hel klauf hausa fǫlva,
hendr tvær jǫfurr spenndi.

prince of the Norwegians, when
the king clasped the shaft with
both hands, and the ruler of
Heaven divided the land; Hel
split pallid skulls.)

The reference in Arnórr's verse to the casting aside of the mail-coat is so brief and unexplained as to suggest that its implications were automatically obvious, and thus, that the motif was one commonly used in eulogistic battle verses.

The theme receives its most extensive treatment in the account of the last battle of Magnús's successor, King Haraldr harðráði, at Stamford Bridge in 1066. The abandoning of armour is more naturalistically motivated here; the king and most of his army are taken unawares by the arrival of the English forces, having gone ashore unprepared for hostility: 'Þá var veðr forkunnliga gott ok heitt skin. Menn lǫgðu eptir brynjur sínar, en gengu upp með skjǫldum ok hjálmum ok kesjum ok sverðum gyrðir, ok margir hǫfðu ok skot ok boga ok váru allkátir.' (Then the weather was remarkably fine, and the sun was hot. Men left their coats of mail behind, but went ashore with their shields and helmets and spears, and were girt with swords. Many of them also had bows and arrows; and they were extremely cheerful).[14] The abandoning of coats of mail is not rendered as entirely accidental, however, since when his danger becomes clear, Haraldr rejects the advice of Earl Tósti that they return to the ships for their armour, and instead prepares for battle. Before the fight begins, Haraldr recites two verses which refer to his unarmed state. The first is simple in metre and diction:

Framm gǫngum vér
í fylkingu
brynjulausir
und blár eggjar.
Hjalmar skína;
hefkat ek mína.
Nú liggr skrúð várt
at skipum niðri.

(We are advancing in battle
array, without coats of
mail, beneath blue blades.
Helmets shine; I don't have
mine. Our gear is lying
down at the ships.)

According to Snorri's narrative, Haraldr is displeased with the artlessness of this composition, and replaces it with one more elaborate:

Krjúpum vér fyr vápna,
valteigs, brǫkun eigi,
svá bauð Hildr, at hjaldri,
haldorð, í bug skjaldar.
Hótt bað mik, þars mættusk,

(We do not cower from the
clashing of weapons in the
curve of a shield; so
commanded the discreet Hild
of the hawk's land (the

---

[14] *Heimskringla III*, pp.184–8.

menskorð bera forðum,
hlakkar íss ok hausar,
hjalmstofn í gný malma.

lady). She told me long ago
to carry my head high in
battle, where skulls were
hewn by swords.)

This verse combines the repetition of the theme that the best warriors scorn the protection provided (in this case) by the shield, with the device common in skaldic verse, of referring from the thick of battle or the discomforts of seafaring, to a woman left behind at home. The lady mentioned in Haraldr's verse is not identified; Roberta Frank has suggested, 'there is always the possibility that the woman the king was addressing was no lady at all but his coat of mail, Emma, who left him high and dry when he most needed her'.[15] The obscurity of skaldic diction renders this *double entendre* possible. If this interpretation is correct, it forms a striking example of the customary personification of a warrior's weapons and accoutrements, which Michael Cherniss characterizes as an important element in the portrayal of the Cross in *The Dream of the Rood*.[16]

An interesting footnote to the account of Haraldr harðráði's fight without armour is the comment of Arnórr jarlaskáld in a commemorative verse that the king's death was the result of 'ofrausn' (excessive magnificence).[17] Diana Edwards remarks of this, 'As with the celebrated *ofermōd* 'high courage/ overweening pride' which makes Byrhtnōþ give up his strategic advantage over a Viking army in the Old English *Battle of Maldon* (ASPR VI 9, l.89), the moral overtones of the word are extremely elusive, but the evidence of usage elsewhere would suggest that Arnórr means the word to indicate a tragic, if heroic, flaw'.[18] Haraldr's decision not to return to the ships for armour is one of several actions in his English campaign to which the specific charge of *ofrausn* could apply.

The number and range of examples cited here suggest that within the body of legendary history which was drawn upon by writers of the Icelandic sagas of Norwegian kings, there was a customary use of the motif of a king, when about to undertake battle, casting aside his coat of mail as a gesture of defiance which testifies to his status as a warrior fit to lead other men. With the exception of the battle of Stamford Bridge, no attempt is made to justify or condemn this action on naturalistic grounds; this fact, and the prevalence of the motif in verse as well as prose, suggest that it was primarily a literary device, perpetuated in formal eulogistic verse acclaiming the Northern kings as traditional Germanic heroes. It is more difficult to establish the motif as one of sufficient antiquity to derive from the shared Germanic heritage of the

---

15 *Old Norse Court Poetry*, p.145.
16 Michael D.Cherniss, 'The Cross as Christ's Weapon: the Influence of Heroic Literary Tradition on *The Dream of the Rood*', *Anglo-Saxon England*, 2 (1973), 241–52.
17 *Den Norsk-Islandske Skjaldedigtning*, edited by Finnur Jónsson, 4 vols (Copenhagen, 1912–15), B I, p.324.
18 Diana Edwards, 'Christian and Pagan References in Eleventh-Century Norse Poetry: the Case of Arnórr Jarlaskáld', *Saga-Book of the Viking Society*, 21 (1982–3), 34–53 (p.44).

Norse and Anglo-Saxon literary traditions. The reference to Beowulf's disarming before his fight with Grendel provides some evidence that it is so; I have tried to suggest that in line 39 of *The Dream of the Rood*, there survives an allusive but deliberate evocation of the same heroic idea.

LONG WILL'S APOLOGY: A TRANSLATION

E .Talbot Donaldson

To offer George Russell, of all people, a translation of a fragment of the C version of *Piers Plowman* for a volume honouring his scholarly accomplishments may well seem like offering a prosperous coal merchant of Newcastle a little lump of coal – Indiana coal at that. My excuse for doing so is, I fear, as flimsy as Long Will's to Reason for not performing honest labour – the passage I have translated. Many years ago when I first fell under the spell of *Piers Plowman* it was with the C version that I was most taken, and in the C version with the so-called 'autobiographical' passage in which Will explains, or rather fails to explain, why he lives as disreputably as he does. It is now more than thirty-five years since I left the C version – in far better hands – and turned to B; and when the edition of B with which I assisted George Kane was – at long last – finished, I undertook the project of translating it into Modern English alliterative verse. But despite this long preoccupation with B, my admiration and love of the C version have never diminished: I await with special impatience the appearance of the edition of it with which George Russell will cap his distinguished career. Will's apology, which appears only in C, seems to me the perfect Langlandian passage, hardly matched even by the greatest glories of A and B. I hope that George Russell shares my enthusiasm and will understand the spirit in which I indulge myself in the passage, even if I do so not entirely in accord with my conscience and reason. Would that in the spirit of my enthusiasm I could come close to rendering Langland's own *esprit*!

The lines describe one of the only two occasions on which the waking Dreamer encounters allegorical figures from his dreams, and both passages (the other describes the encounter with Need in the ultimate passus of B and C) relate the allegorical sense of the poem to Will's own life in a powerful and direct way. We have, of course, no idea whether William Langland ever actually lived in a cottage in Cornhill with a wife named Kit (who seems to have been expected to support herself), but the conception of the character accords so well with the personality that emerges everywhere from the three versions, the sudden turns and tergiversations in the logic are so splendidly Langlandian, that one is almost irresistably lured into believing it true. I find the initial response of Long Will to Reason's questioning about whether he can perform day labour the epitome of Langland's method: 'Certainly!' says he, introducing with an enthusiastic affirmative a denial that he is capable of doing hard work (one is reminded of the words of the old song, 'Yes! we have no bananas'), having just told us, a few lines earlier, that he was perfectly capable of labour at that period of his life. His subsequent justification for being a beggar – a welcome beggar by his own account – is that he is a clerk, and that clerks are scripturally exempted from hard labour. In his defense he cites the 'neck verse' which he characterizes elsewhere as having taken from Tyburn a number of flagrant thieves; furthermore, his own definition of what a well-born clerk – as he claims he is – should do includes some of the offices that Reason asks him why he is not performing, a question to which he gives no reply at all.

His principal defense is that his schooling has equipped him to say prayers for the souls of those who furnish him with food, and he says he will follow St Paul's injunction to remain in that vocation to which he has been called. The same biblical justification is, of course, used by two of Long Will's disreputable near-contemporaries in fiction, Alice of Bath and Falstaff, the former for continuing in the profession of wife and the latter in the profesion of highwayman; like them, Long Will likes his style of life no matter how dubious it may appear to others. Despite being a beggar, he asserts that he knows what Christ wants him to do, and even suggests that he is a perfect man whose prayers and penance are pleasing to God. The nature of this perfectness naturally puzzles readers as it puzzles Conscience. Jesus' second answer to the young man who had inquired how he might gain eternal life was that if he wished to be perfect, he should sell what he had, give to the poor, and come and follow him. That Long Will ever had much to sell seems unlikely, so that he could hardly have stored up treasure in heaven, which Christ says one may be doing by giving one's property to the poor. But Will claims that he is following Christ: in the heavily macaronic lines that follow his assertion of perfectness he half-quotes Jesus' words to Satan that man shall not live by bread alone, but by every word that proceeds from the mouth of God. While this serves as an additional excuse for his not earning his bread, it also is an indirect way of saying that he is living by God's word. The claim is reinforced by his last line before Conscience's interruption, his paraphrase of the Lord's Prayer, 'Let God's will be done.' Presumably, Will is doing it.

Conscience's interruption to question the nature of Will's perfectness is of course a questioning of Will by his own conscience. In continuing his apology he shows complete awareness that in the way he lives he is taking a chance, is gambling with his own soul. He refers to the parable likening the kingdom of heaven to a treasure hidden in a field (which in Matthew immediately precedes the likening of it to a pearl of great price which the merchant sold everything to buy); and he cites also the parable in Luke of the woman who found her lost silver coin, whose joy is compared to the rejoicing in heaven over a repentant sinner, who is then dramatized in the parable of the prodigal son. These scriptural references, glossing Will's eloquent lines expressing the hope that he is like one who has often bargained and always lost but finally makes a bargain that stands him in good stead forever, show Will seeing himself as a gambler and, like many a gambler, as a prodigal son: and in the game he is at once the gambler and the stake, both somewhat tarnished. The paradox of Will's position is splendidly expressed in Conscience's comment on his claim to perfectness:

    'By Christ, I can't see that this lies;
    But it seems no serious perfectness to be a city-beggar.'

Editors quite properly gloss the word *lies* (*lyeth* in the original) as being the verb which in its primary sense describes physical position, here used in the sense 'applies'; but if that is all it means, surely Langland would not have chosen a word which some readers will see as meaning only 'is false', a meaning which all readers will see as a possible meaning, if only to reject it: 'I can't see that this is false.' The word that begins the next line, which I have translated 'but', is *ac* in the original; as an adversative, this would support the meaning 'is false'; but *ac* is a weak adversative, and can actually mean 'moreover', which would fit the meaning 'applies'. Conscience's *double entendre* characterizes Long Will's apology as at once specious and heart-felt, false and true; and Will's confidence in his rectitude and his consciousness of a lack of rectitude show perhaps a divided mind, but a wonderfully unified personality.

Piers Plowman: C Version, lines 1–104
(from Huntington Library MS HM 143)

Thus I awoke, as God's my witness, when I lived in Cornhill,
Kit and I in a cottage, clothed like a loller,
And little beloved, believe you me,
Among lollers of London and illiterate hermits.
For I wrote rhymes of those men as Reason taught me.
For as I came by Conscience I met with Reason,
In a hot harvest time when I had my health,
And limbs to labour with, and loved good living,
And to do no deed but to drink and sleep.
My body sound, my mind sane, a certain one accosted me;
Roaming in remembrance, thus Reason upbraided me:
    'Can you serve,' he said, 'or sing in a church?
Or cock hay with my hay-makers, or heap it on the cart,
Mow it or stack what's mown or make binding for sheaves?
Or have a horn and be a hedge-guard and lie outdoors at night,
And keep my corn in my field from cattle and thieves?
Or cut cloth or shoe-leather, or keep sheep and cattle,
Mend hedges, or harrow, or herd pigs or geese,
Or any other kind of craft that the commons needs,
So that you might be of benefit to your bread-providers?'
    'Certainly!' I said, 'and so God help me,
I am too weak to work with sickle or with scythe,
And too long, believe me, for any low stooping,
Or labouring as a labourer to last any while.'

'Then have you lands to live by,' said Reason, 'or relations with
    money
To provide you with food? For you seem an idle man,
A spendthrift who thrives on spending, and throws time away.
Or else you get what food men give you going door to door,
Or beg like a fraud on Fridays and feastdays in churches.
And that's a loller's life that earns little praise
Where Rightfulness rewards men as they really deserve.
       He shall reward every man according to his works.
Or are you perhaps lame in your legs or other limbs of your body,
Or maimed through some misadventure, so that you might be excused?'
 'When I was young, many years ago,
My father and my friends provided me with schooling,
Till I understood surely what Holy Scripture meant,
And what is best for the body as the Book tells,
And most certain for the soul, if so I may continue.
And, in faith, I never found, since my friends died,
Life that I liked save in these long clothes.
And if I must live by labour and earn my livelihood,
The labour I should live by is the one I learned best.
      (Abide) in the same calling wherein you were called.
And so I live in London and upland as well.
The tools that I toil with to sustain myself
Are Pater Noster and Primer, *Placebo* and *Dirige*,
And sometimes my Psalter and my Seven Psalms.
These I say for the souls of such as help me.
And those who provide my food vouchsafe, I think,
To welcome me when I come, once a month or so,
Now with him, now with her, and in this way I beg
Without bag or bottle but my belly alone.
  And also, moreover, it seems to me, sir Reason,
No clerk should be constrained to do lower-class work.
For by the law of Leviticus that our Lord ordained
Clerks with tonsured crowns should, by common understanding,
Neither strain nor sweat nor swear at inquests,
Nor fight in a vanguard and defeat an enemy:
      Do not render evil for evil.
For they are heirs of heaven, all that have the tonsure,
And in choir and in churches they are Christ's ministers.
     The Lord is the portion of my inheritance.
     And elsewhere, Mercy does not constrain.
It is becoming for clerks to perform Christ's service,
And untonsured boys be burdened with bodily labour.
For none should acquire clerk's tonsure unless he claims descent
From franklins and free men and folk properly wedded.
Bondmen and bastards and beggars' children –
These belong to labour; and lords' kin should serve

33

God and good men as their degree requires,
Some to sing masses or sit and write,
Read and receive what Reason ought to spend.
But since bondmen's boys have been made bishops,
And bastards' boys have been archdeacons,
And shoemakers and their sons have through silver become knights,
And lords' sons their labourers whose lands are mortgaged to them –
And thus for the right of this realm they ride against our enemies
To the comfort of the commons and to the king's honour –
And monks and nuns on whom mendicants must depend
Have had their kin named knights and bought knight's-fees,
And popes and patrons have shunned poor gentle blood
And taken the sons of Simon Magus to keep the sanctuary,
Life-holiness and love have gone a long way hence,
And will be so till this is all worn out or otherwise changed.
Therefore proffer me no reproach, Reason, I pray you,
For in my conscience I conceive what Christ wants me to do.
Prayers of a perfect man and appropriate penance
Are the labour that our Lord loves most of all.
　'Non de solo,' I said, 'forsooth vivit homo,
Nec in pane et in pabulo; the Pater Noster witnesses
Fiat voluntas Dei – that provides us with everthing.'
　Said Conscience, 'By Christ, I can't see that this lies;
But it seems no serious perfectness to be a city-beggar,
Unless you're licensed to collect for prior or monastery.'
　'That is so,' I said, 'and so I admit
That at times I've lost time and at times misspent it;
And yet I hope, like him who has often bargained
And always lost and lost, and at the last it happened
He bought such a bargain he was the better ever,
That all his loss looked paltry in the long run,
Such a winning was his through what grace decreed.
　　　The kingdom of heaven is like unto treasure hidden in a field.
　　　　The woman who found the piece of silver, etc.
So I hope to have of him that is almighty
A gobbet of his grace, and begin a time
That all times of my time shall turn into profit.'
　'And I counsel you,' said Reason, 'quickly to begin
The life that is laudable and reliable for the soul.'
　'Yes, and continue,' said Conscience, and I came to the church.

34

REMARKS ON SURVIVING MANUSCRIPTS
OF *PIERS PLOWMAN*

A.I.Doyle

By the time that this essay is published it will be thirty-nine years since I first met George Russell, when as research students at Cambridge we were both put under the supervision of Bruce Dickins, for all that our subjects were quite dissimilar. At that time George was not involved with Langland but I had begun my research more than a year before with the notion of studying the evidence for the medieval circulation of *Piers Plowman* and had already realised that I could not find enough about it to fill a doctoral dissertation, chiefly because of what he has called the anonymity of the manuscripts, and so had widened my scope to other late Middle English theological literature. Since then there has been more than one briefer survey of the explicit testimonies and circumstantial implications concerning Langland's readers,[1] a few more manuscripts have emerged, and the relationships of the forms of text and all the copies have had very close attention. The publication of fuller descriptions of the manuscripts of this and other Middle English works,[2] of specimen and complete facsimiles of them in greater numbers, advances in the palaeography of the later middle ages and in the history of book decoration, and developments in discriminating the symptoms of written dialects, are broader grounds for hoping that it may not be long before it is possible to delimit the milieux of many more of the producers and owners of copies of the poem than has yet been achieved. I have said elsewhere[3] that it would be premature to embark on a thorough consideration of all of the manuscripts of the poem before the publication of the critical edition of the C text, and it will certainly be more profitable when surveys of the manuscripts of other major works and of recurrent scibes, now in mind or progress, have got further. Nonetheless it may be useful at this stage for me, having seen at one time or another, more or less superficially, all the known manuscipts of *Piers Plowman* except two fragments, and with specimen facsimiles to hand of almost all, to try to relate them to each other and to the wider problems of what sorts of people produced vernacular manuscripts, for whom, where and when, so far as our knowledge yet extends. In this I shall be particularly indebted to the Edinburgh Middle English Dialect Project, in an unpublished

---

[1] J.A.Burrow, 'The Audience of *Piers Plowman*', *Anglia*, 75 (1957), 373–84; Anne Middleton, 'The Audience and Public of *Piers Plowman*', in *Middle English Alliterative Poetry and its Literary Background*, edited by David Lawton (Cambridge, 1982), pp.101–23, 147–54.

[2] Particularly in the editions of the A text by George Kane (London, 1960), for comments on which see my review in *English Studies*, 43 (1962), pp.55–9, and the B text by Kane and E.Talbot Donaldson (London, 1975), which will be generally assumed in what follows here.

[3] 'The Manuscripts' (of other alliterative poems), *Middle English Alliterative Poetry*, pp.88–100 (p.90).

map of the dialectal distribution of thirty-nine manuscripts of *Piers Plowman*, and to Professor M.L.Samuels for letting me see a paper of his on the subject, in advance of publication.[4] The grouping of manuscripts by the orientation of their language as well as by their textual connections and their relative dating may reveal likenesses which might otherwise pass unnoticed and pose questions of importance about the circulation of the poem.

It is inescapable, from the complexity of textual inter-relationships which the editors have explored and from the dialect traces of previous copying, that the surviving manuscripts must be only a small proportion of those that once existed, and it is unlikely that the survivals are representative in every way of those that have vanished, but one cannot be content to explain particular predominances in regard to dating, dialect and states of text as solely the results of general factors of destruction, different perils in particular places, or mere chance. Of the fifty-four known at present, complete and incomplete, earlier than the date of the poem's first printing (1550), it seems to me that up to twenty could be, palaeographically, of the fourteenth century, although at least half of those could equally well have been written after the turn of the fifteenth century. We should always remember that a style of writing, and features in it, once adopted or adapted, could persist not only for the rest one scribe's career but as long again in other hands which had learned from him or his like, especially where there were few alternative models or influences, as was still the situation in many places outside the metropolis in the last third of the fourteenth century. Of the remainder of the manuscripts, only four seem to be of the second half of the fifteenth century, and three of the first half of the sixteenth. If there had been a constantly rising production of copies from the times of the composition of A, B and C, into the fifteenth century, then levelling off till say 1475 (when the supply and demand for books began to be affected by printing), one would expect proportionally more survivors from the mid-fifteenth century than there are, and fewer from the fourteenth. It seems that copying may have dropped notably in the middle of the fifteenth century, perhaps because there were enough copies already available to meet the demand, and perhaps because the demand had diminished. It is probably significant that Caxton and his immediate followers did not think it worth printing: business sense endorsing contemporary taste?

When one takes the probable and possible fourteenth-century manuscripts, however, the earlier-looking are not copies of what may be called for convenience the simple A text, but ones of all or parts of B and C, which on the now usually accepted chronology would make them not earlier than the 1380s or 1390s. It is not unparalleled for the very earliest copies of a work, particularly a very successful on to have disappeared (Richard Rolle's are an outstanding case from the fourteenth century), and it is not surprising that the earliest copies of Langland's A text, composed in the 1360s and perhaps slow to be multiplied, but increasingly sought after, should have been lost, as the other longer texts became available for preference, combination or con-

---

[4] 'Langland's Dialect', in *MAE*, 54 (1985), 232–47. See his 'Some Applications of Middle English Dialectology', *English Studies*, 44 (1963), 81–94 (p.94).

flation. It is apposite to mention here Bodley 851, which happens to be the only manuscript in which one form of combination of large parts (as distinct from continuous transcripts or shorter supplies) is physically apparent. Whether the version of passus I–VIII line 90 in the earlier portion of the volume is thought to be a scribal concoction of A with elements of B and C, or an authentic antecedent, or else revision, of A, palaeographically it could have been copied by 1388, when John Wells, the monk of Ramsey and Oxford theologian (whose ownership inscription accompanies it) died abroad; but there are no obvious reasons for supposing that he was the copyist of the poem, and the very pronounced S.W. Worcestershire spelling of it here (shown convincingly by Professor M.L.Samuels to agree with what could be Langland's own) seems less likely to have been preserved by someone like Wells than by a professional scribe (whom the proficiency of the hand would fit) in Oxford, where Professor A. G. Rigg sees the other contents as pointing.[5] The continuation of *Piers Plowman* by a later and hastier hand, of the earlier fifteenth century, completing passus VIII from A, with some Norfolk spellings (according to the Edinburgh Dialect Project), before proceeding with XI–XXIII from C, without them, plainly from a different source, could have been copied at Ramsey (Huntingdonshire).

It is not only early copies of A which are wanting; the Edinburgh Survey's mapping shows only three in West Midland dialects: Vernon (N. Worcestershire), Harley 875 (Warwickshire) and Lincoln's Inn 150 (Shropshire). Of these the first may be dated mainly, but shortly, before 1400, the second possibly but not far into, and the third probably in the first quarter of the fifteenth century. The state of A in Vernon, where it comes near the end of that monumental and expensive collection (possibly completed after 1400), is peculiar to it and Harley 875.[6] The latter is a different sort of book from the former. It is of the A text alone, of middling size (10¼ × 6¾ inches), on flawed membrane, with a portion of its contemporaneous membrane wrapper, now very defective like the text. It starts, for only the first quire, with ink ruling and an awkward attempt at bastard anglicana, with larger textura for Latin quotations, but then changes to a good standard of anglicana formata, with bastard for the Latin, within frame ruling only, perhaps not by a second scribe but the same one more at ease. In both portions the Latin is

---

[5] *Piers Plowman: the Z Version*, edited by A.G.Rigg & Charlotte Brewer, Studies and Texts, 59 (Toronto, 1983), pp.2–6, 27–33; compare A.G.Rigg, 'Medieval Latin Poetic Anthologies (II)', *Mediaeval Studies*, 40 (1978), 387–407; Hugh White, 'The Z-text: a new version of *Piers Plowman*', *MAE*, 53 (1984), 290–5, referring to a private communication of Mr M.B.Parkes, to whom I am also grateful for letting me see his opinion on the palaeographical evidence.

[6] Kane, *The A Version*, pp.5–6, 17, 39, 82, 85. Besides my difference about the dating of Harley there should be noted the subsequent publication of further accounts of Vernon: K.Savajaara, 'The Relationship of the Vernon and Simeon Manuscripts', *Neuphilologische Mitteilungen*, 68 (1967), 428–39; A.I.Doyle, 'The Shaping of the Vernon and Simeon Manuscripts', in *Chaucer and Middle English Studies in honour of Russell Hope Robbins* (London, 1974), pp.328–41; G.Guddat-Figge, *Catalogue of Manuscripts containing Middle English Romances* (Munich, 1976), pp.269–79; and my introduction to the forthcoming complete facsimile.

also underlined in red, there are red marginal parasigns,[7] indented passus initials and the same rubrication of some headings. Thus it was originally a copy of not the more costly nor the cheapest kind, although now very defective in text. Two citations of the Vulgate on the remains of the medieval wrapper point to the levels of clerical readership to whom Langland is reasonably supposed to have made his main appeal; yet this manuscript is not conspicuously the type of book written by a clerk for himself, so much as one procured from copyists with some experience of literary styles of script and presentation, but not in the higher grades. This is apparently the character of a considerable number of copies of all texts of *Piers Plowman*, whether alone or in volumes with other contents, such as Lincoln's Inn 150, where it follows four romances in the tall narrow 'holster' format which may have been designed for some sort of communal entertainment, as the 'coucher' format of Vernon was for conventual or domestic edification.[8]

What looks like the earliest other simple (but imperfect) copy of A, University College, Oxford, 45, by a hastier anglicana formata of the late fourteenth or early fifteenth century, with some of its defective text supplied by a later hand, is in a medieval binding with earlier Latin theological works. Linguistically linked to Cambridgeshire, textually it is paired with the complete Rawl.poet.137, in which occurs passus XII (lacking in Univ.) with the passage by John But (perhaps the king's messenger who died in 1387) mentioning Langland's death and his other writings (probably B or C).[9] Rawl.poet.137 itself, unlike Univ.Coll.45, was probably copied a good deal later than But's original manuscript, perhaps in the second quarter of the fifteenth century, in an idiosyncratic mixed set hand, signed by Tiltot, with spelling indicative of Sussex, and it belonged to the Franciscans of Canterbury in the late fifteenth or early sixteenth century.[10] It seems likely that this state of the text originated in the south-east of England and one may ask whether other forms of A started their dissemination from that region. The remaining copies of bare A are linked by the Edinburgh Dialect Survey with Suffolk (Society of Antiquaries 687 and Ashmole 1468), the East Midlands (Douce 323), Lincolnshire (Pierpont Morgan 818) and Durham (Trinity College, Dublin 213), and none with the London area, yet it is improbable that it was never copied there, and it seems more likely that some of the extant copies either derive from or are themselves metropolitan products, when one takes into account the possibility of scribes, especially before the establishment of a Chancery standard in the second quarter of the fifteenth century, retaining there some or all of their own or their exemplars' provincial spelling

---

[7] I follow Professor Kane and his colleagues in this usage here instead of the somewhat ambiguous 'paraff' or 'paraph'.
[8] Guddat-Figge, pp.228–31.
[9] G.Kane, *Piers Plowman: the Evidence for Authorship* (London, 1965), pp.50–1.
[10] See *Medieval Libraries of Great Britain*, Royal Historical Guides and Handbooks, 3, edited by N.R.Ker, second edition (London, 1964), p.48 n.6; not recorded in *A Version*, p.14. The Observants had the Canterbury convent from 1498.

practices.[11] The advent of B and C, of which it is usually assumed the first originated in London, where it must also have been easier to be aware of and to be able to procure a longer text, may have superseded much circulation of A there afterwards, except combined with one of the others, and led to the disappearance of early copies of the simple shorter text from the area. The currency of combined texts will be discussed after the simple ones.

Turning to simple copies of B, there are more than of A which may be dated somewhat before or slightly after 1400, and most of them are said to show West Midland dialect characteristics of not far from the author's homelands. One only is placed in Middlesex, Trinity College, Cambridge, B.15.17, written in an anglicana formata which in certain respects resembles that of a prolific Staffordshire scribe of the same period and in others that of the scribe of the Hengwrt and Ellesmere manuscripts of the *Canterbury Tales*, with the language of which it agrees, and the use of bastard anglicana, boxing and bracing for display is similar.[12] It has an illuminated vinet of late fourteenth-century style, not with those features which appear in metropolitan work very soon after 1400. It is altogether a handsome product, which as Professors Kane and Donaldson have said, could well be from a London (or Westminster) workshop. One characteristic of its lay-out, blank spacing between the parasigned passages of the text, is found in several copies of B, all of which are connected by the Edinburgh Project with the West Midlands: Bodleian Laud misc. 581,[13] BL Lansdowne 398 + Bodl.Rawl.poet. 38, BL Add. 35287, and Newnham College, Cambridge, 070 – the first two with S. Worcestershire, the others with Herefordshire and N. Oxfordshire, in a residual way according to Professor Samuels. All four are written in anglicana formata but the first three of earlier types and higher quality, Lansdowne/Rawlinson of the oldest aspect, Laud and Additional incorporating more secretary features and all three (like Trinity B.15.17) having the Latin text boxed in red; while Newnham, which has it rubricated, is of a later and less consistently formal type (probably of the second quarter of the fifteenth century), although it shows signs of superior expense in gold initials and an illuminated vinet (appropriate to that dating) and an enigmatic rebus presumably of ownership, most likely lay. The handwriting of Add. 35287 also varies considerably in grade with different stints, though perhaps all by the same hand, sometimes with strong resemblances to that of Hengwrt/Ellesmere, and has been very heavily corrected by at least two contemporary

---

[11] M.L.Samuels, 'Spelling and Dialect in the Late and Post-Middle English Periods', in *So Meny People, Longages and Tonges: Philological Essays in Scots and Mediaeval English presented to Angus McIntosh*, edited by M.Benskin & M.L.Samuels (Edinburgh, 1981), pp.43–54; M.Benskin & M.Laing, 'Translations and *Mischsprachen* in Middle English Manuscripts', *So Meny People*, pp.55–106.

[12] See W.W.Greg, *Facsimiles of Twelve Early English Manuscripts in the Library of Trinity College, Cambridge* (Oxford, 1913), pl.vii. Kane & Donaldson, *B Version*, p.13, do not make clear that Rolle's *Form of Living* and the devotional poem which follow *Piers Plowman* are an addition; they are found together also in Huntington Library HM 127.

[13] For facsimiles of the soiled first page of Laud see Richard Garnett, *English Literature: an Illustrated Record*, I (London, 1903), facing p.98, and *Piers Plowman: Prologue & Passus I–VII of the B Text*, edited by J.A.W.Bennett (Oxford, 1972), frontispiece (of top half only).

hands and so certified at the end of each quire, very possibly in order to serve as an exemplar for further copying. These corrections are said to be from a source of the genetic group of which Trinity B.15.17 is in part the earliest survivor and to which Add. 35287 also in part belongs. As Kane and Donaldson point out, we may infer a background to these manuscripts where different exemplars were available 'in close proximity such as that of a workshop'.[14] The only other early, though probably not so early, member of the same genetic group is Huntington Library HM 128, a complicated collection of items by a number of collaborating hands, different in aspect from the five manuscripts just discussed, yet also subjected to very heavy correction, in the *Prick of Conscience* as well as in *Piers Plowman*, both of Warwickshire language. This looks more like the work of a clerical group than of a commercial workshop.[15]

One is compelled to ask how many of such copies with West Midlands linguistic characteristics were actually made there or if some or all could be more or less faithful renderings of their exemplars done elsewhere and, particularly, in the metropolis? Langland's mention in B of his residence in London has led naturally to the supposition that its circulation started there, but it was not necessarily exclusively so, for the text could have been released both there and in his previous haunts if he or friends returned home. Since he seems to have chosen to express himself in an irreducible rhythm and idiom of distinctively regional character, he may or may not have concerned himself with any adaptation of more accidental features which copyists could themselves make, or not, according to their circumstances and convenience. In the light of our knowledge of demography and dialects in London and its vicinity in Langland's time, and for some time after, and of varying scribal practice with vernacular texts, it is by no means impossible that strongly provincial language was copied there, not necessarily modified to match or compromise with a range of metropolitan norms or tolerances, in a situation where people from every region of the British Isles met, and many owners of books made there may have been happy with what was familiar.

It is interesting that the only other copy in the same genetic group as Lansdowne 398/Rawl.poet. 38 (mentioned above)[16] is one attributed to Essex, a very different, rougher presentation in most respects, Corpus Christi College, Oxford, 201, in a current anglicana, the Latin in fere-textura, frame-ruled only, on poor membrane with many singletons, yet having, besides coloured initials and parasigns, the only historiated illuminated initial showing the dreamer, with good illuminated extensions of late fourteenth-century style, agreeing with the script.[17] This could be a case of an economical copy with dearer decoration done conveniently in London if it was not

[14] *B Version*, pp.50–1.
[15] *B Version*, pp.9–10, 49–50; Doyle, *Middle English Alliterative Poetry*, p.94.
[16] *B Version*, pp.25–32, 58–9, 63–4, 66–9; and see p.13 for early notes of London interest.
[17] For facsimiles of the top half of the first page with the initial see H.Hecht & L.L.Schücking, *Die Englische Literatur im Mittelalter* (Wildpark-Potsdam, 1927), p.99, and A.H.Bright, *New Light on Piers Plowman* (Oxford, 1928), frontispiece.

actually written there, for the population of the city was of course recruited constantly from the neighbouring counties, as well as from further afield, and there must have been a corresponding return movement of goods and interests. An instance of probable commercial handling of the poem in the metropolis in the second quarter of the fifteenth century is the highly conflated copy of B with C and A, in Huntington Library HM 114, by a fluent scribe in anglicana formata, who is assigned to S.E. Essex by Professor Samuels, and who produced another English miscellany of composite quarto paper and membrane, Lambeth 491, and was responsible for the beginning of BL Harley 3943 of Chaucer's *Troilus & Criseyde*[18] The compiler of these two miscellanies, if not the scribe himself (who supplied passages of *Troilus & Criseyde* in HM 114 missing from his main exemplar, not the same as for Harley, from another), must have had access to a wide range of sources, not least of alliterative verse, and the booklets into which they are divided are of course a flexible arrangement for both production and sale.

A genetic group of three copies of a combination of the beginning of C with a passage of A and the bulk of B, (perhaps a making good of a defective exemplar of the last),[19] Bodley 814, BL Add. 10574, and Cotton Calig.A.xi, of which the second seems to be copied from the first and the third related at one remove, has evoked the hypothesis of a 'strictly but not intelligently regulated workshop', which, from the comparison of the types of anglicana formata in which they are written, with coloured decoration, could have been operating within the first quarter of the fifteenth century. Professor Samuels sees their north Gloucestershire features as retained from a source and in the reasonable presumption that such stratification was most likely in London, but we need more palaeographical (in the absence of external) evidence to support or contradict it.

From the south-east quarter of England comes a genetic pair[20] of simple B texts: Oriel College, Oxford, 79, on poor membrane with frame ruling, but in an anglicana formata of professional quality from the first half of the fifteenth century, of Hertfordshire language, has additions of later in the century which includes lists of London wards and London churches and the privileges of Westminster Abbey; and Cambridge University Library L1.iv.14, with the same state of text, in a more current hand on paper, about the second quarter of the century, followed by the only known copy of *Richard the Redeless*, and popular prose Books of Astronomy and Physiognomy, with various English and Latin items added by other hands, is assigned by language to Cambridgeshire. These could be metropolitan products of differing cost or may represent occurrence of B in East Anglia, where copies of A are also

---

[18] Doyle, *Middle English Alliterative Poetry*, pp.94, 144. See the forthcoming catalogue of medieval manuscripts in the Huntington Library. The watermarks, on which Professor Ralph Hanna has kindly sent me further notes, may point to the 1420s or 1430s.
[19] *B Version*, pp.1–2, 5, 40–2; G.H.Russell, 'Some Aspects of the Process of Revision in *Piers Plowman*', in *Piers Plowman: Critical Approaches*, edited by S.S.Hussey (London, 1969), pp.27–49 (p.48).
[20] *B Version*, pp.4, 11–2, 22–4.

found in the middle and second half of the fifteenth century. There is an odd combination of the beginning of B with the end of A in BL Harley 3954, a prose and verse miscellany in Norfolk English in 'holster' format with a set of (unfinished) illustrations of Mandeville's Travels, perhaps of the second quarter of the century, and linked by other contents with a less ambitious book of plainly Norfolk origin.[21]

Cambridge University Library Dd.i.17 seems to stand apart from other copies of the simple B (save for a small number of agreements with Corpus 201 and Newnham) and its linguistic character is unsettled, but the proficient anglicana formata, bastard anglicana and textura in which this very large volume is written, apparently all by one scribe, are of later fourteenth-century types usually employed in monastic books with contents like the Latin chronicles and other works here, a number of which correspond with items in a few volumes in the library of the Austin Friars at York at the end of that century; some features of the spelling and annotation may support a northern provenance or destination, rather than the older guess of Glastonbury.[22] It is of interest that, although the earliest known bequests of *Piers Plowman* are by and to secular priests of the York Diocese[23] (though the first, in 1396, was of West Midland origins), no extant copy can be located nearer than south Lincolnshire (Pierpont Morgan M818) and Durham (Trinity College, Dublin, 213), both of A, and the latter is of the late fifteenth century.[24] Manuscripts may have been owned in some areas without being copied much or at all, and the relatively rare cases of copying in such areas may have disappeared completely, to the disadvantage of any attempt to trace the whole dissemination.

When we turn to simple copies of C it is remarkable that they include more of the earliest-looking manuscripts than survive for A and B. And by the Edinburgh mapping they appear to cluster, even more than those of B, in the West Midlands. Cambridge University Library Dd.iii.13 is in a rapid anglicana, with Latin in larger formata, suggestive of the third quarter of the fourteenth century or earlier rather than the last fifteen years or so in which this old-fashioned hand must have done it; he might well have been an exact contemporary of the author, his language is located on the borders of Gloucestershire, Herefordshire and Monmouthshire, and the text is carefully corrected and so certified on every page for the first half of the book,[25] which is, unusually, foliated. Though the main initial spaces have not been filled,

[21] *A Version*, pp.7–8; M.C.Seymour, 'The English manuscripts of *Mandeville's Travels*', *Edinburgh Bibliographical Society Transactions*, 4, pt.5 (1966), 167–210 (pp.187–8). The other Norfolk volume is Cambridge University Library Ii.iv.9, including the same group of religious poems.
[22] *B Version*, pp.2–3; A.Middleton, *Middle English Alliterative Poetry*, pp.105–6; compare M.R.James, 'The Catalogue of the Library of the Augustinian Friars at York', in *Fasciculus Ioanni Willis Clark Dicatus* (Cambridge 1909), pp.35–6, 156C.
[23] Not religious, as expressed by Professor Middleton, p.103.
[24] *A Version*, pp.4–5, 8–9; Doyle, *Middle English Alliterative Poetry*, pp.96, 99, 145–7.
[25] Despite the omission of many lines through haste: *The Vision of William concerning Piers the Plowman*, edited by Walter W.Skeat, III, Early English Text Society 54 (London, 1873), pp.xlii–iii.

there is functional yellow-tinting of parasigns, line initials, Latin quotations, passus headings and endings. Bodleian Library, Oxford, Laud misc. 656, where the alliterative *Siege of Jerusalem* is followed by passus I and II only of *Piers Plowman* and some English prose, is a smaller book, in a medieval binding, on rather poorer membrane, frame-ruled, initials red or unfilled, in another utilitarian anglicana of the later fourteenth century, whose spelling is put in north Oxfordshire, where it could have been home-made by a cleric.[26]

In contrast, Digby 171,[27] of south-east Herefordshire, is more handsome, in an anglicana formata of one of the varieties developed towards the end of the fourteenth century chiefly in literary use, probably in more than one centre, and the characteristics of this rounded specimen are reminiscent of some copies of the Southern Legendary, indigenous to this region. A more individual creation, approximating in parts to bastard anglicana (in its minims) or feretextura (in loop-less ascenders), is BL Cotton Vesp.B.xvi, placed in south Warwickshire, though with additions including a Latin note on the Holy Blood of Hailes Abbey (Glos.) and an English poem on Henry VI's visit to St Paul's, London, in 1458 by the same hand, which may or may not have any significance for the location after that date.[28]

The script of Huntington Library HM 143, the copy of C chosen by Derek Pearsall and by George Russell as the basis for their editions, is an anglicana formata of more current characteristics than those cited in the last paragraph, becoming larger and less careful towards the end. It is much corrected, with notes certifying it every few leaves, in the same or contemporary hands.[29] The first initial is illuminated, with a demi-vinet of the end of the fourteenth century; and BL Add. 35157, in a similar type of writing, enlarged for Latin etc., with a possible scribe's name and marks of supervision, has a first initial, though more modest, of the same period.[30] In both of these the language is of south-west Worcestershire, the area of the Malvern Hills, although in Add. 35157 mediated by a copyist from further north in the county, and in HM 143 Professor Samuels sees 'some slight signs of interference typical of a London copying'; thus again we face the question which occurred with copies of B,

---

[26] Doyle, *Middle English Alliterative Poetry*, pp.93, 143; another facsimile of Laud as frontispiece to Skeat, and see his description, pp.xxiv–xxx.

[27] Skeat, pp.xliv–v.

[28] Skeat, pp.xxxix–xl; colour facsimile of first page in Garnett, facing p.96; and reduced, uncoloured, in Hecht & Schücking, p.103.

[29] *Piers Plowman: an Edition of the C-Text*, by Derek Pearsall (London, 1978), pp.20–2. G.H.Russell, 'Some Early Responses to the C-Version of *Piers Plowman*', *Viator*, 15 (1984), 276–8, describes its contemporary annotation; I incline to date the later name of a monk he mentions as fifteenth rather than sixteenth-century. A bifolium of a copy of *Troilus & Criseyde* in a strongly secretary-influenced hand of the early fifteenth century bound in the volume does not seem to offer proof about the earliest provenance, though a somewhat similar hand is responsible for an extract of *Piers Plowman* on f.108r.

[30] Russell, 'Some Early Responses', p.281; *Catalogue of Additions to the Manuscripts in the British Museum in the years 1894–99* (London, 1901), pp.192–3. The name Preston at the end, boxed, in red, is in the same shade as the Explicit boxed above. I know of two other manuscripts with the same name of the probable scribe, but they are both of the mid-fifteenth century, and not in the same hand.

how many of the extant copies may have been produced, more or less faithfully to West Midland exemplars, in other parts of England and especially the London region?

How it could come about is illustrated by one pair of incomplete copies, with good evidence for early dating and localisation: Trinity College, Dublin, 212, in which occurs the unique information about the author's origins by an annotator, probably clerical and about 1412, with special interest in Wales and its marcher lords in the earlier fourteenth century;[31] and London University Library V.17, where *Piers Plowman* is followed by the English verse *Estorie del Evangelie*, both from a dismembered volume in which they were preceded by Robert Mannyng's *Handlyng Synne* and *Meditations on the Supper of Our Lord*, now Folger Library, Washington, V.b.236, and Mandeville's Travels in English prose, now Mr R.H.Taylor's at Princeton University Library, all in the same hand and uniform in decoration.[32] The hand of Trinity is an expert literary anglicana formata of late fourteenth-century character and its spelling is assigned to north-west Gloucestershire, while the equally expert hand of the larger dismembered volume, in which the *Piers Plowman* is assigned to west Worcestershire, is of early fifteenth-century appearance, and has illuminated initials and borders in the metropolitan style of that period, from the first of which hangs an impaled escutcheon (which could be original) probably intended for Sir William Clopton, a landowner in Worcestershire, Gloucestershire, Warwickshire, Staffordshire and Shropshire, and his wife Joan Besford, of a Worcestershire family. They had married by 1403, and he died in 1419, between which dates the book could well have been made.[33] Whereas there is nothing to dissociate Trinity 212 from the West Midland background, it seems not improbable that the more ambitious Clopton collection was illuminated if not also written in the metropolis. Of course on the one hand we must allow for mobility amongst craftsmen, and the spread of artistic styles, and on the other we ought to bear in mind that if an exemplar were transported to a distance to meet such a private commission, and did not remain there, no other progeny need have been generated in the place of manufacture.

There is another possible instance to be adduced, London University

---

[31] E.St.John Brooks, 'The *Piers Plowman* Manuscripts in Trinity College, Dublin', *The Library*, 5th series 6 (1951), 141–53; G.Kane, *Piers Plowman: the Evidence for Authorship*, pp.26–32, pl.I, II (i–ii). A similar hand to that of the historical notes gives that date on p.15 at passus IV line 481 with reference to Antichrist (Oldcastle's rising?).

[32] N.R.Ker, *Medieval Manuscripts in British Libraries*, I (Oxford, 1969), 376–7; A.G.Mitchell, 'A Newly Discovered Manuscript of the C-Text of *Piers Plowman*', *MLR*, 36 (1941), 243–4 for the text.

[33] Ker questions the armorial identification, but although the tinctures of the dexter half of the central pendant shield are incorrect for Clopton (a lapse not unparalleled in medieval manuscripts with correct charges), the impaled coat is right for his wife, who in her widowhood seems to have become a vowess or recluse: compare *Transactions of the Bristol & Gloucestershire Archaeological Society*, 13 (1888–9), 162 foll.; *Victoria County History, Worcestershire*, III, 24, 315, IV, 21, 27, 84–5. Clopton was associated with the entourage of Richard Beauchamp, Earl of Warwick, for whom one manuscript, of an English work of Gloucestershire origin (Trevisa's translation of Higden's *Polychronicon* for Beauchamp's father-in-law) was at least completed, and probably made in the same period in London (BL Add. 24194).

Library V.88 (the former Ilchester MS), written by a prolific copyist in the good rounded literary anglicana formata (conceivably based on something like that of Digby 171 mentioned above) which has been identified in a number of expensive manuscripts of Gower, Chaucer and Trevisa apparently produced and illuminated in London or its vicinity in the first dozen or twenty years of the fifteenth century.[34] Comparative analysis of his spelling throughout his known output has shown personal W. Midland habits amidst a progressive modification by the systems of the texts he transcribed for the most part with close faithfulness to the exemplars.[35] The language of his *Piers Plowman* is south-west Worcestershire, and it has been argued whether some lines peculiar to it may go back to the author.[36] We do not know where it was copied, but the daisy-buds attached to its illuminated initials were customary before 1400 in the metropolis and survived somewhat later elsewhere.[37]

As with B, if C had commenced its circulation, in the author's own dialect, both in London and the West Midlands, there is no problem: in both areas faithful transcriptions and translations into other spelling systems or compromises, were possible. What is difficult to conceive is that, if C had been released by the author in London, or reached it at an early date, no copies of the simple text should survive in other than West or W. Central Midland guise. There is an extract, C.XVII 182–98 with the related Latin, under the heading 'nota bene de libero arbitrio secundum augustinum & ysidorum', in Gonville & Caius College, Cambridge, 669/646, signed by its copyist, John Cok, possibly before he became a brother of St Bartholomew's Hospital, London, in 1421 and certainly before 1456 (since it belonged to John Shirley who died in that year)[38], which agrees specifically in its readings with Cambridge University Library Ff.v.35, a complete copy of C, with Mandeville's Travels, in an excellent textura with good coloured decoration, probably of the first half or middle of the fifteenth century. An ownership inscription of Thomas Jakes, perhaps the man admitted to Lincoln's Inn in 1465, is over an earlier irrecoverable one, and the Oxfordshire language of *Piers Plowman* may mean it was written there, though it could of course be by an Oxfordshire scribe in London or a close copy from an exemplar of that complexion.[39] If Cok shows a characteristically clerical interest in one aspect of the poem it is notable that neither Shirley's own manuscripts, nor those

---

[34] Ker, 377–8; A. I. Doyle & M. B. Parkes, 'The Production of Copies of the *Canterbury Tales* and the *Confessio Amantis* in the Early Fifteenth Century', in *Medieval Scribes, Manuscripts and Libraries: Essays presented to N. R. Ker*, edited by M. B. Parkes & A. G. Watson (London, 1978), pp. 163–210, esp. 17–82, pl. 51.

[35] J.J.Smith, 'Linguistic Features of Some Fifteenth-Century Middle English Manuscripts', in *Manuscripts and Readers in Fifteenth-Century England*, edited by Derek Pearsall (Cambridge, 1983), pp.104–12, esp. p.110.

[36] Russell, 'Some Aspects', pp.28–9; Derek Pearsall, 'The "Ilchester" Manuscript of *Piers Plowman*', *Neuphilologische Mitteilungen*, 82 (1981), 181–93.

[37] Professor Francis Wormald compared this feature with a Winchester manuscript of the 1380s.

[38] A.I.Doyle, 'More light on John Shirley', *MAE*, 30 (1961), 93–101 (p.98).

[39] *Pace* Seymour, p.182, on script and owners. Mr J.J.Griffiths has told me of several other manuscripts owned by Jakes.

derived from his, reveal any, although not devoid of other alliterative compositions.

Unless rather more copies of simple C can be demonstrated to be by scribes operating predominantly in London and its vicinity, we may be forced to conclude that the poem was little known in that form there, but mainly in the southern West and Central Midlands. Since we have seen that copies of B, simply and in combinations, were available in the London area, the not immediately obvious superiorities of the alternative long version might be discovered (as no manuscript advertises the distinction) by only a few people in a position to compare copies; most often in the book-trade, where combination or conflation was quite likely (as in HM 114) to be the result.

To look now at combinations of A and C, there is more than one of which the extant copies suggest the possibility of origin or at least circulation in the southeastern quarter of the country. Connected genetically in their A first half, Liverpool University Library F.4.8 and Trinity College, Cambridge R.3.14[40] are both in good anglicana formata of c.1400, with standard decoration, the former perhaps more provincial in appearance but both linguistically mixed; the latter has been taken as the best base for critical editions of A and most closely related textually to it is BL Harley 6041, a much later and rougher copy, on paper, of the second quarter or middle of the fifteenth century, with penwork armorials (partly added), one perhaps Kentish. The language is south-eastern, and the book belonged subsequently to a monk with a Kentish name, who added an English form of confession to it.[41] It seems as if this line of dissemination could have run through the London area.

A different state of A combined, and conflated, with C is found in the former Duke of Westminster's MS, which is written in an elegant set secretary of the kind employed by Privy Seal and some other official scribes at the beginning of the fifteenth century, with bastard anglicana passus rubrics, coloured initials, parasigns and line-fillers; it is simplest, though not necessary, to guess that this may have been so commissioned and executed in that milieu.[42] Connected textually in part but contrasting graphically is National Library of Wales 733B, on poor membrane and by a clumsy bastard anglicana with perfunctory decoration, of uncertain origin and date, probably not far into the fifteenth century, perhaps where better could not be done or by someone who could not afford better.[43] And Digby 145, written by Sir

---

[40] *A Version*, pp .2–3, 15, 28, 39, 113–4. Facsimile of frontispiece with textura caption 'God spede þe plouȝ ...' in Garnett, p .95.

[41] *A Version*, pp .6–7; besides the early sixteenth-century monk of St Augustine's Canterbury mentioned there was a subsequent namesake at Faversham (*Archaeologia Cantiana*, II, 64).

[42] *A Version*, pp .18, 31–5, 39. Sold at Sotheby's, New Bond Street, 11 July 1966, lot 233, for 28,000 pounds to Messrs B .Quaritch on behalf of an anonymous British collector; reduced facsimile in auction catalogue.

[43] *A Version*, pp. 12–3, 35–6; *National Library of Wales Journal*, 2, pt. 1 (1941–2), 42–3, pl. vii. 'Johannes Staptun', fifteenth-century, on p. 137.

Adrian Fortescue in the 1530s, in the home counties or Oxfordshire, shows the processes of amalgamation still in progress.[44]

That the character of the language of all the copies in the last two groups of combined texts is so mixed that they are not on the Edinburgh map suggests that even by the beginning of the fifteenth century the stages of transcription had been numerous enough to have incidentally destroyed consistency or that by conscious choices the more distinctly regional features had been eliminated. The latter process no doubt happened more frequently in the metropolis than elsewhere.

It will have been obvious how repeatedly one is drawn to discuss the reproduction and diffusion of texts and books in English terms of bipolarity between the provinces and the metropolis, with regard to an author who embodied it in his work and to a period at the start of which, in Langland's own life-time, the balance was only beginning to move increasingly, not yet overwhelmingly, in the latter direction. In most of the manuscripts of *Piers Plowman* we can see the development of formalised cursive scripts, especially for literary use in the vernacular, a universal phenomenon in fourteenth-century Europe which reached its peak here about the turn of the fifteenth. It is too easy to assume that all expert examples of anglicana formata of this kind must be metropolitan because the great growth in expensive book production for the expanding market of lay owners was in or around London. There are enough individual instances, independent of any metropolitan associations, to indicate the contrary, though as yet wanting attachment to other likely centres. Beyond that there is a broader problem of schools of writing and local characteristics, which awaits investigation.

If I ask myself what manuscripts of other works do many of those of *Piers Plowman* most resemble the answer is some of the *South English Legendary*, the *Prick of Conscience* and the *Speculum Vitae*, lengthy religious poems of apparently wide circulation in more than one region, well established by the end of the fourteenth century outside the metropolis, and probably not much handled in later trade there. I should not be surprised if it turns out that more than we have yet noticed of the copies of those poems (for all three Vernon, for the *Prick* Society of Antiquaries 687, Huntington HM 128, and Rylands Eng. 90 by the hand of Add. 34779, attributed to Shropshire)[45] share the same scribes. There are resemblances in some early copies of Trevisa, not unexpected in view of his Gloucestershire connections, but not in the copies in the hands and styles of the illuminated manuscripts of Gower, Chaucer and Lydgate from the second and third quarters of the fifteenth century, most probably London products. And, excepting *Troilus & Criseyde*, their poems are not found copied or bound with *Piers Plowman*. It is hard to avoid the impression that it was not a leading article of commerce in the metropolis

---

[44] *A Version*, pp. 9–10, 36–7; mid-sixteenth-century family memoranda not mentioned there.

[45] R. E. Lewis & A. McIntosh, *A Descriptive Guide to the Manuscripts of the Prick of Conscience* (Oxford, 1982), pp. 84–5, 89–90, 103–4, 146–7. The identification of Add. and Ryl. is owing to the Edinburgh Survey.

after the earlier years of that century, and only somewhat occasionally in cheaper copying.

From the character of the work and its author one would anticipate that many copies were made by individuals of similar education for themselves or their acquaintances, but for only a minority of the surviving manuscripts can the distinctive habits of this segment of society be seen as formative in their origin, and while medieval annotation is not wanting to confirm the interests of early readers, specific evidence of ownership is sparser. A noticeable number of copies give the names of ostensible scribes and possible owners: John But, John Cok and Adrian Fortescue we can identify, but who were Thomas Dankastre (HM 137),[46] Preston (Add. 35157), Tilot (Rawl.poet. 137) and Herun (Harley 3954)? Scribal signatures are comparatively rare in England, and it is my impression that when they occur they more often denote an amateur or part-time copyist of books than a full-time commercial one. That however is not simply related to the levels of competence, so we are still left with few firm facts and too much room for conjecture. A great deal more study of the handwriting of the era is needed, not confined to books containing English, before the outlines of a persuasive picture can emerge.

[46] Skeat, pp.xix–xxiv; R.W.Chambers, 'The manuscripts of *Piers Plowman* in the Huntington Library', *Huntington Library Bulletin*, 8 (1935), 1–27; reduced facsimile of part of a page in James Thorpe, *The Gutenberg Bible* (San Marino, 1975), p.13.

THE ROLE OF *SCIENTIA* IN *PIERS PLOWMAN*

James Simpson

Sister M.C.Davlin has argued in a recent article that Langland found in the word 'kynde', as it is used in the phrase 'kynde knowynge', 'an array of interacting meanings perfectly though paradoxically suited to suggest the kind of knowledge called *gnosis* or *sapientia* in the Church tradition.'[1] As I shall argue, this kind of knowledge is defined, both in *Piers Plowman* and in certain monastic texts, by ironically deflating the terms of human, academic education; beyond confirming Sister Davlin's argument by pointing to these monastic texts, I should like, however, to qualify it by going on to consider the way in which the traditions of *scientia*, or specifically human modes of knowing, are drawn upon by Langland to point towards this divine, 'kynde', sapiential knowledge.

I

In an anonymous twelfth century text, the *Tractatus de Interiore Domo*, which is closely related to one text Langland seems certain to have known, and to another which he may have drawn upon in his description of the soul,[2] we find this passage:

Unicuique est liber sua conscientia: et ad hunc librum discutiendum et emendandum omnes alii inventi sunt. Anima cum de corpore egreditur nullum alium praeter conscientiae suae librum secum portare poterit, atque in illo cognoscet quo debeat ire, et quid debeat recipere. Ex his quae scripta erunt in libris nostris judicabimur, et ideo scribi debent secundum exemplar libri vitae: et si scripti non sunt, saltem corrigendi

---

[1] 'Kynde Knowynge as a Middle English Equivalent for "Wisdom" in *Piers Plowman* B', *MAE*, 50 (1981), 5–18. See also her earlier article, 'Kynde Knowynge as a Major Theme in *Piers Plowman*' *RES*, n.s. 22 (1971), 1–19.

[2] Langland seems certain to have known the influential *Meditationes Piisimae de Cognitione Humanae Conditionis*, *PL*, Vol.CLXXXIV, col.485, which he cites at B.XI.3. For a discussion of Langland's possible indebtedness to this and related texts, see J.S.Wittig, '*Piers Plowman* B, Passus IX–XII: Elements in the Design of the Inward Journey', *Traditio*, 28 (1972), 211–280. It is possible, however, that Langland knew the passage he cites from extracts of the *Meditationes*, which circulated independently of the text as a whole. See, for example, BL Additional MS 41069, f.59b, which begins with the line cited by Langland at Passus B.XI.3 (the opening words of the text), but is only a short extract. The text from which Langland may have drawn his description of the soul is the *Liber De Spiritu et Anima*, *PL*, Vol.XL, col.780. See A.V.C.Schmidt, 'Langland and Scholastic Philosophy' *MAE*, 38 (1969), 134–56, for Langland's possible use of this text. For the textual similarities between all these works, see R.Bultot, 'Les "Meditationes" Pseudo-Bernadines sur la connaissance de la condition humaine, Problèmes d'histoire littéraire', *Sacris Erudiri*, 15 (1964), 256–92, who also presents the evidence for a monastic provenance and a date probably late in the twelfth century for the group.

sunt. Conferamus itaque libros nostros cum libro vitae: et si quid aliter
habuerint, corrigantur, ne in illa ultima collatione ... abjiciantur. ...
Multae sunt scientiae hominum, sed nulla melior est illa, qua cognoscit
homo seipsum. Quamobrem redeam ad cor meum, et ibi stare
assuescam, ut totam vitam meam possim discutere, et meipsum
cognoscere.[3]

What is of especial interest in this passage is the way in which the comparison
between the sciences of men and the natural science of knowing oneself is
made. The monastic writer uses terms derived from the crafts of preparing
and reading books to describe the way in which he should treat the 'book' of
his conscience: that book is to be copied and corrected from the exemplar of
the Book of Life, and it is to be read 'critically' as it were, if we understand
the term 'discutere', as I think we should in this context, as meaning 'to treat
of points in books which are dubious or requiring explanation' (*Thes. Linguae
Latinae* s.v.2b). But if the monk uses these terms, he does so precisely in
order to reveal the relative uselessness of these crafts as applied to literal
books: the burden of the passage is, after all, the superiority of the natural
science of knowing the self to the 'scientiae hominum'.

    The terms of human learning are used, it seems to me, to the same effect in
Piers Plowman. The 'book of conscience' is referred to in the poem: Anima
tells Will in Passus XV that saints lived in the desert with 'no book but
conscience';[4] we do find, however, the terms of book-learning used with more
pointedly ironic effect when placed beside the lessons taught by the
conscience. When Piers first speaks in the poem, for example, he says that he
knows the way to Saint Truth 'as kyndely as clerc doth hise bokes./
Conscience and Kynde Wit kenned me to his place' (V.539). Piers is taught
('kenned') not by books, but by his own conscience and natural understanding. What these faculties teach, we learn from Piers' directions to the
pilgrims, is to 'loven Oure Lord God levest of all thynges' (l.563), which is
what Holychurch had pointed out to Will earlier in the poem as the thing he,
too, knows naturally (B.I.142). That Piers does know this 'kyndely' is clear
from the way in which he compares his manner of knowing with that of
scholars: he knows it as 'kyndely as clerc doth his bokes'. This is not
necessarily damaging to the knowledge of scholars, for in one sense of the
word 'kyndely', Piers is saying that he knows the way to St Truth completely,

---

[3] *PL*, Vol. CLXXXIV, col. 507 (col. 520).
[4] B.XV.534. All references are to the B-Text, edited by A. V. C. Schmidt (London, 1978), except
where the C-Text is specified, when I shall cite from the edition of D. Pearsall (London, 1978).
For the phrase 'book of conscience', see A. V. C. Schmidt, 'Langland's "Book of Conscience"
and Alanus de Insulis', *N & Q*, n.s. 29 (1982), 482–484, and E. Wilson, 'Langland's "Book of
Conscience": Two Middle English Analogies and Another Possible Latin Source', *N & Q*, n.s. 30
(1983), 387–389. To these should be added J. Leclercq, 'Aspects Spirituels de la Symbolique du
Livre au XIIe Siècle', in *L'Homme devant Dieu, Mélanges offerts au Père Henri de Lubac,
Théologie*, 57 (Paris, 1963), 63–72, in which many other examples of the Latin phrase are
adduced.

in the way scholars know their books completely (s.v. *MED* 2(d)).[5] But the potential attack on book-learning is contained in another sense of the word 'kyndely', according to which it can mean 'naturally' (s.v. *MED* 1(a)). For if Piers has been taught naturally by his conscience and natural understanding, this can never be said of the knowledge of scholars, which is necessarily acquired. And that the potential attack on the learning of scholars may become actual is clear from his reply to the priest after the tearing of the pardon. Here the terms of clerical learning are used to very specific and brilliantly ironic effect. The priest mocks Piers by saying that he is 'lettered a litel', and, at VII.131, asks Piers who taught him 'on boke'. In answer, Piers does not deny his ignorance of letters, but disparages the priest's learning in this way:

'Abstynence the Abbesse', quod Piers, 'myn a.b.c. me taughte,
And Conscience cam afterward and kenned me muche moore'.

(B.VII.132)

Piers' manipulation of the terms of human instruction, in the context of the priest's mocking question 'Who learned thee on boke?', is hostile to such learning: he uses such terms ('a.b.c.', 'kenned') to illuminate the fact that one is taught the preliminary lessons of moral knowledge through hardship and the conscience, but also to deflate the claims of any 'lessons' taught by the literal alphabet. The very structure of the words themselves 'Abstynence', 'Abbesse' and 'a.b.c.' contain the argument that the real, moral a.b.c. lies not in school-education, but rather in hardship and discipline.[6]

The monastic texts in which we find this manipulation of school-terms for ironic effect are not necessarily hostile to learning in the way Piers is here. In the *Meditationes Piisimae de Cognitione Humanae Conditionis* (cited by Langland at B.XI.3), for example, the author does allow a place for the reading of books, while at the same time insisting that the real act of reading is one of introspection:

Sed quid prosunt hae litterae admonitionis nisi deleas de libro conscientiae tuae litteras mortis? Quid prosunt haec scripta, lecta et intellecta, nisi temetipsum legas et intellegas? Da ergo operam internae lectioni, ut legas, inspicias, et cognoscas teipsum. (col.508)

The 'litterae admonitionis', like the activities of the scriptorium mentioned by the author of the *Tractatus*, are not being rejected here, so much as placed below the treatment and reading of the *real* 'book', the *liber conscientiae*. The

---

[5] The expression also appears in *Mum and the Sothsegger*, edited by M.Day and R.Steele, EETS o.s. 199 (1936), 1.109.

[6] For word play of this kind, see B.F.Huppé, '*Petrus id est Christus*, Word-Play in *Piers Plowman*, the B-Text', *ELH*, 17 (1950), 163–191. For the strategy of using institutional terms in this way, simultaneously to reveal a moral or spiritual force in them, and to criticize their normal application, see my article, 'The Transformation of Meaning: A Figure of Thought in *Piers Plowman*', *RES*, 37 (1986), 1–23.

terms of school-learning are, however, used in an ironic way, and with hostile intent, by monastic writers when the terms refer specifically to the learning of the schools, as distinct from the *Schola Christi* of the monastery. We find this kind of irony in the *Tractatus*, in this passage, for example:

> Deum namque cognoscere, plenitudo est scientiae ... Ad huius vero scientiae plenitudinem opus est potius intima compunctione, quam profunda investigatione; suspiriis, quam argumentis; crebris lamentationibus quam copiosis argumentationibus; lacrimis, quam sententiis; oratione, quam lectione; gratia lacrymarum, quam scientia litterarum.
> (col.552)

Here the terms of the school (as distinct from the monastery) are compared with, and deflated by comparison with, the means to real knowledge, which is through compunction. This manipulation of the terms of school-learning is commonly found within monastic writings which compare the kind of knowledge gained in the cloister with that of the school. The most vehement of those who oppose school-learning is Peter Damien (d.1072), who writes thus, for example, in his small tract *De Sancta Simplicitate Scientiae Inflanti Anteponenda*:

> Ecce frater, vis grammaticam discere? disce Deum pluraliter declinare[7]

The irony is incisive here, and its basic thrust is developed and extended in larger rhetorical patterns throughout the twelfth century. Thus Petrus Cellensis (d.1183) compares the learning of the university and the monastery in this way, in a letter written to John of Salisbury in 1164:

> Ibi [in the monastery] in libro vitae non figuras et elementa, sed ipsam sicut est divinitatem et veritatem oculo ad oculum cerneres, sine labore legendi ... sine sollicitudine retinendi, sine timore obliviscendi. O beata scola, ubi Christus docet corda nostra verbo virtutis suae, ubi sine studio et lectione apprehendimus quomodo debeamus aeternaliter beate vivere! Non emitur ibi liber, non redimitur magister scriptorum, nulla circumventio disputationum, nulla sophismatum intricatio, plana omnium questionum determinatio, plena universarum rationum et argumentationum apprehensio.[8]

The strategy which Piers uses to deflate the value of human education,

---

[7] *PL*, Vol. CXLV, col. 695. For many other examples, see J. Leclercq, *L'Amour des Lettres et le Désir de Dieu* (Paris, 1957), ch .IX, and 'Etudes sur le Vocabulaire Monastique du Moyen Age' *Studia Anselmiana*, 48 (1961), 1–167, especially ch .II, 'Philosophia' (pp.39–68); H .de Lubac *Exégese Médiévale, Théologie*, 41 (Paris, 1959), p.74; J .de Ghellinck, *Le Mouvement Théologique du XIIe Siècle*, second edition (Brussells, 1948), pp .93–96 and E .Gilson, *La Théologie Mystique de Saint Bernard* (Paris, 1947), ch .III.
[8] *PL*, Vol .CCII, col .519 (col .520).

then, seems to me to derive from the monastic tradition I have briefly described, in which authentic knowledge of the self, and therefore of God, through the conscience, is consistently placed above the knowledge gained through human instruction and books.

II

That Piers is advocating a radical anti-intellectualism at B.VII.132–3 is plausible from evidence both internal and external to the poem. We need only remember that it is the authoritative figure Holychurch who rebukes Will for having asked how he might know Truth, by asserting that he knows it naturally:

> It is a kynde knowynge that kenneth in thyn herte
> For to loven thi Lord levere than thiselve.

(B.I.141–2)

And from evidence external to the poem, the suggestion receives authority from classical and patristic treatments of the liberal arts, and their later medieval reformulations, many of which do state the fact that the unlettered are also capable of wisdom and, of course, of salvation. We read this, for example, in the *De Institutione Divinarum Litterarum*, written by Cassiodorus in the early sixth century:

> Sciamus tamen non in solis litteris positam esse prudentiam, sed perfectam sapientiam dare Deum unicuique prout vult. Nam si tantum in litteris esset scientia rerum bonarum, qui litteras nesciunt, utique rectam sapientiam non haberent. Sed cum multi agrammati ad rerum intellectum perveniant, rectamque fidem percipiant coelitus aspiratam, dubium non est puris ac devotis sensibus Deum concedere, quod eis iudicat expedire. Scriptum est enim: Beatus homo quem tu erudieris, Domine, et de lege tua docueris eum (Psalm 93.12).[9]

We also find the theme stressed by St Augustine in the Prologue to Bk.I of the *De Doctrina Christiana*,[10] and by St Jerome who, in a letter concerning the use of the liberal arts which was widely known in the later Middle Ages, points to the profound wisdom of the 'rustici' Peter and John both of whom were, he says, wiser than Plato.[11] We find re-statements of this letter in Jacques de Vitry (d.1240), Nicolas Lyre (d.1349), and Robert Holcot (d.1349), for example,[12] where the figure of the gifted 'rusticus' would seem to point us in

---

[9] *PL*, Vol.LXX, col.1106 (col.1141).
[10] *PL*, Vol.XXXIV, col.15 (col.17).
[11] *Ad Paulinam De Studio Scripturarum, PL*, Vol.XXII, col.540.
[12] Jacques de Vitry, *Sermo* XVI, *Ad Scholares*, edited by J. B. Pitra, in *Analecta Novissima*, 2 vols (Tusculum, 1886), II, 366; For Lyre, see the Prologue to his postilla on the *Glossa Ordinaria, PL*, Vol.CXIII, col.25; For Holcot, see *Commentum in Librum Sapientiae* (Basel, 1586), pp.324–5.

the direction of Piers.

But if we do find arguments of this kind in both patristic and later medieval texts, it is important to notice that these arguments only come within the context of a *defence* of the use of the liberal arts in a programme of theological learning. Recognition that the unlettered may have wisdom is tempered by the knowledge that this is not the general case, and that, on the whole, humans must be instructed in the traditions of human learning as they move towards an understanding of God. It may have been more difficult for Langland, writing in the later fourteenth century, to see any consistent movement from human to divine learning, than it was for, say, Dante writing early in the same century, in the shadow of thirteenth century scholasticism,[13] but we can, I think, see in the speech of Study in Passus X a bridge for the mind between dogmatic statement, designed to be simply accepted passively by the mind, and an active, 'kynde' understanding of God.

Study erupts into the poem with her splendid invective both against Wit for misleading Will, and, more generally, against all those intellectuals who misuse logic in arid and presumptuous theologicaal debate. It is revealing, I think, that she should introduce herself by this attack on those who misuse the arts in her domain, but this is not to say that she is anti-intellectual, as one recent critic would have it;[14] it signals to us, rather, that the fundamental emphasis of her speech to Will is on the discretion and care with which the human arts of learning must be handled. It is true, however, that the immediate emphasis of her speech is, at the conclusion of her attack on those who misuse logic, against theological investigation altogether, in favour of passive acceptance of basic dogma:

> Wilneth never to wite why that God wolde
> Suffre Sathan his seed to bigile;
> Ac bileveth leely in the loore of Holy Chirche,
> And preie hym of pardon and penaunce in thi lyve,
> And for his muche mercy to amend yow here.
>
> (B.X.119–29)

The verbs in the first line here, 'wilneth' and 'wite', encapsulate the action of the previous Passus, in which Will has been questioning Wit;[15] Study sees this collaboration, however, as obstructive to salvation, and asserts that instead of wishing to know, Will should simply believe and observe the fundamental demands of faith, which she formulates in an uncompromisingly dogmatic way.

And if Study points to intellectual activity as being obstructive to faith, she complements this by stressing the value of moral action above intellectual

---

[13] For a helpful sketch of this context, see D .Murtaugh, *'Piers Plowman' and the Image of God* (Gainesville, 1978), pp .76–82. See also J .Coleman, *'Piers Plowman' and the 'Moderni'* (Rome, 1981), ch .I.

[14] Thus J .Norton-Smith, *Piers Plowman* (Leiden, 1983), p .110.

[15] This point has been made by J .Dillon, *'Piers Plowman*: A Particular Example of Wordplay and its Structural Significance', *MAE*, 50 (1981), 40–48 (p .42).

definition. She turns her attack on her husband Wit, and rebukes his elaborate attempts to define Dowel, Dobet and Dobest in this way:

> And tho that useth thise havylons to [a]blende mennes wittes
> What is Dowel fro Dobet, now deef moot he worthe,
> Siththe he wilneth to wite whiche thei ben alle.
> But if he lyve in the lif that longeth to Dowel,
> I dar ben his bolde borgh that Dobet wole he nevere,
> Theigh Dobest drawe on hym day after oother.
>
> (B.X.131–6)

Langland is clearly fond of the analytical personification–allegory which Wit had used in Passus IX, but he is, it seems to me, aware of its limitations and even prepared to laugh at it.[16] Study's own use of the terms of Wit's allegory undermines that kind of personification-allegory altogether, which she describes as a 'havylon' – a 'wile' or 'deceptive trick'. In response to this attack, Wit's intellectual exuberance is entirely confounded; and in her description of the triad, Study stresses its practical, 'verbal' (as distinct from its 'nominal') aspect: she asserts that Will must 'lyve the lif' which pertains to Dowel, and insists upon this verbal aspect in the next line when she short-circuits the syntax of the 'Dowel's' usage as a noun, and uses it instead as a verb:

> For I dar ben his bolde borgh that Dobet wole he nevere,
> Theigh Dobest drawe on hym day after oother.
>
> (B.X.135–6)

Study's grammatical acumen (which we would expect of her as the instructor of grammar) is used here, then, to undercut precisely the analytical casuistry which Wit had used. If Will does not *do* better, then a mere concept of Dobest will be of no use to him at all.

So, despite the fact that it is *Study* who speaks here, whose function it should be to teach the preliminary arts of reading and writing, her speech does not seem in fact to offer a place for those arts of learning. But it is through her grammatical acumen that Study points Will towards the real and practical nature of Dowel, by using the expression as a verb, then this in itself gives us the clue by which we might understand the exact place of the acquired arts of knowing in the poem; for if Study cannot herself give a complete understanding of truth, she can at least exercise her own grammatical skill to point to her own limitations, and this, in turn, points in the direction of more profound modes of knowing.

That Study does afford a place to the arts over which she has control is implicit in the passage which follows: for here she agrees, in response to Will's

---

[16] See M.Carruthers, *The Search for St Truth, A Study of Meaning in 'Piers Plowman'* (Evanston, 1973), pp.88–89 for a discussion of the limitations of the literary form used by Wit.

humility, to direct him to Clergy and Scripture. Will courteously beseeches
Study's grace, by promising to serve her all his life in this way:

> ... Mercy, madame; youre man shal I worthe
> As longe as I lyve, bothe late and rathe,
> For to worche youre wille the while my lif dureth,
> With that ye kenne me kyndely to knowe what is Dowel.
>
> (B.X.145–8)

Given Study's agreement to Will's request, it would seem clear that to *know*
what Dowel is is in fact distinct from, and above, simply observing the
demands of a faithful life, which are specified in Study's dogmatic command
to believe 'lelly in the loore of Holy Chirche' (X.121). But even here, where
Study does acknowledge a place for the preliminary arts of learning, the
formulation of her acknowledgement insists upon submission to higher forms
of knowledge. She politely refuses Will's offer of life-long service, and implies
thereby that Will must move beyond her domain; instead of teaching Will
'kyndely to know what is Dowel', she uses the same verb Will had used,
'kenne', to specify what she *is* capable of teaching, in this way:

> I shal kenne thee to my cosyn that Clergie is hoten.
> He hath wedded a wif withinne thise sixe monthes,
> Is sib to the sevene arts – Scripture is her name.
> They two, as I hope, after my techyng,
> Shullen wissen thee to Dowel, I dar wel undertake.
>
> (B.X.150–4)

Her modification of Will's request is based on a recognition that Will must
not offer Study life-long service in the way he promises to do. This refusal to
accept such service is consistent with, and intelligible within, a tradition which
defines the appropriate age at which one should study the liberal arts, and it is
this focus on the age appropriate for different kinds of study which provides
one of the compromises, it seems to me, between the importance of the
preliminary arts of learning and the necessity to approach more profound,
theological knowledge. In a sermon of Alain de Lille (d.1202), for example,
we find an elegant formulation of a theme which is also found in classical
discussions of the appropriate age at which the liberal arts should be studied.
In his *Sermo de Clericis ad Theologiam non Accedentibus*, we read this
condemnation of those who offer their greatest powers to the liberal
sciences:

> Non ideo dico quod Deus dampnet naturales scientias a se institutas, a
> se mirabiliter ordinatas, pedissecas theologie, ancillas celestis philoso-
> hie. Non in eis dampnat naturam artis, sed moram desidis. Sunt enim
> quidam in liberalibus scientiis cani, in theologia senes elementarii, qui
> florem iuuentutis offerunt naturali scientie, fecem vero senectutis
> theologie. Sed ... salutande liberales artes a limine, id est, postquam

nos perduxerint ad limen theologie, ad ianuam celestis regine, relinquende sunt in pace; non ut ibi figamus pedem sed ut faciamus pontem.[17]

And Study refuses to teach Will 'kyndely' to understand what Dowel is, precisely because she recognizes that she cannot teach Will to know Dowel 'kyndely' at all. Like her refusal of Will's offer of life-long service, this deference to higher instructors in matters of moral understanding is consonant with classical, patristic and later medieval formulations of the role of the arts, which stress the incapacity of the liberal arts to teach moral virtue. We read this, for example, in a Parisian sermon of Jacques de Vitry, which stresses the same themes as the sermon of Alain de Lille cited above:

Stultus quidem est agricola qui vomerem suum exacuit, et terram nunquam excolit. Ars enim dialectica acuit ingenium et elimat ut ad majora praeparetur. Unde Seneca: Filios nostros liberalibus artibus erudimus, non quia virtutem dare possunt, sed animum ad virtutem recipiendam praeparant. Hieronymus ait: Artes a limine sunt salutandae, debent enim praeparare animum, non detinere (p.362).[18]

In the passage from l.170, after the allegorical directions to Clergie (which resemble, incidentally, the characteristics of Chaucer's Clerk in the General Prologue[19]), Study specifies to Will the subjects over which she does have control, as a kind of password to Clergy. She specifies grammar, rhetoric and

---

[17] In *Alain de Lille, Textes Inedits*, edited by M-Th. d'Alverny (Paris, 1965), p.275. For a brilliant discussion of Alain de Lille's place in the development of theology as an academic discipline, see M-Th.d'Alverny, 'Alain de Lille et la Theologia', in *L'Homme devant Dieu, Mélanges offerts au Père Henri de Lubac*, pp.111–28. The idea of the 'elementarius senex' is found in Seneca, Epistle 36.4, in *L. Annaei Senecae, ad Lucium Epistulae Morales*, edited by L.D.Reynolds (Oxford, 1965). The phrase 'a limine salutanda' is also derived from Seneca (Epistle 49.5–6), used with reference to the way in which dialectic should be studied. The same themes are also expressed in the following passage from a mid-twelfth century text (between 1141 and 1147), the *Sententiae Diuinitatis*: 'Non est autem consenescendum in artibus, sed a liminibus sunt salutandae. De ipsis transeundem est ad sacram paginam, propter quam in eis ad tempus studendum est'. ('Die *Sententiae Diuinitatis*, ein Sentenzenbuch der Gilbertschen Schule', edited by B.Geyer, in *Beiträge zur Geschichte der Philosophie des Mittelalters*, 7 (1901), Prologue, p.7). For an early thirteenth century example, see a sermon of Peter of Poitiers (d.1205), cited by C.H.Haskins, in 'The University of Paris in the Sermons of the Thirteenth Century', *American Historical Review*, 10 (1904), 1–27 (p.9, n.7). Robert Fishacre expresses the same idea in his *Sententiae* (c.1240–3), cited by M-D.Chenu, *La Théologie au Douzieme Siècle* (Paris, 1976), p.92, n.2.

[18] The reference to Seneca is drawn from Epistle 88. The most powerful statement of the fact that the liberal arts do not teach virute is, perhaps, that of Augustine in the *Confessions*, IV.16.

[19] See J.Mann, *Chaucer and Medieval Estates Satire* (Cambridge, 1973), pp.77–8. The tradition I am adducing, in which the progression from the arts to theology is stressed, supports Mann's argument that there is a quiet satire of the Clerk in the *General Prologue*, insofar as the end of his study, theology, is not mentioned: 'Of studie took he moost cure and moost heede' (l.303).

dialectic, music, and some mechanical crafts before going on, at l.182, to declare her incapacity to understand theology.

Study's description of a pedagogic programme designed to serve the study of Scripture (to whom Clergie is married), with its emphasis on certain liberal and mechanical arts, derives in its broad outlines from patristic sources, and in its specific shape from twelfth century formulations of the arts preliminary to an understanding of Scripture. However hostile Augustine might have been towards the literary culture of his time, he does nevertheless formulate his conception of *scientia*, or specifically human knowledge, in terms of literary disciplines in the *De Doctrina Christiana* at least. Whereas *scientia* is presented in largely moral terms in the *De Trinitate*, Augustine formulates an intellectual role for *scientia* when faced with the problem of understanding the content of Sacred Scripture in the *De Doctrina Christiana*. *Scientia* is conceived of here as the preparation for *sapientia*, or the understanding of divine truths, as contained in Scripture.[20] Having defined those human sciences which are not supertitious, he distinguishes those which are 'superflua' and those which are 'necessaria'.[21] Of the necessary sciences the most important is 'litterarum figurae' (col.55); he also includes history (col.55), 'intelligentia animalium, herbarum siderumque' (cols 56–7), the mechanical arts, plus a guarded acceptance of dialectic and the numerical arts (cols 58–60).

This basic programme of study is formalised in the twelfth century by a number of writers, often in a quite uncontentious way, and always within the Augustinian categories of *scientia* and *sapientia*. Thus Honorius Augustoduniensis (d.1156), for example, in the *De Animae Exsilio et Patria*, specifies the place of the human arts of learning in this way, referring to the chosen people of God:

In sapientia autem locati quasi in lucida regione conversantur, ideo et filii lucis (l.Tess.V) appellantur. De hoc exsilio ad patriam via est scientia, scientia enim in rebus physicis: sapientia vero consideratur in divinis. Per hanc viam gradiendum est non passibus corporis, sed affectibus cordis. Haec quippe via ducit ad patriam tendentes per decem artes.[22]

He goes on to specify the ten arts as the trivium and the quadrivium, plus physics, mechanical art, and 'oeconomica', and to say that once these have been passed through, 'pervenitur ad sacram scripturam quasi ad veram patriam'. Rupert of Deutz (d.1129) also, in his *De Sancta Trinitate*, includes the mechanical arts in his description of *scientia* (which he defines as 'omnium bonarum et licitarum artium notitia'), but lays greatest stress on the liberal

---

[20] This discussion is dependent on H-I.Marrou, *St Augustin et la Fin de la Culture Antique* (Paris, 1958), Part III, chs 1 and 2.
[21] *PL*, Vol.XXXIV, col.15. The discussion is found in Bk.II.
[22] *PL*, Vol.CLXXII, col.1241 (col.1243).

arts, which he describes as 'lascivae, garrulae et verbosae puellulae', before they are set to their proper task of explicating Scripture.[23] The most famous of such texts is, of course, the *Didascalicon* of Hugh of St Victor (d.1141); Hugh also includes the mechanical arts, but, like Rupert, lays particular emphasis on the liberal arts as the necessary preparation for the understanding of Scripture. By the arts, he says,

> via paratur animo ad plenam philosophiae veritatis notitiam. Hinc trivium et quadrivium nomen accepit, eo quod his, quasi quibusdam viis, vivax animus ad secreta sophiae introeat.[24]

But if texts of this kind do provide a basic defence of the arts as a preliminary 'pons introductorius' to the reading of Scripture, they do so by consistently reminding the reader of the dangers inherent in the study of secular disciplines, and by insisting on the fact that the study of such disciplines must be 'recte ordinata' towards an understanding of Scripture.[25] This pattern of commending the arts, and then warning against their misuse, is also found in the way in which Study offers her range of knowledge as a password to Clergy and Scripture. The fact that she does offer her own arts as a password itself implies how clearly she sees her role as one of serving Scripture. And the statement of the subjects she teaches would seem to me to imply a strict limitation of her capacities to those subjects which serve scriptural understanding. She does mention music, but her emphasis falls upon the trivium:

> Plato the poete, I put hym first to boke;
> Aristotle and othere mo to argue I taughte.
> Grammer for girles I gart first write.   (B.X.175–7)

---

[23] *CCCM*, Vols XXII–XXIV, p. 2048–382. See also G. Evans, *Old Arts and New Theology: The Beginnings of Theology as an Academic Discipline* (Oxford, 1980), pp. 57–79, for a helpful discussion of Rupert's conception of the relationship between theology and the liberal arts.

[24] ed. C. H. Buttimer (Washington, 1939) Bk. III, cap. 3, p. 53. Although it is true that the liberal arts in the thirteenth century were not thought to provide a complete education in human disciplines (see, for example, Aquinas' statement to this effect in his *In Boethium De Trinitate*, translated as *The Division and Methods of the Sciences*, by A. Maurer, (Toronto, 1963), qu. 5, art. 1, ad 3, p. 11), I have presented twelfth century formulations in particular because Langland seems to me to follow a conservative scheme in Passus X, which does not reflect developments in the universities. For the survival of the liberal arts as a programme of study in schools (as opposed to universities, where they were treated as a propaedeutic to the three philosophies (natural and moral philosophy and metaphysics)), see P. Delhaye, 'La Place des Arts Libéraux dans les programmes scolaires du XIIIe Siècle', in *Arts Libéraux et Philosophie au Moyen Age*, Actes du Quatrieme Congrès International de Philosophie Médiévale (Montreal and Paris, 1969), pp. 161–173. See also J. A. Weisheipl, 'The Place of the Liberal Arts in the University Curriculum during the XIVth and XVth Centuries', in *Arts Libéraux et Philosophie au Moyen Age*, pp. 209–213. For a more general treatment of the development of the curriculum leading to Theology in the twelfth century, see G. Paré, A. Brunet, P. Tremblay, *La Renaissance du XIIe Siècle. Les Ecoles et L'Enseignement*, Publications de l'Institut d'Etudes Médiévales d'Ottawa, 3 (Paris, 1933), pp. 97–108.

[25] The phrase is drawn from Hugh of St Victor's *De Sacramentis Ecclesiae PL*, Vol. CLXXVI, col. 185.

The fact that she lays so little stress on the quadrivial arts may be significant: for in one tradition at least, those arts were not considered to lead to spiritual understanding in the way of the trivial arts. Thus we find in another sermon to Parisian scholars by Jacques de Vitry, an encouragement to study the trivium, 'which prepares the hearer for the science of piety', but a warning against the quadrivial arts since, although they contain the truth, they do not 'lead to piety' (p.368). This theme is also found in the *Speculum Doctrinale* of Vincent of Beauvais (d.1264),[26] and derives from a commentary of St Jerome on the Epistle of St Paul to Titus.[27] The argument that Study is deliberately omitting these arts gains strength from her description of those illicit arts over which she also has control, but against which she warns Will; for here she does include Astronomy and Geometry (ll.207–8).[28]

And just as the twelfth century texts referred to above stress the limitations of secular disciplines within a higher, 'sapiential' kind of knowledge, so too does Study define her own limitations in her description of Theology, which she says is quite beyond her:

> Ac theology hath tened me ten score tymes:
> The more I muse therinne, the myst[lok]er it semeth,
> And the depper I devyne, the derker me it thynketh.
> It is no science, forsothe, for to sotile inne.
> [If that love nere, that lith therinne, a ful lethy thyng it were]
> Ac for it let best by love, I love it the bettre,
> For there that love is ledere, ne lakked nevere grace.
> Loke thow love lelly, if thee liketh Dowel,
> For Dobet and Dobest ben of loves k[e]nn[yng].
>
> (B.X.182–90)

At the heart of the Dowel section, then, we have a passage which carefully defines the limitations of human, analytical learning. But however much Study may have seemed to deny a place to such arts of knowing, it will now be clear that this is not the case, and that she has, rather, given those arts a distinct yet limited place within the movement of knowledge towards 'kynde knowynge'. We can understand, from this perspective, the precise way in

[26] 6 vols. (Duaci, 1624), I.35.
[27] *PL*, Vol.XXVI, col.555 (cols 558–9). This tradition is to be sharply distinguished from another, in which the quadrivial arts are felt to approach most closely to God. For this, see Alain de Lille, *Theologicae Regulae* XXXI, where mathematics is described as being the art most closely approaching the nature of God (*PL*, Vol.CCX, col.636). See also his *Sermo de Sphaera Intelligibili* in d'Alverny, *Textes Inedits*, pp.295–306, and Dante's *Paradiso*, where Dante's final act of comprehending God is likened unto that of a Geometer (XXXIII.133–8). For a discussion of the place of the quadrivium more generally, see P.Kibre, 'The *Quadrivium* in the Thirteenth Century Universities (with special reference to Paris)', in *Arts Libéraux et Philosophie au Moyen Age*, pp.175–191.
[28] Study's description of, and warning against, illicit arts is also characteristic of both the patristic and twelfth century formulations of the human sciences to which I have referred. See, for example, *De Doctrina Christiana*, *PL*, Vol.XXXIV, col.50, and Hugh of St Victor's *Didascalicon*, VI.XV. p.132.

which Study uses the terms of academic learning to describe the most profound kinds of knowledge. When, that is, she comments that 'Dobet and Dobest ben of loves k[e]nn[yng]' (which is changed, in the C-Text, to read 'For of Dobet and Dobest here doctour is dere love' (XI.136)), she is not using the term 'kennying' in an ironic way entirely to deflate her own kind of teaching, just as in the C-Text she is not using the word 'doctour' to deflate its academic sense; her use of these terms is, rather, a discreet recognition of her own limitations when it comes to teaching what love is, while at the same time her speech as a whole does assert the value of her role in pointing towards an understanding of love. Her description of love as one who teaches, or as a 'doctour', exercises only a limited irony towards the idea of academic teaching, unlike the hostile irony of Piers in his description of Abstinence as his teacher of the 'a.b.c.'[29]

III

Study, then, sends Will forward into more profound capacities of knowing, Clergy and Scripture. If there is, however, a deep uncertainty about the value of learning in the poem, the ultimate defence of learning must come not from the acquired arts themselves, who do not have the authority for such a defence within the context of Will's search for 'kynde knowynge'; that defence must come rather from the natural faculties of Will's soul (or, more accurately, the soul of which 'Will' is a part), who do perceive that God can be known naturally, but who recognize, nevertheless, the usefulness of the acquired arts of learning. That Study's very careful defence and placing of those arts is of insufficient authority to convince Will is implicit in the fact that his own attack on learning comes *after* his meeting with Study, in his

---

[29] The strategy is analogous to Dante's use of the terms of scholastic discourse in *Par.*XXIV–XXVI, where the forms of scholastic examination and argument are used to present the exposition of specifically theological concepts, whose nature is beyond the conceptual power of logical discourse. But in describing the 'larga ploia' of the Holy Spirit as a 'sillogismo' (XXIV.91), for example, the intent is not ironically to deflate the proper use of logical exposition. However much the grace of the Holy Spirit is beyond the conceptual power of logic, the forms of scholastic procedure do allow for measure and stability of utterance. (For this effect, see R.Kirkpatrick, *Dante's 'Paradiso' and the Limitations of Modern Criticism* (Cambridge, 1978) ch.3 esp.). It remains true that the terms of logical discourse *can* be used ironically to underline the incapacity of logic to comprehend love, though in a secular context. Thus, for example, Gower's amusing treatment of Aristotle succumbing to love in the *Confessio Amantis* (edited by G.C.MacCaulay (Oxford, 1899)):

> I syh there Aristotle also,
> Whom that the queene of Grece so
> Hath bridled, that in thilke time
> Sche made him such a silogime,
> That he foryat al his logique;
> Ther was non art of his Practique,
> Thurgh which it mighte ben excluded
> That he ne was fully concluded
> To love ...

(VIII.2705–13)

encounter with Clergy, from Passus X.396, which might suggest that progress in intellectual understanding is precisely what provokes doubts about its efficacy. Will relentlessly produces examples of the tradition I cited earlier, that the unlettered may have wisdom. Ploughmen and shepherds, he says, these 'lewed juttes', will pierce the 'palace of heaven' easily (X.456). To support the case that the learned may be damned, he cunningly manipulates the traditional image of the ark representing the Church, where the carpenters, who represent the clergy, were not, Will argues, saved.

These arguments are not without force in the poem as a whole; we have already seen how crucial points of the poem are marked by just such an emphasis on the superiority of natural, as against acquired knowledge. Piers Plowman is himself a 'lewed jutte', and the arguments have force, too, within the patristic tradition I mentioned earlier, in which it is stressed that the ignorant may have wisdom. Like Study, however, Clergy is unable to answer Will's arguments here; instead, a natural faculty of Will's soul, Imaginatif, must offer the most explicit and expository defence of acquired learning in the poem, from Passus XII.64. Imaginatif, like Study, offers a moment at which he both reflects upon what has gone before in the poem, emphasising its limitations, and at which he points Will towards the kind of knowledge he must now approach. He distinguishes between 'Clergie' and 'Kynde Wit', which comprise the lower capacities of knowing (and which would seem to summarize the series of figures Will has encountered: Thought and Wit, on the one hand, comprise 'Kynde Wit', while Study, Clergie, and Scripture comprise 'Clergie'), before he goes on to specify the kind of knowledge upon which Will must now attend in this way:

> Ac grace is a gifte of God, and of greet love spryngeth;
> Knew nevere clerk how it cometh forth, ne kynde wit the weyes.
>
> (B.XII.68–9)

If Imaginatif's exposition (whose force has been carefully defined by D. Murtaugh (pp. 91–96)), provides a theoretical placing of human learning, by defining both its value and its limitations, it is, however, only in the feast-scene of Passus B.XIII that the relation between acquired and natural learning receives its most fully imagined and dramatic treatment, and it is to aspects of this scene I should now like to turn.

The definition of Clergy's limitations offered by Imaginatif points forward to the encounter of Will and Patience; Imaginatif says that grace, which Clergy is unable to comprehend, grows only in 'patience and poverty' (XII.61). It is unsurprising, then, that the limitations of Clergy should again be stressed when Conscience and Patience take their leave of Clergy in Passus XIII; like Study in Passus X (and unlike any other figure in the poem except Study), Clergy discreetly declines to comply with Conscience's request that he define Dowel, and uses instead his analytical skill to underline the limitations of analysis in this way:

'I have sevene sones', he seide, 'serven in a castel
Ther the lord of lyf wonyeth, to leren hem what is Dowel.
Til I se tho sevene and myself acorde
I am unhardy', quod he, 'to any wight to preven it.
For oon Piers the Plowman hath impugned us alle,
And set alle sciences at a sop save love alone;
And no text ne taketh to mayntene his cause
But *Dilige Deum* and *Domine quis habitabit*;
And saith that Dowel and Dobet arn two infinites,
Which infinites with a feith fynden out Dobest,
Which shal save mannes soule – thus seith Piers the Plowman'.

(B.XIII.119–128)

Here again the role of the analytical, liberal arts (Clergy's 'sevene sonnes')
is recognised as being potentially useful in proving what Dowel is; but in this
context, where Clergy is himself aware of a more profound, natural
knowledge (the 'kynde knowynge' of Piers Plowman), the activity of those
analytical arts becomes uncertain, and falters. Clergy, as Anne Middleton has
argued, uses a grammatical term to highlight this inability: for in saying that
Dowel and Dobet are 'infinites', Clergy also stresses, in a technical way, the
active nature of Dowel: precisely as *infinite* verbs, they cannot be analysed
and defined, and they do not cease when Dobest begins.[30] Here, where the
terms of the acquired arts of learning are manipulated to point to their
inadequacy to grasp the most profound kind of knowing (in the same way that
Study had exercised her own grammatical acumen), we can, I think, see that
Clergy is not using 'sciences' in a purely ironic way in saying that Piers has set
'all sciences at a sop save love one'; for while it is true that Clergy is pointing
to the incapacity of those arts one would normally describe as 'sciences' to
comprehend the nature of Dowel, his own use of the terms of those arts shows
how they can be manipulated to point in the direction of a kind of knowledge
which is beyond them.

And if Clergy uses grammatical terms to point towards the domain of
knowledge which is outside his range, so too does Patience, in the speech
immediately following, underline the inadequacy of grammatical knowledge.
His triad of 'disce, doce, diligere' suggests that the Dowel triad involves an
educative, cognitive progress. When he offers his enigmatic riddle, which is
quite beyond Clergy's ken, it is significant that the analytical force of the
grammatical term he uses, 'ex vi transicionis', is lost, and transformed. It is
quite submerged in the typological field of reference opened up by the pun on
transicio (if we accept, as I do, the interpretation of the phrase proposed by
E.C.Schweitzer): the phrase literally means 'by the power of transivity', but
in the context this grammatical sense seems to give way to a historical sense
by the pun on *transitus*, meaning 'passover':

---

[30] 'Two Infinites: Grammatical Metaphor in *Piers Plowman*', *ELH*, 39 (1972), 169–88.

With half a laumpe lyne in Latyn, *Ex vi transicionis*,
I bere ther, in a bou[s]te, faste ybounde Dowel,
In a signe of the Saterday that set first the kalender,
And al the wit of the Wodnesday of the next wike after;
The myddel of the moone is the myght of bothe.

(B.XIII.151–5)[31]

If emphases of this kind confirm the place of the analytical arts as defined by Study in Passus X, Clergy's final leave-taking from Conscience also helps us to understand the place of those arts in a programme of theological learning. Conscience is prompted to go out on pilgrimage with Patience through, he says, Patience's good will; this alerts us to the fact that from this point in the poem it is Will himself, as the human will, who is to be instructed through a more profound kind of knowledge. But this in itself involves a recognition that Clergy is unable to instruct the will; before he leaves, Conscience whispers in Clergy's ear:

Me were levere, by oure Lord, and I lyve sholde,
Have pacience parfitliche than half thi pak of bokes!

(B.XIII.200–1)

Clergy does not see the humour of this remark, and refuses to bid farewell to Conscience. At this point, however, a reconciliation takes place, which imaginatively represents the fundamental, ideal relation between preliminary, acquired knowledge and 'kynde knowynge' in the poem. Conscience assuages Clergy's hurt pride by saying that 'if Patience be oure partyng felawe and pryve with us bothe', then Clergy and Conscience will together convert the entire world to the true faith. 'Partyng felawe', in this context, seems to me to be a revealing pun: on the one hand, it means 'partner', which is the meaning assigned to it in the *MED* (s.v.(e)), and this aspect of meaning is extended in the rest of the line – 'and pryve with us bothe'; on the other hand, at this moment of leave-taking, the phrase would seem to be jolted out of its normal meaning to mean something like 'the fellow with whom we take our leave of each other'. This aspect of meaning, which stresses the fact that Conscience and Clergy must separate for the moment, is strengthened by Clergy's reply, when he accepts what Conscience says, and agrees to content himself with the teaching of children and scholars until Conscience returns,

Til Patience have preved thee and parfit thee maked.

(B.XIII.214)

If I am correct in detecting a pun on 'partynge felawe', then we could explicate the sense of the line by saying that Clergy, Conscience and Patience

---

[31] ' "Half a Laumpe Lyne in Latyne" and Patience's Riddle in *Piers Plowman*', *JEGP*, 73 (1974), 313–27. See also, for the grammatical context of the phrase, R.E.Kaske, ' "*Ex vi transicionis*" and Its Passage in *Piers Plowman*', *JEGP*, 62 (1963), 32–60.

will all be partners in grace, if Clergy patiently takes leave of Conscience. The full power of Clergy is revealed only after Conscience, in 'kynde knowynge', has been made perfect; a perfected Clergy is not felt to lead completely to a perfect Conscience, but is, rather, subsequent upon the perfection of the Conscience. This relation, in which the craft of learning is fully potent only after Conscience has been perfected, is also, we might notice, felt at moments when a perfect commonwealth is being established. Thus it is Conscience who heralds the coming of Grace in Passus XIX; the first crafts which Grace distributes are:

> ... wit, with wordes to shewe,
> Wit to wynne hir lyflode with, as the world asketh,
> As prechours and preestes, and prentices of lawe –
> They lelly to lyve by labour of tonge,
> And by wit to wissen othere as grace hem wolde teche.
>
> (B.XIX.230–4)

In conclusion, then, we can see that however much Piers does embody the inspired figure whose knowledge of God is 'kynde', or sapiential, and however much that tradition of knowing might be expressed through ironic deflation of the terms of human, academic knowledge, it is nonetheless true that Langland does recognize a place for the acquired disciplines of human education, by drawing upon and personifying the traditions of human learning which define its place as a propaedeutic to the study of Scripture. If Langland represents traditions of intellectual history in this way, it is also true that he is concerned to enact rhetorically the way in which human disciplines lead to the point at which they fail, and at which they must attend upon deeper sources of knowledge; he enacts, that is, the way in which the pedagogic figures of Study and Clergy manipulate their grammatical, analytical skill to undercut the confidence of the intellect, and at the same time to promote an awareness, at least, of a 'kynde', sapiential knowing whose 'doctour is dere love'.

LANGLAND'S ORIGINALITY:
THE CHRIST-KNIGHT AND THE HARROWING OF HELL

R.A.Waldron

No reader of *Piers Plowman* can fail to respond to the climactic power of the Passion and Harrowing of Hell sequence in the B and C Versions (B Passus XVIII, C Passus XX). Here with great virtuosity Langland knits together into a unitary dramatic vision many of the patterns of thought and imagery which have threaded through the poem hitherto. The dialectic of salvation which has sent the Dreamer 'about ... and about' from the beginning of the poem is brought for the time being to a triumphant conclusion in the argument of the Four Daughters of God and the debate before the gates of hell. Many dichotomies find their resolution here: truth and deception, mede and charity, the old law and the new, justice and mercy. The Dreamer's long quest, which dramatically quickens pace in the journey through historical and liturgical time to Jerusalem in Holy Week, is brought also to a psychological climax by his falling asleep at the beginning of B XVIII *wery of þe world* and his waking at the end of the passus into everyday life on Easter morning to the reassurance of the Cross and *goddes resurexion* and to the sound of Easter bells.[1]

There is the satisfying finality of a synthesis and an answer to doubt in all this – yet at the same time, perhaps, for the reader, an element of puzzlement in the very relief which he feels in recognition of the familiar. Have we really come through so much questioning to find the answer under our very nose? The answer to *this* question is, of course, partly 'Yes'. Solutions to the Dreamer's difficulties are to be found, as we might have deduced from a careful reading of the speeches of Holy Church in Passus I, among the central tenets of his faith, and the rediscovery of those great commonplaces is a major strand of significance in the poem. Nevertheless we would be unwise to assume that Langland is doing no more than restate the obvious in a reaffirmation, however effective, of Christian commonplaces. His use of traditional material is usually more original than this. There might be a useful analogy in his treatment of the sins in B Passus V (C Passus V–VII): they have often been seen simply as particularly vivid and dramatic embodiments of vice in a long homiletic tradition, searing to the conscience of the reader and introduced to that end. No doubt we have to make allowance in Langland for a number of different poetic aims pursued simultaneously: one of the effects of the confessions of the sins *is* to convict the reader of sin. Nevertheless, in the long run (and perhaps the very length and dramatic power of the scenes

---

[1] Quotations from the B Version are from the edition of George Kane and E.Talbot Donaldson (London, 1975).

has something to do with this, together with the particular combination Langland uses of human everyday reality and larger-than-life abstraction) the effect on the reader is close to the opposite of this – to convince him of the archetypal and inevitable sinfulness of humanity and to bring him close to the despair which is displayed by some of the sins themselves. That this is Langland's design becomes even clearer in the subsequent episodes – the abortive pilgrimage to Truth, and Piers's failure to make the folk of the field stick to their work – to say nothing of the figure of Haukyn, in whom Langland poignantly recapitulates the theme of the apparently incorrigible state of human nature at the end of Dowell.

Some homiletic orientation is undoubtedly present also in the Crucifixion episode; Will's devout impulse at the end is in part a mirror of the reader's response. Yet the passus as a whole is not a single-minded stimulus to devotion but rather, in its poetic and logical complexity, a challenge to the imagination and intellect. In this essay I wish to look afresh at Langland's handling of the three main constituents of the passus: the figure of the Christ-knight, the debate of the Four Daughters of God, and the Harrowing of Hell, in order to reconsider, in the light of what we can know or surmise about his acquaintance with earlier traditions, where his individual emphases lie.

The topic of the Christ-knight has been dealt with at some length, principally with the aim of demonstrating Langland's indebtedness to features of the preceding traditions, by a number of critics, among them Gaffney, Le May, St-Jacques, Woolf and Bourquin.[2] Gaffney's principal contribution to the subject was to propose a specific source for Langland in the Anglo-Norman allegorical Crucifixion poem in fifty rhymed quatrains beginning *Vn rey esteit iadis ke aueit vne amye*, which is attributed to Nicole Bozon in the William Herebert manuscript in which it is copied.[3] He finds two main points of similarity between the two poems:

1. Jesus took the arms of *humana natura* secretly to deceive the devil. 'Christ here [in B XVIII] is represented as following the custom fairly well known in the Middle Ages – at least in chivalric romances – according to which a renowned and formidable knight rides to a tourney in disguise so that his adversaries will not recognize him and consequently decline to encounter him in the lists'.

---

[2] Wilbur Gaffney, 'The Allegory of the Christ-Knight in *Piers Plowman*', *PMLA*, 46 (1931), 155–68; Sister Marie de Lourdes Le May, *The Allegory of the Christ-Knight in English Literature*, Dissertation, The Catholic University of America, Washington DC, 1932, (Xerographic Reprint by University Microfilms Inc, Ann Arbor, Michigan, 1963); Raymond St.-Jacques, 'Langland's Christ-Knight and the Liturgy', *Revue de l'Université d'Ottawa*, 37 (1967), 146–58; Rosemary Woolf, *The English Religious Lyric in the Middle Ages* (Oxford, 1968), pp .44–55; Guy Bourquin, *Piers Plowman* (Paris, 1978), pp .500–26).
[3] Edited by M .L .A .Jubinal, *Nouveau Receuil*, 2 vols (Paris, 1839–42), II, 309; and in *Peter of Langtoft's Chronicle*, edited by Thomas Wright (London: Rolls Series, 1868), pp .426–37, Appendix: 'An Allegorical Romance on the Death of Christ' (from MS BL Cotton Julius A V). Unless otherwise indicated, quotations from both Bozon poems are from British Library Additional MS 46919 (formerly Phillipps 8336), fols 38–40, 90v–91v. I am indebted to Dr Claire Isoz, King's College, London, for linguistic advice on the Anglo-Norman texts.

2. Bozon connects the rescue of the captive lady with the descent of Christ into Hell (and in *Piers Plowman* the Christ-knight proceeds to the Harrowing of Hell while his body is hanging on the cross).

Gaffney is taken to task by both Sister Marie de Lourdes Le May and Raymond St-Jacques[4] for overlooking the fact that Langland depicts Christ as a noble valiant fighter rather than as 'a knight in the amour-courtois convention'. Gaffney, however, does draw attention to this difference, if only briefly:

> If one may regard the poem by Bozon as supplying the basis of the corresponding allegory in *Piers Plowman*, it is interesting to observe the modifications of the story made by Langland. Though he retains a brief reminiscence of the arming of the Knight in the Maiden's 'chamber', he leaves out entirely the espousal motif. The jousting is not undertaken for a lady, but *for mankynde sake*. In other words the romantic features of the story are wholly discarded and attention is centred upon the combat between Christ and the Devil, or between Life and Death. Such a change in tone from the romantic to the heroic is, however, quite in keeping with Langland's general point of view. (p.166)

Gaffney does not further specify what he means by 'Langland's general point of view' but a glance back to the earliest known treatment of all – that in *Ancrene Wisse* – gives a measure of the stylistic distance involved. Here the action of the knight-king, coming after the various other inducements to the lady to give him her heart, is presented above all as an act of self-sacrifice, a powerful inducement to love in return.

> Ich chulle, for þe luue of þe, neome þet feht up o me & arudde þe of ham þe þi deað secheð. Ich wat þah to soðe þet ich schal bituhen ham neomen deaðes wunde; & ich hit wulle heorteliche forte ofgan þin heorte. (p.21)

> His leofmon bihalde þron hu he bohte hire luue, lette þurlin his scheld, openin his side to schawin hire his heorte, to schawin hire openliche hu inwardliche he luuede hire, & to ofdrahen hire heorte. (p.23)

The lady who could not feel gratitude for the sufferings which the king endured for her sake must be *of uueles cunnes cunde*. The focus of attention is on the body of the victim, allegorically represented as the knight's bloodstained shield which is hung in church as a reminder of his death; and the three reasons given for God's choice of such a painful death to free us are to deprive us of every excuse for not loving him, to attract our love, and to

---

[4] St.-Jacques points out the liturgical sources Langland may have drawn on for the imagery of Christ as a warrior-knight. While the article is a valuable reminder of the liturgical level of the allegory, it seems to me, however, to overemphasize by implication the physical battle element in Langland's narrative. Also, the liturgical battle-images themselves do not directly suggest the specifically medieval chivalric features of Langland's treatment.

demonstrate his own love openly.[5] A similar persuasive rhetoric dominates the Bozon poem. Though the king might have sent his army to rescue his lady he deliberately undertakes to free her by single combat *pur atrere le quer de cele alopé* and after the battle and rescue he appeals to the lady's pity:

> Regardez ma face cum est demanglee,
> Regardez moun corps, cum est pur vous plaee,
> Auisez moun escu cum est deberdisé
> E ne quydez ja ke seez refusé.

There is a second allegorical Crucifixion poem, also attributed to Bozon, in the Herebert MS, with the title *Coment le fiz deu fu armé en la croyz* and beginning *Seignours ore escotez haute chiualerye*. This poem, in sixteen quatrains, seems to have been overlooked by Gaffney, but has more recently been referred to by Bourquin as part of an argument that Langland's thought was broadly influenced by the works of Franciscan piety contained in British Library Additional MS 46919 to an extent that suggests that he had access to the MS itself.[6] The second poem incorporates eighteen lines on the arming of the *bacheler* in the chamber of a maiden which are identical to 21–36 and 41–42 in the first poem; but among the allegorical elaborations in this poem is a development of the shield of the knight which is reminiscent of the shield-image in *Ancrene Wisse*:

> & bien deueroyt s'amye en chaumbre courtynee
> Son escu depeyndre qe si est deuisé:
> Il porte l'escu d'argent & tencelé de goules,
> En chef la coroune de verges espynouses,
> Blef la bordure a quatre signes coustouses,
> & en my la fontayne des veynes plentyuouses.

In both of the Anglo-Norman poems, then, the Christ-knight is the suffering saviour of the individual soul and the image is exploited as a spur to devotion. Nevertheless, in spite of the obvious difference of Langland's approach, Gaffney may actually have been too modest in tracing possible connections between the first Bozon poem and *Piers Plowman*, for Bozon touches on some other aspects which Langland was to raise to prominence in his handling of the theme: the lady is abducted by *vn traitour* (so described in the Cotton MS at line 7; the reading of BL Additional MS 46919 is *vn tiraunt*) who takes her away *par un acord*; the action is characterized as a *gylerye* and throughout the poem, the king's *dreit en li clamé*, his *dreit en chose chalengé* is stressed.

---

[5] *Ancrene Wisse: Parts Six and Seven*, edited by Geoffrey Shepherd (London, 1959), pp. 21–3. As Le May and Woolf show, the majority of lyrics on this subject are also poignant presentations (whether successful or not) of a suffering knight. A significant exception is the Herebert poem which is found in BL Additional MS 46919: *What ys he, þis lordling þat cometh vrom þe vyht?*, a paraphrase of Isaiah 63. 1–7.
[6] Bourquin, pp. 702–7. The short extract published by P. Meyer in *Romania*, 13 (1884), 530–1, is printed by Le May, p. 27.

The tyrant *conuseit sun poer, e ses dreite leys*. Moreover, though the lady stands for the individual soul, the poem ends on a note of universal application, with a prayer to

> Dieus, nostre roys, chevaler alosee,
> Qe conquist en bataille tot humayne ligné.[7]

In the second poem, the theme of treason is alluded to directly only once, in the identification of the lady as *l'ame de home qe iadis fu tra[hy]e*, but lines 13–15 of this poem:

> Soul se myst as champ pur reyndre sa amye
> Si venqist la batayle & conqist seygnurye
> Partye par poer & partie par mestrie

seem to bear an antithetical relationship to the passage at B XVIII, 348–9, more explicitly in the slightly expanded version of C:

> So leue hit nat, Lucifer, aʒeyne þe lawe y feche
> Here eny synfole soule souereynliche by maistrie,
> Bote thorw riht and thorw resoun raunsome here myn lege.[8]

Whether these similarities strengthen the case for *Vn rey esteit iadis* as a direct source for Langland or not, they point in the direction of Langland's intellectual and doctrinal (rather than devotional) approach to the subject. Langland's poetry does rise, of course, to the sublime pathos of the Crucifixion:

> Pitousliche and pale, as a prison þat deieþ,
> The lord of lif and of light þo leide hise eighen togideres,
> (B.XVIII. 58–9)

---

[7] The reading of Wright's edition (Cotton MS).

[8] C XX 393–95 (edited by Derek Pearsall (London, 1979)). The words of Christ here (in both B and C) are a direct reply to Lucifer's accusation:
> If he reu[e] me my riʒt he robbeþ me by maistrie.
> For by right and by reson þe renkes þat ben here
> Body and soule beþ myne, boþe goode and ille. (B.XVIII.277–9).

Langland chooses a position close to Grosseteste's:
> Donc dist li duz Jhesu beneit:
> 'Kar iceo est bien reson e dreit,
> Encontre droit ne voil je mie
> Tolir tei rien par mestrie'.

(cited by) *Le Château d'Amour*, ed. J.Murray (Paris, 1918), 1068–71.

The vocabulary is similar enough to suggest that Grosseteste is his direct source here, although the idea that Satan was defeated by justice rather than force was a commonplace. The phrase used in the Pseudo-Augustinian *De Symbolo* (*PL*, XL, 1192) is *non potestate victus sed iustitia*. In a more extended statement Alcuin has (*Liber Caroli*, II, 28; *PL*, XCVIII, 1097): *Ratione potius quam dominatione, et justitia potius quam potentia constrictus, praedam [diabolus] compulsus est evomere*. See Jean Rivière, *Le Dogme de la Rédemption au début du moyen âge* (Paris, 1934), pp.7–40.

but even here at the point where the most intense personal appeal is felt through the dream-observer's sensibility our attention is drawn also to the intellectual paradox of the *lord of lif* who died *as a prison* and of the *lord ... of light* who *leide hise eighen togideres*. The lines take on an even greater depth of paradoxical meaning when read in relation to those that introduce the Passion Week sequence in B XVI 161:

Thoruʒ Iudas and Iewes Iesus was [ynome]
That on þe friday folwynge for mankyndes sake
Iusted in Iherusalem, a ioye to vs alle.
On cros vpon Caluarie crist took þe bataille
Ayeins deeþ and þe deuel; destruyed hir boþeres myʒtes,
Deiede and dee[þ] fordide, and day of nyʒt made.

Although the theme of victory through suffering and sacrifice is present in these passages, the dominant tone of Langland's use of the knight-image in B XVIII as a whole, is triumphant.[9] Le May and St Jacques are right to insist that this is the warrior-knight. They assume, however, that the warfare imagery must be principally hortative, and view the fight of Christ with the devil as an apotheosis of the 'ghostly battle', 'the allegorization of the warfare of man against sin'; Christ is 'the model that the poet presents for imitation ... the ideal knight'.[10] I see little evidence in the structure or texture of the sixth vision that Langland's poetry here is of this particular didactic kind. It seems rather to be directed (though within a poetic statement and couched in terms of the Dreamer's doubt, fear and assurance) towards analysis of the doctrinal significance of the act of redemption.

Undoubtedly the most distinctive aspect of Langland's treatment of the figure of the Christ-knight is the way he makes it the nexus of many strands of parallelism between the feudal society of his time and the transcendental society allegorically depicted in the Prologue.[11] In his initial vision Langland sees the universe as a projection of his social world: as a somewhat simplified

[9] Both the speech of Faith (Abraham) in lines 28ff. and that of the *dede body* in 64ff. point away from the Crucifixion itself to the battle behind the scenes. The triumphant tone is sustained on a more discursive level in Conscience's exposition of the meaning of the name *Christ* as 'Conqueror' in the next passus.

[10] Le May, p.40. St.-Jacques is not so explicit on the question of the function of the image, but appears to accept Le May's assessment in pointing first to Ephesians 6.10–17 and other 'armour of God' passages as instances of the warrior-knight in the liturgy. St.-Jacques, pp.148–9.

[11] For interpretations of the legal and social metaphors used in the Harrowing of Hell sequence, see William J.Birnes, 'Christ as Advocate: The Legal Metaphor of *Piers Plowman*', *Annuale Mediaevale*, 16 (1975), 71–93; John A. Alford, 'Literature and Law in Medieval England', *PMLA*, 92 (1977), 941–51; and Anna P. Baldwin, *The Theme of Government in 'Piers Plowman'* (Cambridge, 1981), pp.55–75. Two earlier papers by P.M.Kean also explore the relationship between Langland's social and religious doctrines: 'Love, Law and *Leute* in *Piers Plowman*', *RES*, n.s. 15 (1964), 241–61; and 'Justice, Kingship and the Good Life in the Second Part of *Piers Plowman*', in *'Piers Plowman': Critical Approaches*, edited by S.S.Hussey (London, 1969), pp.76–110.

diagram of a feudal-age society in which all the space between the two castles of heaven and hell is occupied by agricultural land and an agricultural population. We may see Langland's feudal allegory as a pictorial device common to a lot of medieval poetry in which chivalry, or kingship, or treason are terms in a complex figure of speech – earthly things which signify the supernatural. For Langland, however, the bonds of similarity between earthly and heavenly society are evidently more real than this: in a very positive way the earthly concepts of kingship or justice are themselves reflections of their eternal counterparts. This is true most of all of the moral level (as opposed to the external, pictorial level, where we may be conscious of figure of speech): in the interpretative discourse of Holy Church in Passus I, the duty of the knight to serve truth and bind transgressors is validated by the code of the archetypal heavenly host:

> [And] crist, kyngene kyng, knyȝted ten,
> Cherubyn and Seraphyn, swiche seuene & [anoþer];
> Yaf hem myȝt in his maiestee, þe murier hem þouȝte,
> And ouer his meynee made hem Archangeles;
> (B.I. 105–8)

Langland rarely makes a theological point of the unbounded mercy of God, without turning immediately to the reciprocal responsibility of the earthly ruler to be merciful towards his subordinates (e.g. B.I. 159–84). Conversely, in B XIV, in the discussion by Patience of the chances of salvation for rich and poor, the arguments from double reward and payment in advance seem to be not merely illustrations but proofs, the validity of which rests on the existence of a single moral universe in earth and heaven.

In his account of the Passion of Christ and the Harrowing of Hell, Langland selects those parallels between the feudal society and the transcendental society which will highlight the theological issues of the atonement and the redemption of mankind. I think this explains why (in spite of the lines added in C XX to make more vivid the warlike preparations of the devils) the purely chivalric picture is less prominent than we might expect. (The jousting with the Devil is a literal battle in *Vn rey esteit iadis*). The imagination of the reader is not to be provided with a resting-place in the decorative and dramatic surface of knighthood, for the figure of battle and conquest is only of limited value in the exploration of the theological issues. Langland exploits it chiefly in developing the theme of the submission of Longeus, probably the first time this episode from the *Gospel of Nicodemus* had been dramatised in this consistently chivalric language.[12] Christ's legs are not broken by the officer because Nature forbade it in consideration of his nobility:

[12] Longeus is traditionally a *miles* and hence is frequently referred to as a *knyght* or *blynde knyght* in Middle English. No other writer portrays his action specifically as a joust, however. See Rose J.Peebles, *The Legend of Longinus*, Bryn Mawr College Monographs. Monograph Series, 9 (Bryn Mawr, Pennsylvania, 1911), ch.6.

> Ac was no bo[y] so boold goddes body to touche;
> For he was knyȝt and kynges sone kynde foryaf þat [þrowe]
> That noon harlot were so hardy to leyen hond vpon hym.
>
> (B.XVIII. 75–7)

Instead, Longeus, the *blynde bacheler*, is forced to joust with Jesus as the Jews' *champion chiualer*, and *ȝilt hym recreaunt re[m]yng, riȝt at Iesus wille*. The pictorial dramatization is only the jumping-off place, however, for Faith's development of the social-theological outcome of the Crucifixion in relation to the Jews and the Old Law.

Another significant chivalric addition to the Passion narrative (already foreshadowed in Passus V) is that Jesus is to joust in Piers's 'armour':

> This Iesus of his gentries wol Iuste in Piers armes,
> In his helm and in his haubergeon, *humana natura*;
> That crist be noȝt [y]knowe here for *consummatus deus*
> In Piers paltok þe Plowman þis prikiere shal ryde.
>
> (B.XVIII. 22–6)

One reason for its introduction here (as in the Bozon poems, where the arms are those of Adam) is that it gives visual embodiment to the theme of the deception of Satan, which was already incorporated in the *Descensus* account of the Harrowing of Hell.[13] A more important reason is that in paradoxically dressing the Christ-knight in the 'armour' of Piers Plowman, Langland also stresses the humanity of Christ at his most triumphant moment, as Christ does himself in the dispute with the Devil at the gates of hell:

> 'A[c] to be merciable to man þanne my kynde [it] askeþ
> For we beþ breþeren of blood, [ac] noȝt in baptisme alle.
> Ac alle þat beþ myne hole breþeren, in blood and in baptisme,
> Shul noȝt be dampned to þe deeþ þat [dureþ] wiþouten ende.'
>
> (B.XVIII. 375–8)

This recalls the language used by Piers in Passus VI, when he asks Hunger what is to be done with those who will not work in this world:

> '[And it] are my blody breþeren for god bouȝte vs alle;
> Truþe tauȝte me ones to louen hem ech one.'
>
> (B.VI. 207–8)

The Langlandian reciprocity of earth and heaven is very striking in these two quotations: Christ says that his *kynde*, his experience of human nature, compels him to be merciful in judgement; Piers claims that all men are blood brothers by virtue of the blood of Christ. If the notion of blood-brotherhood is borrowed from chivalric romance, the social implications of the figure are pursued to a theological conclusion.

---

[13] *Quis es tu, tam magnus et parvus, humilis et excelsus, miles et imperator, in forma servi admirabilis praeliator. Evangelia Apocrypha*, edited by L.F.C.Tischendorf (Leipsig, 1876), p.399.

Another strand of social metaphor pressed into service in connection with the theme of knighthood is that of enfranchisement. Here again, the essential notion can be expressed in pictorial terms as a release from the bondage of hell, but beyond that lies another metaphorical extension to the social 'freedom' of *gentil men* (an updating of the older metaphor of citizenship of the city of God).[14] As Conscience explains in the next passus, a knight who is a king and a conqueror can make

> lordes of laddes of lond þat he wynneþ
> And fre men foule þralles þat folwen noȝt hise lawes.
>
> (B.XIX. 32–3)

So that those Jews who became Christian

> Aren frankeleyns, free men þoruȝ fullynge þat þei toke
> And gentil men wiþ Iesu.
>
> (B.XIX. 39–40)

In the Harrowing of Hell sequence itself, although the martial and chivalric aspects of feudalism are present in the background, in his speech to Lucifer the Christ-knight is principally occupied in justifying his action in accordance with the concepts of law, justice, kingship and treason. In effect, the right of Lucifer to *seisin* of the souls is judged by the principles of medieval law. The chief argument used by Christ is that as they were obtained by deceit they are not lawfully his:

> 'For in my paleis, Paradis, in persone of an Addre
> Falsliche þow fettest þyng þat I louede.'
>
> (B.XVIII. 335–6)

This echoes what Gobelyn has already said: *'We haue no trewe title to hem, for þoruȝ treson were þei dampned'* (294). Lucifer's 'treason' is, of course, to be judged as a violation by a subject of his allegiance to his sovereign, rather than as a crime against the state. The new statute of 1350–1 defines it almost entirely in personal terms ('compassing or imagining the King's death, or that of his wife or eldest son, etc.').

At this point it will be useful to glance briefly at Langland's handling of the

---

[14] See Thomas Rendall, 'Liberation from Bondage in the Corpus Christi Plays', *Neuphilologische Mitteilungen*, 71 (1970), 659–73. Langland may have taken a hint from the Middle English *Gospel of Nicodemus* for his social interpretation of release from bondage:

> He lowsed þan þaire bandes all
> þat lang had bunden bene,
> he made þam fre þat are war thrall,
> of care he clensed þam clene.

The Middle-English Harrowing of Hell and Gospel of Nicodemus, edited by W.H.Hulme (London: EETS, ES 100, 1907, reprinted 1961), p.112.

ancient literary topos of the debate between the Four Daughters of God. In her 1907 dissertation Hope Traver traced the evolution of this theme from its beginnings in the Midrash (where the subject at issue is whether God should create man or not), through the developments it underwent in Hugh of St Victor's *Annotations on certain Psalms of David*, St Bernard's sermon *In Festa Annunciationis Beatae Virginis*, Robert Grossetestes's *Chasteau d'Amour*, and the *Meditationes Vitae Christi* of Bonaventura of Padua.[15] Of the use of the theme in *Piers Plowman* she says (after dismissing pronounced resemblance to Grosseteste, Deguileville, 'or indeed to any other version of the altercation of the sisters'):

> To me the work seems to stand apart, an example of the originality and power of its author, who could so transform the material beneath his hand as to prevent recognition of the particular source of which he had availed himself. In my perplexity as to the whole matter, I have merely presented the scene, leaving it to some one else to decide what affiliations with other versions may exist. (p .150)

It is not my aim to take up the challenge of the last sentence. Indeed, the acknowledgement of Langland's creative relation to his sources suggests that a more fruitful approach would be to attempt to determine which features of Langland's treatment of the convention are special to him and thus significant elements in his design for the vision as a whole. One such feature is without doubt the dream architecture of the scene in Langland. Traver notes that the positioning of the debate in *Piers Plowman* is 'peculiar in that it is made the prelude to the Harrowing of Hell', but in fact the structure is more complex than this.

The sixth vision begins and ends as a historical realization of the gospel events within the liturgical framework of the *Gloria, laus* of Palm Sunday and the *Te deum laudamus* of Easter day. Within this historical-liturgical envelope Langland encloses the debate of the Four Daughters of God. Embedded in their dialogue and enacted within their visual space (261–2) is first the testimony of Book and then the dramatization of the apocryphal story of the Harrowing of Hell. (From this episode we return first to the concluding reconciliation of the Four Daughters and then to the liturgical Easter moment). The successive layering of the narrative – which has features of a

---

[15] Hope Traver, *The Four Daughters of God*, Bryn Mawr College Monographs. Monographs Series, 4 (Bryn Mawr, Pennsylvania, 1907). For the development of the 'Processus Belial' variants, see also, by the same author, 'The Four Daughters of God: a Mirror of Changing Doctrine', *PMLA*, 40 (1925), 44–92. More recent discussion of the subject, with particular relation to Grosseteste, is to be found in Sister Mary Immaculate [Creek], CSC, 'The Sources and Influence of the *Chasteau d'Amour*' (unpublished dissertation, Yale University, 1941) – not consulted, but see Sajavaara, below; Sister Mary Immaculate [Creek], CSC, 'The Four Daughters of God in the *Gesta Romanorum* and the *Court of Sapience*', *PMLA*, 57 (1942), 951–65; *The Middle English Translations of Robert Grosseteste's 'Château d'Amour'*, edited by Kari Sajavaara, Mémoires de la Société néophilologique de Helsinki, 22 (Helsinki, 1967). The last-mentioned contains a valuable summary and discussion of Sister Mary Creek's dissertation.

Dantesque journey, as well as reminiscences of the inner visions of Passus XI and XVI – serves the end of both poetic and doctrinal focus. Langland has effectively shifted the jousting of Jesus from the Cross to the gates of Hell and equated it with the legal tournament with Satan there.[16]

As in other versions of the debate of the Four Daughters the outcome is to demonstrate the reconciliation of mercy with justice. In the vast majority of versions their debate takes the form of a court-disputation addressed to God (or the king of the fictionalized examples based on the story of 'Rex et Famulus'). As this is true of the versions commonly regarded as sources for Langland (Deguileville, Grosseteste, *Gesta Romanorum*), we are probably justified in thinking that it was his deliberate choice to cast it instead in the form of an argument among the sisters themselves. The effect is to change them to a very great extent from active participants into a chorus, commenting on the events rather than trying to influence them. Langland also gives a less decisive role in the total drama to Mercy, whose impassioned pleading in many versions is the deciding factor. In those versions in which the debate is combined with the 'Rex et Famulus' story (e.g. in the Anglo-Latin and Middle English version of the *Gesta Romanorum*) it is Mercy's sight of the prisoner in the hands of his tormentors and her compassion for his plight that sends her to the king and starts the whole process. The king's son, moreover, takes Mercy with him on his mission to rescue the serf from his four tormentors.[17]

Though we may deduce from these changes that it is no part of Langland's design to suggest a crude triumph for the softer sisters, *Mercy* and *Pees*, the dramatic presentation does allow him to characterize *Truþe* and *Rightwisnesse* as a touch shrewish: *'That þow tellest', quod Truþe, 'is but a tale of waltrot!'* (142); *'What, rauestow?' quod Rightwisnesse, 'or þow art right dronke?'* (188). Furthermore, the similarity between their point of view and that of Lucifer is underlined by verbal echoes:

> Rightwisnesse:
> [At] þe bigynn[yng god] gaf þe doom hymselue
> That Adam and Eue and alle þat hem suwede
> Sholden deye downrighte and dwelle in pyne after
> If þat þei touchede a tree and þe [trees] fruyt eten.
> Adam afterward, ayeins his defence,
> Freet of þat fruyt and forsook, as it weere,
> The loue of oure lord and his loore boþe.
>
> (B.XVIII. 191–7)

---

[16] The identification is reinforced by the allusions to the legal side of the trial and crucifixion of Christ (36ff.) and by the pun on *Iuste/Iustice*.

[17] See Creek, *PMLA*, 40 (1925), 952–4; *Patrologia Latina*, edited by J .Migne (Paris, 1850), XCIV, 505–7; *Gesta Romanorum*, edited by S .J .H .Herrtage (London: EETS, ES, 33, 1879), pp .132–6.

Lucifer:
If he reu[e] me my riȝt he robbeþ me by maistrie.
For by right and by reson þe renkes þat ben here
Body and soule beþ myne, boþe goode and ille.
For hymself seide, þat Sire is of heuene,
If Adam ete þe Appul alle sholde deye
And dwelle wiþ vs develes; this þretynge [driȝten] made.
(B.XVIII. 277–82)

These gestures towards the denigration of the severer sisters Langland can allow himself in the interests of dramatic life because the main stress of this debate (as well as that of Christ and Satan) is on the truth, justice and legality of the Redemption. Langland has already identified God with Truth, as well as Love, in the speech of Holy Church in Passus I; in Passus XVIII underlines the point by making the devil identify *Truþe* with Christ, the Harrower of Hell:

'Certes I drede me', quod þe deuel, 'lest truþe [do] hem fecche.
Thise þritty wynter, as I wene, [he wente aboute] and preched.'
(B.XVIII. 295–6)

In his dramatization of the Harrowing of Hell Langland highlights the legality of the Redemption by drawing attention repeatedly and insistently to the deception of man by the Devil. The long address of Christ to Lucifer with its theme of *gile ... bigiled, and in his gile fallen* (360) (borrowed, with so much of the word-play and irony of the speech, from the *Pange Lingua* of Fortunatus) is both a paean of justified triumph at the outwitting of evil ingenuity and a serious legal argument undermining utterly Lucifer's claims to the souls of men.

This speech has no counterpart at all in the *Gospel of Nicodemus*. In the Latin A version of the section known as *Descensus Christi ad Inferos* nearly all the discussion about Jesus and his role takes place between the patriarchs and saints who are to be released, and between Satan and Hell (*inferus*) before the approach of Christ. There is in addition a speech by Hell and the demons *to* Christ, marvelling at his appearance. Only in the Latin B version, however, does Christ address words to Satan or Hell, and there only the sentence of condemnation: *Per omnia secula multa mala fecisti, ullo modo non quievisti: hodie te trado igni perpetuo.*[18] Vernacular dramatic versions of the Harrowing of Hell, on the other hand, show a tendency to develop the personal confrontation between Christ and Satan. In the Old French *La Passion du Palatinus* there is a dialogue of twenty-five lines composed mainly of maledictions.[19] In the thirteenth-century Middle-English *Harrowing of Hell*

---

[18] *Evangelia Apocrypha*, p.429; *The Apocryphal Gospels*, edited by M.R.James (Oxford, 1924, corrected reprint 1953), p.137.
[19] Edited by Grace Frank (Paris, 1922). See also D.D.R.Owen, *The Vision of Hell* (Edinburgh and London, 1970), p.233.

there is quite an extended dialogue of some eighty lines, in which Satan bases his claim to the souls of men on the argument that he has bought them: Adam came to him hungry and in return for the apple which Satan gave him he made him do *manred*. Christ easily counters this argument by pointing out that the apple was not his to give.[20]

Grosseteste shares with Langland this emphasis on the deception involved in the Fall. It is noted by Creek and Sajavaara that for his conception of the Atonement as it is expounded in *Le Chasteau d'Amour* Grosseteste goes back to the notion of the 'Devil's rights', a doctrine which took two forms in the early church, the theory of ransom and the theory of the abuse of power:

> In the theory of ransom – it is the juridical variant – God and the Devil are seen as two opposing rulers, who desire man's soul. Adam has the choice, and he chooses the Devil. To make man return to him God must give ransom to the Devil, and this ransom is his only Son. The theory of the abuse of power is a political variant of the basic idea. A contract between God and the Devil stipulated the limits of their spheres and neither of them could infringe on the domain of the other. The life and death of fallen man was in the hands of the Devil, but he used his power on the Son and transgressed the contract. In both cases the Devil fails in his aims.[21]

The theory was superseded in the eleventh century by St Anselm's doctrine of a satisfaction for sin paid to God's righteousness but continued to appear in popular presentations. Grosseteste is of course familiar with the doctrine of satisfaction and introduces it in the exemplum, where the son explains to the father his motives and aims in the rescue of the serf:

> Del serf prendrai la vesteüre
> En verité e en dreiture
> Sustendrai le jugement.   (449–51)

In other parts of the poem the two different (and to some extent conflicting) forms of the 'Devil's rights' are appealed to. He uses first the notion of the Devil's 'abuse of power', specifically in the form that his temptation of man was an act of treason:

> Kar oez donkes ma preere,
> Pur cel dolent, cheitif prison,
> Ke venir peüst a rançon,
> Ke en mi ses enemis
> Avez en grief prison mis
> Ki par premesse li traïrent

---

[20] Edited by W.H.Hulme (see note 14, above), pp.6–13.
[21] Edited by Sajavaara (see note 15, above).

> Par unt trespasser li firent,
> La premesse li fauserent
> Kar fauseté tut tens querent,
> Et fauseté lur seit rendu
> E le prison a mei rendu.   (260–70)

At this point in Grosseteste's poem the argument is part of Mercy's plea to the King in the 'Rex et Famulus' exemplum. It is, however, repeated (in the same feudal language) in the dialogue between Christ and Satan which Grosseteste develops out of the New Testament account of the temptation of Christ in the desert:

> Dont respundi li duz Jhesu:
> 'Li covenanz fu bien tenu,
> Meis tu primes le enfreinsistes,
> Kant en traïson li desistes:
> Tu ne murras pas pur tant
> Einz serez cum Deu sachant.
> De le fet fustes acheson.
> Ores esgardez donc reson.
> Veus tu del covenant joir
> Kant covenant ne veus tenir?'   (1041–60)

(The Christ of the Middle English *Castle of Love* is even more unequivocal: *He agulte þorw þe and elles he wer skere.*)[22] This argument would appear of itself to dispose of the Devil's rights but, surprisingly, Christ goes on to agree to pay Satan's price for the souls of men:

> 'Rendez mei donc ki tant vaille,
> Cum fet ore tut le mund
> E kant k'apres tuz jurs vendrunt.'
> 'Volontiers tut iceo ferei,
> Kar mieuz vaut mun petit dei
> Ke tels cent mil mundes ne funt
> Od tute la gent ki i sunt.'   (1076–82)

Logically and legally this development weakens the case against Satan and must be accounted for, I think, by a wish to recall the poem to its penitential direction at this point by emphasizing the sacrificial nature of Christ's action.

Given the similarity of argument and the feudal language in which it is couched there is good reason to believe that Langland is working closely with

---

[22] Sajavaara, pp.57–8. See also Rivière (note 8, above).

Le Chasteau d'Amour in this section of *Piers Plowman*.[23] It is important, however, to recognize the modifications which he has introduced. He has made the rescue-allegory more comprehensive than it is in *Le Chasteau d'Amour*, where it is confined to the exemplum; he has eliminated the running didactic commentary of the Anglo-Norman poem, along with the admonitory evocation of the punishments of hell and the joys of heaven; he has (possibly taking a hint from the vernacular dramatic treatment of the Harrowing of Hell) transferred the exposure of the Devil's treason from the Temptation in the Desert to the triumphant speech of the Christ-knight at the moment when he is actually breaking open Hell; and in the speech of Christ itself he has transformed the notion of a price paid to the Devil for the souls in hell to one of satisfaction for sin plus a lawful claim on his own property:

> lo! here my soule to amendes
> For alle synfulle soules, to saue þo þat ben worþi.
> Myne þei ben and of me; I may þe bet hem cleyme,
> (B.XVIII. 327–9)

and (by skilfully blending the two arguments) subordinated the whole subject of ransom to that of the Devil's treason.

We may, I believe, interpret these observations on Langland's choice and disposition of the three traditional figures he uses as confirmatory evidence of an emphasis in the sixth vision on the rightness and necessity of salvation. Langland seems to be as anxious to discount the arbitrary exercise over evil of God's mercy as he is the arbitrary exercise of God's power. The mercy which will be shown at the Day of Judgement to any who make the minimum response of penitence is, on the analogy of the earthly law of the king's pardon, itself a legal act, subsumed under justice: '*I [may] do mercy þoru3 [my] rightwisnesse and alle my wordes trewe*'. It will be remembered that *Truþe* and *Mercy* have already agreed, at one point in the debate of the Four Daughters, in giving *Rightwisnesse* a sort of primacy: '*For he[o] woot moore þan we; he[o] was er we boþe*' (166).[24]

---

[23] The influence on this part of *Piers Plowman* of Guillaume de Deguileville's *Le Pélerinage de l'Âme* (edited by J.J.Sturzinger, London: Roxburghe Club, 1895) is much less obvious, in that it relates in the first person the experiences of the individual soul after death; while the attack on the soul by Satan does develop into a legal debate between Justice, Truth, and Mercy, the weighing of the soul in St Michael's balance is to be the deciding factor (Mercy tips the scales by depositing the Charter of Christ in favour of the soul); thus some of the elements of Langland's allegory are present but they are used in quite a different way by Deguileville.

[24] Christ's obedience to the law is noted by a number of critics: 'The poet ... finally demonstrates through the figure of Christ that only one law operates on both a divine and temporal level and to this law even Christ must submit' (Birnes, p.84 – see note 11, above). Baldwin, for similar reasons, calls the Christ of the poem a 'subject-king'. It should be observed, however, that the character *Book* (B XVIII 230–60) is introduced specifically to demonstrate the full divinity of Christ and that in his speech to Satan/Lucifer Christ repeatedly identifies himself with the Father (*ri3t of myselue* 330, *in my paleis, Paradis* 335, *Thow fettest myne in my place* 350, etc.). It is because he *is* justice (it is *my rightwisnesse and right* 397) that he 'submits' to the law.

We are not concerned here, of course, with the totality of Langland's thought about salvation (there is a great deal of emphasis on penitence and the breadth of God's mercy in other passages of the poem); still less are we concerned with Langland's 'beliefs' as a set of dogmas extracted from the poetry. As the scholar and critic whom we honour in this volume has wisely remarked:

> *Piers Plowman* is not a theological treatise and it does not necessarily at any particular point deploy the personal view of its author. It is a poem of exploration and of often agonized reappraisal in which views of almost every shade rightly find their places within a variety of dramatic contexts.[25]

What Langland has produced out of the materials to hand from numerous other treatments of the theme of Redemption is a new amalgam fulfilling even more completely the description *consolatio peccatorum* than did the *Processus Belial* to which the designation was habitually attached. In the dramatic context of the sixth vision, we are shown the dreamer's perception of the necessary triumph of justice over Satan's deceit and its consequent moment of rare assurance in his waking experience.

---

[25] G.H.Russell, 'The Salvation of the Heathen: the Exploration of a Theme in *Piers Plowman*', *Journal of the Warburg and Courtald Institutes*, 29 (1966), 101–16 (p.102).

SOME FOURTEENTH-CENTURY 'POLITICAL' POEMS

George Kane

A number of fourteenth-century English poems have in the last decade or so been read in a political sense as poems of 'protest' and 'dissent'. The most important are first, three from BL Harleian MS 2253, called *Song of the Husbandman*, *Satire on the Consistory Courts* and *Satire on the Retinues of the Great*, then a longer poem variously called *The Simony* or *On the Evil Times of Edward II*, then the two (or is it three) reflexes of *Piers Plowman*, *Pierce the Ploughman's Crede* and *Mum and Sothsegger*, and, finally, by John Ball's 'letters'.[1] They are described as part of a large body of writing exhibiting a common 'temper'; they have been seen as manifesting an increasingly secular concern for political change and reform, or as signalling the genesis of the English-speaking democracies. There is an implication in them of momentum, of a widespread movement of political awakening.[2]

> In an age when all thought was religion-orientated, any criticism of the social order was bound to be criticism of the religious concepts which formed its base. Thus, many of the Middle English religious poems lamenting the sins of the age, although they use the terminology of doctrine, are really political.[3]

No matter that the first premise of that statement is absolutely questionable and the conclusion a non-sequitur, 'The ghost of Langland stands behind Lilburne, and the ghost of Wyclif behind Winstanley'.[4]

These positions are variously unhistorical, that is to say, anachronistic. One main reason is that they do not take into account the prevalence and the character of estates satire, a literary activity unquestionably concerned with the evils of the times and correspondingly denunciatory, but also funda-

---

[1] *Historical Poems of the XIV and XV Centuries*, edited by Rossell Hope Robbins (New York, 1959), pp.7–9, 24–27, 27–29; *The Political Songs of England from the Reign of King John to that of Edward II*, edited by Thomas Wright (London, Camden Society, 1839), pp.323–45; *Pierce the Ploughmans Crede*, edited by W.W.Skeat, EETS 30 (repr. Greenwood Press, NY 1969); *Mum and the Sothsegger*, edited by Mabel Day and Robert Steele, EETS 199, 1936 for 1934; Robbins, *Historical Poems*, pp.54, 55.
[2] Rossell Hope Robbins, 'Middle English Poems of Protest', *Anglia*, 78 (1960), 193–203; Thomas L.Kinney, 'The Temper of Fourteenth-Century English Verse of Complaint', *Annuale Mediaevale*, 7 (1966), 74–89; Thomas J. Elliott, 'Middle English Complaints against the Times: to Condemn the World or to Reform It?', *Annuale Mediaevale*, 14 (1973), 22–34; Rossell Hope Robbins, 'Dissent in Middle English Literature: The Spirit of (Thirteen) Seventy-Six', *Medievalia et Humanistica*, 9 (1979), 25–51.
[3] Robbins, 'Poems of Protest', p.193.
[4] Robbins, 'Dissent in Middle English Literature', p.42.

mentally conservative.[5]

Estates satire, based on a concept of ideal human behaviour, explains the 'evils of the times' not by reference to the inequity of systems, but as a consequence of the failure of people to carry out the duties of what my Victorian grandmother still called, without embarrassment, their 'station in life'. It was the prevalence of such failure that engendered the complaints, reiterated for centuries with little modification except elaboration of detail, about the oppression by temporal lords, denial of access to the law through the rapacity of lawyers, the venality of the ministers of God, particularly the friars, by which the channels of God's grace to sinners were obstructed, the illiteracy or sloth or profligacy of all sorts of clergy, and in consequence God's visitation of calamities upon the world, his deafness to men's prayers, and worst of all, the affliction of the innocent along with the guilty.

The state of mind expressed in such writings is essentially unmodern. The authors of even the most extreme of them had no concept of politics as we understand the term; they had in fact much more in common with the corrupt representatives of the established order whom they were attacking than with us today. The difference begins with the ablolute prevalence of two beliefs: in the existence of a necessarily, if incomprehensibly, benevolent deity, and in the unquestionable authority of scripture as his communication of his will to man. As for the notion that estates satire, 'complaint', had anything of the character of a movement of political reform, this is dismissed by the circumstance that all fourteenth-century English conceptions of a 'reformed', that is an ideal society, had dogmatic and hieratic bases. The general principle of authority as such was never in question. The arguments against degree, the gradation of society, were designed not to produce a democracy in any modern sense, but to emphasize the injustice of fiscal oppression of the common people. The question about Adam and the gentleman did not argue for an equal voice and equal 'social responsibility' (a very modern concept) but against the parasitism of what Langland called *wastours*, drones. And if only half of what the *Historia Anglicana* reports about John Ball and Walter Tyler is true, the *Animal Farm* syndrome existed in the movement of 1381: Ball was to be sole archbishop of England, Tyler to be King of Kent, Litster King of Norfolk, 'the first of many county kings'.[6] The anomalies in the situation were stultifying. The existing, gradated structure of society would function perfectly if all men behaved virtuously: another of Langland's themes. But conversely, because of original sin, in consequence of which most men were disinclined to virtue, no social structure had a chance of being just, or hope of reform.

---

[5] None of these essays takes due account of Ruth Mohl, *The Three Estates in Medieval and Renaissance Literature* (New York, 1933). I have found only three references to her book, one actually concerned with Gower and one with Boccaccio (Robbins, 'Dissent in Middle English Literature', pp.31, 33 and accompanying endnotes).

[6] May McKisack, *The Fourteenth Century 1307–1399* (Oxford, 1959), pp.417–20; *Chronica Monasterii S Albani Thomae Walsingham*, edited by Henry Thomas Riley (London, Rolls Series 28, II, 1864), p.10. See also a recent summary of the scholarship of the subject in R.B.Dobson, *The Peasants' Revolt of 1381*, second edition (London, 1983), pp.xix–xlv.

As to social inequality, both John Ball's case and the opposition to it relied on scripture for their authority, but the opposition had the advantage when inequality, as in the Sermon on the Mount, was actually held to be spiritually advantageous. Even the most violent expressions of social malaise in the English fourteenth century were based on desire for a benevolent paternalism, good rule by the king, or rule by a good king. The concept of individual right and its concomitant responsibility to participate in government had no currency. Indeed, the critical voices of the time made no claims of that kind; the cry was for someone else to fulfil the responsibility of governing them, to their own prescription and advantage. In that sense estates satire derives its energy from envy – in the medieval sense of the term – of those who are getting away with graft.[7]

As to 'protest', the term is inadequate. The dictionary defines it as 'A formal statement or declaration of disapproval of or dissent from . . . some action or proceeding; a remonstrance'.[8] Recent history has given the term connotations inappropriate for medieval application. It suggests demonstrators with placards and banners, crowds throwing cobblestones and homemade firebombs, police behind riot shields, above all, 'causes'. The uprising of 1381 was both more and less. A modern protester in the western world is protected by the legally-enforced tolerance of the system he is angry with; the peasants of 1381 were staking their lives. The modern protester professes to be demonstrating for a principle; the peasants were reacting to conditions that had at length come to seem intolerable. Indeed they were more like their own contemporaries of the 'establishment', the combination of magnates and parliament against Richard in 1386, who reacted to equally intolerable conditions.

As for 'dissent', 'difference of opinion in regard to religious doctrine or worship',[9] this must in a fourteenth-century English application mean denial of the truth of canonical dogma. The only unmistakable instance I know of such rejection in the vernacular is that of Wyclif and his followers who came to be called Lollards in the last decade of the century. His is the one clear position: he was unquestionably a dissenter. But for our modern enthusiasts he was the wrong kind of revolutionary. His proposed reforms would not have been liberalizing or democratizing, for he was resolutely authoritarian, radical only in challenging the prerogatives of authority, not authority itself. And he conducted his arguments about dogma within the terms of the dogmatic system, the authority of scripture, which it did not occur to him to question. He had, moreover, no concept of 'equality' in his religion, which was resolutely determinist, his church on earth 'composed of the *predestinati*,

---

[7] Some perception of this may underlie Elliott's description of simony as an injustice ('Middle English Complaints', p .26). The sin was essentially heinous because of its sacrilegious nature, but no doubt it will have seemed an 'injustice' to those whom it deprived of preferment.

[8] *OED* s.v. sb. 4.

[9] *OED* s.v. sb. 3, the only apt sense in this context.

those who would be saved, and the *presciti*, those foreknown to damnation'.[10] He did not question the essential tyranny.

This is the historical perspective in which the poems named above need to be read, dispassionately and also with respect to their literary relations.

The most prominent is the Harley poem called, by its first and by most subsequent editors, *Song of the Husbandman*. Its language is difficult, but it does respond to study, and a close reading sharply corrects much that has been written about it. It is, first of all, not a complaint by a serf about his miserable lot. This is not where we read about the wretched peasant in his coat of coarse cloth, his hair staring through the holes in his hood, his shoes an imperfect composition of patches, up to his ankles in mud, straining at the plough while his wife, sheltered from the weather only by a winnowing sheet, leaves traces of blood from her bare feet on the ice as she follows the gaunt oxen with the goad, and three hungry children lie whimpering at the end of the tillage strip. That ghastly vignette is from *Pierce the Ploughman's Crede*, which is concerned not about politics but about the failure of spirituality.

Song of the Husbandman is mainly about overtaxation, the doubtless wellfounded grievance of not one but a number of social classes. The speaker of the poem complains, to be sure, but its poet is not what A. K. Moore once called 'the shaping agent through which the mass mind expresses its inclinations';[11] he was evidently a very clever technician, necessarily in view of the date a clerk, and therefore not even subject to the grievance that is his main topic, corruption and high-handedness in the collection of the king's taxes. *The Simony*, possibly a somewhat later poem, describes how the tax-collectors proceed.

> shrewedeliche for sothe hii don the kinges heste;
> Whan everi man hath his part, the king hath the leste.
> Everi man is aboute to fille his owen purs;
> And the king hath the leste part, and he hath al the curs, with
>   wronge.   (331–35)

They carry out the king's orders corruptly, for when every one of them has had his share the king is left with the smallest part. Each of them is concerned to fill his own purse. The king gets least, and with it, unjustly, all the ill-will.

'I paid out my tax more than ten times over' (40) says the speaker; 'there was never a tax-collector who made an honest return.'[12] The name of the poem, given it by Wright, which has been uncritically retained, is inappropriate. It does indeed represent the peasantry as the worst-hit by fiscal oppression (19,

[10] *Selections from English Wycliffite Writings*, edited by Anne Hudson (Cambridge, 1978), p.5.
[11] Quoted by Kinney, 'The Temper', p.76.
[12] *nabbeþ ner budeles boded ar fulle* (59). The last word is mistranscribed as *sille* by Wright (p.152) and as *sulle* by Robbins (*Historical Poems*, p.250). For the sense of *boded* here see *MED* s.v. *boden* v. (1) 2.

21–25). But the speaker of the poem implies that he was formerly a man of substance: 'When I remember my time of prosperity I am almost in tears' (66). And he is not alone: 'People who once wore robes' (that is, did not work with their hands) 'now go in rags' (36). Just as the poor are pillaged and picked clean (25), so

> þe ryche me raymeþ wiþouten eny ryht;
> ar londes & ar ledes liggeþ fol lene.   (26–27)

'The rich are unrightfully despoiled; their lands and households are in a wretched state.' All this is part of the general badness of the times (71–72); religious orders are held in contempt by all classes (29–30); even the crops are failing (3, 68–70).

This poem has been misinterpreted partly because of Wright's title, partly because *the ryche me raymeþ* of line 26 has been either mistranslated or rejected as politically unacceptable. The construction *me raymeþ* is grammatically parallel with *me pileþ* in the line before it; the two impersonal pronouns are used to convey a passive voice. Wright left the pronoun out;[13] Robbins omitted the line from his summary;[14] the Sisams, in *The Oxford Book of Medieval English Verse*, changed it to *men*, and translated, 'Powerful men take at will'.[15] The manuscript reading, however, gives perfectly good sense, and the sense obtained by the various emendations is repugnant to the context, especially to the line that follows: *ar londes & ar ledes liggeþ fol lene*: the peasants who actually tilled the land would not be written of as having estates or a tenantry.[16] This poem does not have the political base claimed for it. Certainly it is a complaint, but one of all classes, against maladministration, but also against the general badness of the times.

Another misrepresented poem is the one Wright and Robbins call *Satire on the Consistory Courts*. The speaker of the poem does indeed express resentment against those courts. But if there is satire here the target is that speaker himself, for he is not favourably represented.[17] The burden of his resentment is suggested in the first three lines, the bitterness of *lewed men* against clerks: 'It is impossible for an unlettered man to live nowadays, no matter how good he may be acknowledged to be with his hands, for the clerics subject us to such harrassment.' Again it must be recalled that the author of

---

13 p.150.

14 Rossell Hope Robbins, 'Poems Dealing with Contemporary Conditions', Chapter XIII in *A Manual of the Writings in Middle English 1050–1500*, vol.5, edited by Albert E.Hartung (New Haven, 1975), p.1404.

15 Celia and Kenneth Sisam, *The Oxford Book of Medieval English Verse* (Oxford, 1970), p.112.

16 This I take to be the original meaning of *londes and ledes*. The meaning 'Land, landed property, landholdings' for *ledes* (*MED* s.v. *led(e)* n. (2) 3) is clearly present only in the last two *MED* citations. *OED*'s 'land and vassals or subjects' (*Lede*. Obs. 1.b) is more likely correct. But in any event the term implies ownership of 'broad acres'.

17 There is a better reading of this poem by Carter Revard, 'Lecher, Legal Eagle, Papelard Priest', in *His Firm Estate, Essays in Honor of Franklin James Eikenberry*, edited by Donald E.Hayden (Tulsa, 1967), pp.61–67.

the poem was almost certainly a cleric, a member of the class against which the lay speaker he creates is expressing his animus. As for that speaker, he may be 'from the lower classes', but to judge by the opening lines he is a man with a craft skill and what he says hardly shows him to be 'incensed by judicial venality', and the treatment he reports can hardly be seen to 'corrode the very foundations of a just society.'[18]

The speaker resents having to turn up on a particular day in answer to the summons. He resents the number of law books that are brandished. He dislikes the appearance of the Official or Archdeacon. He fears that, to save his good name, to keep out of the Archdeacon's book, he may have to try a bribe. He hates the sight of the summoners sitting there, everyone's enemies. It infuriates him that the most useless clerk who is in trouble can claim privilege, insolent, black-habited swine. And the beadle's voice is infuriatingly loud!

But he is in court for having tumbled a girl – two, actually, as it turns out. And there is loud altercation between them about which one he is to marry. For his part he would like to get clean away, and escape his *fere*, his playmate. She didn't care what sort of a man it might be, so long as she had it. Worst of all he is now treated like a dog *At chirche ant pourh chepyng*, all over the community. And he has to submit to being married to one of them – his last resentment – by a priest as proud as a peacock!

> Wyde heo worcheþ vs wo
> for wymmene ware.

'Look how these clerks make trouble for us because we have to do with women.' What we have here is more social comedy than 'complaint'. The poem needs a new title, and it should not be classified, as Robbins does in the *Manual*, among the political poems.

Then there is the *Satire on the Retinues of the Great*. The title creates expectation of criticism of the vanity of huge households, extravagantly maintained to swell the pride of grandiose magnates. Of course pride is sinful but the notion that it was sinful to maintain large households has an element of anachronism about it. For it could be held to be commendable: a lord should study, says Langland's poem,

> how he myȝte mooste meynee manliche fynde,   (B.X. 94)

'how he would be able to support the largest possible household generously'. This poem is actually about something else: it is a brilliantly malicious, very scurrilous lampoon against grooms, stable lads, horseboys, a companion

---

[18] 'Middle English Complaints', p .27. For Robbins too the poem is a satire 'on the venality of those concerned with administering the law'. (*Manual*, p. 1406) As to the speaker's status, Revard (p .62) misreads the text. The speaker does not 'claim' to be *neuer in hyrt so hauer of honde* (2), only implies that he is such a person. He is not a household servant, but a skilled craftsman. The expression means 'known generally to be a man of exceptional skill'. (*MED* s.v. *hired* n .3c).

piece to *The Blacksmiths*. This lot are louse-ridden, scabby, whoremongering gamesters, vain, overdressed, insolent.

> whil god wes on erthe & wondrede wyde
> whet wes þe resoun why he nolde ryde?
> for he nolde no grom to go by ys syde.　　　　　(33–35)

Here indeed we have a genre, and it is not complaint. Still, Robbins in the *Manual* calls this a political poem and *The Blacksmiths* a vignette on contemporary life.[19]

What we have been looking at is instances of Middle English satirical verse in varying degrees of seriousness. These poems do exemplify a genre, satire, which is most likely to have developed in England soon after 1154 in imitation of the *sirventes*. One can argue this influence from Bertran de Born's involvement with the sons of Henry II, and from a number of Provençal *sirventes* relating to English royal policy that have survived.[20] In English there is a fine, early instance of a strictly political *sirventes*, *The Song of Lewes*, which must have been written shortly before the Battle of Evesham in 1265.[21] An equally clear example, considerably later, is the poem called *The Follies of the Duke of Burgundy*.[22] This importation had a long life: what some scribe mistakenly called 'Lenvoy de Chaucer' at the end of *The Clerk's Tale* is a flawless *sirventes* in *coblas unissonans*. The satires I have discussed just now are in a derivative tradition, and characteristically English in their elaborate use of ornamental alliteration.

There is one further, notable poem in this tradition, *The ʒeddingus of Prest Papelard*, from the West Midlands like the Harley poems, and dated before 1349.[23] This poem, like the *Satire on the Consistory Courts*, is developed from the sermon convention by which a capital sin exposes its character. In the *Consistory* poem it is possible to see *Ira*, here we have *Accedia*.[24] The speaker is a clerk in higher orders who has, in his time, worn *robes of ray*, that is been a practitioner of (presumably) civil law, but has let himself be persuaded to take on a cure of souls. Now he has had to give up riding to hounds; he does not know his way about the order of services; his household and the men who work his glebe ignore his instructions; and so he runs on: a wholly unspiritual person represented in a position of spiritual responsibility.

There is wit, both stylistic and intellectual, in these poems, considerable

---

[19] pp.1403, 1467.

[20] Wright prints examples on pp.3, 36, 39.

[21] Carleton Brown, *English Lyrics of the XIII Century* (Oxford, 1932), pp.131–32.

[22] Robbins, *Historical Poems*, pp.50–53.

[23] A.H.Smith, 'The Middle English Lyrics in Additional MS 45896', *London Mediaeval Studies* vol.II part 1 (1951), pp.42–45.

[24] The range of sophistication with which this convention was put to literary use in fourteenth-century England is great. We find it at its most elementary in *Speculum Christiani* (edited by G.Holmstedt, EETS 182, 1933 for 1929, pp.58ff.) and in developed form in *Piers Plowman* and *The Canterbury Tales*. Here one might identify *ira* (*Consistory Courts*) and *accidia* (*Papelard Prest*).

dramatic skill, and a very high level of technical ability. But only the two about extortionate tax collection and the ill-suited parish priest are deeply serious. There are, of course, some deeply serious poems about contemporary conditions in Middle English, but of a very different character, and all distinctive. Three are outstanding: *The Simony*, also called *On the Evil Times of Edward II*, *Pierce the Ploughman's Crede* from the latter end of the fourteenth century, and what I believe to be two poems, possibly by a single author, that now go by the name *Mum and Sothsegger* and fall early in the reign of Henry IV.

The Simony is the least complex of the three, a straight theodicy, that is, a demonstration that the present sufferings of people are divine visitations for their sins. It instances a system of homiletic formulation increasingly prevalent as the eschatological crisis mounted in fourteenth-century England. 'I will tell you', says the speaker, a critic but not in any modern sense a satirist, 'why the times are so bad'. He then runs through the estates, beginning with the clerical, and gives each its deserts of formulaic criticism, the best brand of by now highly developed estates satire. The tenor is anti-monastic and anti-fraternal both: we seem to have here a secular cleric. This poem is not revolutionary: the theodicy it instances is by its very nature a defense of the existing theocratic structure. What makes it exceptional is that the quality of the writing is high for this kind of work, that Langland thought well enough of it to take some of its personifications into *Piers Plowman*,[25] that its author evinces genuine compassion for the poor, and that he includes himself among those who by their sins are bringing down God's wrath.

By contrast *Pierce the Ploughman's Crede* is untypical. Two things stand out about it. First, the term 'creed' as the poet uses it has nothing to do with disputes about dogma or the articles of faith, but relates to the fulfilment of belief in action, as in the Pauline definition of true religion and undefiled. Second, the dependence on Langland is extreme: the poet has been fired by the symbol of Piers as mankind regenerate. His ragged peasant ankle-deep in mud which, by the way, he has no business trying to plough – Langland would never have made such a gaffe – stands for a life in whole accord with spiritual values by contrast with that of self-indulgence exemplified by the friars. The poem is enigmatic but not impenetrably so: its contradictions are more apparent than real. Illustrating the virulence of the friars' reaction to criticism the poet refers favourably once to Wyclif who, *in goodnesse of gost*, admonished them, and once to Walter Brute[26] who *seyde hem þe soþe*. Both men, the text says, the friars maliciously pursued with accusations of heresy (528–32, 657–62). By contrast the creed Piers teaches at the end is, article by article, the Apostles Creed. We tend to oversimplify the opposition. Here is a poem from a time and place where a contemporary of Wyclif found his proposals for moral reform commendable, and was not yet aware of, or alarmed by, his heterodoxy. The poem is primarily anti-fraternal, innocent of

---

[25] Elizabeth Salter, *'Piers Plowman* and *The Simonie'*, *Archiv*, 203 (1967), 241–54.
[26] Skeat, *Pierce the Ploughmans Crede*, pp .x, xi; McKisack, pp .519, 20.

any dissent. It is not revolutionary, and not so much a satire as a straightforward polemic. Its author was certainly not, as Janet Coleman suggested, a member of the 'proletariat',[27] but an educated man and a good plagiarist.

There remains the other striking imitation of *Piers Plowman*, nowadays called *Mum and Soothsegger*. This is straightforward political writing. We have here two incomplete, conceivably even unfinished poems. There is a formal difference between them: one fragment is divided into sections, passus, and the other not. And there is a difference in the position of the two speakers which seems to reflect political development. They may be by a single author: my ear tells me that they are closer to each other stylistically and metrically than either is to any other imitation of *Piers Plowman*. Fragment I, which Skeat called *Richard the Redeless*, is apparently thinly-veiled propaganda justifying the deposition. It is cast in the form of recommendations to Richard for better government. But these are quickly seen to have been made after the event, therefore to be retrospective criticism of his rule after 1389, criticism of the favourites, the excessive maintenance, the lack of central control, the misuse of the law courts, the acquiescence of the 1397 parliament in Richard's programme of revenge, all in excuse of Henry. The political theory is simple and conventional. Fragment II is a debate between Mum, 'Discreet Silence', and Soothsegger, 'Plain Speaker', in which the argument prevails that if a man is concerned about the state of the realm and in a position to be heard he has an obligation to speak out. Keeping silent about abuses is a main reason why they persist. Compelled by this argument the speaker of the poem sets down his reckoning of the troubles of the times, and it turns out to be the commonplace list of estates satire. Both fragments are thoroughly royalist and authoritarian, without a trace of revolutionary thinking.

There is in fact no genuinely revolutionary writing in Middle English prose or verse except that of Wyclif and the Lollards. The only evidence that John Ball was, as Robbins affected to call him, 'the priestly theoretician' of the 1381 rising is reports in contemporary chronicles, and does not amount to much. According to Walsingham Ball preached that God created all men equal by nature: so had many a friar for many a year. He was not the originator of the couplet about Adam digging and Eve spinning. It was a preacher's commonplace, a warning against pride. According to Walsingham, Ball made it an attack on the concept of degree. If God had wished to create serfs he would have done so at the outset: it was man who unjustly introduced serfdom, against God's will. No priestly theoretician was needed to formulate that proposition, or the actual demands of the rebels, which varied from region to region and had in some parts already been realized following the labour shortages. As for the revolutionary implications of Ball's two 'letters',[28] they have been exaggerated. One actually admonishes against precipitous

[27] Janet Coleman, *Medieval Readers and Writers 1350–1400* (New York, 1981), pp.61–62, 168.
[28] Robbins, *Political Poems*, pp.54, 55; see also *Manual*, pp.1511, 1512, 1710, 1711.

action: *be war or ye be wo*, 'be cautious before you bring unhappiness upon yourselves', and *haueth ynow and seith hoo!*, 'When you have a sufficiency, say "Stop" '. 'Flee sin', it proposes, 'seek peace, keep yourselves in peace'. The other is in effect a complaint about the prevalence of six of the seven capital sins (the absent one is, significantly, anger) followed by prayer, *God doe boote for nowe is tyme*, 'May God effect a remedy, for the moment has come.' For Robbins that prayer is 'a summons to man the barricades';[29] more accurately, it is a commonplace of apocalyptic thinking. It would be sounder not to romanticize John Ball. He was ready to become archbishop of all England after the death of the prelates whose killing he recommended.[30]

Some of the error that has characterized discussion of the so-called Middle English literature of protest and dissent has come from the difficulty of the language, especially that of the Harley poems. Some has come from not looking closely at the texts; thus Wright's titles were taken at their face value. Some misreading seems to have been induced by a political disposition. The poems are in fact a highly miscellaneous body of writings. The serious ones have only one common element: concern about the inadequacy of human conduct, the consequent malfunctioning of the social order, the loss of hope.[31]

[29] 'Dissent in Middle English Literature', p.37.
[30] McKisack, p.421.
[31] 'The notion of the 'sovereignty of the proletariat' was wholly absent, and indeed inconceivable for centuries to come'. V.H.Galbraith, 'Some thoughts about the Peasants' Revolt', in *The Reign of Richard II: Essays in Honour of May McKisack*, edited by F. R. H. Du Boulay and Caroline M. Barron (London, 1971), p.56.

THE NON-TRAGEDY OF ARTHUR

H.A.Kelly

William Matthews's book, *The Tragedy of Arthur*, published in 1960,[1] signaled a new tendency to consider the *Alliterative Morte Arthure* as a deliberately intended tragedy. Matthews was anticipated by a few years by Karl Höltgen,[2] and followed by many others, including Helaine Newstead,[3] John Finlayson,[4] J.O'Loughlin,[5] Karl Göller,[6] Larry Benson,[7] Hanspeter Schelp,[8] Robert Lumiansky,[9] John Gardner,[10] George Keiser,[11] Maureen Fries,[12] Jean Ritzke-Rutherford,[13] Anke Janssen[14] and Russell Peck.[15]

---

[1] William Matthews, *The Tragedy of Arthur: A Study of the Alliterative 'Morte Arthure'* (Berkeley, 1960).

[2] Karl Josef Höltgen, 'König Arthur und Fortuna', *Anglia*, 75 (1957), 35–54; see also his 'Die "Nine Worthies"', *Anglia*, 77 (1959), 279–309, esp. 298–99.

[3] Helaine Newstead, review of Matthews, *Romance Philology*, 16 (1962–63), 118–122.

[4] John Finlayson, review of Matthews, *Medium Aevum*, 32 (1963), 74–77; see also his partial edition of the *Morte Arthure* (London, 1967; Evanston, 1971), esp. pp.14–15.

[5] J.L.N.O'Loughlin, review of Matthews, *Review of English Studies*, 2.14 (1963), 179–82.

[6] Karl Heinz Göller, *König Arthur in der englischen Literatur des späten Mittelalters*, Palaestra 238 (Göttingen, 1963), pp.104–21; *Romance und Novel: Die Anfänge des englischen Romans* (Regensburg, 1972), pp.151–53, 165.

[7] Larry D.Benson, 'The Alliterative *Morte Arthure* and Medieval Tragedy', *Tennessee Studies in Literature*, 11 (1966), 75–87.

[8] Hanspeter Schelp, *Exemplarische Romanzen im Mittelenglischen*, Palaestra 246 (Göttingen, 1967), pp.16, 169–80, 246–47.

[9] Robert M.Lumiansky, 'The Alliterative *Morte Arthure*, the Concept of Medieval Tragedy, and the Cardinal Virtue Fortitude', *Medieval and Renaissance Studies* 3, edited by John M.Headley (Chapel Hill, 1968), pp.95–118.

[10] John Gardner, *The Alliterative Morte Arthure, The Owl and the Nightingale, and Five Other Middle English Poems in a Modernized Version* (Carbondale, 1971; repr. 1973), pp.239–56.

[11] George R.Keiser, 'The Theme of Justice in the Alliterative *Morte Arthure*', *Annuale Mediaevale*, 16 (1975), 94–109.

[12] Maureen Fries, 'The Poem in the Tradition of Arthurian Literature', in *The Alliterative Morte Arthure: A Reassessment of the Poem*, edited by Karl Heinz Göller, Arthurian Studies 2 (Cambridge, 1981), pp.30–43, 159–61.

[13] Jean Ritzke-Rutherford, 'Formulaic Macrostructure: The Theme of Battle', Göller (n.12 above), pp.83–95, 169–71.

[14] Anke Janssen, 'The Dream of the Wheel of Fortune', Göller (n.12 above), pp.140–52, 179–81.

[15] Russell A.Peck, 'Willfulness and Wonders: Boethian Tragedy in the Alliterative *Morte Arthure*', in *The Alliterative Tradition in the Fourteenth Century*, edited by Bernard S.Levy and Paul E.Szarmach (Kent, Ohio, 1981), pp.153–82. I might mention also that Valerie Krishna in her 1976 edition (see n.39 below), pp.21–22, speaks favourably of Matthews's 'theory' that the poem is a tragedy. In *The Alliterative Morte Arthure: A New Verse Translation* (Washington, 1983), pp.xiii–xiv, she continues to favour the view of critics who see it as a medieval tragedy.

In my view, these and similar studies that analyze medieval works as tragedies are misguided: they are based on a series of mistaken assumptions and lead to false conclusions. In the following essay, I wish to set the record straight on tragedy, and then analyse the *Alliterative Morte Arthure* and other Arthurian works on their own terms; with one exception, these terms do not include a notion of tragedy. Finally, I will give some specific examples of how scholars have been led astray by classifying the *Alliterative Morte* as a tragedy.

The fundamental error from which the other mistakes flow is the supposition that tragedy was a common word and idea in the Middle Ages, and that it was common for authors to think of themselves as writing tragedies. The truth of the matter, which I intend to show in detail elsewhere, is that the word tragedy – that is, the Latin *tragedia* or its vernacular equivalents – was comparatively rare in the Middle Ages, and had a variety of meanings to those who used it. So far as I have been able to discover, the word appears in the writings of only four English authors in the last half of the fourteenth century, namely the poet Geoffrey Chaucer, the chronicler Thomas Walsingham, the translator John Trevisa, and the surgeon John Arderne. I will speak of Chaucer and Walsingham below. Trevisa, writing about 1387, simply passes on Ranulf Higden's list (which he got from St Jerome) of the works of 'Seneca', without translating *tragedie* or even taking it out of the accusative case: 'Also he made bookes de Beneficiis, de Clementia, declamaciones, tregideas, de naturalibus questionibus', and so on. The mistaken form *tregideas* (later manuscripts have the correct *tragedias*) is a sure sign of incomprehension on the part of Trevisa or his early scribes.[16] Arderne, writing in 1379 or a bit later, specifies 'the Bible and other tragedies' as likely sources for the kind of good and decent stories that medical persons should tell to their patients to make them laugh and put them in a joyful frame of mind.[17] The only usage that comes close to this is that of Herman Alemannus's translation of Averroes's commentary on Aristotle's *Poetics*, where tragedy is defined as the praise of virtue, instances of which can be found in the Bible and collections of *exempla*; though there is some stress on

---

[16] See *Polychronicon Ranulphi Higden*, edited by Churchill Babington and J.L.Lumby, Rolls Series 41.1–9 (London, 1865–1886), 4.402–3. I am grateful to Dr Lister M.Matheson, Associate Editor of the *Middle English Dictionary*, for pointing out Trevisa's usage to me, and for providing me with the whole *MED* file on 'tragedy' and related words.

[17] John Arderne, Preface to his *Practica*; I give the text from Bethesda, Maryland, National Library of Medicine MS acc. no. 146304 (Microfilm reel 58–27), fol. 65v (=25v): 'Expedit eciam vt medicus sciat confabulare de bonis fabulis & honestis que pacientes cogant ad risum tam de biblia quam de alijs tragedijs & alijs quibuscumque de quibus non sit curandum dummodo pacienti letum inducant animum.' (I wish to thank Mr Mark Infusino for helping me locate this text.) A crude rendering of the passage can be found in the early fifteenth-century translation edited by D'Arcy Power, *Treatises of Fistula in ano, Haemorrhoids, and Clysters*, EETS, os 139 (1910), p.8. The sense of the passage is that the 'fables' that the surgeon is to tell can be taken from the Bible or from other tragedies or from any other source, it matters not what, so long as the tales serve to make the patients joyful. For the date of Arderne's Preface (which would have to be after 8 February 1379), see Power's note to p.1 on p.107.

unmerited misfortunes, the two biblical examples cited (namely, Abraham and Isaac and Joseph and his brothers) end joyfully.[18]

Most frequently, Isidore of Seville's lead was followed in considering tragedy to designate a literary or dramatic genre once practiced by the ancient Romans or Greeks but now extinct. Dante in his *De vulgari eloquentia* was unusual in considering tragedy to be a current form (namely, poetry in high style about elevated subjects).[19] And, apart from Dante, who considered his own lyrics to be in that form, Chaucer was the first vernacular author anywhere in Europe who not only considered tragedy to be a living genre but also thought of himself as a writer of tragedies.

Chaucer as a 'tragedian' was anticipated by several Latin authors, including John Garland with his feeble attempt at narrative tragedy and Albertino Mussato with his imitation of Senecan tragedy; but it is highly improbable that Chaucer knew anything about them.[20] Boccaccio was a Latin author who did not anticipate Chaucer in the field, for contrary to 'popular scholarly opinion' Boccaccio did not regard the episodes of his *De casibus* as tragedies. There was, however, an author of Latin tragedies who was Chaucer's contemporary and who like him lived in the London area: I mean the Benedictine monk Thomas Walsingham, who began working on his great chronicle of St Albans around 1376. He preferred to write comedy, he says, but he recorded a 'more than tragic matter' that occurred in 1378, namely the pollution by bloodshed of Westminster Abbey.[21] When he tells of the Peasant Revolt of 1381, at one point he says that he is scarcely able to finish the tragedy of the crimes committed at London without having to write of similar events at St Albans,[22] and he calls the combined accounts a 'tragic history'.[23] One cannot tell whether he used these terms in the annals he kept at the time of the events or only later, in 1392–1394, when he put this early part of his

---

[18] See H.A.Kelly, 'Aristotle-Averroes-Alemannus on Tragedy: The Influence of the *Poetics* on the Latin Middle Ages', *Viator*, 10 (1979), 161–209, esp. 166–72.

[19] Kelly, 'Aristotle', p.186. I agree with those scholars who consider the *Epistle to Cangrande* to be spurious.

[20] John Garland, *Parisiana Poetria* 7.11–153, edited and translated by Traugott Lawler, Yale Studies in English 182 (New Haven, 1974); on the lack of influence of Garland's work, see Susan Gallick, 'Medieval Rhetorical Arts in England and the Manuscript Traditions', *Manuscripta*, 18 (1974), 67–95. For Mussato, see Kelly, 'Aristotle', 187–94; for another possible precedent (a prose lament over the capture of King John of France in 1356), see Kelly, p.172 n.44.

[21] Thomas Walsingham, *Chronicon Angliae*, edited by Edward Manude Thompson, Rolls Series 64 (London, 1874), p.206: 'Rem scripturus sum plus quam tragicam, qui comoediam scripsisse semper optaveram.' For Walsingham's works, see V.H.Galbraith, *The St Albans Chronicle, 1406–1420* (Oxford, 1937), esp. pp.ix–x, xlvi–xlvii.

[22] Walsingham, *Chronicon Angliae*, p.301: 'Ecce enim dum magna et nimis magna facinora scribo diebus Veneris atque Sabbati gesta Londoniis, vix eorum explicare possum tragoediam quin eisdem diebus occurrunt scribenda similia apud Sanctum Albanum, ut praetactum est.'

[23] Walsingham, p.312: 'Scripsimus, non sine labore, in praecedentibus tragicam historiam, ad posterorum notitiam et cautelam, de dominatione rusticorum, debacchatione communium, insania nativorum.'

chronicle into final form. Decades later, around 1420, he sums up his whole history of the rebellion as 'the rustic tragedy'.[24]

It does not seem likely, however, that Chaucer knew of Walsingham's history, or was inspired by his conception of tragedy as an account of horrendous events. Where, then, did he find out about tragedy? There is no doubt that he got his main notion from Boethius's *Consolation of Philosophy*, in the passage of the second prose of Book II where Fortune asks, 'What else does the cry of tragedies bewail but Fortune's overthrow of happy kingdoms by an unseen and unseeing stroke?' Chaucerian scholars go further and affirm that Chaucer was also drawing on Nicholas Trevet's learned commentary on Boethius. Trevet glosses *tragedia* by giving the 'villainous' definitions of Isidore of Seville and William of Conches, who both regarded tragedy as an obsolete genre of the ancients. According to Isidore, tragedy was a mournful poem of the deeds and crimes of wicked kings. According to William, tragedy was a writing about great iniquities beginning in prosperity and ending in adversity.[25] But in my opinion Chaucer never saw Trevet's gloss, did not use Conches's gloss or Isidore's *Etymologies*, did not know about Seneca's tragedies, and had not read Horace's *Ars poetica*. Rather, his main additional source of information was a simple gloss contained in his own text of the *Consolation*. The glosses that Chaucer's text must have contained are pretty much preserved in the manuscript that John Croucher gave to Cambridge University within a generation after Chaucer's death. The gloss at *Quid tragediarum clamor* reads as follows: 'Tragedia dicitur carmen de prosperitate incipiens et in aduersitate terminans'. The unknown glossator took over Conches's definition as provided by Trevet, but removed the *de magnis criminibus uel iniquitatibus* to make it fit the Boethian context of disasters caused by Fortune. Chaucer in his *Boece* (which is given section by section after the Latin text in the Croucher volume) translates the gloss closely:

---

[24] Walsingham, *Ypodigma Neustriae*, Henry Thomas Riley, Rolls Series 28.7 (London, 1876), p. 335: after telling briefly of the events that occurred in London, he says: 'Caeterum quis nebulonum debacchationes in aliis locis explicare posset ad plenum? Certe, nullum posse referre puto plenarie malitias et nequitias, homicidia et sacrilegia, crudelitates et scelera, quae gesserunt. Quae quia tractatum expetunt specialum, praesenti compendio non impono, remittens ad nostra Maiora Chronica videre cupientes tragoediam rusticam.' In my text above, I interpreted the *explicare* of the passage quoted in n. 22 to mean 'finish', but in the present passage *explicare* clearly means 'give all the details of', and it may be that this meaning applies in the earlier case as well. If so, it is possible that Walsingham is using *tragedia* (to give the medieval spelling) metaphorically, to mean the events themselves rather than the record of the events. In the last-cited text, his reference to 'seeing' the tragedy may indicate that he is aware of the dramatic nature of tragedy in antiquity.

[25] For Isidore's definition, found in *Etymologiae* 18.45, see Kelly, 'Aristotle', p. 171 n. 41, and for background see H. A. Kelly, 'Tragedy and the Performance of Tragedy in Late Roman Antiquity', *Traditio*, 35 (1979), 21–44. For the glosses of Trevet and Conches, see Alastair Minnis, 'Aspects of the Medieval French and English Traditions of the *De consolatione Philosophiae*', in *Boethius: His Life, Thought and Influence*, edited by Margaret Gibson (Oxford, 1981), pp. 312–61, esp. 336–37, 359 n. 82.

'Tragedye is to seyn a dite of a prosperite for a time þat endith in wrecchydnesse'.[26]

When Chaucer first applied himself to write tragedies of his own, in the series of stories he later gave to the Monk in the *Canterbury Tales*, he showed persons falling from prosperity for all sorts of reasons. Some fall because of foolish miscalculations or heedlessness or overconfidence; some are cast down by God for their sins, others are betrayed by friends or overcome by enemies; some are entirely wise and virtuous but fall nevertheless for no other reason than the whim of Fortune – or, translated into real terms, they fall because of overpowering odds or unfortunate circumstances.

There is not the slightest indication that any other author of Chaucer's time or later shared his ideas on tragedy or was influenced by them until John Lydgate took them up. Of the historians and poets who told the story of King Arthur, only Lydgate considered his account a tragedy. It is true that in the twelfth century one writer, Aelred of Rievaulx, followed by Peter of Blois, seems to have considered Arthurian stories of heroism under fire (though not, perhaps, stories of Arthur's end) to be tragedies.[27] But there is no reason to think that the authors of the stories shared any such notion.

It follows, therefore, that anyone who assumes that the author of the *Alliterative Morte Arthure* was consciously writing in a genre of tragedy is very probably distorting his meaning.

When the story of Arthur was first elaborated, by Geoffrey of Monmouth in his *History of the Kings of Britain*, it was mainly a story of the king's unparalleled triumphs. But, like the ninety-odd other kings described by Geoffrey, he died. The occasion of his death was a Pyrrhic victory over his nephew Mordred. Mordred was killed outright, but Arthur himself was lethally wounded and taken to Avalon to be healed; there he handed the crown of Britain over to his cousin Constantine. Constantine, after defeating Mordred's sons, was killed by Conan – or, according to a variant reading, he was struck down by the sentence of God (presumably for killing Mordred's sons in church).[28]

Wace, in his Anglo-Norman verse paraphrase of Geoffrey's Latin prose, adds the report that Arthur would one day return, and he admits that there was no assurance that he had really died. Lawman, doubtless using an expanded version of Wace, gives Arthur a dream predicting the trouble with Mordred and his own departure to Avalon. As Lawman tells the story, Mordred and his own departure to Avalon. As Lawman tells the story, Arthur

---

[26] Cambridge University Library MS Ii.3.21, fols 37–38. See the edition by Edmund Taite Silk, *Cambridge MS. Ii.3.21 and the Relation of Chaucer's Boethius to Trivet and Jean de Meung* (Yale University dissertation, 1930: Ann Arbor, University Microfilms 1970, no. 23,051), pp. 142, 146.

[27] Aelred of Rievaulx, *Speculum caritatis* 2.17.50–51, edited by C. H. Talbot, *Aelredi Rievallensis opera omnia*, I (Turnhout, 1971), 90; Peter of Blois, *Liber de confessione sacramentali*, PL, Vol. CCVII, cols 1088–89.

[28] Geoffrey of Monmouth, *Historia regum Britanniae* ll. 2–4, edited by Acton Griscom (New York, 1929), pp. 501–503.

bestows the rule on Constantine before going to Avalon; at Avalon he expects to be healed of his wounds and to return.

In none of these accounts is there any reason given for the final turn of events, apart from Mordred's betrayal, and there is little or no time spent in lamenting Arthur's fall.

The Arthurian stories produced by Chrétien de Troyes are all episodic and do not deal with Arthur's end. It is only in the prose *Mort Artu* that the themes and settings elaborated by Chrétien, particularly the love of Lancelot and Guinevere, are combined with Geoffrey's account of the treachery of Mordred. The *Mort* is a work of great originality and genius, and it goes into the circumstances of Arthur's death with abundant detail. It seems to draw on the same source as Lawman, but to much different effect. Arthur is given two dreams near the end, but they come after he has learned of Mordred's betrayal and after he has returned to England to fight him. In the first dream, the dead Gawain appears to him and warns that the battle with Mordred will go badly. The second dream, which occurs on the following night, centres around a woman whom we are to identify as Fortune, though she is not named as such. Arthur dreams that a beautiful lady comes to him and lifts him from the earth, carries him to a high mountain, and seats him on a wheel. She catechizes him gently, and tells him that he is on the wheel of Fortune, and that all of what he can see, which seems to him like the whole world, is ruled by him, the greatest of all kings; but, she says, such are the prides of earth that there is no one seated so high that he is not forced to fall from the power of the world ('mes tel sont li orgueil terrien qu'il n'i a nul si haut assiz qu'il ne le coviegne cheoir de la poesté del monde'). Up to this point, the lady has seemed very sweet and sympathetic, and we almost hear a touch of sadness in her voice. Nevertheless, she now takes Arthur and whirls him to the ground so roughly (*felenessement*, literally, 'feloniously') that his body and limbs feel completely broken and powerless.[29]

'Thus', the author says, 'King Arthur saw the misfortunes that would befall him'. In the morning after the second dream, Arthur first attends mass and then goes to an archbishop and confesses as best he can all the sins of which he feels guilty before God. Next he recounts his visions, and his confessor tries to dissuade him from joining battle, but Arthur refuses.

Arthur's perseverance in his course does not seem to be regarded primarily or entirely as a moral fault, of the sort that would require further confession or would prevent the archbishop from giving him absolution. The archbishop does, it is true, appeal to the safety of Arthur's soul and body and kingdom (similarly, Gawain in his dream had told him that all noble men would suffer great harm from his failure to wait for Lancelot). However, when Arthur says he cannot comply, the archbishop does not make it a matter of sin but a question of honour: the king will dishonour himself if he does not follow his advice. But Arthur clearly feels bound by a different sense of honour and

---

[29] *La mort le roi Artu* sect. 176, edited by Jean Frappier, ed. 2, Textes littéraires français, 58 (Geneva, 1954, repr. 1964). For the theory of an expanded Wace as the common source for Lawman and the *Mort Artu*, see p .xvii n .3.

obligation. He swears on the soul of his father that he will not turn back, and he tells the archbishop that he will not retreat for all the honour of the world.[30] We might be tempted to say that it is Arthur's pride, in the vicious sense of the word, that holds him from turning back,[31] but the author refrains from drawing this harsh conclusion, at least explicitly. We must remember that Arthur's quarrel with Mordred is completely justified, and that the archbishop differs from him only in the matter of strategy.

When Arthur comes to Salisbury Plain and sees Merlin's prophecy inscribed in stone, foretelling a great battle that will orphan the kingdom of Logres, the archbishop loses hope of Arthur's winning even with reinforcements. He tells the king that he will be killed if he fights Mordred under any circumstances. No other outcome is possible, he says, for Merlin's prophecies have always come true. Arthur now says that if he had not advanced so far, he would turn back. Instead, however, he prays to Christ for aid, for he is determined not to stop until Our Lord gives the honour to him or to Mordred; and, in a mood of great desolation, he says that if he falls, it will be because of his sin and his folly ('ce sera par mon pechié et par mon outrage'), for he has more good knights than Mordred.[32] He is not defeated, of course, but his victory results in fearful losses. He attributes these losses not to sin but only to folly, for failing to send for Lancelot.[33] At the end, his only comment on his desperate state is that Fortune, who had been a mother to him, has now become a stepmother, and he must spend the remnant of his life in grief and anger and sorrow. He says this in great anger, after seeing that his fervent embrace of one of his wounded knights has killed him.[34] Arthur's last knight, Girflet, looks on as the king is taken away in a boat by Morgan, and later he finds a tomb with the inscription, 'Here lies King Arthur, who through his valor conquered twelve kingdoms'. Girflet remains all day at the tomb in great grief,[35] and the story goes on to tell of the return of Lancelot and his forces, and their dispatch of Mordred's two sons and their allies, and it ends with an account of Lancelot's pious death.

According to this version of the story, then, Arthur believes that he came to grief for not heeding the warning of Gawain in his dream and for not taking his confessor's advice to wait for reinforcements. His interim statement that failure would be the result of his sin should not be taken as a serious expression of belief, since he does not return to the idea again. Rather, it should be interpreted rhetorically, as expressing his confidence in his superior forces. From the point of view of the author and the reader, Arthur cannot be convicted of overconfidence, since it is abundantly clear that he is quite apprehensive; he is nevertheless determined to carry on in spite of possible defeat, because of his sense of personal honour. We can surmise, from

[30] *Mort Artu*, sect. 177.
[31] Such is the judgment of Larry D .Benson, *Malory's Morte Darthur* (Cambridge, Mass., 1976), p .239.
[32] *Mort Artu*, sect. 178.
[33] *Mort Artu*, sect. 186.
[34] *Mort Artu*, sect. 192.
[35] *Mort Artu*, sect. 193–94.

Arthur's second dream and the archbishop's reaction to it and to Merlin's prophecy, that Arthur could not have averted his destiny even with Lancelot's help – and that therefore Arthur was not right to blame the disaster on his folly. We are no doubt meant to conclude that Lady Fortune is right, that Arthur will fall simply because his time of 'pride' or greatness is past, and that he undergoes the same fate as the virtuous Zenobia in the tragedy that Chaucer devotes to her in the *Monk's Tale*.

There were, of course, sins involved in Arthur's downfall, but they were mainly not his sins. They were above all Mordred's sins of betrayal and rebellion, and more remotely Gawain's insane desire for revenge and Lancelot and Guinevere's sins of adultery. Arthur could be said to share some of the blame himself – his desire to punish Lancelot and Guinevere was doubtless excessive at first; but on balance his was a moderating influence in the face of Gawain's excess. One could find other causes for Arthur's fall in the pre-history of the *Morte Artu*; Arthur would not have fallen if he had not married Guinevere or if he had not sinfully begotten Mordred, or if his father with Merlin's connivance had not sinfully begotten Arthur. This is as much as to say that Arthur would not have fallen if he had never been born, or that he would not have fallen if he had not risen.

This sort of speculation is irrelevant for a work of literature unless the author or his characters encourage it. We must limit ourselves to the statements of causality, responsibility, or blame that are actually present in the text, particularly at critical junctures and at the end of the work, and to the lessons and morals that the author clearly intended to be drawn.

If Chaucer had known the *Mort Artu* and wished to write a tragedy from it in synoptic form as he did with his 'Modern Instances', he could hardly have avoided treating the story of Arthur as a simple tragedy of betrayal. Just as Pedro of Castile was undone by his brother, Bernabò Visconti by a nephew who was also his son-in-law, and Pierre Lusignan by his own lieges, so Arthur was brought down by the man who was his son, nephew, knight, viceregent, and the would-be lover and husband of his queen.

To come to the *Alliterative Morte Arthure* itself, we must admit that the circumstances of its composition and textual history are obscure. It has usually been dated around 1360–1375, though a date of around 1400–1402 has recently been suggested.[36] As far as the manuscript evidence goes, it could have been written as late as 1450.[37] But if it was written after Chaucer's time, it shows no sign of his influence. In general, the poem follows the story as set forth by Geoffrey of Monmouth. The author is usually thought to have known the French traditions, but for the most part to have ignored them. However,

---

[36] Larry D .Benson, 'The Date of the *Alliterative Morte Arthure*', in *Medieval Studies in Honor of Lillian Herlands Hornstein*, edited by Jess B .Bessinger, Jr., and Robert R .Raymo (New York, 1976), pp .19–40. Mary Hamel in her edition (n .39 below) supports Benson's dating for the final form of the poem, but suggests that the author may have started it in the 1370s (pp .56–58).

[37] The watermark of the Thornton manuscript indicates that it was copied between 1420 and 1450; see George R .Keiser, 'Lincoln Cathedral Library MS 91: Life and Milieu of the Scribe', *Studies in Bibliography*, 32 (1979), 158–79, esp. 159.

it seems highly likely that the dream of Fortune that he gives to Arthur was partially inspired by the *Mort Artu*.[38] The dream may also be indebted to Lawman or to Lawman's source, since it comes at the place that he assigns it, before Arthur is told about Mordred's treachery.

I believe that a proper understanding of the meaning and function of Arthur's dream is crucial for our understanding of the whole work, and I wish to analyse it at length.

The author has combined the *Mort Artu*'s dream of Arthur's encounter with Fortune with the tradition of Nine Worthies. Arthur first sees the six Worthies who lived before him (though he does not yet know their identity). The six together, or separately, pronounce the following lament:

> That euer I rengnede on þir roo me rewes it euer!
> Was neuer roye so riche that regnede in erthe;
> Whene I rode in my rowte, roughte I noghte ells,
> Bot reuaye and reuell and rawnson the pople;
> And thus I drife forthe my dayes, whills I dreghe myghte,
> And therefore derflyche I am dampnede for euer.[39]

(3272–77)

The last line must not be taken as indicating eternal damnation in hell, for that would mean the loss of the three Hebrew champions (Judas Maccabaeus, Joshua and David) as well as the three pagans (Alexander, Hector and Julius Caesar). It must mean something like 'condemned to suffer in this way and never to rise on the wheel again', or, as Caesar puts it, 'dampnede to þe dede' (3299), that is, condemned to death or condemned to join the dead. For these heroes are not enduring their 'days' in a real (that is, Christian) cosmos; they are not in hell or purgatory. Rather, they exist in the same sort of visionary world as the hosts of walking wounded that flock to Boccaccio's study to beg for inclusion in the *De casibus*.

Similarly, the apparent stress upon crime and punishment is to be taken as so much rhetorical exuberance or alliterative distortion. For the main emphasis is upon the richness and untroubled prosperity of their reigns, not upon their misdeeds. The shock of their loss is great, and it is 'thus' and 'therefore' that they mourn.

This reading is confirmed by an examination of each of the individual lamentations that follow. With one exception, sin is not mentioned as a cause for their falls. The exception occurs in the case of Joshua, who should by

[38] So J.L.N.O'Loughlin, 'The English Alliterative Romances', in *Arthurian Literature in the Middle Ages*, edited by Roger Sherman Loomis (Oxford, 1959), pp.520–27, esp. 524; so too Höltgen, *König Arthur* (n.2 above), p.44.
[39] I follow the text of Valerie Krishna, *The Alliterative Morte Arthure: A Critical Edition* (New York, 1976), but consult also that of Mary Hamel, *Morte Arthure: A Critical Edition* (New York, 1984), and the facsimile, *The Thornton Manuscript (Lincoln Cathedral MS 91)*, introduced by D.S.Brewer and A.E.B.Owen (London, 1975, 2nd edition, 1977), as well as the normalized edition of Larry D.Benson, *King Arthur's Death: The Middle English Stanzaic Morte Arthur and Alliterative Morte Arthure* (Indianapolis, 1974).

rights be considered the most saintly of the lot. Instead, he is described as a fierce man who madly struggles against his fall:

> The fifte was a faire man þan fele of þies oþer,
> A forsy [MS: forsesy] man and a ferse, with fomand lippis;
> He fongede faste on þe feleyghes and falded his armes,
> Bot ʒit he failede and fell a fyfty fote large;
> Bot ʒit he sprange and sprente and spradden his armes,
> And one þe spere-lenghe spekes, he spekes þire wordes:
> 'I was in Surrye a syr and sett by myn one,
> As souerayne and seyngnour of sere kynges londis;
> Now of my solace I am full sodanly fallen,
> And for sake of my syn, ʒone sete es me rewede'.
>
> (3306–15)

I maintain that Joshua is the victim not of punishment for sin, but of character assassination by alliteration. It was his fate to be the fifth fellow to fall. The fourth had used up most of the good f-words; and while some are repeated ('faire', 'forsy'), Joshua is burdened with the implications of intemperate fury ('with fomand lippis'). His illustrious career as achiever of the Promised Land is then subordinated to the next alliterative need, and it is the row of sibilants that must bear the blame for his 'syn'. When a different letter is pressed into service in the philosopher's explanation, we are given a much truer picture:

> The fyfte was Iosue, þat joly mane of armes,
> þat in Ierusalem oste full myche joye lymppede.
>
> (3414–415)

After Arthur describes his dream, the philosopher interprets it:

> 'Freke', sais the philosophre, 'thy fortune es passede;
> For thow sall fynd hir thi foo – frayste when the lykes.
> Thow arte at þe hegheste, I hette the forsothe;
> Chalange nowe when thow will, thow cheuys no more.
> Thow has schedde myche blode and schalkes distroyede,
> Sakeles, in cirquytrie, in sere kynges landis.
> Schryfe the of thy schame and schape for thyn ende;
> Thow has a schewynge, Sir Kynge – take kepe ʒif the lyke;
> For thow sall fersely fall within fyve wynters.
> Fownde abbayes in Fraunce – þe froytez are theyn awan –
> Fore Froill and for Ferawnt and for thir ferse knyghttis,
> That thowe fremydly in Fraunce has faye beleuede'.
>
> (3394–405)

This admonition has usually been taken as meaning that the philosopher is attributing Arthur's fall to his unjust methods of waging war. Why, then, when the philosopher goes on to warn him to take heed of the other kings in his dream, does he tell only of their glories? Why does he single out France as the site of Arthur's sins, when it is his Italian campaign to which modern critics have given the worst marks?[40] Why pick on Frolle, who was killed in the French wars that occurred before the action of the poem?[41] One could argue that Geoffrey of Monmouth shows Arthur conquering France and defeating Frollo for no other reason than desire for conquest and glory; but if our author intended to find particular fault with this phase of Arthur's career, would he not have made more of a point of it? When we expect examples of the innocent men that Arthur has killed, why does the philosopher name Feraunt, whose father, we have been told, was none other than 'the Fende' (2761)?[42]

Since I view the poet as rather crude in his priorities, I believe that the F-foes were chosen for the sake of the alliteration,[43] as was the period of 'fyve wynters' for the limit of Arthur's good fortunes. Later, when t's are tyrannizing the tiers, the philosopher says that bad tidings will come 'within ten dayes' (3450), but they come immediately, and Arthur's downfall follows in rapid sequence. I also believe that much of Arthur's apparent savagery in Tuscany, which I will take up below, is to be accounted for in the same way, that is, as caused by alliteration taking precedence over sense and nuance.

Even if these points are conceded, however, it is clear that Arthur has committed some sins along the way, whether or not they were noted as sins when they occurred. The philosopher says so, and Arthur does not deny it.

[40] For example, Matthews (n.1 above), pp.133–34; Lumiansky (n.9 above), p.112. See also Mary Hamel, 'The Dream of a King: The Alliterative *Morte Arthure* and Dante', *Chaucer Review*, 14 (1979–80), 298–312, esp. 310 n.8.
[41] The Lady in Arthur's dream takes credit for Arthur's victory over Frolle (line 3345).
[42] For 'Ferawnt' Hamel substitutes '(his) fernet', holding that one of the versions of the *Awntyrs off Arthur*'s line 275, viz., 'Freol and his farnet, fey ar þey leued' (Ireland MS; the Douce MS reads 'Freol and his folke', and the Thornton MS has 'Freol and his farnaghe'; see the edition of Ralph Hanna (Manchester, 1974), who preserves the original reading of both poems. But this would leave the line with the meaning, 'Frollo and his knights and their knights'. Perhaps because of this Hamel also suggests that 'thir' should be emended to 'othir'. It is my guess, however, that *Awntyrs* 275 has simply compressed *Alliterative Morte* 3404–05, that that 'farnet' (or 'folke' or 'farnaghe') corresponds not to 'Ferawnt' but to 'ferse knyghttis'.
[43] Keiser (n.11 above), p.101 n.23 admits that Feraunt 'seems to be only a convenient name the poet uses when he is working in patterns of alliteration on *f*. An outlandish example of an inappropriate word chosen for the sake of alliteration comes in line 37, where the poet is telling of Arthur's previous conquests of 'Gyan and Gothelande and Grece the ryche'. F.Holthausen's suggestion, which Krishna accepts, that 'Grece' does not mean 'Greece' but is a mistake for 'Grace' and refers to Grasse, is not convincing. Grasse was an obscure bishopric in Provence near Monaco, whereas it is clear that some well-known place was intended and called for by the context. Other examples can be seen in the names Sir Priamus throws around: his father is the uncle of Alexander's grandfather, Sir Ector of Troy, he is descended from Judas (Maccabaeus) and Joshua, and he holds possession of Alexandria and Africa (2602–8). Mary Hamel, 'The "Christening" of Sir Priamus in the Alliterative *Morte Arthure*', *Viator*, 13 (1982), 295–307, attempts to make sense out of Sir Priamus by seeing him as a schismatic (Byzantine) Christian, but this interpretation asks too much of the author. However, I do agree that he is a Christian and not a pagan. The latter view is argued by Lee W.Patterson, 'The Historiography of Romance and the Alliterative *Morte Arthure*', *Journal of Medieval and Renaissance Studies*, 13 (1983), 1–32, esp. 21.

Are these sins, then, the cause of his fall? Most readers, as we will see, say yes. But Benson says no: 'We know that Arthur's end is near, that he is now at the zenith of fortune's wheel and will inevitably fall, not because of some fate seeking retribution of his sins, and not because God's justice demands that he be punished for the excesses of his campaign, for his cruelty is necessary even in a just war and he remains noble in his kingship.' Nevertheless, Benson believes that he falls because of a fault: 'He will fall because the zeal essential to the attainment of his present success has led him to forget his own mortal limitations.'[44] Arthur might well exclaim with the *Exultet*, 'O certe necessarium peccatum!'

The fact is, of course, that everyone has to fall, and, as the adage has it, 'The higher you rise the harder you fall'. Sometimes caution can prevent premature falls, sometimes not. Being aware of one's mortal limitations does not make one any less mortal; it only makes death less of a surprise when it comes. The philosopher does not tell Arthur that he will fall because of his sins, and Ward Tonsfeldt is surely right when he concludes that Arthur's fall is entirely unconnected with his faults, whether moral or intellectual: 'The dream is a warning of death, not of sin.'[45] Arthur falls because it is time to fall; and Edmund Brock's marginal summary gives us the whole theme of the passage: 'The philosopher interprets the dream, and tells Arthur that his good fortune is passed. He is to prepare for his end, and to found abbeys in France'.[46] The philosopher points to another reason as well: Arthur falls because of wicked men in his realm (3447). Arthur will go down because others sin against him and against God, but he will do his utmost to see to the punishment and destruction of these sinners.

After explaining to Arthur the identity of the other eight Worthies, the philosopher repeats his counsel to repent of his great misdeeds before it is too late:

> I rede thow rekkyn and reherse vnresonable dedis,
> Ore the repenttes full rathe all thi rewthe werkes.
> Mane, amende thy mode, or thow myshappen,
> And mekely aske mercy for mede of thy saule.
>
> (3452–55)

These words could be taken to mean that Arthur is to desist from his present sinful course, in order to prevent his predicted mishap, or to prevent it from

---

[44] Benson (n.7 above), pp.83–84.
[45] Hugh Ward Tonsfeldt, *Medieval Narrative and the Alliterative Morte Arthure* (University of California, San Diego, dissertation, 1975), p.227.
[46] *Morte Arthure*, edited by Edmond Brock, EETS, os 8 (1871), p.100. Hamel, 'Dream' (n.40 above) 300–7, notes that the sinfulness of the Worthies is 'a central oddity of the dream', and though she also finds it odd that the philosophers 'recount only the Worthies' fame and accomplishments', she concludes that the dream-Worthies are meant to be regarded as sinful; their sin lies in 'the heedlessness and oppressiveness of their lives', and the philosophers deduce Arthur's similar sinfulness from the dream.

being worse than it otherwise would be. But we know from the context that his fall is inevitable; the philosopher's meaning therefore is that he is to prepare for his end while he can still do so properly – for instance, by founding abbeys in France and benefiting from their prayers; for, as the philosopher tells him, the fruits are his own. If Arthur was previously 'forgetful of his own mortal limitations', he is not so now. Death will not take him unawares.

The fact that the poet neglects to tell us of Arthur's preparations for death until he lies dying does not warrant our thinking that Arthur himself has been negligent in the matter. The author simply takes it for granted that Arthur agrees to comply, that he does confess his sins, and does determine to follow the philosopher's other prescriptions; and he moves on to tell of Arthur's moody anger at his coming decline from glory. We must keep in mind that it is not necessarily a sin to be depressed over one's misfortunes; one may rail against Fortune without fear of divine punishment. Undoubtedly, perfect resignation to the will of God would be admirable and expected in a saint's life, but the poet is not a hagiographer, and it would not be seemly for his hero to take his coming reversal with equanimity.

We find a similar instance of narrative foreshortening in the scene of Arthur's last moments:

The Kyng sees by asaye þat sownde bese he neuer,
And sone to his sekire men he said theis wordes:
'Doo calle me a confessour, with Criste in his armes;
I will be howselde in haste, whate happe so betyddys.
Constantyn, my cosyn, he sall the corown bere,
Alls becomys hym of kynde, ȝife Criste will hym thole;
Beryn, fore my benyson, thowe berye ȝone lordys,
That in baytaille with brondez are broughte owte of lyfe;
And sythen merke manly to Mordrede children,
That they bee sleyghely slayne and slongen in watyrs;
Latt no wykkyde wede waxe, ne wrythe one this erthe –
I warne fore thy wirchipe, wirke alls I bydde.
I foregyffe all greffe, for Cristez lufe of Heuen;
ȝife Waynor hafe wele wroghte, wele hir betydde'.
He saide *In manus* with mayne one molde whare he ligges,
And thus passes his speryt, and spekes he no more.

(4312–27)

Once again, we might expect to see Arthur confess his sins, since he calls for a confessor, but the author shows him going on in the same final speech to take care of other matters before commending his soul to God and dying. We must simply assume that he does go to confession and receive the viaticum. It would be a distortion of the author's obvious intention to interpret the lines otherwise.

It would be a worse distortion to see any relapse or hard-heartedness or vicious desire for revenge in Arthur's speech. On the contrary, Arthur is exemplary in what he says. He first passes on the rule to Constantine, speaking of him in the third person and then, I take it, addressing him directly: he is to see to the proper burial of his men, and to the destruction of Mordred's 'children', who are to be denied burial. No enemy, no 'wicked weed', is to be allowed to survive.

Readers have been misled into thinking that Arthur is referring to Mordred's children by Guinevere.[47] But though Mordred is said to have married Guinevere and 'wroghte hire with childe' (3552, cf. 3576), there would not have been time for her to have borne him even one child, let alone more than one (let us not speak of twins or triplets). Arthur has been gone for less than a year, and though the poet is unrealistic about the enormity of Mordred's accomplishments before word of them is brought to Arthur, he shows Arthur as wasting no time in returning; he arrives as quickly as he can in Flanders and assembles his fleet within fifteen days (3598). When Mordred warns Guinevere to 'flee with hir childire' (3907), he is referring to her maidservants, for she 'passes owte of þe palesse with all hir pryce maydenys' (3913).[48]

Arthur is most likely referring to Mordred's grown children, since his order comes after he has appointed Constantine. As we have seen, Geoffrey of Monmouth tells how Constantine pursued Mordred's two sons and killed them (in the *Mort Artu* Lancelot does the job). But the reference could be to Mordred's knights in general. The poet tells us earlier that Arthur's army hunts down the enemy,

> Mourtherys in the mowntaygnes Sir Mordrede knyghtes;
> Thare chapyde neuer no childe, cheftayne ne oþer.
>
> (4259–60)

There are other examples in the poem where 'child' means 'knight'. Arthur even calls Mordred himself 'a childe of my chambyre' when he leaves him in charge of his kingdom (690). The two kings awaiting their turn on Fortune's

---

47 Some scholars who accept this idea nevertheless hold Arthur excused of wrongdoing. For example, Krishna in her note to the passage, p .205, suggests that Arthur is motivated by prudence rather than revenge, and Hamel's note (p .396) is similar. Jörg O .Fichte, 'The Figure of Sir Gawain', ed. Göller (n .12 above), pp .106–16, says that 'neither Arthur nor the poet seems to find any moral fault' with the order to exterminate Mordred's offspring (pp .114–15). In contrast, Göller in one of his own essays ('The Dream of the Dragon and the Bear', pp .130–39), considers the order to kill Mordred's children as a sign that Arthur 'remains recalcitrant, entrapped in worldliness to the end' (p .139). This contradiction between essayists in Göller's collection is noted by James L .Boren in his review in *Philological Quarterly*, 61 (1982), 491–94; Boren clearly thinks that the reader is meant to condemn Arthur for ordering 'child-murder'. Peck (n. 15 above, pp. 173–77) asserts that Mordred is Arthur's son and that Arthur therefore orders the death of his grandchildren.

48 A similar usage is given in the *Middle English Dictionary*, s.v. 'child', no. 13a, from the earlier Wycliffite Bible: 'Judit seide to hir child womman' (translating *puella*). Hamel in her notes (p .382) thinks either that the plural of child is a mistake or that Guinevere also has charge of Mordred's older children, who would accordingly be portrayed as still young. Later (p .396) she affirms the second alternative.

wheel (who turn out to be Charlemagne and Godfrey of Bouillon) are also called 'childire' (3328).[49]

Arthur ends by forgiving, out of love for Christ, all wrongs that have been done to him, and he specifically wishes Guinevere well if (I interpret him to mean) she has truly repented.

Arthur's earlier lament over the dead Gawain, who, he says, was killed 'for syn of myn one' (3986), is not to be taken for anything more than it is, a heartfelt cry of sorrow. This is not to say that Arthur does not have some further sins to confess on his deathbed, but only that the poet does not tell us what they are and does not present his fall and death as in any way the result of his sins.

In spite of a certain lack of finesse and occasional lapses of tone and nuance, the author of the *Alliterative Morte Arthure* achieves a powerful effect in his story of Arthur's triumphs and subsequent death. But he does so according to his own lights, which are not those of an anti-war moralist but those of a patriot. His treatment is similar to that of Shakespeare when he portrays the deaths of the Earl of Salisbury and Sir Thomas Gargrave in *I Henry VI* 1.4.70–97. It is assumed by both Talbot and by Salisbury himself that Salisbury has sinned during his life and that he repents and will be forgiven; it is assumed that his military record was wholly admirable, that it was cut short through sheer chance but also through a malevolent enemy; it is assumed that he is still admirable and virtuous, and not sinful, when he desires vengeance on the French, even when Talbot compares him or himself to Nero playing the lute while Rome burned.

Talbot declares that Salisbury's death is a woeful tragedy, since by Shakespeare's day it had become second nature not only to think of certain poems and plays as tragedies but also to speak of unfortunate events as tragedies. Such usages and ideas were uncommon two centuries earlier, and there is no indication that they figured in the frame of reference of the *Alliterative Morte Arthure*.

I should emphasise that even if the author of the alliterative poem had heard of some definition of tragedy and had kept it in mind while writing his work, it need not have influenced the way he told his story or the lessons he drew from it. Let me illustrate this point by looking at the accounts of Arthur given by Boccaccio, Premierfait and Lydgate. All three of these authors, like the author of the *Alliterative Morte*, ignore the French complications of the Lancelot-Guinevere affair and tell only of Arthur's betrayal by Mordred.

Boccaccio's stated intention at the beginning of the *De casibus* is to give examples of great men who were wicked or who became wicked and fell as a consequence of their wickedness. His idea was to provide cautionary lessons to his readers so that they would avoid similar falls. But when he comes down to telling his histories, he includes as many men who fell for no fault of their own as those who deserved to fall. Arthur, it turns out, is one of the blameless

---

[49] See the other examples given by Krishna in her glossary. The eight-score 'childrenne' that Arthur receives as hostages from Rome (3188) should also be taken for adults, contrary to James L .Boren, 'Narrative Design in the Alliterative *Morte Arthure*', *Philological Quarterly*, 56 (1977), 310–19, esp. 315.

ones. Boccaccio recounts, with obvious approval, Arthur's exploits by which he increased his kingdom and his glory, and says that he was so successful that even savage Fortune could not prevent his glory from shining with great brilliance down to the present time. Arthur's downfall was caused by Mordred, his own son by a concubine. Mordred had been beguiled by Fortune into thinking that he could supplant his father. The sad result was that a single nefarious man in a short time destroyed Arthur's great kingdom, and when the king died his Round Table was broken up and its history debased to the level of popular fable. 'The great glory and fame of the king was brought by this desolation to ignominy and obscurity, so that men can, if they wish, recognise that nothing on earth can endure except what is lowly.'[50]

This moral, which contradicts Boccaccio's earlier statement that Arthur's glory still shines *claro cum fulgore*, and which overlooks the fact that the lowly perish just as surely as the great, was repeated by Laurence of Premierfait: Arthur's name and fame were reduced in desolation to infamy and obscurity.[51]

Lydgate, though convinced that he is writing a tragedy in English from a tragedy written in French (and before that in Latin), follows the main lines of the story that Premierfait hands on from Boccaccio. He adds some conventional remarks about Fortune: Arthur had a better chance than anyone to control her, but she is most to be feared when she is most favourable, and there is no certainty in her.[52] But instead of repeating the moral that his fame has diminished, Lydgate indicates that just the opposite has occurred: Arthur has a heavenly constellation named after him, and Christians speak of him as the first of the Nine Worthies.[53] He then adds 'a Lenvoye', the only one in his eighth book, which begins with the lines:

> This tragedie of Arthour heer folwyng
> Bit princes all bewar of fals tresoun.[54]

His earlier practice has been to refer to the previous account as the tragedy, to which the envoy draws the moral. 'Folwying' then should no doubt be understood to mean 'continuing' or 'concluding'. Lydgate, like Chaucer and

---

[50] Boccaccio, *De casibus virorum illustrium*, Book 8; see Louis Brewer Hall's reprint of the Paris ca. 1520 edition (Gainesville, 1962), pp.205–6 (fol.99r–v). This edition follows Text A, which was composed ca. 1357–60, slightly revised ca. 1370, and first circulated ca. 1373 or just after Boccaccio's death in 1374; it is the version that was used by Laurence of Premierfait. For Text B (Boccaccio's revision of 1373–74), see the edition of *De casibus* by Pier Giorgio Ricci and Vittorio Zaccaria in the Mondadori *Tutte le opere di Giovanni Boccaccio*, edited by Vittore Branca, vol.9 (Milan, 1983), pp.728–34 (Book 8, chap. 19). For the dates of the texts, see Zaccaria, 'Le due redazioni del *De casibus*', *Studi sui Boccaccio*, 10 (1977–78), 1–26, esp. 25, and his edition, p.883.
[51] The relevant passage is given by Henry Bergen in his edition of Lydgate's *Fall of Princes*, 4 vols, EETS, es 121–4 (1924–7), IV, p.334.
[52] Lydgate, *Fall of Princes*, 8, 2661–67, 2861–63, 3088–89.
[53] *Fall of Princes*, 8, 3102–8.
[54] *Fáll of Princes*, 8, 3130–32. The envoy goes on to elaborate the dangers of betrayal.

unlike Shakespeare, never uses tragedy to mean 'tragic events' but only 'tragic history' (in written form).

If the idea of tragedy did not affect the way in which Lydgate retold the story of Arthur, it has affected the way in which modern scholars have understood the *Alliterative Morte Arthure* (though I am far from saying that it is the only reason for their mistaken interpretations of the poem).

Some tragic readings of the *Alliterative Morte Arthure* begin with the supposition that the author was writing a Chaucerian tragedy, but since there are different scholarly opinions about Chaucer's ideas of tragedy, the interpretations vary accordingly.

The most extreme (and, in my view, the most distorted) idea of Chaucerian tragedy is that of D.W.Robertson, who sees all of Chaucer's tragedies as 'moral', that is, as telling the stories of persons whose falls are caused by some sort of 'cupidity' on their part.[55] Lumiansky's view is somewhat similar, except that he contrasts the Monk's supposedly shallow view of tragedy with 'true tragedy', which Chaucer and the author of the *Alliterative Morte* must have deduced from Boethius: the Monk laments wordly loss, while true tragedy laments moral loss.[56] Lumiansky considers the alliterative poem to be a deliberate non-tragedy, because Arthur is saved from a tragic end by exercising the virtue of fortitude.[57] But Lumiansky's conception of fortitude as 'temperance-in-adversity'[58] is not verified in any medieval source.

Lumiansky is speaking in opposition to Benson's more accurate assessment of Chaucerian tragedy (though he too extends it to 'medieval tragedy' in general), namely, that the loss of human possessions is painful for everyone, even for the most flawless hero.[59] However, I think that both Benson and Lumiansky are flawed in their statements of Chaucerian tragedy, but that, of the two, Benson errs on the side of the angels. His fault consists only in leaving little or no room, on the level of theory, for self-inflicted tragic disasters. But when it comes to the practical level of assessing Arthur's fall as a tragedy, Benson does say, as we have seen, that it was caused in part by his own fault.[60] It would have been better, in my judgment, if he had reversed his points, by allowing for the possibility of fault-induced falls in Chaucer's tragedies and by presenting Arthur as an example of a hero who does not fall because of a personal failing.

Matthews also begins by assuming the universality of the Chaucerian genre of tragedy in the Middle Ages, and though he admits that there are various kinds of tragedies within the form, he sees the *Alliterative Morte* as the tragedy of a king who falls at least in part because of his martial deeds.[61] This

---

[55] D.W.Robertson, Jr., 'Chaucerian Tragedy', *English Literary History*, 19 (1952), 1–37, reprinted in *Chaucer Criticism*, vol.2, edited by Richard J.Schoeck and Jerome Taylor (Notre Dame, 1961), pp.86–121: see esp. p.91.
[56] Lumiansky (n.9 above), pp.98–99, 101.
[57] Lumiansky, p.117.
[58] Lumiansky, pp.103–04.
[59] Benson (n.7 above), p.79.
[60] See above at n.44.
[61] Matthews (n.1 above), pp.116–17.

view is shared by Finlayson and Gardner, neither of whom develops ideas of medieval tragedy, and both of whom rely to some extent on modern notions of tragedy.[62] The same is true of O'Loughlin, who however denies all wrongdoing on Arthur's part in the poem itself and says that his tragedy is caused by the Aristotelian *hamartia* of his begetting of Mordred.[63]

Höltgen contrasts what he sees as the tragedy of worldly knighthood in the *Mort Artu* with the *Alliterative Morte Arthure*'s individual tragedy of Arthur, a medieval Christian tragedy in which the hero falls because of his knightly deeds. These deeds are considered reprehensible from a Christian point of view, but praiseworthy from a human and nationalistic perspective.[64] Though Höltgen has a moralistic conception of tragedy, and Benson a nonmoralistic conception, they arrive at a similar interpretation of the *Alliterative Morte*: in splendidly fulfilling the obligations of his kingly office, Arthur is guilty of sins or faults that contribute to his downfall.

Göller follows the lead of Höltgen: all Nine Worthies in the *Alliterative Morte* neglected the welfare of their souls because of their good fortune, and were punished for it. The author shows Arthur suffering a tragic *casus* or fall.[65] Schelp agrees: Arthur is a good man who becomes sinful through pride. Fortune is not the fickle pagan goddess in this poem but rather the Christian figure who executes God's punishment.[66]

Keiser takes issue with Benson for following Chaucer's Monk and putting too much emphasis on misfortune, while he himself follows Willard Farnham in alleging that medieval tragedy often stressed personal responsibility: 'Because of his sin, the fall that Arthur, like all men, must suffer, seems more just.'[67] As can be readily seen, Keiser's assessment of Arthur in the *Alliterative Morte* turns out to be quite similar to Benson's in spite of their theoretical differences over medieval tragedy.

Of more recent scholars, Fries considers the *Alliterative Morte* as a tragedy of a hero who falls because of his own faults,[68] whereas Janssen, who thinks that medieval tragedy told only of undeserved falls, holds that the poet intentionally removed his poem from the genre of tragedy by making Arthur responsible for his fall.[69] Ritzke, writing in the same collection as Fries and

---

[62] Finlayson (n.4 above) in his review regards Matthews's tragedy interpretation as tenable; in his edition, he embraces it. He differs from Matthews only in seeing Arthur's early battles as completely just. Gardner (n.10 above), esp. p.244, follows suit.
[63] O'Loughlin (n.5 above), p.180; he had already expressed the notion of Arthur's *hamartia* in his 1959 essay (n.38 above), p.524.
[64] Höltgen, 'König Arthur' (n.2 above), pp.45–50.
[65] Göller, *König Arthur* (n.6 above), 118–21.
[66] Schelp (n.8 above), pp.174, 179. Schelp disagrees with Matthews's contention that the poem was influenced by a moralistic Alexander tradition (pp.177–78). Göller, *Romance* (n.6 above), pp.151–53, follows Schelp in speaking of the *casus* or tragedy genre with a rise-and-fall structure in which the falls come about through a variety of causes.
[67] Keiser (n.11 above), pp.100, 102. I should note that Willard Farnham's book, *The Medieval Heritage of Elizabethan Tragedy* (Berkeley, 1936), bears a large share of the blame for fostering the view that there was a widespread idea of '*de casibus* tragedy' in the Middle Ages.
[68] Fries (n.12 above), p.42.
[69] Janssen (n.14 above), pp.144–56, 151.

Janssen, after some wavering over whether the poem fits the *casus*-schema of
Schelp and Göller,[70] blames Arthur's downfall on 'his pride and sin of greed
for power', and says that the work resembles not only a medieval tragedy but
also a classical tragedy. She concludes: 'It is quite possible that the poet was
familiar with these features of the Senecan model of tragedy, or Italian
adaptations of it.' In support of this suggestion, she says, 'It is worth noting
that Lydgate, the poet's near contemporary, was an admirer of Seneca as a
writer of tragedy.'[71] On this last point, which she attributes to Farnham, I
must enter a demurrer; I believe that Lydgate's acquaintanceship with
Seneca's tragedies extends no further than his knowledge that he wrote
tragedies, and that he only pretends to know what is in them. Thus, he refers
us to Seneca's tragedy on Oedipus to read how he fell into a dotage and was
mistreated by his sons; and he names Seneca's tragedies as telling of Medea's
restoration to Jason.[72]

Finally, Russell Peck strikes out on his own and starts from an analysis of
Boethius's *Consolation*. He asserts that Boethian ideas of good rule are
prominent in the fourteenth century, and, in addition, the two subtopics of
fate and tragedy 'likewise figure largely in literature dealing with the will'. He
fails to establish that any attention at all was paid to tragedy, and therefore his
conclusion that Arthur's tragedy 'lies in his misunderstanding of his proper
domain'[73] is without basis.

All of the writers discussed above who have considered tragedy as pertinent
to the *Alliterative Morte Arthure* agree that Arthur's fall is presented, at least
in part, as the result of his own failings. They only differ in the extent to which
he is guilty of causing his own destruction. I must confess that I too formerly
took it for granted that the author meant us to see Arthur as falling in
consequence of his wrong-doing, until Ward Tonsfeldt's analysis convinced
me otherwise, that the poem presents Arthur as only incidentally sinful.[74]

But Tonsfeldt does not go far enough, I believe, for he shares the view of
those who think that the poet shows Arthur to be sinful in the latter part of his
war against the Romans. I hold rather with Helaine Newstead, who, in spite
of approving of Matthews's classification of the *Alliterative Morte* as a
medieval tragedy, not only rejects his attempt to explain Arthur's reversal of
fortune as divine retribution for his sinful ambition to conquer the world, but
rejects also any condemnation of Arthur by the poet. The poet is on Arthur's
side, she says, and Arthur's enemies are the poet's enemies. It is true that 'the
philosopher refers to bloodshed and the destruction of warriors as he exhorts
the king to repent in preparation for his coming downfall', and his
philosopher's naming of Arthur's sins 'fits into the context of the fateful

[70] Ritzke-Rutherford (n.13 above), pp.89–90, 170 n.18.
[71] Ritzke, 94–95.
[72] Lydgate, *Siege of Thebes*, 994–1001 (Oedipus); *Fall of Princes*, Book 1, lines 2384–87 (Medea).
[73] Peck (n.15 above), p.172; see pp.154–55.
[74] See n.45 above, where I cite Tonsfeldt's dissertation; I first encountered Mr Tonsfeldt's views shortly before he filed his dissertation, when he made a guest appearance in a seminar that I conducted at UCLA in the winter term of 1975.

prophecy'. However, 'it does not overshadow the dominant impression of Arthur's greatness in the poem as a whole', and it is a mistake to read it otherwise by attributing to the author 'a subtly ironic intention, expressed in ambiguities and complexities of meaning'.[75]

Those who see Arthur as initially just and only unjust when he crosses the Alps into Italy must face the fact pointed out by Janssen, who considers him unjust from the beginning; namely, that Italy and Rome figure in Arthur's plans from the start.[76] Arthur asserts his 'title to take tribute of Rome'(line 275), and announces the following time-table: they will join battle by June 1, stay in Lorraine or Lombardy on August 1, spend six weeks in the Vale of Viterbo, send riders to the 'price toun' (rightly glossed by Brock as Rome)[77] and besiege it unless peace is offered in due time (344–56). Peace, of course, means unconditional surrender. These plans are confirmed by the speeches of the Welsh king (325–28) and Lancelot (379).

The poet has Arthur give a different schedule later: he will be in France on February 1, reign in Lucius's lands on August 1 and hold his Round Table by the Rhone, turn into Tuscany when he deems it opportune and besiege Rome within seven winters (421–40). This last wildly innapropriate time-limit does not even have an alliterative excuse, but perhaps can be explained as broadly ironic, since he is now addressing the Roman delegation.

When Arthur sends two captive senators to Rome, the senators make it clear that they are Christians (they escaped death 'thurghe þe helpyng of Criste', 2316), and they promise to deliver their message without being hindered by pope, potestate, or prince (2327). Arthur expresses his intentions concerning Italy and the pope thus:

> Than will I by Lumbardye, lykande to schawe,
> Sett lawe in þe lande, þat laste sall euer;
> The tyrauntez of Tuskayn tempeste a littyll,
> Talke with þe temperall, whills my tym lastez.
> I gyffe my protteccione to all þe Pope landez,
> My ryche pensell of pes my pople to schewe;
> It es a foly to offende oure fadyr vndire Gode,
> Owþer Peter or Paule, þa postles of Rome.
> 3if we spare the spirituell, we spede bot the bettire;
> Whills we haue for to speke, spille sall it neuer.
>
> (2406–15)

In due course, the poet tells us how Arthur deals with the tyrants of Tuscany:

---

[75] Newstead (n.3 above), p.120. This is also the view of Elizabeth Porter, 'Chaucer's Knight, the Alliterative *Morte Arthure*, and Medieval Laws of War: A Reconsideration', *Nottingham Medieval Studies*, 27 (1985), 56–78. Porter's excellent essay has the additional virtue of not referring to the *Morte* as a tragedy.
[76] Janssen (n.14 above), pp.146–48.
[77] Brock (n.46 above), p.12.

Into Tuskane he tournez, when þus wele tymede,
Takes townnes full tyte, with towrres full heghe;
Walles he welte down, wondyd knyghtez,
Towrres he turnes and turmentez þe pople,
Wroghte wedewes full wlonke wrotherayle synges,
Ofte wery and wepe and wryngen their handis;
And all he wastys with werre, thare he awaye rydez,
Thaire welthes and theire wonny[n]ges, wandrethe he wroghte.
Thus they spryngen and sprede and sparis bot lyttill,
Spoylles dispetouslye and spillis theire vynes,
Spendis vnsparely þat sparede was lange,
Spedis them to Spolett with speris inewe.

(3150–61)

These lines are not as finely shaded as our delicate sensibilities would dictate if the author shared our ideas of the horrors of war and wished to keep Arthur as clear of blame for them as possible; but, given what has gone before, it is obvious that he means Arthur to be dealing death-blows against the oppressors: they are the 'people' he torments and it is their wives he turns into widows. It is not Arthur but the author who should be convicted of brutal heavy-handedness, for attacking his matter with the blunt instrument of these zestful alliterative verses.

After his successful sweep of Northern Italy, Arthur awaits word from Rome, as planned. The expected peace offer comes from a cardinal, who

Prayes hym for þe pes and profyrs full large,
To hafe pete of þe Pope, þat put was at vndyre.

(3179–80)

Arthur, of course, complies, in keeping with his stated intention of protecting the pope. After taking over Rome, he intends to go on crusade to the Holy Land, 'to reuenge the Renke that on the Rode dyede' (3217). Is this the picture of a power-mad killer who wars even against the Church?

Many of the critics who interpret Arthur's conduct as morally flawed do so because they consider the poet to be protesting against war. But, as Valerie Krishna points out, such passages have been a part of heroic poetry since Homer, and 'though the poet leaves no doubt of the ghastly consequences of Arthur's battles, he also … cannot conceal his enthusiasm for those battles'.[78] I might also adduce Gaston Paris's reasoning as to why the tellers of stories about morally questionable heroes like Odysseus or Tristan pass over their faults without condemning them. It is typical of 'less aware epochs', Paris

[78] Valerie Krishna, reviewing the book of essays edited by Göller (n.12 above), *Speculum*, 58 (1983), 177–80, esp. 180; she is specifically addressing Göller's essay, 'Reality Versus Romance: A Reassessment of the *Alliterative Morte Arthure*', pp.15–29. Cf. Patterson (n.43 above), p.13.

says, that authors are the slaves of their matter and therefore sympathize with their heroes in all circumstances.[79] I allow that the author of the *Alliterative Morte Arthure* has at least progressed in awareness sufficiently to admit that some of Arthur's actions are retrospectively sinful. Such actions, according to Tonsfeldt's reading, are not said to be the cause of Arthur's loss of worldy good fortune, nor are they seen as diminishing his glory in any way. But if the collapse of Arthur's empire because of Mordred's rebellion is not to be considered a spectacular *exemplum* of divine overkill against Arthur, it remains true that his various excesses will receive temporal punishment here or in purgatory unless the punishment is mitigated or waived by the standard practices of penitence and reparation outlined by the philosopher.

Tonsfeldt shows that this interpretation is available even to those who believe that the poet portrays Arthur as becoming gradually sinful in his campaign against the Romans, since Tonsfeldt himself takes this moralistic view. Except for Newstead, O'Loughlin and perhaps Benson, it is a view that is shared by all those who impute an idea of tragedy to the author. However, their willingness to blame Arthur for his fall is not entirely caused by their mistaken views about medieval tragedy, I believe, but also by a widespread view of what 'tragedy in general' should be according to Aristotle's *Poetics*. As careful students know, Aristotle in Chapter 13 states that the best kind of tragedy deals with a man neither completely good nor evil who falls because of some flaw (while in the next chapter this kind of tragedy turns out to be second-best). Most people, however, by a strange simplification assume that Aristotle insisted on such a plot for all tragedies, and they refuse the name of tragedy to anything that does not conform. In one or other form this Aristotelian ideal has put great pressure upon literary critics to upgrade the works they admire to the level of tragedy or great tragedy. Hence, I suggest, comes the emphasis on human responsibility in discussions of medieval tragedy. The supposition is that an operative flaw in a hero will make for a more artistic story.[80] Arthur is not the only protagonist who has fallen victim to this tendency; Beowulf and Troilus have suffered as well.

The main moral I wish to be drawn from this essay is that readers of the *Alliterative Morte Arthure* should put from their minds all alleged theories or influences of tragedy and assess the work for what it is. My personal assessment is that it is the product of an often ham-fisted alliterator who lacked a sense of proportion and subtlety.[81] It is not the kind of work that invites close reading, except with great caution. Nevertheless, in spite of its flaws, some of which are doubtless to be attributed to clumsy or interfering scribes, the poem has many merits, not the least of which is its portrait of the life and death of the greatest of the Nine Worthies. While good fortune was with him, no man was his equal. At the point when his fortune changed

---

[79] Gaston Paris, 'Tristan et Iseut', *Revue de Paris*, 1894, reprinted in his *Poèmes et légendes du moyen-âge* (Paris, 1900), pp. 113–80; see pp. 172–73.

[80] Benson (n.7 above), p.79 also deplores this Aristotelianizing tendency and the bad effect that it has had on interpretations of the *Alliterative Morte*.

[81] Cf. Newstead (n.3 above), p.120: 'Subtlety is hardly a striking characteristic of the *Morte Arthure*'.

(through no fault of his own), he was favoured with a dream that enabled him to repent of his sins and make provision for his death. He fought valiantly to the end and died like the good Christian king that he was.

Newstead says of the work, 'It is a passionate poem on a grand scale, with epic effects, if not truly an epic; it celebrates the heroic character of Arthur revealed in his glorious victories and his equally glorious death. Such an approach is not incompatible with a powerful sense of pity for the tragic fall of so mighty a king'.[82] If we are not allowed to call it a tragedy in intent, that is, as written in a genre of tragedy or drawing on medieval notions of tragedy, we are permitted to call it a tragedy in effect, if we wish, by bringing to it whatever ideas of tragedy suit our fancy, whether ancient, medieval or modern, so long as we do not thereby falsify the poet's message or misrepresent his sentiments.

[82] Newstead, p.120.

ISRAEL GOLLANCZ'S 'WYNNERE AND WASTOURE': POLITICAL SATIRE OR EDITORIAL POLITICS?

Stephanie Trigg

Until very recently, the composition of the alliterative poem *Wynnere and Wastoure* in the winter of 1352–1353 seemed to be one of the few 'facts' about the alliterative revival of the fourteenth century on which we could rely, a fixed point around which we could chart the early growth of that movement. This dating depends on an argument from internal evidence first proposed by Israel Gollancz in his edition of the poem in 1920,[1] and remains an important feature of, and, indeed, a frequent starting-point for many histories of the alliterative revival.[2] It nevertheless depends heavily, as I hope to show, on a prior interpretation of the imperfectly preserved text as a topical pamphlet, a satirical critique of the social and economic problems of the early 1350s and the failure of Edward III and his son, the Black Prince, to deal with them. While the particulars of Gollancz's dating have been severely criticised, particularly by Elizabeth Salter and David Lawton,[3] its theoretical and methodological presuppositions, and the implications of Gollancz's interpretation and generic classification of the text are harder to dislodge from their position of institutional and pedagogical authority. A very recent, general survey of the period reiterates Gollancz's date along with the common corollary argument, reinforcing the idea of an evolutionary pattern of literary influence, that *Wynnere and Wastoure* represents the high stylistic achievement of a literary mainstream established at least a decade earlier, a style

---

[1] *A god schorte refreyte bytwixe Wynnere and Wastoure*, edited by Israel Gollancz, Select Early English Poems III (London, 1920; rpt. Cambridge, 1974). Second edition, revised by M.Day (London, 1930).

[2] For example, see T.Turville-Petre, *The Alliterative Revival* (Cambridge, 1977), pp.1–6; D.J.Williams, 'Alliterative Poetry in the Fourteenth and Fifteenth Centuries', in *The Middle Ages*, edited by W.F.Bolton, History of Literature in the English Language, 1 (London, 1970), p.114; D.Everett, *Essays on Middle English Literature*, edited by P.Kean (Oxford, 1955), p.55; J.Speirs, *Medieval English Poetry: The Non-Chaucerian Tradition* (London, 1957), p.264. See also D.Pearsall, *Old English and Middle English Poetry*, The Routledge History of English Poetry, 1 (London, 1977), p.153.

It is only recently that doubt has been cast on the accepted dating of this poem. See David Lawton, 'Middle English Alliterative Poetry: An Introduction', in *Middle English Alliterative Poetry and Its Literary Background*, edited by David Lawton (Woodbridge, Suffolk, 1982), pp.1–19, 125–29, esp. pp.3–4, and Anne Middleton, 'The Audience and Public of *Piers Plowman*', also in this volume, pp.101–23, 147–54, esp. p.152, n.34.

[3] E.Salter, 'The Timeliness of *Wynnere and Wastoure*', *MAE*, 47 (1978), 30–65; and D.Lawton, 'Literary History and Scholarly Fancy: The Date of Two Middle English Alliterative Poems', *Parergon*, 18 (1977), 17–25.

against which Langland in turn was to define himself and his poetic style approximately ten years later.[4]

Within the poem's critical history, there has simply never been scope for an examination of the basic assumptions under which Gollancz worked, or the impact of his text on subsequent studies of the alliterative revival. Largely because there has been no other readily available, fully annotated edition of the poem since Gollancz's pioneering work, the most scrupulous scholarly research has not been able to dislodge a view of *Wynnere and Wastoure* established by its first editor. It is my intention here to explore the poem's editorial and textual history, to examine Gollancz's work in its historical context, considering his understanding of the editorial rôle, and even his political allegiances which, it can be argued, served as a strong motivation for his wish to identify the herald in the poem as Edward, the Black Prince. I wish to argue that received opinion about the relationship between *Piers Plowman* and *Wynnere and Wastoure* depends on a chronological order which has not been conclusively established, and which is underwritten by Gollancz's prior notions about the subject matter of the shorter poem. His interpretation is not *per se* so very improbable, although it can be criticised on its own terms: my intention is to question its status as literary dogma, and to consider some alternative possibilities for editing and interpreting the poem. I also wish to question the assumption Gollancz seems to make that a *topical* poem must be read *literally*, and to suggest that while the poet might make use of contemporary conditions to illustrate his argument, and those of his two protagonists, he himself is primarily concerned with the moral and indeed, linguistic implications of what he initially posits as two opposing principles of economic management.

The key to the interpretative history of *Wynnere and Wastoure* can be identified as Gollancz's first reading of the poem as a topical satire. With this generic decision as his starting point, much of the introduction and commentary in his edition is devoted to finding the correct historical grid over which the poem might be set to fit exactly, as an accurate, literal statement about current events. The poet, we are told in the Preface, is 'evidently writing concerning events which are just happening, or are fresh in his memory', and the poem is 'a pamphlet ... of the hour'.[5] Gollancz thus invokes a single, constant relation between the personages and events

---

[4] D. S. Brewer, *English Gothic Literature*, Macmillan History of Literature (London, 1983), esp. pp. 143–6. For the earlier statements of this case, see J. A. Burrow, 'The Audience of *Piers Plowman*', *Anglia*, 75 (1957), 373–84; S. S. Hussey, 'Langland's Reading of Alliterative Poetry', *MLR*, 60 (1965), 163–70, and also N. Coghill, 'The Pardon of *Piers Plowman*', *PBA*, 30 (1944), p. 37. A. C. Spearing also writes, in the fullest statement of this case, 'I think it likely that when Langland began to compose the A version of *Piers Plowman* he intended a poem which would not differ too greatly in kind from *Winner and Waster*, and that what we have in the poem's three versions is, among other things, the record of how he came to see that he would have to go further, and create a radically new kind of dream-poem'. *Medieval Dream Poetry* (Cambridge, 1976), p. 140.

[5] Gollancz, p. vi.

referred to in the poem and the people and politics of a particular year, or season, in fourteenth-century English history.

Valorising the literal level of the text, its editor had no difficulty in dating and localising the poem. The king who summons the two leaders to debate their grievances before him was identified through references to the Order of the Garter, overseas wars and his love of hawking as Edward III, and some wishful argumentation from heraldry, including a less than literal reading of the charges on the herald's escutcheon, suggested that this herald represents Edward of Woodstock, the Black Prince. The reference to William Shareshull at line 317 inspired Gollancz to find a precise reference at lines 130–3 to his Statute of Treasons of 1352, 'evidently recently promulgated', even though these lines seem to misunderstand the terms of the Statute.[6] Nevertheless, the statement of Wynnere and Wastoure at line 206 that the king has protected them for twenty-five years (even though this line, *And hase vs fosterde and fedde for fyve and twenty wyntere*, is highly formulaic and hypermetrical by Gollancz's own standards)[7] seemed to confirm the setting of the poem in the twenty-fifth year of Edward's reign, that is, 1352. From this point, most other general allusions to the Pope, the activity of the friars, and economic or climatic conditions could be argued to be appropriate to this year.

There was some initial dispute about this dating, principally from James Hulbert, whose objections to Gollancz's date were by and large ignored by later scholars, who have also ignored Gollancz's previous cases for the years 1347–48 or circa 1350.[8] His last hypothesis passed into orthodoxy with the publication of his edition, and *Wynnere and Wastoure*, a comparatively late discovery (the manuscript was purchased by the British Museum only in 1879) took its place at the head of the extant fourteenth-century poems in

[6] Salter observes that if the poet is referring to the Statute, he in fact shows himself unsure about the very distinction between high and petty treason, and the appropriate punishments for these offences it was the Statute's aim to clarify, 'The Timeliness of *Wynnere and Wastoure*', 41–43.

[7] All quotations from the poem, unless otherwise specified, are taken from my edition, '*Wynnere and Wastoure*: A Critical Reconstruction with Commentary' (unpublished PhD. dissertation, University of Melbourne, 1984).

[8] J.R.Hulbert, 'The Problems of Authorship and Date of *Wynnere and Wastoure*', MP, 18 (1920), 31–40. A year later, J.M.Steadman supported Gollancz's date and in a note mentioned Hulbert's retraction, never to be published, of his later dating, in 'The Date of *Wynnere and Wastoure*', MP, 19 (1921), 211–19. In his edition of *The Parlement of the Thre Ages* for the Roxburghe Club (London, 1897), Gollancz had argued that *Wynnere and Wastoure*, which he had presented as a virtually unemended Appendix, was written in 1347–48, and then, during the course of a lengthy debate with George Neilson in the pages of *The Athenaeum*, he maintained only that the poem was written before 1357, in 'A note on *Wynnere and Wastoure*', *The Athenaeum*, 24 August 1901, pp.254–55. Later accepting the poet's failure to mention the Black Death of 1349, he proposed a date *circa* 1350, in *The Athenaeum*, 14 September 1901, p.351. Gollancz first proposed the season of 1352–53 in his edition of the poem in 1920, but Henry Bradley, who had also bought into the debate, was the first to interpret Wynnere and Wastoure's account of their years of service at line 206 (see above) literally, maintaining the poem was written in 1352 (*The Athenaeum*, 18 April 1903, pp.498–99).

Thus, while Gollancz's edition gives the impression of presenting a complete and consistent argument, it must be considered against this background of hesitation and speculation about the interpretation of these lines so crucial to Gollancz's dating.

unrhymed alliterative verse, accepted almost immediately as a kind of 'missing link' in the literary tradition that had previously seemed to burst into full flower only with *Piers Plowman*. Gollancz, indeed, seemed to regard the shorter poem as merely incidental to Langland's vision, also commonly regarded in the early decades of this century as a poem primarily concerned with social and political criticism:

> When *Wynnere and Wastoure* was a new poem, it seems to have stirred the heart of a young western man, and perhaps to have kindled in him the latent fire of a prophet-poet, destined to deliver a weightier message to his fellow-countrymen.[9]

Even though Langland 'denounced even greater evils than those dealt with dramatically and dispassionately by our poet', Gollancz offers further reasons why one should read the poem, appealing to its 'relevance' to twentieth-century readers.

> [The] poem is in fact a topical pamphlet in alliterative verse on the social and economic problems of the hour, as vivid as present day discussions on like problems. Indeed, nothing is more striking than the parallel between the national questions affecting England in 1352 and in 1920.[10]

These parallels eventually give rise to an extraordinary expression of nationalistic fervour in the editorial note on Wynnere's exhortation to Wastoure to cultivate his lands:

> Increased tillage was the pressing problem of the time. The Statute of Labourers, in the previous year, had attempted to deal with the question of labour, disorganised by the ravages of the Black Death, social changes and especially by war conditions. It is the problem of the present day. The Prime Minister, in a speech delivered to the Chairman of·County War Agricultural Committees on Dec. 21, 1917, made a stirring appeal to landowners – 'Land is life to the nation now, land is victory to Great Britain now; therefore, the man who stands on his land and does not cultivate it now is guilty of treason. Deal relentlessly with men who do not make the best of the land, because they are robbing the people of food, and they are robbing the nation of victory'. (*The Times*, Dec. 22, 1917, p.4)
> (Note to lines 286–88)

Gollancz seems to be seized with the same reforming fervour he detects in the poet, as his political message takes precedence over artistic or literary, even historical considerations, and also, perhaps, distracts him from fully

---

[9] Gollancz, p.xvii.
[10] Gollancz, pp.vi–vii.

exercising his editorial judgement. Certainly, he presents little discussion of his textual policies, and in matters of metre, alliteration, grammatical agreement and syntax, his programme of editorial correction is large-scale and heavy-handed, although he rarely offers a reasoned defence of his position. His practice is, moreover, often inconsistent, although again, his text and emendations give the impression of conforming to a preconceived, recognised standard of metrical form and textual quality. We are told that the manuscript represents one of the most corrupt versions of any Middle English text, and the scribe is assumed to have found his text in a 'copy of the poem carried in a minstrel's wallet, which had become illegible in many places … The task of dealing with the many errors has necessitated very bold treatment of the text, as may be seen from the long list of emendations'.[11]

A glance at this list and the accompanying text will illustrate the extent of his alterations to the text, and an illuminating comparison can be made with the extremely conservative, yet in the main, intelligible text offered by Thorlac Turville-Petre.[12] We are concerned here, however, only with editorial activity of a particular kind, of which the examples are few, but telling, since they show Gollancz correcting the text to accord with his prior interpretation of the poem. His reading also led him to find corruption where, in all probability, none exists, correcting the text to provide further proof of his interpretation.

At the very least, this circular method can blind the editor to other possibilities for textual reconstruction. For example, lines 90–91 in the manuscript clearly demand correction:

> This kynge was comliche clade in kirtill and mantill
> Bery-brown was his berde brouderde with fewlys.

In Gollancz's text, willingness to identify the king as Edward III at the age of forty by linking this description to an illumination of the king in a Statute Book, in which his ' "bery-brown beard" is noteworthy', led the editor to locate the scribe's error in the word *was*, which he emends to *as*, where another editor might find greater likelihood of error in the similarity of the forms *berde/brouderde*, or the repetition of the half-line *brouderde with fewles* at line 96 below. The appeal to the illumination has since been proved misguided, but this small detail in Gollancz's corrected text confirms the identity of the king for many readers.[13]

Other changes may affect our understanding of the poem's concerns and the poem's very subject matter, as in line 446, where the word *make* 'mistress, mate' is changed to *makande* 'living', in Wastoure's *'I hold hym madde that mournes his make for to wyn'*. Gollancz compares similar lines from the *Parlement of the Thre Ages* in an argument which seems to confirm both his

[11] Gollancz, p.i.
[12] 'An Anthology of Medieval Poems and Drama', edited by T.Turville-Petre in *Medieval Literature: Part One: Chaucer and the Alliterative Tradition*, edited by Boris Ford, The New Pelican Guide to English Literature, 1 (Harmondsworth, 1982), pp.398–415, 600.
[13] Salter, p.49.

emendation and his view of the common authorship of the two poems. The undoubted similarities between the poems are not, however, sufficient grounds for emending one to form a closer parallel with the other.

As far as the study of literary history is concerned, Gollancz's changes to the Prologue have also had a profound influence on subsequent scholarship and deserve consideration here. Scribal carelessness allegedly warrants this substantial re-organization of the prologue (twelve changes in thirty lines), but Gollancz seems motivated principally by a wish to confirm the popular, oral origins of alliterative poetry, writing of the 'recitative (if not lyrical) character of this fourteenth-century *archaic* poetry' (my italics). His reconstructed text leaves three lines which seem to record a lament for the decline of oral poetry and its appreciation:

> Whylome were lordes in londe þat loued in thaire hertis
> To here makers of myrthes þat matirs couthe fynde
> Wyse wordes within, þat wr[iten] were neuer.
> (lines 20–22 in Gollancz's text; lines 19,20,22 in ms.)

From these lines, and his emendation of manuscript *wroghte* to *writen*, Gollancz now deduces that the author of the poem was 'certainly a professional minstrel, of humble rank', although he does not discuss minstrelsy at all, and we are not told how a humble rank of minstrel might be distinguished from a minstrel of more exalted rank. His treatment and discussion of the prologue also support his hypothesis of the casual transmission of the text, folded many times, in a minstrel's wallet; but most importantly, this reading of the prologue seems to confirm that the poem *was* topical in inspiration, a widely-circulated and quickly written political pamphlet, and not the more bookish, learned work that Thomas Bestul, for example, would argue it to be.[14] The degree of corruption in the text can be explained simply as the inevitable result of approximately one hundred years of transmission, as the text made its way from the North Central Midlands to the hands of Robert Thornton in the North Riding of Yorkshire. Moreover, to judge from the other contents of the manuscript (British Museum Additional MS. 31,042), Thornton regarded the poem as a moral treatise, for it finds company, not only with the *Parlement of the Thre Ages* but also a number of moralities, religious histories, romances and lyrics, including the lyric, 'Waste makes a kyngdome in nede'.[15]

The most crucial emendation, however, is that which affects line 108, the herald's response to the king's command. The manuscript reads *3is lorde*, and Gollancz argues that the scribe's exemplar read *Y serue* in a northern contracted form *Y ser*, abbreviated in a manner which would have suggested

---

[14] Thomas Bestul's book, *Satire and Allegory in Wynnere and Wastoure* (Lincoln, Nebraska, 1974), is the only full-length study of the poem. Bestul emphasises the poem's Aristotelian schema and its debt to the Latin tradition of psychological debate-poetry.
[15] For the fullest account of the Thornton manuscript, see K.M.Stern, 'The London Thornton Miscellany: A New Description of BM. Addit. MS. 31042', *Scriptorium*, 30 (1976), 26–37, 201–18.

the reading *3is*. Salter criticises this logic, commenting that Thornton experiences no difficulty in adapting any northern forms behind other occurences of *serue* which use this abbreviation; and of course, most of the northern forms in the text derive from Thornton himself. Gollancz's correction obscures the formulaic nature of the second half-line, *while my life dures*, which according to Salter,

> may depend on our recognition of another model – that, perhaps, of the heraldic motto, or of the 'devise', with its elliptical structure: for example, *dum varior, whyll lyf lastyth*.[16]

Gollancz's defence for his correction of a reading which offends no standard of sense, style, metre, grammar or alliteration rests on his proposal that *Y serue* may be conscious English translation of the Black Prince's motto, *Iche dene*, and he appeals to the English version of the Garter motto which appears at line 68, *Hethyng haue the hathell þat any harme thynkes*. The herald had been confidently identified as the Black Prince, from the narrator's praise of his illustrious appearance, and an interpretation of his escutcheon as the ostrich feathers of the Prince of Wales's 'badge for peace':

> Thre wynges inwith wroghte in the kynde
> Vmbygon with a gold wyre
>
> (lines 117–18).

Salter argues convincingly that Gollancz's reading of *wynges* as feathers is untenable, but not before this identification of the herald had been accepted by most students and readers of the poem, even though there is no suggestion of any familial relationship between herald and king; and even the identification of the king rests on an unreasonable insistence that the poem's king must 'be', in the fullest, most literal and personal sense, the king on the throne at the time of the poem's composition.[17]

In tampering with the herald's response, Gollancz is certainly guilty of conflating his interpretative and editorial tasks in the manner of an interfering and rather meddlesome scribe, with enormous effects on subsequent readings of the poem. Another even more serious charge can be levelled at him,

---

[16] Salter, p.55.

[17] Salter rejects Gollancz's reading of the herald's charge as ostrich feathers in favour of a more literal reading, the wings of the Wingfield coat of arms, arguing that the poet intended a compliment to a member of that family. She thus accepts Gollancz's methodological presuppositions, and disagrees only over details. Admittedly, it is often difficult to know how to read heraldic references in medieval poetry: the authors often indiscriminately mix recognisable references, such as the royal coat of arms at lines 76–80, with more fanciful or suggestive ones. Much scholarly attention has been given to the banners of the armies in the prologue to the poem, attempting to identify the arms of patrons of the various mendicant orders. Only some of these seem tenable, and then, only as suggestive, not historical charges. For the most recent attempt to link these banners to historical charges, see Nicholas Havely, 'The Dominicans and their Banner in *Wynnere and Wastoure*', *N&Q*, n.s. 30 (1983), 207–9.

though, that in identifying the herald as the Black Prince and introducing an English translation of his motto into the poem, he intended a deliberate compliment to the Prince's namesake, Edward the Prince of Wales, son of George V, thus drawing another 'striking parallel' between the fourteenth and twentieth centuries.

Several years before, Gollancz had researched the motto for peace of the Prince of Wales, arguing that *Iche dene*, not *Iche diene*, was its correct form.[18] On philological grounds, he had eliminated the possibility of its German or Dutch origin, tracing it to the Netherlands, to Gelderland or Cleves. Now in 1921, as Chairman of a Presentation Committee comprised of members of the University of London, Gollancz presented a manuscript of the Chandos Herald's *Life of the Black Prince* to the Prince of Wales on the occasion of his becoming an Honorary Doctor of the University. This manuscript, soon given back to the University for safe-keeping, features an illumination of the Black Prince kneeling in prayer, surrounded by the ostrich feathers and motto of his badge for peace, the motto in the form Gollancz had predicted, 'ich dene'. The illumination was later reproduced as the frontispiece of a collection of essays by members of King's College, London, where it is accompanied by a note by Gollancz in which he records his delight in this confirmation of his research.[19] He stresses the connection of the motto with the Low Countries, and draws another parallel between the fourteenth and early twentieth centuries:

> Edward III's alliances with the peoples and rulers of the Low Countries were, indeed, the prelude to the Anglo-Belgian relations so triumphantly attested during the past years.[20]

Gollancz concludes his note with a record of the closing words of his address to the Prince of Wales, comparing him to his fourteenth-century counterpart:

> 'In our choice of a gift worthy of your acceptance we have been inspired by a joyous recognition that the ideals of courage, reverence, and service, acclaimed in the life of Edward Prince of Wales, the Black Prince, are so nobly exemplified in Your Royal Highness yourself; and we fervently pray that for long years to come it may be vouchsafed to you, by the side of His Majesty the King, to bear the Badge of Peace, and to continue your high offices and graceful service for England, for the Empire, and for humanity'.[21]

We recall that Gollancz's speech was made in the same year as the first publication of his edition of *Wynnere and Wastoure*. Even if line 108 was not

[18] See his letters to the *TLS* 1, 8 and 22 August 1918.
[19] *Chivalry: A Series of Studies to Illustrate its Historical Significance and Civilising Influence*, edited by E.Prestage (London, 1928).
[20] Prestage, p.x.
[21] Prestage, pp.x–xii.

reconstructed or the herald's shield identified as the Black Prince's 'badge for peace' deliberately to compliment the Prince of Wales, the emendation was certainly made at the same time as the discovery of the manuscript of the French poem, and its presentation to the Prince. Gollancz's desire to dissociate the motto from any form of German militarism can perhaps be attributed in part to the prevailing political climate, and to discover this confirmation of his hypothesis in the French manuscript would certainly have delighted his scholar's heart, but to find an anglicized form of the motto in a fourteenth-century English poem would be even more gratifying, perhaps irresistible.

In considering these circumstances, and the many comparisons Gollancz makes between England and her prince in 1352 and in 1920, we can see how his interpretation of the poem as a topical satire was strongly conditioned by his own historical situation, royalist loyalties, and his sense of urgency in making his own economic and moral 'complaint against the times'. He relies upon a literal reading of the poem which admits little, if any, allegorical or moral interpretation, or even a more general application to fourteenth-century conditions than to just one year. This literalism, and the edition which supports it, have inhibited the development of a full range of critical possibilities for the poem, since it is difficult to resist such an insistent and at times very attractive programme of changes when reading the poem in his edition. Gollancz's list of emendations and original readings is inconveniently confined to a separate section before the notes, instead of appearing at the foot of each page of the text, where square brackets do not always fully indicate the extent of editorial activity. Many textual changes go unmarked in the notes, while many others are recorded without any discussion of the problems involved.

The chief faults of Gollancz's interpretation, independent of its influence on the text, are its literalism and circularity. Many of his 'time-indications' depend on previous assumptions, and, in themselves, do not indicate composition in a particular year. But general 'questions of labour, wages, prices, dress, food' are made to recall the Statute of Labourers of 1351, and vague 'allusions to questions resulting from the Black Death of 1349' refer to the period immediately following the plague, even though these effects were felt for many years.[22] Climatic conditions mentioned in the poem allegedly indicate composition in the winter of 1352–53, and a drought recorded by Knighton under the year 1353. Burrow, however, suggests that the 'greater cold that is to come' (*the more colde es to come*, line 293) is an apocalyptic reference to hell,[23] while the 'great drought' is Gollancz's mistranslation of the *droghte* or dryness that will never come to save the judges whom Wastoure would see drowning in the ocean (line 312).

Another of Gollancz's points has received little comment but in fact represents an inconsistent reading of the king's final speech, an objection

---

[22] Gollancz, pp .iv–v. Compare also n .8 above.
[23] See *English Verse, 1300–1500*, edited by J .A .Burrow, Longman Annotated Anthologies of English Verse, Vol.1 (London, 1977), 32–45.

raised by Hulbert in 1921. In this speech, the king is shown to be at home, attending to domestic matters, and preparing for war. He bids Wynnere return from exile immediately he is summoned, and specifically commands him to come to serve him when he goes to war in the future and holds his court in Paris (lines 466–71, 496–503). When Gollancz was first pressing for a date of 1347–48 for the poem, he linked these lines to the truce which followed the capture of Calais in September 1347.[24] But now, wanting to place the poem in the winter of 1352–53, he claims that they were written in a time of war, *between* periods of truce with France, and during a period of hostility which lasted from September 1352 until March of the following year. We thus find a major inconsistency: if Gollancz wishes to argue from a strictly literal viewpoint, then the king, Edward III, is shown in *Wynnere and Wastoure* at peace or in a state of truce, preparing for war, and the time cannot be the winter of 1352. This inconsistency, and the fact that Gollancz was able to change his interpretation of these lines according to his changing views on the poem's date, should cast doubt on the rest of his methodology: nevertheless, his misreading has been regarded as authoritative.

Gollancz's text held sway for several decades as the only published version of the poem, and even when *Wynnere and Wastoure* came under closer critical scrutiny from writers such as Everett and Speirs in the 1950s[25] and became a more popular choice amongst anthologists of Middle English verse, no more work was done on the text, and most anthologists, modernisers and translators have been content to follow Gollancz's text.[26] In this way, his interpretation and date have passed into critical orthodoxy, supported by his own heavily emended and virtually unchallenged text.

Bestul, one of the first to examine the rich intellectual heritage of the poem and its author's debt to tradition, discusses this aspect of its critical history:

With the passage of time, it is possible to see that the eagerness to explain *Wynnere and Wastoure* by reference to contemporary events reflects certain critical biases current during the time in which most criticism of the poem appeared, or roughly from 1897, when it was first printed, to about 1930. The same readers who measured Chaucer's

[24] Hulbert, 'The Problems of Authorship and Date of *Wynnere and Wastoure*', pp.36–37.
[25] See Everett, pp.49–50; J.Speirs, '*Wynnere and Wastoure* and *The Parlement of the Thre Ages*', *Scrutiny*, 17 (1950), 241–49, and *Medieval English Poetry*, pp.263–89.
[26] Compare the text of the passages of the poem edited by Rolf Kaiser, in his *Middle English* (West Berlin, 1958, rev. 1961), Francis Berry, in 'An Anthology of Medieval Poems', in *The Age of Chaucer*, edited by Boris Ford, The Pelican Guide to English Literature, 1 (Harmondsworth, 1959), and Ann S.Haskell, in *A Middle English Anthology* (Garden City, NY, 1969). A more carefully edited selection of the debate proper was published by John Burrow (see n. 23 above), and before Turville-Petre's recent printing, two post-graduate dissertations, as yet unpublished, presented editions of the poem. See Karen M.Stern, 'A Critical Edition of *Wynnere and Wastoure*' (unpublished M.Phil. dissertation, University of London, 1973) and Lon M.Rosenfield, '*Winner and Waster*: A Critical Edition' (unpublished PhD dissertation, Columbia University, 1975).

progress as a poet by his discarding of 'outmoded' and 'sterile' conventions and valued him most when it appeared that he was writing from real life would naturally find most interesting that aspect of *Wynnere and Wastoure* by which it seemed that the poet was recording his own experience.[27]

There is no doubt of course that *Wynnere and Wastoure* was 'very much conditioned by the time in which it was written', and several treatises, including Bestul's, outline the background of social and economic upheaval against which the poem must be considered.[28] Gollancz's extreme literalism, however, can be likened to that which seeks to name citizens of London amongst the Canterbury pilgrims: it is a refusal to allow the light and shade of idealisation and caricature, or iconography and literary or rhetorical precedence to play on poetic figures and structures. While scholars like Charles Muscatine and Robert Payne successively charted and then proceeded to lead the movement in Chaucer studies away from realism as the predominant aesthetic, *Wynnere and Wastoure* studies have lagged far behind until the publication of Bestul's study in 1974.[29] For all its interest, however, this is principally a source and background study, and Bestul does not offer any authoritative reading of the text.

It is possible to read the poem somewhat differently, however, taking account of its historical context and its undoubted topicality, without insisting that its references be interpreted literally. I believe the poet to have been principally concerned, not to criticise Edward's economic management of England, but to come to an understanding of the terms *winning* and *wasting* and the relationship between them. On a tropological level, the debate takes as its theme the opposition between these qualities, represented in their extremes by avarice and prodigality, in relation to a man's way of life. Throughout the debate, of course, the disputants refer to general and specific economic and social issues; for example, profiteering in grain, complaints against the friars and the practice of leading private armies, all by way of illustrating the activities to which both extremes of winning and wasting can lead.

We should also remember that it is the debate proper which is the ethical heart of the poem, not the elaborate prologue to which Gollancz gives so much attention. Its dominant philosophical scheme is Aristotelian, whereby the virtue, generosity, is seen as the desirable mean between the two extreme vices of avarice and prodigality. The poem owes an indirect debt to the

---

[27] Bestul, p .2.
[28] See Stern, Rosenfield and William B .McColly, 'The Audience of *The Parlement of the Thre Ages* and *Wynnere and Wastoure*' (unpublished PhD dissertation, University of California, 1957).
[29] C .Muscatine, *Chaucer and the French Tradition: A Study in Style and Meaning* (Berkeley, 1957); R. O. Payne, *The Key of Remembrance A Study of Chaucer's Poetics* (New Haven, 1963). For an interesting and comprehensive account of changing fashions in medieval literary criticism, especially as it relates to Chaucer, see Joerg O .Fichte, *Chaucer's 'Art Poetical': A Study in Chaucerian Poetics* (Tübingen, 1980), 11–21.

Secreta secretorum and the 'advice to rulers' genre, borne out by the poet's claims for the role of the poet as counsellor in his prologue. He is also indebted to other encyclopaedic and moral treatises, as Bestul demonstrates.

The poet draws heavily on the connotative range of both words and concepts in English, according to which winning can be seen as prudent and virtuous productivity or selfish acquisition; good management or the pointless accumulation of wealth. Wasting is similarly ambiguous, and can take the form of thoughtless consumption of goods with no thought for the future, or the lavishness and generosity which are important to maintain a lord's honour. Wynnere and Wastoure accuse each other of personifying each behavioural extreme, to the point where, in the final speeches, the terms of the debate become clouded. The confusion attains its highest irony when Wastoure accuses Wynnere of wasting his time (line 439) by not maintaining his property and cattle. The scene is then set for the king's inconclusive arbitration and his ultimate failure to discriminate between them on a moral level.

Wynnere and Wastoure must also be seen in the tradition of psychological battle poems, exemplified by Prudentius' *Psychomachia*, but because winning and wasting can be two different ways to make use of one man's wealth, the conflict is presented in civil terms, as an oppositon of classes within the one kingdom, or two departments of a royal household.[30] Another strong theme that runs through the debate, particularly in Wynnere's criticisms of Wastoure, shows the poet's awareness of changes in the social fabric. Wastoure is presented as the leader of one of the armed and often violent bands that proliferated in the 1350s; and as the squanderer of his inherited estates, envied and despised by Wynnere, who seems to represent the rising middle class of wealthy merchants.[31] The poem thus enacts several basic economic and social tensions, but debates them in primarily moral terms. We can also detect an uneasiness in the poet, as to how traditional moral schemes and homiletic *exempla* can apply to changing economic conditions and social structures, as each disputant accuses the other of various of the Seven Deadly Sins, and condemns his opponent to eternal damnation several times.

The poet seeks an authoritative resolution to his problem, trusting in the formalities of debate and traditional schemes of morality to settle the dispute which has brought these armies together. Interestingly, even the setting attempts to contain the issues by evoking the conventions of theatrical pageant.[32] Nor do the assembled armies ever come to blows, of course, not

---

[30] For a persuasive account of this background to *Wynnere and Wastoure*, see David Starkey, 'The Age of the Household: Politics, Society and the Arts, c.1350–c.1550', in *The Later Middle Ages*, edited by Stephen Medcalf, The Context of English Literature (London, 1981) pp. 224–90, esp. 256–7.

[31] See Gardiner Stillwell, '*Wynnere and Wastoure* and The Hundred Years' War', *ELH*, 8 (1941), 241–47 and also Dennis V. Moran, '*Wynnere and Wastoure*: An Extended Footnote', *NM*, 73 (1972), 683–85.

[32] See Ralph W. V. Elliott, 'The Topography of *Wynnere and Wastoure*', *ES*, 48 (1961), 65–76.

even through the single combat of the two leaders, who agree to debate their grievances, again, under quite formal conditions. For while their armies are described in warlike terms, Wynnere and Wastoure appear and kneel before the king as two loyal knights, perhaps even stewards, indistinguishable from each other. They speak in turn, in four speeches of similar length, not interrupting each other, and following a fairly strict rhetorical plan of attack, defence and rebuttal. Finally, as the linguistic element of the debate exhausts itself in paradox and hyperbole, the poet looks for resolution in another tradition; specifically, that of the wise and generous ruler, the figure in whom Gower, the poet's near contemporary, places so much faith. The king, no more than the poet, can resolve their dispute, however, and they must both resort to the traditional 'resolution' of the literary debate; the inconclusive or suspended judgement. The poem thus attempts to conceal or normalise, through its reliance on literary and philosophical tradition, the very tension in other aspects of those traditions it has been exploring.

A full analysis of the manner in which the poet plays off these different semiotic or linguistic codes against each other is unfortunately beyond the scope of this paper. Such an analysis would also be severely hampered if it were confined to Gollancz's edition. Nevertheless, it opens up alternative possibilities for reading the poem, and also makes us less dependent on a precise dating. I have argued elsewhere that *Wynnere and Wastoure* can be dated only approximately between 1352 and 1370, the year of the death of Judge Shareshull.[33] But if we lose *Wynnere and Wastoure* as a definite and immediate precursor of *Piers Plowman*, we may gain, on the other hand, a more subtle perception of one medieval poet's attempts to make sense of a changing world within formal poetic structures. The question is this: why do we still value literary history over literary interpretation?

[33] Trigg, pp. 271–74.

SOME DISCARNATIONAL IMPULSES IN THE CANTERBURY TALES

Penelope Curtis

Although I believe that the *Canterbury Tales* is chiefly incarnational in character (a term it would be absurd to try to define in a short article), there are several tales which seem to run counter to the work as a whole: tales I will start by calling 'discarnational', and which I want to consider here. For, while the stress of the incarnational-discarnational dialectic in the Christian heritage is not central to the *Tales* as it is to *Piers Plowman*, it does appear in Chaucer's poem, and on terms which show how much more the *Tales* does than merely reflect or monumentalize a mature civilization: how fully it enters into the processes which make and unmake such a civilization. The 'discarnational' tales do contribute in special ways to the overall character of the *Tales*. Contrast is only the beginning of their function; but the contrast is stark.

The *Tales* first orients itself in an earthscape of renewals and pilgrimages, pilgrimage being imagined as a way towards a sacred source which may actually be reached. History is possible and so are multiple perspectives. The pilgrims' contest for a 'soper' is based on sharing: they exchange whatever is in their male, in a 'feest' far richer than the one competed for. Style provokes style, one genre confronts another or a rival version of itself, an enriching and self-interrupting process in which the pilgrims make not only common cause but a communal culture. That purpose is challenged, extended, re-defined along the way, but always on a basis of pluralism; and the tales evoke a range of stable contexts from a world which is, or comes to be, held in common.

Jill Mann, it is true, finds an 'absence of a sense of social structure in the general ethic of the *Prologue* ...',[1] 'a world of specialist skills, experience, terminology and interests ...'[2]

> The haphazard groupings in the *Prologue* suggest ... a specialised, blinkered approach, in which an individual's relation to the rest of society does not extend beyond his immediate family or friends.[3]

But, even if she is right about the *Prologue* (and I think she is only partly so), these are the very conditions which most change in the free intra-group exchanges of the link sections, and in the local dynamics of tale interacting with link and/or tale.

Of course, each tale taken singly is partial or limited, and breaks or

[1] *Chaucer and Medieval Estates Satire* (Cambridge, 1973), p.115.
[2] *Medieval Estates Satire*, p.200.
[3] *Medieval Estates Satire*, p.147.

modifies the Canterbury narrative, which itself has only seeming continuity. It is through the breaks and the contrasts that the tales and other pieces interact and achieve pluralism. Some tales, however, secede from the feast of multiplicity even while taking part in it. The stanzaic and prose tales, and one or two others, do most to diversify the work, yet they also all practise some radical exclusion, limitation or rejection. They do this, of course, in very different ways. One instance is the monolithic nature of the rhetoric and logic (or rhetoric as logic) in the prose tales. Another is the fact that *Sir Thopas* is not understood by the Canterbury company and so is not shared with it. Perhaps in the end one may measure the poem's pluralism by the ways in which it accommodates such exclusions and even rejections. This is no place to consider the special functions of these special cases (such as the ways in which the Manciple's tale demythologizes story-telling) but together they bring into prominence a dramatically recessive feature of the work: the fact that the pilgrims' oral entertainment is enriched by the silent communications of writers.

The *Tales* plainly is what it declares itself to be, a literary compilation as well as a folk-experience; even though much of the time its dominant conventions suggest the second, the immediate creative exchange. Most of the tales, however finished they may be as literary products, evoke an audience which may plausibly be identified with the pilgrim group: their literary-dramatic qualities are assimilable to those created for the pilgrim-journey. Some tales, however, withstand that assimilation. They exist as written works first or in some obtrusive way, or as works directed to a different audience, which reach the pilgrim audience through the indirections of literary traffic. These tales insist on the remote or alien or intransigent components of experience; on the vastness of creation, especially in its aspect of time; and on the objective character of works. The exchange of tales, which is concentrated in the pilgrims' forum, is thus also seen as laterally spread through space and time.

The four stanzaic tales which interest me as a group are the pious legends[4], which call up a special audience (such as the silent credulity of the convent) or a general audience in a special mood. They are the Man of Law's, Clerk's, Second Nun's and Prioress's tales. These tales exaggerate the idea of breaking off the journey, transmuting or projecting it into another mode or tempo. They insist on their own value-structures, on their sometimes painfully exclusive terms of reference. And they are founded on a different principle from that announced in the *Prologue*: a purifying, abstracting and disheriting impulse (which in extreme forms tends towards Manicheism). This principle is very close to that of 'Truth', which declares man an exile both from the world and his own body.

---

[4] I use this term provisionally, for convenience. I am not engaging with Paul Strohm's interesting distinctions ('*Passioun, Lyf, Miracle, Legende*: Some Generic Terms in Middle English Hagiographical Narrative', *ChauR*, 10 (1975), 154–71), in particular his distinctions between the 'lyf of Seinte Cecile' and the 'tale' of Constance. All quotations are from F .N .Robinson's second edition (London, 1957).

Her is non hoom, her nis but wildernesse:
Forth, pilgrim, forth! Forth, beste, out of thy stal!
Know thy contree, look up, thank God of al;
Hold the heye wey, and lat thy gost thee lede ...

(17–20)

The Christian is allegorized as a lonely figure in perpetual passage through a hostile world, through the wilderness of his own fleshy being. Among its many representations, his 'gost' or *anima* may drive, like Custance, through a 'see' or pass ecstatically to its release through a cut throat.

This purifying, abstracting impulse is at work (indeed at struggle) continuously in *Piers Plowman*. In the *Tales*, Chaucer isolates, even attenuates it, and attaches it strictly to genre; at the same time he explores its genre-characteristics and investigates certain of its roles in a worldly civilization which in some lights represents Christendom at the full and in others verges on being post-Christian.

Two of the four tales have female tellers; three have women as central figures and one has a child (closely protected by two mothers, or even three). One factor in this cluster of tales around the 'feminine' principle is the traditional gender-casting of the soul: which in turn reflects the cultural 'disembodiment' of the sex disfranchised through the centuries. (The corollary, of course, is the over-fleshly stereotype of Eve, Lilith behind her, which is the target of massive anti-feminist attack, superbly dramatized in the *Tales* in the Wife's *Prologue*.) In the complex civilization which the pilgrims evoke and embody, the degree to which a purist Christianity is itself perceived as minor, at best a leaven in the dough, is seen in its limiting association with feminine stereotypes. These are silent, self-suppressing, outwardly conforming, emotionally vulnerable especially through the feelings of a 'moodir'; and in turn they are associated with the infantile and the infantine. That is not to say that strong men cannot enjoy manipulating or even assuming them: these stereotypes, and the tales which focus on them, are among the options current in the community, as the poem's structure indicates, and they coexist with very different levels of religious insight, such as that which dramatizes the Pardoner's bi-spirituality. But thus they are characterized, and the Host's jibes at the Monk (after his exaggerated deference to the Prioress) amount to a demand for something masculine embodying his own authoritive vitality, something which bears on the real matters of life. Those do not include the way of dispossession.

All four pious legends emphasize the forms of voyage, journey, passage. They disrupt ordinary time patterns:

Yeres and dayes fleet this creature ...

(*Man of Law's Tale*, 463)

'... I sholde have dyed, ye, longe tyme agon'.

(*Prioress's Tale*, 651)

130

There is a suppression or a transcendence of feeling in the victim; a disorienting loss of context; patterns of repetition; a fluctuating emotional temperature, and a play of binary opposites which takes different forms, such as the alternation between the lonely composure of the central figure and a hectic paranoia both in the vipers' nests themselves and the apostrophes against them.

The group is, of course, formed from two complementary pairs. It hardly needs saying that the Man of Law's and Clerk's tales of exemplary wives emphasize the religious content of the female stereotypes, while the Second Nun's and the Prioress's emphasize a body-soul division. The first two are histories of suppressed martyrdom over many years, while the latter two present actual bodily martyrdoms in which the instant of the soul's release is miraculously prolonged, over days or hours. But the four are sufficiently alike to create a feeling of recurrence in the *Tales*, and strong enough to impress a special experience on the general one. At the same time each appears on terms which define its status as minor, even marginal.

Michael Stugrin and Carolyn P.Collette evidently do not think so. Stugrin claims that the pathetic voice 'takes on a power and significance greater than the individual contribution of each of the tales' and speaks of 'the common ground on which we find not only Chaucer's pathetic tales, but the Passion sequences of the vernacular plays, the Passion lyrics, and so much religious visual art'.[5] Collette locates at least the Prioress's tale in a mainstream: 'Her concern with emotion, tenderness, and the diminutive are part of the late fourteenth-century shift in sensibility'.[6] However, Stugrin's claims, though interesting, remain speculative, and Collette reduces hers to something minor after all: 'The Prioress's stress on love, emotion, and pity are all consonant with what we might call a fashion in religious taste'.[7]

The otherness and strangeness of Custance's experiences among the far-off heathen find a form in the urgent and repeated images of voyage.

> She dryveth forth into oure occian
> Thurghout oure wilde see, til atte laste
> Under an hoold that nempnen I ne kan,
> Fer in Northhumberlond the wawe hire caste ...
> The wyl of Crist was that she sholde abyde.

(505–11)

> Forth gooth her ship thurghout the narwe mouth
> Of Jubaltare and Septe, dryvynge ay
> Somtyme west, and somtyme north and south ...

(946–48)

---

[5] 'Ricardian Poetics and Late Medieval Cultural Pluriformity: the Significance of Pathos in the *Canterbury Tales*', *ChauR*, 15 (1980), 153–67 (p.159).
[6] 'Sense and Sensibility in the *Prioress's Tale*', *ChauR*, 15 (1980), 138–50 (p.138).
[7] 'Sense and Sensibility', p.149. John C.Hirsh ('Reopening the *Prioress's Tale*', *ChauR*, 10 (1975), 30–45) also uses the word 'fashion' (p.38) in connection with the 'background of affective piety which informs the tone throughout'. (p.37).

This sea is much like the chaotic emblem Auden speaks of in *The Enchafed Flood*,[8] its imagined power to shift and overwhelm increased, if anything, by the Sultaness's scornful references to baptism and Custance's to the 'Lambes blood . ../That wessh the world fro the olde iniquitee . ..'. The tale portrays a world riddled with the old iniquity.

In the flux of the narrative and its main emblem there are precarious images of stability: the ship of Custance's soul, the chamber of her pregnancy, and the coastal forts her ship fetches up beneath. These are ambiguous images of safety, especially the last. One such place materializes only long enough for the rapist to appear and be forced overboard, and on she drives again. And Hermengyld is slain beside her in the other. The sea itself provides the nearest thing to a continuum in Custance's experience, but, while she survives indefinitely and the rapist quickly drowns, it is not an easy sea to negotiate. Custance seems to survive by a quality of self-immolating fearlessness which enables her at times to drive with the sea's movement, and not merely be driven. At every crisis point there is some initiative for her to take or to retain.

> She kneleth doun and thanketh Goddes sonde;
> But what she was she wolde no man seye . . .
> *(Man of Law's Tale*, 523–24)

William C.Johnson Jr. takes this idea much further in his somewhat confusing and highly metaphorical case that:

> The Christianity that remains in the *Man of Law's Tale* and in similar tales told by the Prioress, the Clerk, and the Second Nun, provides the literary idiom of feminine inwardness. Custance's alloy of hagiographic piety reveals beneath its surface an incipient individualism that necessitates the tale's multiple viewpoints, elusiveness, and ambiguity – the rhetorical richness of texture against which her character collides.[9]

The tale seems to me to move much more clearly and potently between polarities than that language suggests, but he is right about the inwardness, and perhaps the incipient individualism. In fact, the human value of the Man of Law's and Clerk's tales can be largely judged by the discriminations with which Custance and Grisilde partly yield to, and partly oppose, the tides of chance and human malice, not to mention the inscrutable 'sonde'.

> Therwith she looked bakward to the londe,
> And seyde, 'Farewel, housbonde routhelees!'
> And up she rist, and walketh doun the stronde . . .
> *(Man of Law's Tale*, 862–64)

---

[8] W. H. Auden, *The Enchafed Flood*, Virginia (1950), eg. pp. 6–7, where some pre-Romantic ideas of the sea are summarized.
[9] 'The *Man of Law's Tale*: Aesthetics and Christianity in Chaucer', *ChauR*, 16 (1982), 201–21 (p. 217).

In both tales, the verse finely establishes the *gravitas*, the dignity and bodily reality, of the central female figure.

> And as she wolde over hir thresshfold gon,
> The markys cam, and gan hire for to calle;
> And she set doun hir water pot anon,
> Biside the thresshfold, in an oxes stalle,
> And doun upon hir knes she gan to falle,
> And with sad contenance kneleth stille,
> Til she had herd what was the lordes wille.
>
> (*Clerk's Tale*, 288–94)

In this composed sequence of gestures, signifying a version of *Ecce ancilla Domini*,[10] Grisilde is not a passive figure, though she has a largely passive role: it is rather that her considerable energy is given over to achieving silence and stillness, the 'stille' that matches 'wille'.

In each tale the *gravitas* of the central figure is developed as an increasing isolation, until that figure, into which are shut increasingly mute strengths, comes to have the character of a fort: a defensive image in a threatening, chaotic environment, most unlike the world-view presupposed and enjoyed by the pilgrims. Auden believed that, before Shakespeare, the sea was almost universally seen as hostile: 'so far as I know, the pilgrimage of the pious soul is never symbolised in early Christian literature by a sea-voyage';[11] and, while Custance's years at sea do counter that dictum by having many features of a soul's pilgrimage, it is also true that Custance the free pilgrim can act only within the circumstances imposed on Custance the victim. She is free under constraint, and that constraint gradually works its way into her characterization, as does the even greater constraint placed on Grisilde by her over-special marriage vows. By the end of the tale the victim is immured in herself. She is dumb, maimed, paralysed.

> And she, for sorwe, as doumb stant as a tree,
> So was hir herte shet in hir distresse,
> Whan she remembred his unkyndenesse.
>
> (*Man of Law's Tale*, 1055–57)

> And in hire swough so sadly holdeth she
> Hire children two, whan she gan hem t'embrace,
> That with greet sleighte and greet difficultee
> The children from hire arm they gonne arace.
>
> (*Clerk's Tale*, 1100–3)

[10] Long noted, and referred to by Francis Lee Utley as 'what we may now call without blush the Annunciation passage in the *Clerk's Tale*' ('Five Genres in the *Clerk's Tale*', *ChauR*, 6 (1972), 198–228 (p. 224)).
He cites Sister Rose Marie ('Chaucer and his Mayde Bright', *Commonweal*, 43 (1940–41), 225–27) as the first to take note of Chaucer's allusion, but it is, I think, immediately apparent.
[11] *The Enchafed Flood*, p.8, note.

Those lines attest a partly irreversible condition. Grisilde and Custance have lost *time* and

'It wol nat come agayn, withouten drede ...'

The *Man of Law's Tale* follows a linear movement, through a monotonous world, of ever-recurring suffering, irregularly punctuated by crises in which the victim's survival is inseparable from self-repression. Michael Paull sees in it a conscious and consistent management of genre-effects, in particular, 'repetition and intensification'.[12] I see rather an instinctual craft, not unlike that of *Pericles*, where the repetitions reflect a working of folk-material for not fully recognized imaginative ends. The emphases in the tale are on time lost, strangeness, remoteness, isolation.

These effects are much heightened by its framing. It is a one-tale fragment, whose introductory 'wordes' are very substantial, formal and literary ('Aprill' is reinterpreted as 'messager to May'). They take new bearings from the heavenly bodies, independently of the *General Prologue*. The pilgrimage is seen from a distance, freshly bathed in light and through the unexpectedly silent cognitions of the Host. When he does speak, his monologue on time casts a new shadow of necessity on the pilgrim's game. The Man of Law's responding monologue – his precedent-ridden literary biography of a Chaucer not known to the pilgrims – is teasing and opaque. Whatever linking characterization of the Man of Law one may see in the 'wordes', prologue and tale,[13] these three stand in disjunct, oblique relations to each other; all the while with an air of being consciously arranged. The sophistication of all of this is both a barrier to the tale and a claim on it: it is treated as a communal possession, which moves according to its own alien laws. Custance is locked away in her hostile geography, the Man of Law in his spiritual destitution, and the pilgrimage itself moves in a distanced, almost lonely way, under the yard of time.

Custance (a partly allegorical figure) is put to sea like an errant wife but endures there as an exemplary Christian. The *Clerk's Tale* is more 'earthed'

---

12 Michael R.Paull, 'The Influence of the Saint's Legend Genre in the *Man of Law's Tale*', *ChauR*, 5 (1971), 179–94 (p.183).
13 For example, Robert Enzer Lewis ('Chaucer's Artistic Use of Pope Innocent III's *De Miseria Humane Conditionis* in the Man of Law's Prologue and Tale', *PMLA*, 81 (1966), 485–92), who finds that the prologue shares common ground with the introduction, in 'developing more fully the character of the Man of Law as presented in the *General Prologue*', and that it serves as 'a bridge from the Introduction to the Tale', p.492; Alfred David ('The Man of Law vs. Chaucer: A Case in Poetics', *PMLA*, 82 (1967), 217–25) who also finds that the Prologue expresses the 'blunt materialism' of its speaker, and that its unlikeness to the tale is designed to demonstrate that 'those who insist most loudly on morality in art are often morally insensitive'. (p.221); and Rodney Delasanta ('And of Great Reverence: Chaucer's Man of Law', *ChauR*, 5 (1971), 288–310), who sees the Man of Law's character as being developed in several ways throughout the tale itself: especially in his literary pretension and inaccuracies, his 'intrusive declamation' (p.300), and his 'legalistic attitude toward humankind' which is 'defective, alternately on the side of sentimentality or on that of anathema'. (p.303).

but even more hybrid.[14] Its action also can be charted as a series of journeys or translations, but the action is limited because there is one central place and people (Grisilde has a father to return to), and it is complicated because its very substance is a subterfuge (whose effect is that she does not recognize her children). Walter's unstable presence is a source both of power and instability in the narrative. The verse shows the sophistication needed to present him and to make the proper discriminations, but the rhetoric is somewhat differently managed, in a way which partly deprives the audience of a vent for its anger. Grisilde's great divorce speech, where she strips herself of everything but honour, is all the more passionate for her life-long silence and for the constraints under which she is still labouring; and even so it is partly thwarted and thwarting, since its very nobility excites Walter perversely.

The tale is balanced and sane in its feeling for the body: as in the episode where her father comes to meet Grisilde and tries to cover her with her old coat, which movingly suggests the limitation of the body's powers to be the soul's raiment. However, its sense of the world as almost completely hostile is more chilling than anything in the Man of Law's tale (where the world's hostility is that of heathens to the true faith). Walter puts Grisilde away, in what is allegedly a Christian world, with a cruel ease which betrays it as an alien world masquerading as familiar.

The Clerk's tale challengingly imagines the strain placed on someone trying to 'Be perfect ...' in an experientially unChristian world. The strain of keeping even inner silence, the waste of years, the moral and mental cost of continuing to love, are all the more painful to witness because they lack the correlative, the exteriorization, of, say, Hermione's statue. There is a gulf between Grisilde's values (with their defect of formalism) and the Canterbury-ward world to which they are introduced: a gulf which, as the Lenvoy shows, is best crossed by irony and self-deprecating play. This tale admits more consciousness of other value-systems than the Man of Law's, partly through its own internal strains and tensions; and that, no doubt, is one reason why it can be set in dialogue with another tale, the Merchant's, though it is the dialogue of irreconcilable opposition.

To return to the purer version of the type: Sheila Delany and Eugene Clasby clash over the meaning and value of Custance's survival, but they over-generalize it in similar ways. Delany finds that 'Constance's particular type of femininity serves ... as an emblematic model for men and women alike'[15] and, though she adds that 'it is precisely in her sexual role that Constance's main virtue is best seen: the acceptance of fate and authority',[16] she does nothing to decide the force of that 'precisely'. Clasby's argument is rigorous and eloquent,

---

[14] Francis Lee Utley finds harmony and balance between the tale's various influences or dimensions ('Five Genres'), but I think that there is tension which often becomes unease.
[15] 'Womanliness in the *Man of Law's Tale*', ChauR, 9 (1974), 63–72 (p. 64).
[16] 'Womanliness in the *Man of Law's Tale*', p .66.

> Not once does she express the essential sentiment of submission: that those who injure her are justified in doing so.[17]

but, like Delany, he sees Custance the exemplary human being as a simple extension of Custance the exemplary woman or wife.

> Her virtue is human virtue, and her suffering is human suffering.

> It is not her femininity, as such, that makes her 'wayke' but the circumstances imposed on her by Fortune.[18]

In fact, nearly all the powerful worldly figures in both tales are men, and all Custance's evils, like Grisilde's, derive from men who want to marry, dominate or rape her. Among the binary oppositions involving Custance (*contra* fathers, Mohammedans, heathen, seas, husbands, rapist-traducers, mothers-in-law) it must be admitted that mothers-in-law loom fairly large; they are so extremely drawn that the teller hesitates to call them female, yet in such a way as to emphasize their connection with Eve. But they are plainly power-brokers for men, figures belonging to masculine structures of interpretation. As Delany suggests, they are the other half of the Constance fiction,[19] figures in a system of male oppression of which she is a victim. And, in so far as she does not submit to this system, the *mode* of her non-submission necessarily grows out of the mode of the suffering imposed on her. It is, to say the least, a relatively silent and 'stille' mode.

If one asks the obvious question, why a principle of accepting authority *or* enduring oppression should be commended to everyone *via* the obedience peculiarly expected of wives, the obvious answer is that these things are acceptable when they take a female form and not when they don't. The 'circumstances imposed on' Custance are of a kind typically imposed on women rather than men, and/or on Christians in a heathen world, and/or on exiles. Indeed, in the patterns of associations shared by these stanzaic legends, women are made correlative to early Christians and both are seen as exiles.

Custance, Grisilde and Cecilia are all, in fact, strong figures. Custance battles alone for years at sea, and lacks all male support in her crises, while the worthlessness of Walter's countenance and support is immediately exposed when he removes them from Grisilde. But those two are nevertheless disherited beings, wanderers on the face of the earth and sea. To a large extent the impulse towards radical Christianity in the *Tales* is narrowed to that of the alienate and disfranchised soul, whose emblem is the pious woman, and deflected into the patterns of a minor art. One might even say that the second sex is used to provide models for a second metaphysic.

---

[17] 'Chaucer's Constance: Womanly Virtue and the Heroic Life', *ChauR*, 13 (1979), 221–33 (p.226).
[18] 'Chaucer's Constance', p.223.
[19] 'The characters of Mary and Eve live symbolically in Constance and her antagonists', 'Womanliness in the *Man of Law's Tale*', p.69.

In the Second Nun's and Prioress's tales, women and children represent the weakness (somewhat notional in Cecilia's case) of the flesh through which the spirit must pass, and the weakness of the chosen instrument through which God manifests His power. The two tales share a central image: the head not fully severed (unlike the pagan Virginia's, whose *anima* disappears abruptly mid-line), the spirit preternaturally potent in the body's pain. Indeed, while the role models for Christian life in the first pair of stanzaic legends are feminine, the models for Christian death in the second pair are more nearly genderless: that is, gender more or less disappears, but does so from a feminine context. Cecilia transcends the fleshly bondage of a wife and ends a potent, scarcely gendered saint,[20] while the Prioress's little mother-oriented choirboy voices an impersonal ecstasy after the crisis. The trappings of these tales are female, but their central experience – of soul subduing, or ecstatically inhabiting, its prison – has no more gender than formally belongs to the *anima* itself, and perhaps not so much.

The two tales differ markedly, however. Cecilia is a strong martyr, in a formal, orthodox[21] and pragmatic tale undeflected by considerations of the 'weye'. Its series of distancing (though ardent) introductions are all quite impersonal, and it enters the Canterbury story only retrospectively. The Second Nun's tale offers a pivotal memory for Christendom, since it recalls an otherworldly phase of Christianity which was also a period of transition from Roman Antiquity to the different *imperium* of the Roman Church. Though she takes her stand on a truth seen only by the inner eye of faith, Cecilia's role is really to bring Christianity out of the catacombs into the light, the public world.

What Clasby argues about the Man of Law's tale is also true of this: while it is neither dualist nor Manichean,[22] it does have a subversive force, it does affirm 'a hidden order of values against which the values of the world are to be judged'.[23] In the Second Nun's tale that hidden order is expressed first in mystical signs and located in the historical church 'lotynge' under the city. And it must be said that as a poem of mystical experience it largely fails. The historical memory is lively:

> 'Ne menestow nat Urban,' quod he tho,
> 'That is so ofte dampned to be deed.
> And woneth in halkes alwey to and fro,
> And dar nat ones putte forth his heed?',
>
> (*Second Nun's Tale*, 309–12)

too lively, in fact, to be subsumed into the pattern of mystical tokens. Those

---

20 So that the possibility that she spends the last three days (sheeted, of course) preaching from her bath, does not matter.

21 See Carolyn P .Collette ('A Closer Look at Seinte Cecile's Special Vision', *ChauR*, 10 (1976), 337–49) for an account of the tale's harmonious relation with its theological/philosophical background, and of the care and consistency with which it presents that theology.

22 'Chaucer's Constance', p .232.

23 'Chaucer's Constance', p .231.

tokens are offered with an assurance that they *are* the reality, that faith has overcome the world. The old man and book with letters of gold, Cecilia's angel, the sweet-smelling crowns of lily and rose, are presented in a calmly triumphalist spirit, but their theological explanations are flatly prosaic, while the tokens themselves come and go. They do not engage with the very different 'real' world of hostile political force, nor even with their own counterparts in it, the old living pope, the poor folk, the sheets which catch Cecilia's blood. There are, in effect, two sets of sense impressions, which correspond without being adequately differentiated or connected; they are only mutually displacing. Only the saint's pain, 'half deed ...', seems to belong at once to the unseen order and the seen.

The tale's dual character, of otherworldliness and public confrontation, shows as a tension in Cecilia's double citizenship of the hidden Rome and the external one. As a 'weak' woman destined for marriage, she is fitted to represent an order whose signs are invisible savours, disembodied crowns, night journeys made in fear: fit to bring strong men to God. At the same time she is patently a leader, active and unyielding (she can retain her virginity though she cannot avoid marriage), with full confidence in the might of her invisible contacts to overcome the world. She has a public identity and presence; like St Paul, she is a Roman citizen and has a rhetoric to suit the fact. She is a powerful speaker (no Galilean fisher she) and even so she has the spirit to deride her worldly strength as weakness. She is the embodiment of the old Rome and a pioneer of the new one.

It is at her trial that her real power to implement the 'hidden order' is declared, not in symbols but in argument.[24] She dominates proceedings,

> 'Ye han bigonne youre questioun folily,'
> Quod she, 'that wolden two answeres conclude
> In o demande ...'

(428–30)

insisting on a vast separation, of which her judge knows nothing, opening up in the world between imperial Rome and God's invisible kingdom. The two world-views are set in a counterpoint in which Cecilia turns the trial around and makes of it a trial of the pagan world, doing so with all the rational energy that the old Rome has bred in her.

> 'Ther lakketh no thyng to thyne outter yën
> That thou n'art blynd; for thyng that we seen alle
> That it is stoon, – that men may wel espyen, –
> That ilke stoon a god thow wolt it calle.

[24] See Paul E .Beichner's account ('Confrontation, Contempt of Court, and Chaucer's Cecilia', *ChauR*, 8 (1974), 198–204) of the way Chaucer adapted his chief Latin source for that section to shift the centre of the tale more completely to the trial scene.

> I rede thee, lat thyn hand upon it falle,
> And taste it wel, and stoon thou shalt it fynde,
> Syn that thou seest nat with thyne eyen blynde.'
>
> (498–504)

This proof, not that Christianity is true, but that pagan confidence is false, represents an interesting moment in the history of Christianity: what Auerbach called 'a to and fro of the pendulum';[25] the moment immortalized by Bede, as a turning from a known treachery to a brave trial of things unseen. It represents the moment of the annunciation, before Christianity puts on flesh, before the new *imperium* takes on a worldly content from the life-process itself. And it is here that the tale finds its chief strength as a corporate memory: in its form of a rhetorical confrontation.

The body-soul polarity is expressed in a direct, traditional way which arouses no unreasonable fears such as we find in the Prioress's tale.

> And of thy light my soule in prison lighte,
> That troubled is by the contagioun
> Of my body, and also by the wighte
> Of erthely lust and fals affeccioun ...
> Now help, for to my werk I wol me dresse.
>
> (*Second Nun's Tale*, Invocacio, 71–77)

The *Invocacio* balances the powerful 'contagioun' with the 'fals affeccioun' which is the crux of both tales in the fragment, and the saving 'werk' which is, in two senses, 'The lyf of Seinte Cecile'.

In fact the ideal exemplified in Cecilia is of a body and mind naturally strong (as minds and bodies go) and strengthened further by the energy of her soul. Her powers in argument are raised by faith to the dimensions of a spiritual battle. Her body itself is very hard to kill: she cannot be burnt, and her head cannot be severed within the legal limit of three blows. What we see is the body 'inspired', possessed by spirit:

> For al the fyr, and eek the bathes heete,
> She sat al coold ...
>
> (520–21)

her pain a point of junction between worlds:

> But half deed, with hir nekke ycorven there,
> He lefte hir lye ...
>
> (533–34)

in which condition she is more than ever active. The 'hidden order' is strongly manifest here too.

---

[25] Or 'the birth of a spiritual movement in the depths of the common people' which 'sets man's whole world astir'; *Mimesis*, translated by W.R.Trask (New York, 1957), pp.36–37.

The tale looks back to a starkly politicized world and its shadowy outlaw, the church in hiding, in what might be called a pre-incarnational phase of Christianity, and it finds links with both. This appears particularly clearly in its own overt character as a literary document, which belongs to a linguistic and rhetorical tradition that has become the property of the new patricians, i.e. the Fathers. Like the prose, the tale emphasizes the alternative aspect of the *Tales* as a literary compilation, an expression of a civilization in which literacy is a mark of power over others. The Latinate clerical tradition remains enshrined and powerful within the larger vernacular civilization which Chaucer is presenting.

The Second Nun's tale stands in a quasi-historical relation to the Canon's Yeoman's: hers being 'purer', simpler, the verse itself seeming abstract beside the walking corpses of the Yeoman's tales.[26] Bruce A .Rosenberg claims that 'only when this life of St Cecile is read in conjunction with and in the light of the *Canon's Yeoman's Tale* will the Nun's story gain literary stature',[27] and that 'The paradoxical aspects of vision ... sum up the philosophy of the tales, relate them to each other, enrich each story with dramatic irony, and give the *Second Nun's Tale* much of whatever complexity it has'.[28] I do not believe that complexity is thus imported into a poem which does not otherwise have it (though its function may be complicated if it becomes a unit in a larger entity). 'The lyf of Seinte Cecile' is not itself made more complex by being placed with the Canon's Yeoman's: if anything, its limitations are exposed, not only its prosaically decorative trimmings but the externality of its procedures. Beside the Yeoman's reliving of past tumults in a present crisis, Cecilia's legend has the clear but simple outline of a revived debate: something retained in the archives and raised to the status of a semi-drama.[29] But each tale represents an aspect of the *Tales*, and in particular it is represented by their coexistence. It is the juxtaposition itself – the Fragment – which becomes a complex statement.

It is also true that the purity and stability of the genre in the Second Nun's tale free one's analysis of its other exposition, by the Prioress. Perhaps of all the group the Prioress's tale alone might fairly be said to show a Manichean sensibility. It is also the tale which most intricately expresses its teller and is most precisely her genre-equivalent; the one that is most completely 'placed'

---

[26] This is not to undervalue the work done on thematic links between the tales by such critics as Joseph E. Grennen ('Saint Cecilia's Chemical Wedding: The Unity of the *Canterbury Tales*, Fragment VIII', *JEGP*, 65 (July, 1966), 466–81) and Bruce A. Rosenberg ('The Contrary Tales of the Second Nun and the Canon's Yeoman', *ChauR*, 2 (1968), 278–91) and on structural links in the Fragment by Glending Olson ('Chaucer, Dante, and the Structure of Fragment VIII (G) of the *Canterbury Tales*', *ChauR*, 16 (1982), 222–36). But, against such linking pressure, stands a quasi-dramatic difference in literary quality and mode.

[27] 'The Contrary Tales of the Second Nun and the Canon's Yeoman', p. 279.

[28] 'The Contrary Tales of the Second Nun and the Canon's Yeoman', p. 283.

[29] John C. Hirsh's interesting suggestion that the middle section contains a political allegory on the papal Schism ('The Politics of Spirituality: The Second Nun and The Manciple', *ChauR*, 12 (1977), 129–46) may be well-founded but, if so, that allegory does not give a contemporary feeling to the tale; it remains spirited but historically remote.

and clearly seen in its ambivalence, in this case as the perfect artefact of a weakly pious sub-culture and as a genuine vessel of the numinous.

All the pious tales are given considerable social protection, which adds to their prominence and isolation. The Prioress's sequence in particular occupies a charmed circle, created for her by the Host; on the other hand, it is fully contained within the Canterbury narrative, and her stanza appears less eccentric than the array of forms which follow, from 'Chaucer' and the Monk. Her portrait in the *General Prologue* was full of claustrophobic and claustrophiliac tension, personally voiced. That voice is instantly recognizable in her *Prologue*, but the direct address, beyond the social circle, is marked by a new amplitude:

> 'O Lord, oure Lord, thy name how merveillous
> Is in this large world ysprad,' quod she ...
> *(Prioress's Prologue, 453–54)*

With 'this large world' she is entering a new region of consciousness. When she compares herself with a child 'on the brest soukynge',

> 'But as a child of twelf month oold, or lesse ...
> Right so fare I ...'
>   (484–86)

the unmistakable signs of her sensibility, the sensual emphasis on 'soukynge' (both like and unlike 'hir smylyng' or 'wyped she'), and (her very hallmark) the intensifying diminuendo, 'twelf month oold, *or lesse*', are seen in the context of new possibilities 'the truth will set you free'. Her identification with small, helpless creatures is made openly and frankly, in fact it becomes her theme: Instrumentality. Donald W .Fritz and Albert B .Friedman both make the point that, in Friedman's words, 'the tale was her *Alma Redemptoris Mater*'.[30] Some implications of this clear parallel are, I think, that the Prioress is a vessel for the genre, and for the mystery which speaks through both her and it. In a similar way her *Prologue* is both hers and not hers: 'the *Prologue* is something of a *tour de force* since the significant phrases and the very cadences echo the Office recited daily by nuns at their private devotions'.[31]

Perhaps the free spirit of the *Prologue* is not only enabled by the Host's protection and the impersonal dimension in her language, but also associated with the safety of the child's position 'on the brest'. For the *Prioress's Tale* is marked from the beginning by constriction and fear. At seven years, the clergeon has reached the traditional age for separation from the mother, the age for a martial cooption, or the symbolic puberty of Blake's Lyca who finds herself among lions and tigers. In the Prioress's tale that separation is

---

[30] Albert B. Friedman, 'The *Prioress's Tale* and Chaucer's Anti-Semitism', *ChauR*, 9 (1974) 118–29 (p. 125). Donald W. Fritz, 'The Prioress's Avowal of Ineptitude', *ChauR*, 9 (1974), 166–81 (p. 173).
[31] Friedman, 'The *Prioress's Tale* and Chaucer's Anti-Semitism', p. 124.

minimal, highly ritualized, and well guarded by 'th'ymage' which is the mother's proxy: it amounts to a brief, regular passage through an alien street. Nevertheless, the tale is founded on the experience of enclosure and threat, as its opening images suggest.

> Ther was in Asye, in a greet citee,
> Amonges Cristene folk, a Jewerye,
> Sustened by a lord of that contree
> For foule usure and lucre of vileynye,
> Hateful to Crist and to his compaignye;
> And thurgh the strete men myghte ride or wende,
> For it was free and open at eyther ende.
>
> (*Prioress's Tale*, 488–94)

A Christian community, which apparently surrounds a 'Jewerye', is experienced as itself under threat. That Christian community is portrayed in the image of a 'litel scole'. The basis of its faith is delicately ambiguous – by inheritance or adoption, 'ycomen of Cristen blood'. What is taught is tautology: custom and usage are both the substance and the mode. It is a beautiful little ghetto, a refuge.

> A litel scole of Cristen folk ther stood
> Doun at the ferther ende, in which ther were
> Children an heep, ycomen of Cristen blood,
> That lerned in that scole yeer by yere
> Swich manere doctrine as men used there,
> This is to seyn, to syngen and to rede,
> As smale children doon in hire childhede.
>
> Among thise children was a wydwes sone,
> A litel clergeon, seven yeer of age,
> That day by day to scole was his wone,
> And eek also, where as he saugh th'ymage
> Of Cristes mooder, hadde he in usage,
> As hym was taught, to knele adoun and seye
> His *Ave Marie*, as he goth by the weye.
>
> (495–508)

Each stanza is as tightly enclosed and self-referring as the 'Cristen' life it is describing (the sentence never continues past the stanza, so that any developments or repercussions are internal). The characteristic part of any construction is likely to be 'as', which least disturbs a perfect stasis.

> This litel child, his litel book lernynge,
> As he sat in the scole at his prymer,
> He *Alma redemptoris* herde synge,
> As children lerned hire antiphoner;

> And as he dorste, he drough hym ner and ner,
> And herkned ay the wordes and the noote,
> Til he the firste vers koude al by rote.
>
> (516–22)

That stanza is typical. It produces a prolonged echoing moment in which the walls between two states are experienced as very thin. Such action as there is takes place in the extension of the moment: here, the action of a type of nervous system, the child trembling and inching towards his object. The child's nervous system is a high-profile manifestation of genre. At the same time, of course, it bears a very strong likeness to the teller's in her portrait; and the tale brings the vibrations of his nervous system very close.

However, the tale, unlike the portrait, works according to two principles, the first being that of the protectively closed system based on fear, whereby the child is formed according to his culture, and the second being the principle of instrumentality, whereby the child is made the innocent instrument of divine force.

> Twies a day it passed thurgh his throte . . .
>
> (548)

> The swetnesse hath his herte perced so . . .
> He kan nat stynte of syngyng by the weye.
>
> (555–57)

Those two principles together produce the rhythm of enclosure and release which verges on a kind of undeclared Manicheism. The lines just quoted are immediately followed by a reaction,

> Oure firste foo, the serpent Sathanas,
> That hath in Jues herte his waspes nest,
> Up swal . . .
>
> (558–60)

a recoil from ecstasy to a fearful didacticism whose terms are conditioned and predictable, and directly represent the speaker's culture or sub-culture.[32] There are two instrumentalities in the tale: the Prioress deems childhood to be especially vulnerable to grace, and 'Jues herte' to be vulnerable to the forces of darkness. The first instrumentality involves a free passage of the spirit through the flesh, and the second a quasi-material obstruction ('Up swal') from some force inimical to the spirit.

When the support of the enclosed community breaks down, in a disaster worse than anything the child anticipated, and he is caught in a 'trappe' of the lowest kind of matter,

---

[32] Friedman gives a balanced account of the Prioress in her time ('The *Prioress's Tale* and Chaucer's Anti-Semitism') and Hardy Long Frank ('Chaucer's Prioress and the Blessed Virgin', *ChauR*, 13 (1979), 346–62) of the Prioress and 'the cult of the Virgin Mary' (p.346).

> I seye that in a wardrobe they hym threwe
> Where as thise Jewes purgen hire entraille,
>
> (572–73)

his song takes on an aspect of power, of the numinous. A strong vibration replaces the weaker one of the child's (and its mother's and the narrator's) nervous dread:

> Ther he with throte ykorven lay upright,
> He *Alma redemptoris* gan to synge
> So loude that al the place gan to rynge.
>
> (611–13)

In the frieze-like mourning procession, the ecstatic moment is prolonged and amplified so that the onlooking community can take up and hold a relation to it.

> This child with pitous lamentacioun
> Up taken was, syngynge his song alway,
> And with honour of greet processioun
> They carien hym unto the nexte abbay.
> His mooder swownynge by the beere lay;
> Unnethe myghte the peple that was theere
> This newe Rachel brynge fro his beere.
>
> (621–27)

In the abbot's and people's slow acknowledgement of the wonder, a process is enacted by which emotional energy is converted into a still, passive worship. Even so, there is a temporary harmony between the tale's unlike and opposed interests: in a supporting, forming, ethnic-cultural group with its own minor art, and in that which resonates out of it, a divine 'showing' which has considerable otherness and force.

> 'My throte is kut unto my nekke boon,'
> Seyde this child, 'and, as by wey of kynde,
> I sholde have dyed, ye, longe tyme agon.
> But Jesu Crist, as ye in bookes fynde,
> Wil that his glorie laste and be in mynde,
> And for the worship of his Mooder deere
> Yet may I synge *O Alma* loude and cleere.'
>
> (649–55)

That stanza is Manichean neither in feeling nor in outlook. Pain and violence have by no means been escaped. The prolongation of the ecstatic moment here is also the prolongation of his agony. Yet the peculiar piercing resonance of his voice seems connected with the child's absence of fear. 'Yet may I synge' rings out confidently, beyond any fears of obstruction in or by the flesh.

The *General Prologue* portrait links this tale with an adult who appears to have a strong and probably neurotic interest in remaining childish. We recognise her accents in the tale and recognise at the same time that they are the accents of a specific religious literature. The *Prioress's Tale* exemplifies, among other things, a thin strain of cultivated piety and an intolerance of adult issues; and Chaucer tacitly invites us – *via* the teller, as well as through the challenge of other tales – to see it as systematically bounded by the infantine, with a defensive interest in being beautiful and faultless.

Yet the tale is shaped with a degree of moral pressure and intelligence which gives it simultaneously another function. If we see the tale as creating states of consciousness, which resemble the Prioress's patterns of behaviour and consciousness in the *Prologue* but take another course, then there is an enabling shift of consciousness that demonstrates a 'miracle' of faith; and the tale becomes a vessel of a genuine (though still infantine) sense of the sacred within the culture.

The Prioress's tale has a part in the complex and bizarre development of Fragment VII. The Host's rebound from it into 'game' provokes a series of unexpected reactions. He first asks 'Chaucer', whom he characterizes as a sexless and/or feminized 'popet' and 'elvyssh wight', for a 'myrthe', and Chaucer provides one or two that do not wholly serve. Then the Host (comically invoking his wife as the embodiment of masculine force) taunts the Monk with his virility and asks him to 'be myrie': the Monk haughtily refuses. Finally the unknown Nun's Priest accepts the commission and, picking up a suggestion from the Host's word 'tredefowel', constructs a magnificent mirth around it: in return for which the Host, repeating the compliment which the Monk rejected, elaborates it into a fantastic portrait of the Nun's Priest in Chauntecleer's likeness; the tale, in this case, making the man. The Prioress's tale, then, helps create the vacuum which produces the Nun's Priest's: a hymn to creativity, sexuality, and, before both, virility, the forces which move the poem as a whole from its first lines.

The other three pious legends all have a primitive vigour, and all, to some extent, represent encapsulated memories or layers of the corporate past. The most contemporary tale (in manner, feeling and concerns), and the most nearly discarnational of the four, is also the tale most fully integrated into the *Tales* as a whole and into the particular dynamic of its fragment: a fragment which culminates in the most incarnational example of the storytelling art.

CHAUCER'S CLERICAL VOICES

Ralph W.V.Elliott

The theme of this essay was suggested, as is wholly fitting, by G.H.Russell's stimulating study of the *Prioress's Tale*, more particularly by this sentence:

> The supple couplets and the lithe, if rather chilly, movement of *The Shipman's Tale* yield now to those statuesque, formal stanzas which recall an earlier, 'courtly', phase of Chaucer's creative work and which he was to use on only three other occasions in *The Canterbury Tales* – the first in a tale told by a nun, the second in another tale told by an ecclesiastic, the Monk, who is provoked into telling a tale of monumental solemnity by the mockery of the Host, and the third by yet another churchman, the grave and idealized Clerk.[1]

The fact that the *Man of Law's Tale* is cast in the same metrical mould does not disprove Russell's thesis that there is something distinctive about these clerical tales. The seven-line rhyme-royal stanza which Chaucer uses in these tales – except for the Monk's eight-line stanza – may well have been Machaut's gift to him. Chaucer uses it also in several of his shorter poems,[2] and in *Troilus and Criseyde* where it encompasses a much wider range than in the clerical tales. It remains for us a stanza form with strong medieval associations, as well as royal and Shakespearean ones, not least because of its revival by William Morris in *The Earthly Paradise* a little over a century ago.

While the primary difference between the stanzaic clerical tales and those of the less reputable clerical pilgrims in the *Canterbury Tales*, whose narrations are in heroic couplets, is metrical, a comparison of the two groups reveals more important distinctions. By choosing to talk about clerical 'voices' I am permitting myself a form of shorthand, which includes not merely whatever individual speech mannerisms Chaucer cares to mention, nor just the range of linguistic and stylistic resources at the story-teller's command, but more especially the deeper issues, moral, satiric, and 'affecting' – in the sense of Aristotle's *páthe* – raised by the tales themselves and by the didactic or homiletic stances of their tellers. For it is, presumably,

---

[1] G. H. Russell, 'Chaucer: *The Prioress's Tale*', in *Medieval Literature and Civilization: Studies in Memory of G. N. Garmonsway*, edited by D. A. Pearsall and R. A. Waldron (London, 1969), p. 213. I also wish to acknowledge valuable criticism received in the preparation of this paper from Professor J. P. Hardy.
[2] Compare for example Wolfgang Clemen, *Chaucer's Early Poetry* (London, 1963; repr. 1968), p. 172.

no accident that Chaucer's clerical tales divide into two clearly separable groups: on the one hand, there are the stories of saints and sufferers, statuesque, solemn, full of pathos; on the other hand, there are the fables, fabliaux, and felonies of Chaucer's clerical rogues, the Friar and the Pardoner, as well as that more shadowy cleric, the Nun's Priest, quite capable, we are told, of being a 'trede-foul' himself, had he been secular. The Summoner, although not himself a cleric, was a minor Church official whose tale of a hypocritical friar places him squarely into this latter group. Only the *Parson's Tale*, being in prose, stands deliberately and conspicuously by itself.

The speech mannerisms of Chaucer's pilgrims, as far as the poet mentions them at all, are part of Chaucer's *ars descriptionis personae*. He drops a sufficient number of hints to make us aware of distinctions, whether of choice of words or of accent or of speech defects like the Friar's lisp. The Man of Law's verbal sagacity, the Summoner's inebriated Latin, the Merchant's 'solempne' speech are not so much gratuitous titbits as hints to the audience of Chaucer's own awareness of the different speech habits he encountered among his fellows. How far it is possible to relate what Chaucer says about his pilgrims' modes of talking to the manner of their story-telling, I have discussed elsewhere.[3] Some of his hints are taken up later, as Chaucer so obviously does with the Wife of Bath's deafness, whence presumably her loud voice. Others are not developed. Thus there is no audible indication of the Prioress's Stratford French in her tale, unless we are meant to hear her speech 'entuned in hir nose', but nasalized articulation was not only a French characteristic. As Muriel Bowden has reminded us, 'chanting the service has always demanded a nasal quality to avoid strain on the vocal chords';[4] nor did the characteristic vowels and diphthongs of fourteenth-century Anglo-French lend themselves as easily to transcription in manuscript as the dialect speech of the Reeve's libidinous students from the north country.

Chaucer was obviously not deaf to such linguistic distinctions: he had, in Dorothy Everett's pithy phrase, a 'good ear',[5] and it is worth while considering for a moment how he indicates in his poetry the different vocal characteristics of tone and pitch and mood which he heard in the course of a busy life. There are the small voices of the Pardoner and the Miller's Absolon, the latter 'gentil', the former goat-like. There are the loud voices of the knights addressing large gatherings in the Wife's and the Squire's narratives, and even strident voices clamouring for war in pilgrim Chaucer's *Tale of Melibee*. The Miller's evident familiarity with contemporary miracle plays is revealed not only by his references to Absolon playing Herod 'upon a scaffold hye' and to

> The sorwe of Noe with his felaweshipe,
>
> (*Miller's Tale*, 3539)[6]

[3] *Chaucer's English* (London, 1974), ch.7.
[4] *A Commentary on the General Prologue to the 'Canterbury Tales'*, 2nd edition (New York and London, 1967), p.102.
[5] *Essays on Middle English Literature* (Oxford, 1955), ch.6.
[6] All Chaucer quotations are from Robinson's second edition.

but very pointedly by letting us hear the loud echoes of Pilate's voice, as the Miller enters upon the scene with one of those blasphemous oaths which we soon discover to be characteristic of him.

> Peas, carles, I commaunde,

shouts Pilate at the opening of the Towneley 'Conspiracy', following this up with a goodly selection of forceful oaths by the devil and 'by Mahowns blood', and by yelling at the folk around in such phrases as

> Go hence, harlot! Hy mot thou hang!

or

> The dwill, he hang you high to dry!

It takes little imagination to hear the Miller declaim 'a twenty devel wey!' or 'By Goddes corpus' in Pilate's voice as he studs his narrative with such expletives.

There are other loud voices in the *Canterbury Tales* of course, like that of the young king of India which sounded like 'a trompe thonderynge' or that of the people, also in the *Knight's Tale*, shouting up to the skies 'with murie stevene', but Chaucer responds as readily and especially in his stanzaic tales, to sweet, soft, humble, and piteous voices. He had, after all, given us already in his early poem *Anelida and Arcite* an unforgettable line that was to echo down the centuries of English poetry:

> thou Polymya ...
> Singest with vois memorial in the shade.

Not the least important characteristic of such sweet, soft, humble, and piteous voices is the words they use. In the *Prioress's Tale* there is a delicacy of idiom, a 'simple and undemonstrative' vocabulary, as Russell says, which is wholly in keeping with the martyrdom of an innocent that is being narrated. And equally appropriate to this particular clerical voice are the liturgical echoes which reverberate throughout the tale, including those fittingly derived from the mass of Innocents' Day.[7] Moreover, in pointed contrast to the mouth-filling oaths of most of her fellow-pilgrims, clerical and secular, the Prioress's mentions of the divine personages are invariably devout. Here indeed is a pious 'voys of aungel' such as Chaucer's dreamer had heard in the birdsong in the garden of the *Parliament of Fowls*. The Prioress achieves much of the pathos of her tale by repeated use of evocative adjectives, some of them reiterated with powerful cumulative effect. The positioning of these adjectives, varied according to the demands of metre and rhyme, adds yet further emphasis by allowing such Italianate doubling as 'his litel body swete',

---

[7] Russell, p.216; see also B.Boyd, *Chaucer and the Liturgy* (Philadelphia, 1967), ch.5.

'the white Lamb celestial'. The Mariolatrous tone of the tale is another important ingredient of the Prioress's narrative voice, skilfully sustained not only by the recurrent references to the Blessed Virgin, but also by the emotive juxtaposing of the heavenly mother and the grief-stricken earthly one:

> With moodres pitee in hir brest enclosed,
> She gooth, as she were half out of hir mynde,
> To every place where she hath supposed
> By liklihede hir litel child to fynde;
> And evere on Cristes mooder meeke and kynde
> She cride ...
>
> (*Prioress's Tale*, 593–98)

Like the Prioress's tale, that of the Second Nun is a story of martyrdom. Whatever sources or version of the *Legenda aurea* Chaucer may have drawn upon for his Life of St Cecilia, the Nun's voice is, like her stanzas, akin to that of the Prioress. There are parallels in the respective opening invocations of the two nuns to the Virgin:

> O mooder Mayde! o mayde Mooder free!
>
> (*Prioress's Prologue*, 467)

> Thow Mayde and Mooder, doghter of thy Sone ...
>
> (*Second Nun's Prologue*, 36)

Chaucer was drawing on the same sources for his Marian prayers, and at the same time he was establishing appropriate diction and cadences for the nuns' pathetic tales, for the Clerk's story of Griselda, and for the Monk's lamentable anthology of which the most pitiable story is that of Ugolino. That Dante's influence is apparent in the shaping of this linguistic register is beyond doubt; what is of interest is Chaucer's creation, early in his poetic career, of a distinctive narrative voice to suit both tellers and tales in similar metrical forms which are audibly different from those of the other pilgrims. Although the Second Nun also begins with a prayer to Mary, she does not imitate the Prioress's mother-child motif, for Cecilia is a nubile maiden, so that the appropriate juxtaposition in this tale is that of the maiden and her two bridegrooms, one human, the other divine. Hence the repeated references and invocations to Christ by name or periphrasis – 'Goddes Sone', 'Fadres Sone' – and to God Himself – 'The rightful Judge', 'the Kyng of grace' – which create a devotional tone akin to that of the Prioress, although the Nun's tale tends as much towards theological disquisition as towards narrative pathos.

It is in the 'tragedie' of Ugolino of Pisa that the Monk approaches closest to the narrative voices of the two nuns. He here shares with the Prioress the advantage of a compellingly pathetic story and he tells it with comparable economy of language and use of evocative diction:

> Thus day by day this child bigan to crye,
> Til in his fadres barm adoun it lay,
> And seyde, 'Farewell, fader, I moot dye!'
> And kiste his fader, and dyde the same day.
> And whan the woful fader deed it say,
> For wo his armes two he gan to byte,
> And seyde, 'Allas, Fortune, and weylaway!
> Thy false wheel my wo al may I wyte.'
>
> (*Monk's Tale*, 2439–46)

The same affecting tone is heard repeatedly in the two long stanzaic tales of suffering womankind, those of Constance and Griselda; for example, in the latter's tearful leave-taking of her child, part of the 'tormentynge' of this long-suffering wife and mother:

> And thus she seyde in hire benigne voys,
> 'Fareweel my child! I shal thee nevere see.
> But sith I thee have marked with the croys
> Of thilke Fader – blessed moote he be! –
> That for us deyde upon a croys of tree,
> Thy soule, litel child, I hym bitake,
> For this nyght shaltow dyen for my sake.'
>
> (*Clerk's Tale*, 554–60)

The formality of the stanza provides apt vehicle for the emotive diction. This is, for the most part, the essentially simple vocabulary of native stock which has ever been the hallmark of strong emotion in English. J .D .Burnley is right in referring to the Clerk's plain style, 'employing simple vocabulary, and exhibiting a marked sobriety in the use of rhetorical figures';[8] but I cannot agree with his view of Cecilia's speech in the *Second Nun's Tale*, that 'Chaucer loads it with polysyllabic words of Romance origin, and couches it in rhetorical phrasing'.[9] The theological arguments of the story certainly necessitate some learned words, although these cannot stand comparison with the ponderous diction to be found in the tales of our other group of clerical pilgrims. Nor is there any evidence of 'loading', as Burnley suggests. In fact, Cecilia's diction is more accurately represented by a passage like the following, with its homely image:

> 'Youre myght,' quod she, 'ful litel is to dreede,
> For every mortal mannes power nys
> But lyk a bladdre ful of wynd, ywys.
> For with a nedles poynt, whan it is blowe,
> May al the boost of it be leyd ful lowe.'
>
> (*Second Nun's Tale*, 437–41)

[8] *Chaucer's Language and the Philosophers' Tradition* (Cambridge, 1979), p .86.
[9] *ibid.*, p .84.

or by this stanza, with its strong appeal to the senses:

> 'Ther lakketh no thyng to thyne outter yën
> That thou n'art blynd; for thyng that we seen alle
> That it is stoon, – that men may wel espyen, –
> That ilke stoon a god thow wolt it calle.
> I rede thee, lat thyn hand upon it falle,
> And taste it wel, and stoon thou shalt it fynde,
> Syn that thou seest nat with thyne eyen blynde.'
> (Second Nun's Tale, 498–504)

The affecting nature of these stanzaic tales leaves little room for direct moralizing. If the Clerk is one who would 'gladly teche', it is certainly not by any overt didacticism, but rather by the direct impact of Griselda's undeserved sufferings, broken only occasionally by the narrator's critical comments that enough is enough:

> He hadde assayed hire ynogh bifore,
> And foond hire evere good; what neded it
> Hire for to tempte, and alwey moore and moore,
> Though som men preise it for a subtil wit?
> (Clerk's Tale, 456–9)

Even the conclusion of the *Clerk's Tale* refrains from overmuch moralizing, leading instead to a light-hearted envoy as the Clerk offers to 'lat us stynte of ernestful matere'. As for the Prioress's eagerness 'to ben holden digne of reverence', this relies as much on the simple dignity of her narration as upon the courtly manners and 'semely' deportment to which the General Prologue draws attention. Her tale, like that of the Second Nun, is sufficiently affecting to require no moralizing appendage. The Monk may have been 'provoked', as Russell says, 'into telling a tale of monumental solemnity by the mockery of the Host,' but once embarked on it, he proceeds to warn his listeners against putting their trust in blind prosperity by letting his 'ensamples trewe and olde' speak for themselves.

The similarities which link these tales into a recognizable group suggest a distinctive narrative genre, distinguished by the affecting nature of the narrative itself, sustained by a simple, emotive diction and a solemn, formal stanzaic structure, and characterized by an avoidance of overt moralizing or preaching. It is worthy of note that Chaucer's successors were by no means insensitive to these characteristics, and that similar tones can be heard in *The Kingis Quair* or in a stanza like this from Henryson's *Testament of Cresseid*:

> Quhen scho ouircome, with siching sair and sad,
> With mony cairfull cry and cald ochane:
> 'Now is my breist with stormie stoundis stad,
> Wrappit in wo, ane wretch full will of wane!'

Than fel in swoun full oft or euer scho fane,
And euer in hir swouning cryit scho thus,
'O fals Cresseid and trew knicht Troylus!'[10]

It is when listening to the second group of clerical voices that we detect notes of 'sermonyng', a fact which has prompted not a few critics to seek parallels and to establish links between Chaucer's more openly homiletic tales and medieval *artes praedicandi* as well as actual sermons. Charles E .Shain, for example, has asserted that 'no one will want to dissent from the generally held opinion that he (Chaucer) was steeped in the lore of pulpit rhetoric';[11] a theme developed more selectively in Susan Gallick's discussion of specific tales, based upon her premise that 'when a pilgrim adopts a certain theme, tone, and style of speaking, the audience reacts to him or her as a preacher.'[12] She here includes not only Pardoner, Nun's Priest, and Summoner, but also the Reeve's 'sermonyng' and the Wife of Bath's memorable performance as 'a noble prechour'. The note of irony which is detectable in such words and phrases probably owes a good deal to Chaucer's familiarity with contemporary sermons, not least those which condemned the clerical abuses which nourished his own satire. G .R .Owst notes Richard Fitzralph, archbishop of Armagh from 1348 to 1360, accusing prelates in his sermons of being fornicators, gluttons, plunderers, thieves, robbers, and men of merchandize – a tailor-made catalogue of Chaucer's own clerical rogues.[13] That the tales told by such dubious 'worthies' should be suffused with irony is a necessary concomitant of the satiric approach to the characters themselves. The very fact that they should be preaching at all is richly ironic, and Chaucer takes pains to sharpen the contrast between the 'sermonyng' clerics and the 'affecting' ones in several ways.

The metrical contrast is the most obvious one. The formal stanzas with their intricate rhyme patterns now give way to the steady onward movement of the decasyllabic lines arranged in couplets. There is no harking back to an earlier rhyme word as in rhyme royal, less scope for that lingering within the formal structure which makes for a more leisurely narrative pace. We thus come much closer to what must have been the conversational English of Chaucer's time:

'Nay, olde stot, that is nat myn entente,'
Quod this somonour, 'for to repente me
For any thyng that I have had of thee.
I wolde I hadde thy smok and every clooth!'
(*Friar's Tale*, 1630–33)

Although Chaucer generally pauses at the end of a line, there are countless

10 *Testament of Cresseid*, edited by Denton Fox (London, 1968), lines 540–46.
11 'Pulpit Rhetoric in Three Canterbury Tales', *Modern Language Notes*, 70 (1955), 235.
12 'A Look at Chaucer and His Preachers', *Speculum*, 50 (1975), 456.
13 G .R .Owst, *Literature and Pulpit in Medieval England*, 2nd edition (Oxford, 1961), pp .243–48.

instances where he does not, with the result that rhymes, once so important in the stanzaic verse, become less insistent and may even be thought to be lacking altogether:

> For whan I dar noon oother weyes debate,
> Thanne wol I stynge hym with my tonge smerte
> In prechyng, so that he shal nat asterte
> To been defamed falsly, if that he
> Hath trespased to my bretheren or to me.
>
> (Pardoner's Tale, 412–16)

The conversational flow of words in such passages fully justifies the comment by D.W.Robertson, Jr., that 'in the more accomplished passages of his later poetry Chaucer achieves an easy and conversational manner, spiced by the rhythms of vigorous speech. Neither Gower, who spreads relatively long and somewhat 'literary' sentences over many rhetorically unbroken octosyllabic lines, nor the alliterative poets, constrained by the regular emphasis of their heavily stressed verses, were capable of the free and rhetorically emphatic rhythms which Chaucer was thus able to produce.'[14] Chaucer's decasyllabic lines arranged in rhyming couplets allow a great diversity of moods and tones entirely suited to the characters of their speakers. The voices of Pardoner and Summoner's friar, the exemplars of this group, are sonorous one moment and wheedling the next; they range over the entire gamut of linguistic registers, from the Summoner's crudities and the Pardoner's oaths to the Nun's Priest's courtly rhetoric and all the technicalities of contemporary theological disquisition, often with a strong admixture of irony as in the Summoner's hypocritical friar's use of terms like 'misericorde', 'abstinence' and 'contemplaunce', or the nonce 'persecucioun'. The devotional references to God and Christ and the Virgin now become the body-tearing oaths of blasphemers, be they story-tellers themselves or characters in their tales. The sober and solemn mood gives way to worldly concerns with money and sex, and the diction becomes crude, often coarse, although there are of course passages of 'heigh style' as well, especially in the tales of those who knew how to 'wel affile' their tongues. Yet it would be wrong to conclude from the often conversational homiletic tone of Chaucer's 'noble prechours' that the sermons of his time were but impromptu effusions; on the contrary, as Siegfried Wenzel writes: 'The entire performance of the Pardoner, the tale of the Nun's Priest, and the speeches of the begging friar within the *Summoner's Tale* quite obviously reflect the professional training and activity of preachers'.[15] Reflections are but mirror images of reality, and Chaucer's sermonizing rogues, for all their homiletic postures, are not preaching authentic sermons, however much they may be copying their structural arrangement, scriptural echoes, *exempla*, imagery, and technical terminology.

---

[14] *A Preface to Chaucer* (Princeton, 1963), p. 278.
[15] 'Chaucer and the Language of Contemporary Preaching', *Studies in Philology*, 73 (1976), 138.

The tales of the second group of clerical pilgrims possess none of the evenness of homiletic tone that characterizes the *Parson's Tale*, nor do they sustain the statuesque solemnity of the stanzaic tales.

If Chaucer had wished any of his pilgrims to preach a genuine sermon, to which the *Parson's Tale* comes closest, there was nothing to prevent him, except the danger of courting the undesirable effects of preaching noted by some of the pilgrims, including himself in the *Tale of Melibee*, 1043:

> 'For soothly, he that precheth to hem that listen nat
> heeren his wordes, his sermon hem anoieth.'

Harry Bailly is even more outspoken:

> 'But precheth nat, as freres doon in Lente,
> To make us for oure olde synnes wepe,
> Ne that thy tale make us nat to slepe.'
>
> (*Clerk's Prologue*, 12–14)

The fact that Harry responds to the Monk's gloomy catalogue in similar terms does not, of course, brand the *Monk's Tale* a sermon. It is rather the monotony of misery that prompts the Knight to put an end to it and that makes the Host exclaim that 'Youre tale anoyeth al this compaignye' and assert that but for the Monk's bell-tinkling bridle he would long since have fallen asleep. Such reactions to boring harangues were not by any means original. St Ambrose had said that a dull sermon arouses anger, and in his *Liber quo ordine sermo fieri debeat* Guibert de Nogent had warned preachers against courting boredom. He had also, we might recall, offered much sound counsel on the proper use of pathos as part of the art of effective preaching. There are moments of pathos even in the Pardoner's racy tale, such as the old man's moving cry 'Leeve mooder, leet me in!', but the tone of pity is but a momentary intrusion into a story of greed and blasphemy and murder. The Pardoner and his ilk are more adept at 'saffroning' their 'predicacioun' by other means, be they snatches of Latin to impress the 'lewed' folk, or grandiloquent rhetorical figures, or lively *exempla*. It is most unlikely that anyone could have slept through the Pardoner's performance any more than through that of the Prioress, albeit for quite different reasons.

These two tales, the Pardoner's and the Prioress's, are the antipodes of Chaucer's clerical voices in verse. They demonstrate prosodically and stylistically the profound differences in tone and diction between the two groups of clerical pilgrims. The schema is of course not simply one of black and white: neither the Monk nor the Prioress is an idealized religious as the Parson is, nor are they as singlemindedly virtuous as Chaucer's Clerk; as for the Second Nun, we know her only through her story as a devout woman with a theological bent. The case is more straightforward with the others, birds of a feather, except perhaps for the Nun's Priest whom Harry Bailly may well be maligning and whose story, while certainly neither devotional nor affecting, conveys in its genial tone, diversity of interests, and gentle ironies aspects of character which may well have been Chaucer's own.

And yet Russell was right in gathering the 'stanzaic' clerics into one fold, for they share, as we have seen, a good deal more than their metrical kinship. As theirs are probably among Chaucer's earlier tales, as most critics have tended to assume, they display a narrative art largely innocent of irony, although no one would wish to dismiss them as mere apprentice work. The homely diction, the powerful emotional appeal of the suffering children and women are by no means artless. There is in these tales, on the contrary, a controlled use of language and of rhetorical colours as well as of the stanzaic metres that is capable of evoking powerful responses. Even Chaucer's later undisputed mastery of the decasyllabic couplet cannot erase the reader's haunting memory of the unmerited sufferings inflicted upon Constance and Griselda; of the little innocent Christian boy singing his way through the hostile 'Jewerye'; of the dying Cecilia staunchly continuing to preach the gospel of the true God; or of the sweet young 'briddes' starving in their cage at Pisa. What we find in the later tales is added bonus: the couplets' inexhaustible scope for narrative and stylistic variety; for discourse, human or gallinaceous, that has widened the range from the most 'gentil' to the unashamedly bawdy; for a moral tone which now embraces wit and humour, irony and satire.

But even as we revel and rejoice in Chaucer's mature masterpieces, of Pardoner and Nun's Priest, we need to remember that his genius for language did not have to wait for the decasyllabic couplet to give it voice. It is unmistakably present, in a different register and with different emotional appeal, in those earlier solemn tales with their own distinctive clerical voices. As this essay honours a distinguished medievalist whose work and insights have greatly enriched our understanding of the fourteenth century, it is appropriate that George Russell, speaking of the Prioress's verse should have the last word:

> Chaucer has given to the Prioress a verse which, in his best manner, is deceptively easy and simple, with a total control over a demanding rime scheme and a rhythmical pattern attuned to respond sensitively to the needs of the narration. Its use of language is unaffected and unobtrusive, deriving its hidden strength from the command of a series of words that are resonantly strong and evocative in his hands – *blisful, deere, sely, reverence*. Words like these recur through the poem and serve to remind us of the depth and the density of the verbal complex that the best late-fourteenth-century religious poetry in England has achieved. It embodies a mature management of language which enables the fullness and richness of a series of recurring words and phrases to suggest the depth and mystery which underlie this simple and otherwise merely pathetic story. Its success is intimately involved with this co-existence in its language of the apparently simple and that which is conceptually and emotionally rich and dense.[16]

[16] 'Chaucer: *The Prioress's Tale*, p. 226.

CHAUCER'S RELIGIOUS CANTERBURY TALES

Stephen Knight

This paper's title can be read in two ways: are there some tales which are religious, or is the whole *Tales* to be seen as an ultimately religious work? The evidence of the eighty-six manuscripts suggests that both views were held in the fifteenth century. Twenty of them are selections of notably religious or moral tales. Favourite narrators in these clerical digests are the Clerk and the Prioress, both occurring six times, and Chaucer himself with Melibee's five appearances. Man of Law, Monk and Parson are twice selected, and the Second Nun once.[1] Apart from indicating a substantial audience for a specifically Christian *Canterbury Tales*, this evidence suggests that modern critics who treat Melibee and the tales of the Prioress and Monk as inadequate or satirical offer a view not shared by devout fifteenth-century readers.

But other evidence implies that some early owners of the *Tales* found it possible to accommodate the entire text in a religious and moral context. Five of the complete or near-complete *Tales* are bound with religious material – and Ellesmere's addition of Chaucer's 'Truth' might put it close to that category. Nine other *Tales* were bound with Lydgate and one was coupled with Gower.[2]

Evidently, while there are isolable 'religious' tales, the *Tales* as a whole was seen as having a distinct religious impact. That conclusion, the sense of the title to be pursued in this paper, fits well with my recent work in studying the whole poem in terms of its relation to the history and society of its original period.[3] But the fit is not a simple one: the religious tales are not separable from the whole movement of the *Tales* and its relation to its sociohistorical matrix. The variously religious tales act as the medieval church acted, in a complex and dialectical way both as part of the ambient world and also providing a major interpretation and evaluation of that world.

The religious Canterbury tales are elements of the process by which through the mediations of art Chaucer realised the conflicts of his period, transmuting the dynamic forces of history and society into an artistic creation with such vigour and inherent power that it has both demanded and provided

---

[1] For this and following information about manuscripts, see *The Text of The Canterbury Tales*, edited by J.M.Manly and E.Rickert, 8 vols (Chicago, 1940), I.

[2] There is hardly a trace of an alternative 'secularising' reception, though one manuscript (Royal 17 D.XV) has the *Tales* bound with historical and political material, and one other (Harley 1239) makes what could be interpreted as a 'courtly' digest, copying only the tales of the Knight, Man of Law, Wife of Bath, Clerk and Franklin, and adding to them *Troilus and Criseyde*.

[3] See the forthcoming *Geoffrey Chaucer* in the *Re-Reading Literature* series, edited by T.Eagleton (Oxford, 1986).

continuous reinterpretations from the different and changing positions of later readers.

To see this process at work through the religious tales, it is first necessary to establish that the *Canterbury Tales* has a clear order and progress. This has seemed doubtful because of the startling variety of tale-order found in the manuscripts.[4] The problem has apparently been exacerbated by the widening recognition that the Hengwrt manuscript has a particularly accurate text, while its contents and order are markedly different from those of Ellesmere – the source of the text and order in the best-known modern editions. It has recently been argued that Hengwrt's order should be accepted as well as the text, and this would radically alter perceptions of the *Tales*.[5] But the case founders on weaknesses in Hengwrt's *ordonnance* evident through traditional methods of editorial scrutiny. The links provided (during the scribal process) in Hengwrt before both the Franklin's and the Merchant's tales are plainly spurious.[6] The distinctly unusual order thereabouts cannot stand as authoritative – and so doubt is cast on all of Hengwrt's other arrangements, including its lack of the Canon's Yeoman's tale. Hengwrt's structure must yield to the evidently authorial links which bind together the Ellesmere order in that area, and, by extension must yield to the order found there and elsewhere in Ellesmere and in the textually quite accurate group of manuscripts called *a* by editorial tradition, and also in several others of early date which are not textually affiliated to either Ellesmere or *a*, especially Harley 7335 and Bodley 686. These manuscripts and some others together comprise the A tale-order group; their order is taken in this paper to be authoritative.

A second methodological question would ask how to define the religious tales: are they just those told by clerics, regular and secular, or do they include tales by minor functionaries of the church such as Summoner and Canon's Yeoman – and might they also embrace moral tales by laymen like those included in the manuscripts that make a religious selection? The following discussion avoids a pre-emptive definition on this point and considers the varying roles of all those tales; they are all religious, but in differing degrees and directions.

In general, the role of all the tales with religious connections of any sort is only comprehensible through a grasp of the complex process of action and interaction between tales and across the *Tales* as a whole. When the tales are read in sequence and in an awareness of their sociohistorical relations, the varying character of the religious tales is seen to develop through a dominating quadripartite structure in the poem, which does not entirely mesh with traditional divisions of the *Tales* into 'fragments'. This structure might conveniently be sketched in as a preliminary to discussing the role of the religious tales in and through those patterns.

[4] See the tale-order charts in Manly and Rickert, II, pp .494–95.
[5] See the Introduction to N .F .Blake, *The Canterbury Tales* (London, 1980).
[6] For a discussion of this point see my review of Blake's edition in *Parergon*, 31 (1981), 31–36; a detailed rejection of Blake's opinions and a defence of the A group tale-order as 'Chaucer's final arrangement' is given by L .D .Benson, 'The Order of the Canterbury Tales', *Studies in the Age of Chaucer*, 3 (1981), 77–120.

In the *Tales* as a whole (and to be explicated in the later discussion) there are four major sequences representing Chaucer's varying engagement with the conflicts of his period. The first sequence runs from General Prologue to Man of Law's Tale and sets out the main lines of traditional social structure and the forces that press historically against it. In the second sequence, from Wife of Bath's tale through to Pardoner's tale, this dialectical complex is explored through narratives which project the inherent sociopolitical positions of particular pilgrims; this process operates with an extraordinary power that produces most of the tales thought to be inherently great – that is, the tales which have most successfully transmuted into art the apprehended dynamism of sociohistorical forces.

The complete Fragment VII or Group B², from Shipman's to Nun's Priest's tale, forms the third sequence, in which the tales are less ambitious and less potent, tending to fill out rather than project the General Prologue account of the pilgrim or to create in other ways a steady closing down of the historical imagination. With that process of withdrawal comes a developing rejection of art as a medium of social analysis. Finally, the last four tales create both the voice of the orthodox church in full power and also the concomitant rejections of secular conflict and art as its mediator. The journey from London to Canterbury, which fails to be the promised return trip, is both a way into and out of the turbulent social world of the fourteenth century.

The General Prologue opens with a famous and inherently religious passage that is curiously at odds with most of the poem which follows. It asserts with all the subliminal power of poetic art that the religious impulse in humans is as natural as the drive of birds to mate and of nature to revivify the world. An influential article speaks of the 'two voices' of this opening,[7] but it is the silence of a third voice that is most striking, because it is to dominate long sequences of the *Canterbury Tales* – the voice of human secular experience and conflict. That voice is dramatically raised during the whole General Prologue, including when those who belong in some way or other to the church are being described. Indeed the prologue is itself structured through that voice, since the groupings within it respond to types of work and social function. After the opening feudal group of the Knight's *familia*, the figures of the second group are regular religious. Secular over-emphasis makes them all deficient in terms of their clearly implied roles – Prioress in conscience, Monk in Augustinian rigour, Friar as mendicant preacher. The following group of pilgrims, from Merchant to Wife, are all socioeconomically self-supporting, not part of a feudal or religious commune; they live by the exercise of personal skills – they are professionals, in a word. Only the Clerk is to any degree religious, and his interest is scholarly not spiritual, however admirable he may appear. The Franklin belongs here because his position depends on legal and administrative skills, not birth or property, whatever his feudal aspirations might be; the Wife stands as a weaver, as has been clearly

[7] A.W.Hoffman, 'Chaucer's Prologue to Pilgrimage: The Two Voices', *ELH*, 21 (1954), 1–16, reprinted in *Chaucer: Modern Essays in Criticism*, edited by E.Wagenknecht (New York, 1959), pp.30–45.

expounded recently.[8] The fourth group is composed of non-independent workers, best seen as servitors of various kinds. The first sub-group fulfil their roles admirably and fraternally, Parson and Plowman (the parson must be serf-born to have a Plowman brother). Then follow role-abusing secular servitors, Miller, Manciple and Reeve, and last come those who exploit their positions deep in the institutionalised church, Summoner and Pardoner.

The Parson is unquestionably an admired figure, but the emphasis of his description is upon secular enactment of a spiritual duty: his is very much the active, not contemplative or prelatic life, and the voice of distinctly religious and spiritual feeling remains silent. So it does throughout the first fragment of tales. The Knight ends his story with Theseus's thoughtful and broadly speaking Christian speech; critics differ as to whether it plumbs the depths of divine order, or is at best a patched up *modus credendi*,[9] but neither it nor the tale has any spiritual range. That ghostly absence is starkly evident in the next tales, where both the narrative mode and its treatment of love develop the view of a society in material conflict. Nicholas, Alan and John are scholars and so in some sort of orders, but they value nothing beyond a sensually pleasing use of their sharp wits; other clerical officers, whether servile like Absolon or in full orders like the miller's father-in-law, have the same attitude without the secular grace of cunning or success. The Cook's tale is a positive sump of urban artisan sensuality and there, for most critics, the fragment ends – never very religious at all and moving dramatically away from any sense of Christian morality.

Yet the tale which consistently follows in the A tale-order group is to some degree religious and should be seen as a relief and containment of the preceding godless social conflict. The Man of Law's tale has normally been treated as a puzzling precursor to the long sequence beginning with the Wife of Bath's tale – its enigmatic endlink has intrigued scholars so much that they have only looked after it for connections. But the evidence is that no sure link was ever constructed at an early stage (the neat idea of linking the tale to the Shipman's is an editorial brainwave revealed in the late Selden MS). The tale's relations are strong with its predecessors (a point Kolve has recently made with some weight[10]). The Man of Law's tale establishes both secular Christian morality and conservative political order together. It advocates constancy, a value very close to Langland's 'patient poverty' and notable for its absence in the previous churlish tales; by making a queen its subject, the tale reverts to the aristocratic register subverted by the Miller in his literary peasant's revolt.

---

[8] D.W.Robertson discusses the historicity of the Wife and her work in '"And for my land thus hastow mordred me?": Land Tenure, the Cloth Industry and the Wife of Bath', *Chaucer Review*, 14 (1980), 403–20.

[9] For the positive view, see Charles Muscatine, *Chaucer and the French Tradition* (Berkeley, 1957), pp.189–90; on the negative side are E.Salter, *The Knight's Tale and the Clerk's Tale* (London, 1962), pp.31–32, and David Aers, *Chaucer, Langland and the Creative Imagination* (London, 1980), p.187.

[10] V.A.Kolve, *Chaucer and the Imagery of Narrative* (London, 1984), Ch.5.

But the Man of Law was not religious in the General Prologue, and his tale has a mercantile taint in its opening (122–33); his version of moral order achieves no control over the surging forces of the *Tales*; quite the reverse, in fact, as the second major sequence follows his tale, distinct from the first in that it works not by viewing society in conflict but by projecting the inherent positioning of the narrators in remarkably powerful and historic ways which can either be traditional or distinctly radical. The Wife of Bath is a potent anti-Constance, in no way royal, patient, or passively feminine. A small businesswoman of a sharply credible kind, she disrupts both masculine and clerical hegemony with her prologue which begins like a 'quasi-Lollard sermon'[11] then develops steadily into a quite remarkably individualised account of one woman's claim to authority, both intellectual and personal, through the medium of human experience. Subverting as she does the wisdom of the antifeminist fathers and the authority of her husband, she is also seen as a threat by those clerical highwaymen, Pardoner and Friar: she is not the sort of woman they like to encounter because her money will not be prised away by religiose melodrama nor by personal flattery.

Her tale is far from being the simple wish-fulfilment of an 'essential' woman, as modern criticism from Kittredge has preferred to imagine; it is, rather, a realignment of the 'fairy mistress' structure to give that figure of masculine wish-fulfilment new authority in both religious and social terms: 'gentillesse' in her account is as inherently anti-feudal as were her own business practices.

After her onslaught on men and the church among other aspects of power, it would not be surprising for the voice of religion to be heard. And so it is, but with depressing depravity, as Friar and Summoner wrestle in their chosen slough of financial obsession and vicious competition. The Clerk's tale which follows is an essentially secular and moral response to what he identifies ultimately as disorder induced by the Wife. In this respect the Clerk fills a role not unlike that of the Man of Law, but as he is closer to being a true religious, so the Clerk's moralism is more potently conservative, more explicitly Christian and finally more discomforted by the threat he attempts to contain. His tale fulfils a double role, realising a lucid and responsible voice for a man connected with the church, so containing the worst implications of the previous two tales, and also countering the Wife of Bath by imposing the virtues of patience and political quiescence through the medium of a classical story and a nerveless heroine. The brief final raising of the story to the tropological level suggests that Griselda represents the Christian soul and Walter figures forth Christ himself, but this seems no more than a gesture towards a world of fully religious values, effectively swamped as it is by the *envoi* which in its riot of irony, rhetoric and conscious controversy, returns the tale to the conflicted world where the Wife established her challenge to authority.

The clerical secular moralist can do no more than make his voice heard in

11 See Robertson, 'And for my land', 415.

the hubbub; he is restricted both by the force of the disorder and his own basically secular positioning, his lack of a sacerdotal or spiritual terrain on which to argue. Neither Host nor Merchant make more of his tale than a stimulus for their own distinctly personal and conflictive concerns. The Merchant's tale projects the reification of personal relations with brilliant venom and shows how the finest structures of courtly culture, such an important element of aristocratic and feudal hegemony, are, in a world of mercantile values, no more than top-dressing. The Squire's tale itself accepts those cultural values as an absolute (which his father did not) and seems a deliberately overblown construction which falters of its own inauthenticity and inertia.

The Franklin, who comments on the Squire's tale, if not precisely interrupting it, is another of the conservative moralists who come from the professional group of pilgrims, where his work-skills place him, though his aspirations shape his tale as the work of an aristocratic ideologue. Like the bulk of the romances,[12] it creates various threats for male aristocratic patriarchy and resolves them through a complex set of imposed imitations of traditional conservatism by husband, lover and the distinctly professional scholar (who is the actual agent of the most disturbing forces of threat). But these firm assertions of feudal security and general social acceptance of Arveragus' moral leadership all stand on nothing more secure than the Franklin's own self-interested fascination with social mobility and the possibilities of an unhierarchical set of evaluations.[13] The tale is hardly the sonorous ending to a 'marriage group' that Kittredge dreamed into being as part of his humanistic and novelistic re-reading of the *Tales*; after all, the tale is based both on a quizzically treated piece of aristocratic ideology and also on a marriage that, for all the protestations of mutuality (by critics more than by Chaucer), must adopt an authoritarian structure to survive.

Nor, if the consistent pattern of the A tale-order group and the inherent dynamic of this sequence of the tales is to be taken into account, is the Franklin's tale even the end of a group. Physician and Pardoner always come next in the A tale-order group and they continue the realisation of an increasingly feeble secular conservatism and an increasingly powerful disruption. The Physician's tale is another classical moral fable from a 'professional' but it has never been found particularly convincing. Nor is it, but not because it is a weak tale or a deliberate parody, the normal ahistorical critical responses. It starts with a rather strained harangue urging the control of daughters, that central anxiety of patriarchal families, found in ballad, folk-tale, romance and novel; then follows a distinctly drastic story about how one man resolved the threat made by the legal process through a churl to his own family's future.

Throughout the medieval period a man with only a daughter had reason to fear the loss of his familial property as well as his name, and the combined

---

12 This pattern is discussed in my forthcoming essay, 'The Social Function of the Middle English Romances', in *Re-Reading Medieval Literature*, edited by David Aers (Brighton, 1986).
13 For a fuller discussion, see my article, 'Ideology in *The Franklin's Tale*', *Parergon*, 28 (1980), 3–35.

threat of legal trickery and churlish pressure realises contemporary anxiety more vividly than the hygienised and readily solvable problems of the Franklin's tale. The Physician's tale combines the voice of the Miller with the legally empowered ascent of the Franklin himself – and the prologue's description of a Manciple alluded to the real and encroaching power of lawyers over the aristocracy in the period (576–85).

Against such a complex of vivid forces, the tale's constrained tone and spare realisation seem themselves part of a containment. There is certainly no ready narrative solution to such pressure, as there was none in sociohistorical reality. When Virginius beheads his daughter and the 'people' all concur, the text offers an incredible and desperate remedy to the impingement on feudal stasis of new forces which were increasingly powerful in the contemporary world, which were the dynamic of the disorder that the tales so far had in varying degrees recognised, and against which the conservative tales had offered a decreasingly effective opposition and containment.

The Pardoner's tale which follows is no more than the most powerful and thoroughly imagined projection of disruptive forces. It is blatantly individualistic, explicitly cash-obsessed, insidiously anti-conservative in its mastery of rhetorical and ecclesiastical techniques of persuasion and – as its confessional prologue and highly dramatic ending make clear – deeply revolutionary in clerical, economic and ontological terms. The only containment that is offered other than moral disgust and promises of hell-fire, is the Pardoner's sexual peculiarity, which is planted in the General Prologue and reaped by the crude instrument of the Host. This is not medieval intolerance, nor yet deep-laid religious allegory (though both have been suggested): it is rather a somewhat overstrained projection of the medieval use-economy commonplace insisting that cash dealing was sterile; it should have no progeny in the form of profit on capital. The exchange economy, this and similar images urgently state, was unnatural and without future. Chaucer develops this banal defensive notion with the imagination of the great artist into the Pardoner's individualist vanity and mysterious, off-putting lack of normal masculinity.

This ends the sequence of tales from which most of the famous and much-read *Canterbury Tales* have come, a series in which Chaucer has demonstrated the great artist's power to make dynamic through the medium of art the historical and social forces of the contemporary world. He has also indicated his personal positioning in the consistent attempt to construct a conservative opposition to those tales but, still a historically veracious artist, has not found in the world of the secular and professionally employed moralists any solid ground on which to oppose and contain those forces. No specifically religious voice has been heard yet, through the limitations of the professionals (including the Clerk) and the dereliction of the Summoner and the Friar.

As if in response to the disruptive power of the work so far, Chaucer creates in the third major sequence of the *Tales* a set of narratives which are distinctly less ambitious in their projections and so less disruptive sociohistorically. They tend both towards a rejection of the means of art itself (which has produced the power of the preceding two groups) and also towards the beginnings, at least, of another voice, that of religious feeling and so of an alternative ground on which to work, believe and find peace. The Shipman's tale is a muted re-creation of the monetary, sexual and anti-clerical themes already presented. The world of commodity values is realised, but without the uncontrollable dynamism found in the Miller, the Wife of Bath, the Merchant and the Pardoner. By any other artist it would be a masterpiece, but by Chaucer's demonstrated standards it is quiescent, resolving in a neat, vulgar pun on 'tailling' rather than in visions of a shattered feudal and Christian social contract.

The Prioress's tale operates against the Shipman's tale, and establishes for the first time the voice of religious feeling, making available the impact of liturgical writing and of a distinct, if limited, sense of spirituality. Schoeck's 'anti-semitic' reading of the tale has vivid twentieth-century bases, but other scholars have shown that the tale stands in its own right as a small gem of affective religion, a force which in the period was itself historically dynamic, as is indicated by the growth of mysticism and *devotio moderna*.[14] The Prioress's tale certainly has limits: it is much closer to the teller's General Prologue description than are the searching projections of the previous sequence of tales, and its religious sense is no more than affective and, for a prioress, close to infantile. But it does deal in categories not heard before, apart from a brief and overshadowed gesture by the Clerk at the end of his tale. The power of Mary and her name, the innate devotion of an innocent, the possibility of force quite at odds with secular normality – these are all introduced, through however restricted and even frail a vessel. They will be empowered by sterner figures of religion in the last group of tales.

In this context, though, the Prioress's tale has the immediate impact of an under-dynamised, though not parodic, version of a child martyr story, and is therefore part of the literary self-consciousness and self-limitation that permeates this group. That force is immediately made prominent as the author-pilgrim himself produces a magisterial pastiche of Middle English romances as they appeared to a writer of European and philosophical sophistication. But there is more than literary self-definition at work here; the Host's words 'thou shalt no lenger ryme' have both immediate and distant reverberations. Chaucer in response tells the first of the prose tales: yet another classical moral tale from one who, rightly, would be in the professional group of pilgrims. But this time the tale is not limited in effect either by its positioning or its inherent characteristics. If read with care in its sociohistorical context, the tale of Melibee is evidently a carefully composed

---

[14] R.J.Schoeck, 'Chaucer's Prioress: Mercy and Tender Heart', *The Bridge: Yearbook of Judaeo-Christian Studies*, 2 (1956), 239–55, reprinted in *Chaucer Criticism*, edited by R.J.Schoeck and J.Taylor, 2 vols (Notre Dame, 1960), I, pp.245–58. The other view is put most forcefully by G.H.Russell, 'Chaucer: *The Prioress's Tale*', in *Medieval Literature and Civilization: Studies in Memory of G.N.Garmonsway*, edited by D.A.Pearsall and R.A.Waldron (London, 1969), pp.211–70, and John C.Hirsh, 'Reopening the *Prioress's Tale*', *Chaucer Review*, 10 (1975), 30–45.

piece of advice on how to respond to dramatic social disorder. It speaks to the English aristocracy of the 1380s, recommending neither total repression nor total despair in the wake of the political incursions and crises of that period, especially the events of 1381, but offering a response based on the prudence of the powerful, not some notional patience of the powerless, and on a carefully moderated mixture of authority and tolerance. This tale also finally shifts its ground into religion, but lacks any equivalent of the Clerk's countertonal *envoi*, and rather suggests that the lineaments of religion are, as the tale's sermon-like structure suggests, concordant with this powerful and intensely practical piece of secular containment of anti-aristocratic activity.

The tales that follow give an increasing voice to religion and religious speakers, but their full authority is deferred in favour of more intellectual ground-clearing. The Monk is interrupted; his series of tragedies has an unsubtle quality, a lack of applicability to the modern world made evident by its location after Melibee, its banal repetitiveness and the distinct implication in the opening that the whole thing is learned by heart. This unconsidered application of Benedictine tradition is not so much a gibe at Lydgate as a statement, like the Prioress's, of another distinctly limited religious position, another genre to be realised and shortly surpassed. But religious forms that fall short of adequacy are not all, and not the most central, of the literary modes to be dismissed as of no lasting value.

Rejections of a much more wide-ranging character are the essence of the Nun's Priest's tale. The fact that he, Second Nun, Canon and his Yeoman are characters presented in no detail or not at all in the General Prologue indicates that a change of plan at this stage led Chaucer to introduce some more religious story tellers. The Nun's Priest's tale, however, is not so much a work of religion as a thorough clearing of the secular ground in terms of the literary and scholarly terrain on which this group has basically operated, though the author lets his own Melibee stand without assault from the detemporalising priest.

The first manoeuvre is to create a figure of real peasant patience, a 'povre wydwe', and from the culturally indigestible names of food she eschews the tale moves through a whole series of intellectual and cultural complexities, finding them all comical or inadequate in one way or another. Dreams, courtly culture, astrology, philosophical speculations, rhetoric, these are the major casualties of the Nun's Priest's light but biting wit, and they are of course major structural forces in Chaucer's own work. It is in the context of such drastic rejections that the author is able to phrase his only direct reference to the Peasants' Revolt, a phenomenon and a force that has underlain so much of the earlier disruptive material, and is now exorcised by clerical skill. The final moral, offered by the priest as his allegorical 'fruyt', is no more than judicious silence and watchfulness. A priest performs the fullest and the most effective piece of containment in the whole poem so far, but Chaucer's art assists his power. It is only because the range and impact of the previous tales is so carefully reduced that this piece of literary quietism can seem so effective and even, to suggest its incorporation of the values of Melibee, ultimately both prosaic and prudential.

The fourth major sequence of tales, consistently gathered together in the A tale-order manuscripts, both exploits and reproduces the position arrived at so far. The Second Nun's tale is, as has been widely recognised, a religious genre offered in full power and with inescapable authority. It develops the affective piety of the Prioress's tale into a weapon of a dynamic church; faith and works are a condensed instrument of a determined and busy saint. Using the poetic power of the rhyme royal in a much fuller register than the rather dilute lyricism of the Prioress, unflinchingly grasping the nettles of celibacy and martyrdom, here the *Tales* erects its first strong structure of the Christian religion.

Against this, the Canon's Yeoman's tale is no more than a *rechaufé* of the themes of clerical greed and misapplied skills; indeed it draws into itself the themes of mercantile values and the mode of urban realism, both previously so disruptive. As has been observed,[15] the tale itself is not dynamic, but a tame restatement of the themes established in its prologue. This lack of a developmental, non-Gothic narrative mode and the actual silence of the Canon himself are formal elements of the containment performed implicitly by this deliberatively negative tale.

Such negativity is taken a stage further in the Manciple's tale. In its headlink the final motif of secular conflict between Cook and Manciple sounds again in *diminuendo* the potent drama of the first two sequences, but this comes to nothing – determinedly and consciously to nothing. The voice of the crow who told too much truth may be taken as a symbol of the poet who created so much, and so much disorderly reality as well. Though the headlink offers an insubordinate flutter of the old disruptive mode, the tale narrates in rather automatic verse and then states overtly in obsessive and even liturgical repetition the need for silence, for a state of patient intellectual poverty. An absence of art is all this tale finally offers, a Chaucerian rejection of poetic in the crisis of realising what a truly historicised poetry can produce.

Now the Parson can speak, as the pilgrims arrive at Canterbury and the aura of the place is invoked. The road from London curves down from Harbledown and the cathedral suddenly comes into view, presenting directly its western front. As Chaucer sets the scene, the Caen stone catches the late afternoon spring sunshine, and as it still does, it would shimmer with pale golden light. Regular travellers to Dover and Sandwich like Chaucer and his friends could hardly have missed the sight or its anagogical implication: here is the imagistic setting for the words that redirect this pilgrimage to celestial Jerusalem.

The Parson fulfils the religious impulse that was asserted through nature in the opening lines of the poem and brings forward his primary religious function, which was overlaid in the social concerns of the General Prologue. The second prose tale of the *Tales* rejects all poetry and unlike Melibee develops wisdom beyond secular limits. The Parson's tale is a firm, thoughtful

---

[15] For a survey, see P .Brown, 'Is the *Canon's Yeoman's Tale* Apocryphal?', *English Studies*, 64 (1983), 481–90.

and above all readily accessible account of the necessary details of Christian confession; a steady and confident path through secular and personal chaos is outlined – just like that the pilgrims are now taking. Although the cathedral is ahead as the traveller leaves Harbledown, not even the modern road goes directly there. Before the Canterbury moat became a ring road the approach was even more circuitous. The pilgrims turned north away from their view of the cathedral, along the Stour and down into the dismal suburbs of the city, then across the river through the austere still-standing West Gate and the narrow hubbub of Canterbury's business area. Only then, as they turned up Butchery Lane or Mercery Lane would the cathedral and its peaceful close come within reach.

The Parson's tale ends with a sonorous paragraph that promises relief from all the confusions of medieval butchery and mercantilism; it is the full establishment in the tales of a religious voice that has subsumed all pastoral and secular attempts to control such disorder, and that brings to a head Chaucer's creation of and ultimate withdrawal from a sociohistorical veracity. That withdrawal was not itself unhistorical, of course. Chaucer's own circle contained 'Lollard knights', whose wills speak in austere, even strained language of the need to avoid all the disastrous entanglements of a secular world.[16] Chaucer's poem has itself predicated the need for withdrawal by presenting unsuccessful attempts to impose moral order by professional men on a world of flux in which they were themselves agents of change.

There are religious of all sorts in the *Tales*, and religious tales from low to high. That the *Tales* as a whole is finally religious is evident, and the opening lines predict that. The Retractions indicate that even so, there was a residual strain, a feeling that what had been produced did not really tend so easily towards Canterbury or Jerusalem. The presence, absence, degradations and sublimities of the various religious pilgrims and tales are a series of markers to the depth, the range, the veracious and ultimately disturbing power of Chaucer's historical imagination.

---

[16] See K.B.MacFarlane, *Lancastrian Kings and Lollard Knights* (Oxford, 1972).

'TAKING KEEP' OF THE 'BOOK OF THE DUCHESS'

Andrew Lynch

Charles Muscatine first popularized in Chaucer criticism the idea of 'Gothic form'. His quotation from Arnold Hauser serves as a useful definition:

> The basic form of Gothic art is juxtaposition. Whether the individual work is made up of several comparatively independent parts, or is not analyzable into such parts, ... it is always the principle of expansion and not of concentration, of co-ordination and not of subordination, of the open sequence and not of the closed geometric form, by which it is dominated.[1]

Muscatine goes on to speak himself of 'the co-ordinateness and linearity of Chaucer's form, with its various juxtaposed versions of experience.'[2] Such descriptions have an obvious application to framed collections of stories, such as the *Canterbury Tales* and, to a lesser extent, the *Legend of Good Women*. Even in poems with no clear formal divisions of the narrative, such as the *Parliament of Fowls* and the *Book of the Duchess*, a linear series of discrete episodes and descriptive foci can be identified, some established by changes in 'matere', others by shifts in narrative viewpoint, rhetorical style, or registers of vocabulary.

So, in the *Book of the Duchess*, the narrative seems divided into the following broad sections:

1. The narrator's self-description and preoccupation with sleep (1–43)
2. His reading of Ovid's story of Ceyx and Alcyone, followed by his prayer to Juno and Morpheus (44–290)
3. The ensuing dream, comprising these sub-sections:
   (i) descriptions of the weather, bird-song and decoration in the dreamer's chamber (291–343)
   (ii) a hunt (344–386)
   (iii) a walk through the spring landscape into the woods, until the sorrowful Man in Black is encountered (387–513)
   (iv) a series of conversations between the dreamer and this Man in Black:
   a. the narrator greets him and offers help (514–557)

---

[1] Arnold Hauser, *The Social History of Art*, translated by Stanley Godman (New York, 1952), I, pp .272–73, quoted in Charles Muscatine, *Chaucer and the French Tradition* (Berkeley and Los Angeles, 1957), pp .167–68.

[2] Muscatine, *Chaucer and the French Tradition*, p .168. His view is cited approvingly in Robert M .Jordan's influential *Chaucer and the Shape of Creation* (Cambridge, Mass., 1967), p .148.

b. the Man in Black denies that he can be helped, explaining that he is the victim of Fortune, who has stolen his queen (558–709)

c. rejecting further attempts at consolation, the Man in Black describes this lost woman, White, and praises her many virtues (710–1125)

d. in answer to further questions, the Man in Black describes the course of his long love for White, his final acceptance by her, and their happiness together, revealing in the end that she is dead, at which moment the dream ends (1126–1313)

4. In a short coda, the narrator describes his reawakening and subsequent decision to put his dream into verse (1314–1334).

Fragmented as the poem appears in this view of its narrative outline, it is even more divided as a piece of rhetoric by the introduction of many digressions and purple passages.[3] One sees readily why J.A.Burrow considers the *Book of the Duchess* a prime example of 'Ricardian' verse narrative form, that is, 'a ... sharply and dramatically articulated structure, with the constituent parts marked off and enclosed.'[4]

Not surprisingly, criticism of such a text has usually meant the attempt to connect its various segments in a unifying interpretation. The very lack of explicit connections within the poem has been taken by its modern readers as a challenge to supply them, and in that task several apparently connective features of the narrative and its presentation have been appealed to, especially these four. First, the narrator's helplessly disoriented and imperceptive state in the poem's beginning seems reflected and thematically resumed in the Ceyx and Alcyone story and in the description of the Man in Black. Secondly, many images provided by the Ceyx and Alcyone story are, as Stephanie Hollis says 'confusedly refracted by the dream in various guises and disguises'.[5] Thirdly, within the dream, the Emperor Octovyen's hunt for the 'hert' seems parallelled with the dreamer's attempt to 'ease' the Man in Black's 'hert', and their end is simultaneous, on the explanation that White is dead. Finally, when the narrator reawakens, he finds his Ovid still firmly in his hand, as if to suggest a close connection between book and dream.[6]

In short, although the text occurs in a sharply segmented, linear form, the four features mentioned above, together with Chaucer's teasingly abrupt signing-off – 'This was my sweven, now hit ys doon' – return readers to the beginning, as Burrow observes,[7] in an attempt to break down the text's reticence and lack of explicit controlling connections by constructing unifying patterns out of situational, thematic and verbal cross-references.

---

[3] For example, the description of the Cave of Sleep (153–77); the Man in Black's tirade against Fortune (598–709); the list of exempla in 1052–87; the episode of the Man in Black's 'firste song' (1155–82). All line references are to Robinson's second edition.

[4] *Ricardian Poetry* (London, 1971), p.63.

[5] 'The Ceyx and Alcyone Story in *The Book of the Duchess*', *Parergon*, 19 (1977), 3.

[6] The connection between book and dream is Chaucer's addition to the dream-vision genre. See M.W.Stearns, 'Chaucer Mentions a Book', *Modern Language Notes*, 57 (1952), 28–31.

[7] *Ricardian Poetry*, p.65.

As the wide range of critical interpretations of the *Book of the Duchess* shows us, it is not difficult to make such patterns. The problem lies rather in finding some way of controlling the process. J .I .Wimsatt applies E .D . Hirsch's term 'the hermeneutic circle' to describe this difficulty: 'We move from the parts to the whole, then back to the parts, with no resolution.'[8] One could state matters in another way by saying that critics have set themselves the task of privileging or subordinating a set of impressions juxtaposed in linear form without a readily apparent controlling order.

This interesting task of subordination has been approached in various ways, but very largely through attempts to establish a controlling irony in the narrative, usually coupled with an appeal to notions of genre. By these means, the narrator's apparent failure to understand his experiences – both his reading of Ovid and his dream – can be understood to make him the victim of an irony that privileges the elevated sorrow of Alcyone and the Man in Black, and permits a corrective instruction in the virtues embodied in White, and hence in the significance of her 'loss'. Generically, the poem is thus an elegy for Blanche of Lancaster, under the influence of the French dream-poems of love to which it bears some similarities. On the other hand, the genre can be seen as Boethian consolation, in which the narrator functions as a therapist, easing the Man in Black's heart by drawing him out of a hopeless posture of grief, and, by permitting an examination of White's moral virtues, endorsing for the audience a rational-cum-Christian view to which Alcyone's grief, and the Man in Black's, are subordinated as wrong-headed. This position also allows critics, by means of typological reference, to privilege a thoroughly 'spiritual' reading of the text as an instruction in divine love over a literalism caught up in worldly pleasures and sorrows. Generically, the poem becomes an elegy subsumed by a spiritual vision.[9]

Typological readings, of which J .I .Wimsatt's are the best and best-known,[10] need separate consideration, for they claim to give the vexing questions of coherence and genre a full resolution. Wimsatt first concluded that the poem's celebration of Blanche as a type of Mary effectively displaced grief at her death, becauce Blanche was already enjoying her reward in Heaven. His later article develops this approach in a more subtle way, suggesting that the *Song of Solomon* was 'Chaucer's model for a composition with separate and simultaneous secular and religious interpretations ... The *Book of the Duchess* carries meaning as a topical love poem of the complaint-and-comfort type, and also as a spiritual vision like *Pearl* and Dante's Eden cantos.'[11]

[8] James I .Wimsatt, '*The Book of the Duchess*: Secular Elegy or Religious Vision?', in *Signs and Symbols in Chaucer's Poetry*, edited by J .P .Hermann and J .J .Burke (Alabama, 1981), p .115. The quotation from Hirsch is taken from *Validity in Interpretation* (New Haven, 1967), p .76.
[9] Wimsatt, p .128.
[10] Wimsatt, pp .113–29, and his 'Apotheosis of Blanche in *The Book of the Duchess*', *JEGP*, 56 (1967), 26–44.
[11] Wimsatt, p .127.

Despite the dual approach of his later critique, Wimsatt's conception of genre as the key to the *Book of the Duchess* ultimately remains single, and his two genres co-exist peacefully. The secular poem is questionably accounted for in terms of B .H .Bronson's well-known thesis, in which the Man in Black is led to 'resignation and human acceptance of life and death'.[12] The spiritual poem discovers, on the one hand, the 'desperate' state of the Man in Black's soul 'and of all souls in a world that seems cut off from grace'.[13] On the other hand there is a 'celebration' of 'the heavenly status of Blanche's soul'.[14] In effect, Wimsatt bridges the gap between his two genres by his explication of the spiritual sense, concluding that the poem 'instructs' the dreamer, and by implication the perceptive reader, 'in the nature of the paradisal and heavenly', as Dante and the Pearl-dreamer are instructed.[15] The dominant sense of the text, as Wimsatt's kernel-and-nut method ensures, is found to be a Christian message that *characterizes* in a familiar way the Man in Black and the dreamer as, respectively, despairing and ignorant in the eyes of a privileged reader. To this extent, Wimsatt's apparent openness to disjunction and variety in the text is deceptive; his major perceptions display a hierarchical view of various possible meanings that disallows conflict and subordinates differing perceptions in the manner of the other critical strategies outlined above, with which Wimsatt's may fairly be included.

I do not have space to outline in detail here the many variant and hybrid forms of all these views. (Joerg O .Fichte's *Chaucer's 'Art Poetical'* provides a good recent survey.)[16] Instead, I wish to draw attention to, and call in question, two features which these common critical approaches to the poem share: (i) the belief that the text permits and encourages an understanding of synthesis between the various elements of the 'matere' – waking, reading, dreaming and reawakening; (ii) the belief that through irony and/or an appeal to genre, a reader can unify the poem by hierarchically opposing to perceived states of misunderstanding, failed communication or personal imbalance, correct models that the text makes accessible. I shall argue instead that this poem stoutly maintains a more than superficial disjunctiveness by stressing both the lack of communion between different states of being, even within the one supposed 'character', and an all but complete failure of communication between individuals. Its sharply articulated yet cross-referencing form is, I shall argue, a model for its view of life: one in which differing states or apprehensions of being may be contiguous or have confused dealings, but never effectively interpenetrate and resist all synthesis. Ironic perceptions of misunderstanding in the poem do not privilege any other views. Critical appeals to the poem's genre are subverted by its emphasis on the arbitrariness of decisions about 'kind', whether in life or literature. Finally, though the *Book of the Duchess* does suggest an ideal of perfect wholeness and communion, it goes on to tell us that the ideal is lost.

12 'The *Book of the Duchess* Re-Opened', *PMLA*, 67, (1952), 881.
13 Wimsatt, p .128.
14 Wimsatt, p .128.
15 Wimsatt, p .128.
16 *Chaucer's 'Art Poetical': A Study in Chaucerian Poetics* (Tübingen, 1980).

II

The poem begins with a statement by its fictional narrator that he cannot concentrate on anything, or even distinguish between opposed conditions:

> I have gret wonder, be this lyght,
> How that I lyve, for day ne nyght
> I may nat slepe wel nygh noght;
> I have so many an ydel thoght,
> Purely for defaute of slep,
> That, by my trouthe, I take no kep
> Of nothing, how hyt cometh or gooth,
> Ne me nys nothyng leef nor looth.
> Al is ylyche good to me –
> Joye or sorowe, wherso hyt be –
> For I have felynge in nothyng.
>
> (1–11)

The phrase 'take kep', used here for the first of several times in the text, appears to mean 'listen' or 'observe carefully'.[17] In Chaucer's usage, not to 'take keep' of something is not to listen to it, or not to note it attentively, either through lack of interest, or insensitivity, or both. The Shipman, for instance, 'took no keep' of the promptings of 'nice conscience', both in the sense that he cared little for the idea, and because his heart was hardened by greed.[18] It is notorious that the narrator of the *Book of the Duchess*, obsessed with and weakened by his lack of sleep, subordinates both his actions and his narrative to that preoccupation, which he calls 'our first mater' (43; 218). The story is told in an apparently distorted manner, and it is tempting to oppose to its quirky narrative emphases and failure to connect impressions some synthesis of what is related. And yet, a perception of the narrator's failure to 'take keep' does not necessarily privilege strategies of our own. Indeed, by providing this unlikely person to tell the tale, interposing him between ourselves and its supposedly 'true' meaning, the text emphasises the unreliability of utterance and the difficulties of reading in general. The lines of communication between experience, narrator, text and audience are exposed as extremely fragile. Beyond the question of an unreliable narrator conceived of as a single character, the poem's pre-dream section introduces and sustains a general interest in the difficulty of 'taking keep' of, let alone 'understanding', experience; I shall try to sketch its operation in the text.

First of all, we observe a lack of communication between the waking and sleeping states, between the narrator's 'wonderful', 'ynly swete' dream (276–77) and his waking life. The gloomy introduction is in the present tense,

---

[17] See *A Chaucer Glossary*, edited by Norman Davis, *et al.* (Oxford, 1979), *ke(e)pe(n)*, n.

[18] *General Prologue*, 398.

showing no influence from the 'sweet' dream, whilst at the poem's end, the dream is referred to only as 'queynt', a luke-warm term of aesthetic appreciation. Neither state, waking or sleeping, has more than a limited and confused access to the other. To be awake is to lose one's grip on sleeping experience, and vice versa. A consequence of this is that the wonderful dream is not understandable:

> Me mette so ynly swete a sweven,
> So wonderful, that never yit
> Y trowe no man had the wyt
> To konne wel my sweven rede;
> No, not Joseph, withoute drede,
> Of Egipte, he that redde so
> The kynges metynge Pharao,
> No more than koude the lest of us;
> Ne nat skarsly Macrobeus,
> (He that wrot al th'avysyoun
> That he mette, kyng Scipioun,
> The noble man, the Affrikan, –
> Suche marvayles fortuned than)
> I trowe, arede my dremes even.
>
> (276–89)

No one, not even Joseph or Macrobius, could interpret the dream, says the narrator, and one might be tempted to apply his comment on the dream within the narrative to the 'sweven' as poem (290; 1330–334). Of course, the disclaimer can be, and always is, seen as a form of 'outdoing' comparison, expressing the marvellous nature of the dream/poem and almost patently encouraging interpretation. There may be good reasons, however, for reading it more literally, perhaps as a joke at the expense of Macrobian confidence. The narrative distinguishes in an interesting way between the 'sweet', 'wonderful' *experience* of the dream and *interpretations* (readings) of its utterance, between the existential and the aesthetic, as David Aers puts it.[19] It is *because* the dream/poem is so sweet and wonderful that it cannot be 'read'. It can be experienced ('taken keep of') but the experience is resistant to discourse, just as the vivid dream-section of the poem is framed in a narrative darkness that does not comprehend it.

Even the personality of the narrator undergoes a complete change – from melancholiac to sanguine extrovert – during the dream. The text takes no account of this alteration, referring only to the change from the waking to the dreaming *state*, and rather busily, four times in sixteen lines (276–92). If readers insist on significant change in the narrator as a feature of character, the perception is easily assimilated into syntheses based on ironies at his expense, or on the clash between Boethian philosophy and unconsoled

[19] 'Chaucer's *Book of the Duchess*: An Art to Consume Art', *Durham University Journal*, 38 (1976–77), 205.

slavery to Fortune. But the narrative, by suggesting that totally different, even antagonistic, states, can be inhabited successively by the same so-called 'character', without any clear communication or relationship between them, effectively breaks down belief in stable and integrated characters, hence in reading-strategies based on that concept, including irony at the expense of a fallible narrator. Some other approach must be sought, one which recognizes an irony in all attempts to 'read' a dream.

This narrative emphasis on the barriers between waking experience and dream resembles, and is virtually equivalent to, a second emphasis on the difficulties of reading a literary text, explicitly Ovid's Ceyx and Alcyone story, and implicitly the *Book of the Duchess* itself. Once again, it may be argued that the narrator's apparent errors define by ironic contrast true concerns in the tale he reads – married love, the pain of bereavement, and, in this version of Ovid, the necessity of consolation. Indeed, this is the normal critical reaction. However, it is also possible to see in this section of the poem a warning about arbitrary conceptions of a text's function and genre. Taking up Ovid as a sex-filled 'romance' (48)[20] to pass the sleepless night, a collection of poetic 'fables' and 'tales' from the Age of Nature, (53–56) the narrator concludes by treating it as a manual for insomniacs (221–37), yet all the time with a parade of his attention and readerly purpose.

> For thus moche dar I saye wel,
> I had be dolven everydel,
> And ded, ryght thurgh defaute of slep
> Yif I ne had red and take kep
> Of this tale next before.
> And I wol telle yow wherfore;
> For I ne myghte, for bote ne bale,
> Slepe, or I had red thys tale
> Of this dreynte Seys the kyng,
> And of the goddes of slepyng.
> Whan I had red thys tale wel,
> And overloked hyt everydel,
> Me thoghte wonder yf hit were so.
>
> (221–33)

How shakily the 'book' conveys its ancient wisdom to a later age! Reading is here made the creature of circumstance, and the ordering of diverse narrative 'matere' is conducted on a narrow and random principle. But if readers are tempted to oppose an ordering of their own, this Ceyx and Alcyone story itself offers them striking discouragement. Alcyone's prayer to be helped out of her distress by tidings from Juno (101–21) ends disastrously in her death from grief (212–14). It is 'answered' through three intermediaries

---

[20] See the pun on 'thinges smale' (59), with reference to the Wife of Bath's Prologue, *Canterbury Tales* III, 121.

– Juno, her messenger, the sleepy Morpheus – four, if one includes the corpse of Ceyx which Morpheus inhabits to deliver his message. Despite Juno's warning to the messenger – 'Now understond wel, and tak kep!' (138) – Morpheus does *not* carry out her instructions exactly, but changes his mission from one of bare information to one of consolation as well. There is a cumbersome inefficacy in communication, through the line of prayer, intercession, go-between, agent, dream, disguise and pretence. Morpheus' decision that he must console, as well as inform, Alcyone results in an intolerably mixed message:

> My swete wyf,
> Awake! let be your sorwful lyf!
> For in your sorwe there lyth no red.
> For, certes, swete, I nam but ded;
> Ye shul me never on lyve yse.
>
> (201–5)

Against the image of sweet and shared 'blysse' (211) in Ceyx and Alcyone's former experience is set one of cruel distance and deceit in language, suggested by the simulated living voice in the dead body. Ultimately, we see language as incompetent, unable to bridge the disjunctions in Alcyone's experience, and most inadequately responding to her prayer. The former 'blissful' communication between King Ceyx and his wife is irretrievably lost, a conclusion forced on us by this version's omission of Ovid's metamorphosis and reunion of the couple.

When we enter the world of the dream itself, with its notoriously abrupt transitions, the changes of descriptive focus themselves draw attention to a lack of subordination of the various parts of the 'matere'. Before we encounter the Man in Black, there are four major narrative interests. Firstly, the heavenly 'accord' and 'swetnesse' of the anthropomorphized birdsong which awakens the narrator into his dream (291–320). Secondly, a description of the decorations in his bedroom (321–35). These tell the story of Troy: the text fills with proper names – Hector, Priam and Achilles – which function as shorthand for discord and distress. The narrator neither connects nor opposes the two different impressions, but attends to both with equal interest and pleasure. They are contiguous, but not interrelated, in his experience. The third narrative focus is the hart-hunting, with much joyful bustle and noise (344–86); the fourth is a landscape description, occasioned by the narrator's wandering off after one of the hounds (387–442). He follows it down a 'little used' path (401) into a forest. Once again, by succeeding images of movement and stillness, human and non-human life, the narrative associates the quality of 'swetnesse' (399; 415) with a complete isolation from other states of being. And although the same consciousness may experience both 'swetnesse' and its opposite at different times, there is a 'forgetting' between.

Hyt had forgete the povertee
That wynter, thorgh hys colde morwes,
Had mad hyt suffre, and his sorwes,
All was forgeten, and that was sene.
For al the woode was waxen grene.

(410–14)

Nature's unfrequented sweetness exists beyond the reach of human purpose –
the hunt; it is found as accidentally at the narrator's 'ynly swete' dream, and
has as little communication with other perceptions of life. This section of the
poem offers no more encouragement than those preceding it to the notion of
an adequate synthesis of its disparate experiences.

The human states of bereavement and 'being in love' offer a close analogy.
As the Man in Black's laborious series of contrasts indicates (598–616), his
bereaved condition maintains no link with his former happiness. Indeed, it is
only by his gradual suppression of the fact that White is dead that he can
recapture any sense of his past. Similarly, as one who loves, he is completely
unconscious of any possibility of not loving (1108–1111). Chaucer's lovers
frequently exhibit this inability to commune with their past or potential selves
as non-lovers. Troilus cannot 'unloven' Criseyde 'a quarter of a day' (*Troilus
and Criseyde*, V.1698). Conversely, Theseus (*Knight's Tale*, 1785ff.) is
amusedly detached from his past 'peyne' as a lover. In the triple roundel
known as 'Merciles Beaute' (*Works*, p.542), the speaker passes from
complete infatuation to complete indifference, but gives no indication of how
the change could have taken place. The one state knows nothing of the other.
In the *Book of the Duchess*, then, the inexplicit juxtaposition of opposed
states may well represent an appropriate formal response to the 'matere' of
love and bereavement, rather than an implied appeal for an holistic
reading.

The centre of the poem, and by far its longest section, deals with the Man in
Black and with White, first separately and then in union. As their names
indicate, these personages represent ideally extreme states – one of total
disorientation and violent imbalances, the other of perfect 'mesure' and
integration (881–82). By means of the fictional narrator's attempt to console
the Man in Black, to make him 'hool' (553), their exchanges painfully
recover, with much insistence on the necessity to be attentive (749–57), and
much failure to be so (1137–138), an image of perfect human accord, a union
with White in which, as the Man in Black says, 'Al was us oon' (1295). This
forms the poem's only extensive icon of human communion, showing at
length the 'bliss' before associated with Ceyx and Alcyone. And yet, like all
images of such 'sweetness' in the text, it is framed by statements of its own
inaccessibility, as we shall see.

White's description is formed from the perfect and sustained resolution of
various antitheses – light and dark, stasis and motion, variance and constancy
– that the text has foregrounded strongly in both its narrative structure and its

rhetoric.[21] She is both 'glade, and sadde' (860). This principle of balance saturates each aspect of the description, from the consistent use of *correctio* (861; 874–75; 954) to the larger structure of the portrait. Its first thirty lines hold White in an effulgent stillness, like 'the someres sonne bryghte' (821) with her 'wel set gladnesse' (828), 'stedfast countenaunce' (833) and 'noble port and meyntenaunce' (834). After this effect of statuesque composure:

> By God, and by his halwes twelve,
> Hyt was my swete, ryght as hirselve,
>
> (831–32)

the next thirty lines are suggestive of motion:

> I sawgh hyr daunce so comlily,
> Carole and synge so swetely,
> Laughe and pleye so womanly,
> And loke so debonairly.
>
> (848–51)

In her perfect unity of opposites, White is the human embodiment of the elusive 'sweetness' in experience hinted at before in the text.

The Man in Black demands that the dreamer believe and acknowledge the truth of his description of White (1042–47), whilst the dreamer's interruptions show us that he thinks it the mere expression of biased opinion (1042–43; 1046–51). The doubting narrator wishes to know how a real person – this young knight – could ever have found such perfection. The proofs and answers put forward bear not only on the Man in Black's 'tale', but on Chaucer's; in them the Man in Black indicates the failure of language to achieve this union, and the ultimate success of a mysterious, quasi-religious 'understanding'.

> And whan I had my tale y-doo
> God wot, she accounted nat a stree
> Of al my tale, so thoghte me.
> To telle shortly ryght as hyt ys,
> Trewly hir answere hyt was this;
> I kan not now wel counterfete
> Hir wordes, but this was the grete
> Of hir answere: she sayde 'nay'
> Al outerly.
>
> (1236–44)

---

[21] For example, in the contrast between the ideal dream weather (339–42) and the dark forest (425–26), between the speed of the hunt (363, 379, 385) and the stillness of the Man in Black (443–60), between Fortune's inconstancy (618–75) and the 'truth' of Alcyone, the Man in Black, and White herself.

This 'tale' fares no better with its listener than Ovid's did, or the narrator's 'tale' to the Man in Black (536), or, for all we know, Chaucer's to us. When White does accept the young man, her act is a gratuitous extension of mercy, admitting him to her state of perfection in which all antitheses are balanced.

> So hit befel, another yere,
> I thoughte ones I wolde fonde
> To do hir knowe and understonde
> My woo; and she wel understod
> That I ne wilned thyng but god,
> And worship, and to kepe hir name
> Over alle thyng, and drede hir shame,
> And was so besy hyr to serve;
> And pitee were I shulde sterve,
> Syth that I wilned noon harm, ywis.
> So whan my lady knew al this,
> My lady yaf me al hooly
> The noble yifte of hir mercy,
> Savynge hir worship, by al weyes, –
> Dredles, I mene noon other weyes.
> And therwith she yaf me a ryng;
> I trowe hyt was the firste thyng;
> But if myn herte was ywaxe
> Glad, that is no nede to axe!
> As helpe me God, I was as blyve
> Reysed, as fro deth to lyve,
> Of al happes the alderbeste,
> The gladdest, and the moste at reste.
>
> (1258–80)

In this passage the poem presents for the first time an image of perfect communication, understanding and accord, but only by means of a system of intercession and redemption that withdraws the issue from the sphere of the merely human, and hence beyond language. When the dreamer calls on the Man in Black to verify the existence of White in fact, as well as in words – 'where is she now?' (1279), the only answer is that she is dead, 'lost'. The highly artificial and conventional portrait of White's virtues and of perfect union with her must be taken on faith. In such a context, typological readings cannot claim more than a partial and provisional value. As I have tried to show, many formal features of the *Book of the Duchess*, and some of its major thematic currents, increase, rather than diminish the states of uncertainty which typological reference attempts to transcend. Far from enjoying an 'instructed' confidence in pursuing such strategies, the reader is almost as 'cut off' from full understanding as Wimsatt's Man in Black is 'cut off' from grace. Indeed, the reader's position seems much like the dreamer's. Despite hints of an enduring sweetness beyond ordinary perception, the moment in which he realizes what the happiness of union with White means is also the moment in which he realizes that it no longer exists, that White is dead and the union is broken. 'Is that youre los? Be God, hyt ys routhe!' (1310) His lament for the 'loss' of White is equivalent to a lament for the loss of human ability to connect and understand as one the apparently fragmented phenomena of existence. For the person who has known her, the truest analogy is, as Wimsatt says[22], the ultimate loss of despair. But for those who have never known White – the dreamer, and the even more removed readers of his dream – this 'loss' enforces a critical agnosticism, to which all such images of perfection are unreliable 'tales'. Although inklings of accord and sweetness can be fleetingly experienced, in dreams, in nature, in literature, they are as soon lost, and form no controlling relationship with other experiences.

To conclude, the 'Gothic form' of this poem, its 'various juxtaposed versions of experience', gives it a radical resistance to critical attempts at synthesis. Neither ironies at the expense of character nor generic classifications can remove the many disjunctions that form a wider irony at the expense of utterance itself. In the end, the *Book of the Duchess* can only permit us to 'take keep' of experience, not to understand it, to see life steadily, but not as a whole.

---

22 Wimsatt, p.128.

PENANCE AS POETRY IN
THE LATE FOURTEENTH CENTURY

John Wall

The territory of the Sacrament of Penance is a land native to any catholic literary artist. For within a quasi-judicial framework, the penitent is both defendant and prosecutor as he rehearses the failures of his life before a tribunal both of God and of the whole Church represented in the person of the priest. Nevertheless complete objectivity is never possible; confession involves admitting the disruption of the spiritual life. The causes of dereliction may be obfuscated, so deeply are they embedded in a person's constitution and in the circumstances, both internal and external, of his life. Considered from the standpoint of faith, sin occurs because man's free-will entails the ability to choose what is wrong. By the same token, the weight of culpability varies according to the degree of attachment to evil on the part of the will. It is not surprising then that the three major authors of the last quarter of the fourteenth century all deal with the moral act and penance (both as virtue and sacrament) not simply theologically but poetically. The relationship of the works to the penitential tradition has been noted often enough,[1] but the way in which it operates deserves closer attention.

Cleanness[2] explores the idea of moral and spiritual cleanness by a series of typological connections in Adam, Noah and Daniel. Ultimate reward or punishment will come on Judgement Day. Meanwhile a dialogue between God and man unfolds as the poem ingeniously presents balanced contrasts of loyalty and disloyalty, courtesy and discourtesy, purity and impurity, righteous wrath and unrighteous wrath. The remedy while there is yet time consists in penance:

> þus is He kyryous and clene þat þou His cort askes:
> Hov schulde þou com to His kyth bot if þou clene were?
>
> (1109–10)

> 3is, þat Mayster is mercyable, þa3 þou be man fenny,
> And al tomarred in myre whyle þou on molde lyuyes;
> þou may schyne þur3 schryfte, þa3 þou haf schome serued,
> And pure þe with penaunce tyl þou a perle worþe.
>
> (1113–16)

---

[1] See for example, *Piers Plowman: An Edition of the C-text*, edited by Derek Pearsall (London, 1978), Introduction, p.18; A.C.Spearing, *The Gawain-Poet: A Critical Study* (Cambridge, 1970), p.221; D.R.Howard, *The Idea of the Canterbury Tales* (Berkeley, 1976), pp.43–45.
[2] *The Poems of the Pearl Manuscript*, edited by Malcolm Andrew and Ronald Waldron (London, 1978), pp.111–84.

So if folk be defowled by vnfre chaunce,
þat he be sulped in sawle, seche to schryfte,
And he may polyce hym at þe prest, by penaunce taken,
Wel bryȝter þen þe beryl oþer browden perles.

(1129–32)

Pearl[3] deals with the innocence of the maiden and the dreamer's need for purification. By means of the shifting signification the pearl is at various times literally a lost jewel, allegorically the pure maiden, tropologically the search for innocence, and anagogically Christ, himself the final goal, who makes

vus to be his homly hyne
Ande precious perleȝ vnto his pay.

(1211–12)

Patience[4] stresses the patient acceptance of God's will,

For ho quelles vche a qued and quenches malyce.

The story of Jonah's impatience is dramatically presented. Interesting in itself, the example also contrasts allegorically with the patience of Christ while at the same time being a parallel to Satan's impatience. The moral lesson of repentance for disloyalty is crowned by recognising God's sovereign purpose. God reminds Jonah that trials elicit repentance necessary for eternal salvation:

'þenne wyte not Me for þe werk, þat I hit wolde help,
And rwe on þo redles þat remen for synne;

(501–2)

Wer I as hastif as þou hiere, were harme lumpen;

(520)

Forþy when pouerté me enprecez and paynez innoȝe
Ful softly with suffraunce saȝttel me bihouez;
Forþy penaunce and payne topreue hit in syȝt
þat pacience is a nobel poynt, þaȝ hit displese ofte.'

(528–31)

The concern for 'trawþe' in *Sir Gawain and the Green Knight*[5] is what makes Gawain outstanding in Arthur's court which is itself a noble flower. The opening of the poem establishes the sweep of history from the destruction of

[3] *Pearl*, edited by E.V.Gordon (Oxford, 1953).
[4] *The Poems of the Pearl Manuscript*, pp.185–206.
[5] *Sir Gawain and the Green Knight*, edited by J.R.R.Tolkien and E.V.Gordon, 2nd edition, revised by Norman Davis (Oxford, 1967).

Troy to the origins of Britain, embodying man's struggle with sin, as a preamble to Sir Gawain's quest. The allegorical journey through the wilderness results in the moral *casus* provided by the bedroom temptations and the exchange of spoil. The author adroitly poses Gawain's use of the Sacrament of Penance as a challenge to the final judgements by the knight, Sir Bertilak, the court and not least the readers. There is not the slightest hesitation in the text to imply that Gawain made anything but a good confession.

> þere he schrof hym schyrly and schewed his mysdedez,
> Of þe more and þe mynne, and merci besechez,
> And of absolucioun he on þe segge calles;
> And he asoyled hym surely and sette hym so clene
> As domezday schulde haf ben diȝt on þe morn.
>
> (1880–84)

He confessed himself conscientiously of those misdeeds that he was aware of. Significantly he had asked the priest

> Þat he wolde lyste his lyf and lern hym better
> How his sawle schulde be saued when he schuld seye heþen.
>
> (1878–79)

Even Gawain has to grow in self-knowledge through the grace of repentance, and the encounter at the Green Chapel is the occasion when he discovers what he could not previously see. He now accuses himself bitterly of 'cowarddyse' and 'couetyse' which contradict 'larges and lewte'. Nor does the diagnosis stop here: the deepest wound has been dealt his very nature as a knight 'my kynde to forsake' (2380). With explicit echoes of the Sacrament of Penance Sir Bertilak proffers a type of absolution:

> þou art confessed so clene, beknowen of þy mysses,
> And hatz þe penaunce apert of þe poynt of myn egge.
>
> (2391–92)

Sir Gawain is indeed repentant, but the accomplishment of the grace will be bitter. Those with less acute Christian vision of sin's malice may reasonably seek to comfort him by stressing the definitive forgiveness of God now made clear. Gawain, however, cannot rest easy in that consolation although it would have sufficed the last confession made before the Green Chapel. We are not privy to the movements of his soul, but he goes on a further stage of his spiritual journey to the court and beyond. The concluding recapitulation of the perduring state of the world made for glory and touched by sin indicates both the absolute goal of salvation and also individual man's contingent state.

John Wall

The concerns and spiritual itinerary of *Piers Plowman*[6] coincide substantially with those of the Gawain Poet. The dreamer's vision of a corrupted world as 'a fair feld ful of folk' displays the need for repentance that unhappily would not be fostered by priests, friars or bishops. Among the worst defaulters was a pardoner who preached

> as he a prest were
> And brouth forth a bulle with bischopis selys,
> Sayde þat hymself myhte assoylen hem alle
> Of falsnesses of fastynges, of vowes ybrokene.
>
> (Prol. 66–9)

At least Conscience continued to reproach evil-doers, and the dreamer

> parsceyued of þe power that Peter hadde to kepe,
> To bynde and to vnbynde, as þe boke telleth,
> Hou he it lefte with loue as oure lord wolde
> Amonge foure vertues most vertuous of vertues
> That cardinales ben cald and closyng-ʒates
> Thare Crist is in kynedom to close with heuene.
>
> (Prol. 128–33)

The contrast with the cardinals in Rome is only too clear. The vast sprawl of the poem and its unannounced switches from a world of personified abstractions to the naturalistic pictures of daily life are necessary strategies for conveying the consistent action of grace in the world. Although man will never be forced to accept grace, God's grace is never frustrated. The world seems helplessly a-jangle, but reconciliation is possible. Even teachers like the Friar Doctor, unworthy in their personal lives, speak truth almost despite themselves. Holy Church suffers frequent check, but is indomitable. Reason aided by Conscience preaches confession and repentance. In Passus VI, in a waking episode, the dreamer offers his own confession before the people come to repentance. Pearsall calls it 'more in the nature of an *apologia pro vita sua* than a confession, since it combines contrition with pugnacious self-justification in a characteristic way.'[7] The opinion asserts that the traits are characteristic of one person's psychology. More persuasively one can discern them as traits that characterise a man in the sacrament of Penance. As we see in Sir Gawain, the grace of repentance works on the person as he is and helps him to grow from that existential point. That no case is beyond remedy is explicit in offering confession even to the Seven Deadly Sins, incarnated in readily recognisable individuals (Passus VI).

Piers the Plowman becomes the sign of regenerate man. Unlike the despicable pardoner he can procure from Truth a pardon *a pena et a culpa*

[6] Quotations are from Pearsall's 1978 edition of the C-text.
[7] Pearsall, p.97.

(Passus IX). It cannot be applied to those who withhold repentance, like the merchants who profane the holy days; it is not efficacious when men do not strive to live a full Christian life. For this reason the poem presents the visions Dowel, Dobet and Dobest. These visions correspond aptly with the judgments of Arthur, Sir Bertilak and Sir Gawain respectively in the other poem. In addition, the endings of both poems coincide on every level of meaning apart from the literal. Gawain fares forth into a dark night of the soul which is paradoxically a sign of progress not of abandonment by God. In *Piers Plowman* Sloth and Pride continue to assail Conscience who calls Clergy and Contrition to his aid. When Peace gives the daunting news that the latter has been drowned by 'the frere with his fisyk' (XXII. 378), Conscience rallies his forces to

> bicome a pilgrime,
> And wenden as wyde as þe world regneth
> To seke Peres the plouhman, þat Pruyde myhte destruye,
> And þat freres hadde a fyndynge.

> (XXII. 380–83)

He shouts after Grace and wakes the dreamer. The search is not ended but the ultimate goal of life has been illuminated through penance.

The General Prologue of the *Canterbury Tales*[8] establishes the same grounds for a drama of Penance as the previous poems. Two things are generally accepted. Firstly, Chaucer placed the revised General Prologue at the start, and at the end 'The Parson's Tale' with its coda of the Retraction. Grouping the pilgrims has exercised many writers despite the narrator's claim that he has told

> soothly, in a clause,
> Th'estaat, th'array, the nombre, and eek the cause
> Why that assembled was this compaignye.

> (I[A] 715–17)

Jill Mann has usefully demonstrated that one of the principles for grouping them is that of the medieval estates.[9] Described with individualising detail the participants represent society in a way that parallels Langland's caste. When some of them tell stories which are supposedly accounts of actual experiences in their past lives, 'aventures that whilom han bifalle' (I[A] 795), the tales are inescapably coloured. Since Harry Bailly points out that the stories have to be

> Tales of best sentence and moost solaas

> (I[A] 798)

---

[8] *The Works of Geoffrey Chaucer*, edited by F.N.Robinson, 2nd edition (London, 1957).
[9] Jill Mann, *Chaucer and Medieval Estates Satire* (Cambridge, 1973).

he establishes that they have to be interpreted to yield meaning beyond literal biography and anecdote. The final way in which the interpretation will take place is governed by the penitential nature of pilgrimage. Peterson has cited an interesting parallel from *L'Ymage du Monde*:

> Saint Pierre dit que nous sommes tous pelerins en ce monde cy et alons iour et nuyt sans arrester en nostre pays quie est au ciel. Et pour recreation auoir comment les pelerins qui parlent voulentiers en alant leur chemin aussi en alant a nostre pelerinage, cest en paradis, nous parlerons ong petit; car nous cheminons fort et nauons mais que trois iournees a cheminer: l'une des dictes trois iournees est Contrition et l'aut Confession, et la tierce est Satisfaction.[10]

Baldwin calls the access to the heavenly homeland by means of contrition, confession and satisfaction 'the trope central to the fiction'.[11] Moreover he draws attention to the Parson's intention

> To shewe yow the way in this viage,
> Of thilke parfit glorious pilgrymage
> That highte Jerusalem celestial.
>
> (XI 49–51)

Although Baldwin acknowledges the 'pilgrimage to Canterbury ... to be the spiritual, that is anagogical, figure for the pilgrimage to the heavenly Jerusalem',[12] he denies the possibility of arguing for the application of the medieval four-fold meaning; he draws the line by creating a new category – 'a metaphorical prosecution of the *sensus anagogicus*.' It is not clear what is to be gained by the innovation, for indeed the dismissed opportunity has much to recommend it.

A similar abstention is observable in Robertson's reading. Rightly he warns of a crudely technical application of the distich

> Littera gesta docet, quid credas allegoria,
> Moralis quid agas, quo tendas anagogia.[13]

At the same time he has established that the same kind of tradition was common to Biblical exegetes and literary men of the period: the Italian stream of Dante, Mussato, Petrarch, Boccaccio and Salutati is consistent: 'and the writings of Philippe de Mézières in France, and of Gower in England, are filled with echoes of traditional allegorical exegesis.'[14] He reminds us of the number of exegetes in the *Canterbury Tales*, including the

[10] K.O.Petersen, *The Sources of the Parson's Tale* (Boston, Radcliffe College Monographs 12, 1901), p.3.
[11] R.Baldwin, *The Unity of the Canterbury Tales* (Copenhagen, 1955), reprinted in *Chaucer Criticism*, edited by R.Schoeck and J.Taylor, vol.1 (Notre Dame, 1960), p.23.
[12] Baldwin, p.34.
[13] D.W.Robertson, Jr., *A Preface to Chaucer* (Princeton, 1962), p.293.
[14] Robertson, p.310.

more prominent ones, the Wife of Bath, the friar in the *Summoner's Tale*, the Pardoner and the Parson.[15] His aim of directing all medieval meaning to an exposition of charity dismisses the possibility of at least intermediate and concomitant preoccupations.

I think that the *Canterbury Tales* is neither a rhetorical collection of disparate stories nor an illustration of one theme. It seems to reflect substantially the 'quaternity of reality' in which Penance is not the main theme but the dynamic conceptual and structural element in a way that accords substantially with what we have seen in the poems discussed already.

That the first thirty-four lines of the General Prologue are self-contained is obvious. Baldwin's description is happy:

> Even the conventional metaphor, the springtime, has fostered one conspicuous, symbolic tree, the tree of Penitence, whose roots thrust through and whose branches overspread the world of the Canterbury pilgrims.[16]

Yet his attention to the *reverdie* form leads him only to emphasise the symbolic parallel between the season of annual physical regeneration and the Easter season of spiritual rebirth.[17] While the comparison is apt, the tacit understanding of symbolism is modern and unduly restrictive. Rather as the opening of *Sir Gawain* and *Piers Plowman*, the lines present in paradigm the macrocosm of God's creative action and the microcosm of individual experience as the preamble to representative individuals and their stories. Literally the lines present the 'aventures' past and present of a particular group of 'nyne and twenty in a compaignye' on pilgrimage to the shrine of the martyr

> That hem hath holpen whan that they were seeke.
>
> (I[A] 18)

When their journey is allied to the world whose stars, crops and 'smale foweles' also advance in ordered course, we are invited to consider allegory. When their journey exhorts everyone to be grateful for God's grace given through the saint's intercession, the meaning is clearly tropological. Since the goal is heaven, the prize that 'the hooly blisful martir' has already won, a full anagogical meaning is urged. The poem's data are clear: God works in his creation which encompasses the free participation of individual human beings; that these participants are themselves limited and sinful is calmly accepted; since they are sinful, the grace that they will often most need is repentance (although whether they will look for it or accept it is another matter). Since the pilgrims are themselves representative of the estates in society, any lesson is to be applied to society as it exists. When later the

---

15 Robertson, p.317.
16 Baldwin, p.49.
17 Baldwin, pp.17–18.

narrator defends his procedure by explicit comparison with the examples of Christ and Plato (I[A] 739–42), he means that both faith and reason demand the form of presentation that we have, for both faith and reason applied variously provide truths of different although complementary kinds. When the Knight accepts responsibility for the first tale, his exclamation is like the invocation that launches a religious procession, *Procedamus in pace in nomine Domini*.

The dubieties of the pilgrims' nature and performance both leave room for more than a single meaning and also prevent the rigidities that too slavish an application of literary system could entail. The necessity of seeking several meanings is signalled throughout the *Tales*. The Wife of Bath entertains the pilgrims but also touches

> In scole-matere greet difficultee.
>
> (III[D] 1272)

The Nun's Priest urges his audience,

> Taketh the moralite, goode men.
> For seint Paul seith that al that writen is,
> To oure doctrine it is ywrite, ywis.
>
> (VII[B²] 4630–32)

Nevertheless, taking the fruit and leaving the chaff are made deliberately difficult, not least because there are so many lessons proposed by his several fictional teachers who are of varying competence and prejudice. The same is true of all the moral questions when looked at *singly*. Not even the original audience could have found all the tales easy to understand. The *Knight's Tale*, the *Clerk's Tale*, the *Merchant's Tale* shape a moral to elicit the response, 'But that's impossible ... do you really expect me to accept that?' The same is true of *Sir Thopas* and the *Tale of Melibee*, although for reasons of apparently inept literary form. Even when tales like the Franklin's, the Prioress's, the Miller's and the Reeve's seem transparent, their resulting meaning turns out as a 'sentence' in the medieval sense of the term – an opinion or proposition which of its nature invites disputation. I think that modern readers have been so beguiled by the range of isolated moral questions in the *Tales* that they have made impossible that harmony which a classic four-fold meaning relies upon. If however we take the varied performance as examples of grace and sin, the catalyst for unifying them is the demonstrated need for repentance which is itself a union of 'sentence' and 'solaas', judgement and solace.

The only sermon that the *Tales* finally endorse is foreshadowed by the Host's characteristic jeer at the Parson's rebuke for swearing:

> I smelle a Lollere in the wynd ...
> This Lollere heer wil prechen us somwhat.
>
> (II[B¹] 1173,1177)

In the event, that 'predicacioun' is delayed and has to wait until the very end of the collected tales. Yet clearly the poem faces the possibility that it could be accused of Wyclif's heresy. And not without reason.

Wyclif had exalted the ministry of preaching (in which he himself excelled) and saw two major impediments. The first was the begging friars:

> & heere breken out þes freris ordris, for al ʒif þei han no wordly lordchip as han prestis þat ben dowid, ʒit þei spuylen men of moeblis and wasten hem in noumbre and housis, and þis excees is more synne þan synne of þe fend in o persone. & þus þey turnen þe ende of þer preching for-to gete hem siche godis. & þis entent mut nedis make falsed in maner of þer preching, for þei shapen þer sermouns more to gete hem good þan to profite to þe chirche.[18]

The second was the sacrament of penance, where the friars were also to blame although not solely:

> þat prelate þat shriueþ shuld preche þe puple, and he þat is shriuen shuld here goddis worde; but bi þis shriften ben boþe þise lettid.[19]

He attached canon 21 of the Fourth Lateran Council (1215):

> and þus it semeþ a feendis presumpcioun, þat hiʒeþ himself a-bouen god, to make þus a newe lawe … þis lawe of confessioun þat iche man mut nedis shryuen oonys in þe ʒer priuely to his propur prest.
>
> (p.329)

He had nothing good to say for 'þis roten lawe þat was þus late made of antecrist' (p.330), and preferred the old way of confession 'opynly & generaly, as men confesseden in þe oolde lawe' (p.327), not private confession of specific sins to a priest. In fact it is simply an excuse for fornication, for 'bi þis priueye shrift a frere & nunne may synne togidre' (p.330). In his contempt for unworthy priests as ministers, he claimed that the sacrament would be better served by good laymen: 'lewed men þat weren bettur myʒten þus assoyle bettur þenne wickid prestis' (p.333). Besides, 'boþe in þe oolde lawe, & in þe newe, men tolden commynly her synne' (p.335). On this latter score he espoused the commentaries on St James's injunction, 'Confess your sins to one another that you may be saved' (James 5:16), that were in part used to explain the persistent albeit infrequent practice of confession to laymen.

Although Wyclif's influence remained after his death in 1384 not least among the circle of Chaucer's acquaintance with Clanvowe and the Lollard Knights, Chaucer's coincidence of concerns stopped short of Wyclif's

---

[18] *De officio pastorali*, c. XXVI; in *The English Works of Wyclif Hitherto Unpublished*, edited by F.D.Matthew, EETS os 74 (London, 1880), p.445.
[19] *Of Confession*, Matthew, p.332.

heterodoxy, as does also Langland's because they preserved the unity and authority of the Church while still attacking patent abuse. The *Canterbury Tales* mocks Friar Hubert for working the penitential system to his own profit as he plays on the culpable bourgeois seekers of easy penance. Carefully restrictive legislation would have difficulty in catching him; so the parody of him in the *Summoner's Tale* convicts and punishes his twin. Hubert's glibly self-interested interpretation of the sign-value of monetary alms without tears is aptly countered by the appalling alms that Thomas gives to Friar John groping tenderly down the old man's back. The crowning insult is the machine for sharing equally between thirteen friars Thomas's derisory gift. That the plan comes from a page may be some redress for all those poor widows without a shoe whom Hubert fleeces so ruthlessly.

Wyclif despised unworthy ministers, and Chaucer provides one in the Pardoner who is not only corrupt but glories in his corruption. Just as the legislation of the Fourth Lateran Council could not be proof against Hubert's determined greed, so the fulmination of popes and the law cannot control absolutely an avaricious pardoner and equally avaricious customers who want remission without hardship. By choosing such a figure as the Pardoner, Chaucer intensifies what the *Tales* were doing with the friars. Whereas the effect of Wyclif's attacks was to set apart 'the People' from the institutional Church especially in its ministers, Chaucer insists on the unity of the Church in which all contribute to or diminish 'commun profyt'. As a result he puts on trial both the Pardoner who represents an individual embracing evil while fully aware of what he is doing and without any hint of likely contrition; and also the Pardoner's three audiences – the country parishioners of his ordinary tours, the pilgrims, and the readers. The sins attacked in the Pardoner's sermon are all notably those to which the pilgrims are liable. No one can deny the need for contrition, renewed and deepened as often as possible amid the known risks of a pilgrimage. The relics are false, the pardons may not be. In any case use of them depends finally on the penitent's own disposition, not the worthiness of the agent. The pilgrims unjustifiably use the Pardoner's corruption to distract themselves from the need to examine their own consciences. The Knight comes down on no one's side, since this is still a game, but insists that the Pardoner and Host kiss and be reconciled. No one is asked to believe that they felt any more kindly to each other. Rather the minimum peace is an armistice, however temporary, and Chaucer parodies dramatically the psalm-text much loved by medieval commentators in which the four daughters of God seem to have mutually exclusive claims; yet through repentance which is itself God's gift,

> Mercy and Truth have met each other;
> Justice and Peace have kissed.
>
> (Vg Ps. 84:11)

The descriptions of sin and repentance (or lack of it) are as trenchant as anything that Wyclif might compose, but Chaucer stays within orthodoxy in the same way that Langland does. Heterodoxy seeks reform and purification usually for the benefit of a gnostic elite; there is no room for dissenters from new dogmatism. Both Chaucer and Langland are no less clear-eyed in seeing the failure of sinful man, but salvation remains possible for the penitent. That is why *Piers Plowman* begins with the vision of the field and ends with the shout after Conscience; although the vision of charity and Christ's Passion are definitive, salvation still has to be worked out within the individual and social pursuit of grace. Similarly the *Canterbury Tales* open with the hymn to God's grace-filled creation in which man, its crown, is moved to go on pilgrimage; the rest of the General Prologue, the other prologues and the tales present a selective and representative variety of human experience.

With this view the *Parson's Tale* stands at the end of the *Canterbury Tales* to fulfil a particular function. It could plausibly have stood first in the series, but that would have changed the *Tales* into a sermon whose moral propositions were then deduced by the following tales. By standing at the conclusion, we have a means not for deduction, but for induction. The signification of the performance operates, not dealing serially with separate vices and virtues but simultaneously on several levels. The *Parson's Tale* is the means for judging consistently the examples of the pilgrims and their tales told in a world where, although (as in Langland's work) Redemption has definitively taken place already in Christ's death and resurrection, salvation has yet to be worked out in successive ages and individuals. It is the vision of St Paul whereby 'the whole world groans in an act of giving birth' (Romans 8:22). The tales are the material that must be shaped and judged so that the inherent integrity of God's creation announced in the General Prologue may be realised at the end of time. The *Parson's Tale* is both an invitation to such a penitential task, and an instrument for achieving the metanoia that transforms human life.

The sources of the *Parson's Tale* are the thirteenth-century *Summa* of Raymond of Peñaforte and a treatise on the Seven Capital Sins perhaps by Guilielmus Peraldus. However, Chaucer's adaption is significant. Raymond's work was a handbook for priests to help them hear confessions, whereas the *Parson's Tale* bears the marks of having been adapted for the lay penitent who is to make his confession. In other words it is an aid for examining one's conscience before approaching the Sacrament of Penance. The schematic ordering of areas of life where sin is likely and a limited specification of sins are attempted. Above all, Capital Sins are those basic disorders which are the *capita* or heads and sources of individual derelictions. But to identify them is not enough. A penitent also needs true contrition, adequate confession to a priest in self-accusation, and, having received absolution, a work of satisfaction or atonement (prayers, fasting or a work of charity). Consequently, the *Parson's Tale* is a devotional work that seeks to persuade and convince as well as teach.

For this reason its literary qualities are not mere adornments. Where Raymond's Latin speaks of the way of penance (*viam rectam, necessariam, &*

infallibilem),[20] Chaucer's version uses the devices of *amplificatio* and *repetitio* to stress the many forms of penance and the discernment needed to appreciate them:

> Manye been the weyes espirituels that leden folk to oure Lord Jhesu Crist, and to the regne of glorie. Of whiche weyes, ther is a ful noble wey and a ful convenable, which may nat fayle to man ne to womman that thurgh synne hath mysgoon fro the righte wey of Jersusalem celestial; and this wey is cleped Penitence, of which man sholde gladly herknen and enquere with al his herte, to wyten what is Penitence, and whennes it is cleped Penitence, and in how manye maneres been the acciouns or werkynges of Penitence, and how manye speces ther been of Penitence, and whiche thynges apertenen and bihoven to Penitence, and whiche thynges destourben Penitence.   (X[I] 78–83)

In that passage are many more rhetorical devices than the two mentioned earlier, including alliteration and an elegant use of the rhythmic *cursus* at the end of each main clause. In the tale as a whole, examples are shrewd and lively: for example, excess in fashionable male dress is pilloried for the superfluous material trailing wastefully in the dung, all the more ridiculous since it accompanies an exaggeratedly skimpy cut elsewhere for the sake of immodest, particoloured display 'that semeth lik maladie of hirnia, in the wrappynge of hir hoses' (X[I] 422 ff.). Likewise, the account of backbiting is as vivid as similar expositions in such older English devotional works as *Ancrene Wisse*.[21]

Although the tale is austere in the high standards it proposes, the constantly repeated motivation is far from gloomy. Not fear alone, but love of God and gratitude for ceaseless generosity are the reasons for the penitent's self-accusation.

The climax in the hymn about the fruits of penance (X[I] 1075 ff.) is memorable in its highly wrought exultation. The Parson had disclaimed literary skill:

> But trusteth wel, I am a Southren man,
> I kan nat geeste 'rum, ram, ruf' by lettre,
> Ne, God woot, rym holde I but litel bettre.
>
> (X[I] 42–44)

With aplomb he cuts down to size all those with literary pretensions, including that other southerner, Chaucer himself, who as author of the *Tales* has shown ample literary invention. The Parson says he does not need to tell fables, and

[20] *Summa Sti Raymundi de Penafort Barcinonensis Ord. Praedicator. De Poenitentia, et Matrimonio cum glossis Ioannis de Friburgo* (Rome, Ioannis Tellini, 1603), p .437.
[21] *The English Text of the Ancrene Riwle: Ancrene Wisse*, edited by J .R .R .Tolkien, EETS os 249 (London, 1962), pp .44–47.

his own tale is in fact in the first rank of traditional English prose with all its sophisticated techniques. We are dealing with a performer no plainer than that other selfstyled 'burel man', the Franklin. It is fitting that the Parson be the one to proclaim that meaning of the *Canterbury Tales* which is indisputably anagogical:

> ... thilke parfit glorious pilgrymage
> That highte Jersusalem celestial.
>
> (X[I] 50–51)

Added to it as closely as a coda to a musical composition is the Retraction. It is no example of mock modesty, nor of recanting by way of death-bed insurance. Rather, we have a serious parody of the Pardoner's sinful exhortation to his several audiences which was followed by the approach to individuals; for the Parson's 'predicacioun' bears fruit in the individual poet's formal act of penitence. Certainly the form could not be otherwise than conventional, since no words of confession and contrition fully convey the secrets of a self-accusing conscience before God's tribunal. Nor does any outsider have the right of access to Chaucer's soul. Nevertheless, the form is both sincere and adequate exactly because Chaucer, by profession a writer, makes a responsible distinction between all his works: some are unarguably edifying, but the secular works will always be that same fallible mixture of good and evil which we have seen portrayed in the 'synful folk unstable' (VII[B²] 1877) of the pilgrimage. Chaucer the writer as penitent acknowledges firmly that his works are the best he was capable of and yet *must* be flawed because of 'worldly vanitees'. In that sense only does he disown his works, and ask that

> thurgh the benigne grace of hym that is kyng of kynges and preest over
> alle preestes, that boghte us with the precious blood of his herte; so ... I
> may been oon of hem at the day of doom that shulle be saved.
>
> (X[I] 1090–91)

In this context then, the Retraction provides a true tropological meaning.

In short, penance and multiple meaning are more than equal yoke-mates. Perhaps the right apprehension of them is that, without being the proscriptive, exhaustive explanation of the poetry, their union constitutes the animating principle for the mind's perennial delight in 'the one and the many'.

> Ac fre wil and fre wit foleweth men euere
> To repenten and to arise and rowe out of synne
> To contricion, to confessioun, til he come til his ende.[22]

---

[22] *Piers Plowman*, C, Passus X, lines 51–53.

'INNER' AND 'OUTER': CONCEPTUALIZING THE BODY IN *ANCRENE WISSE* AND AELRED'S *DE INSTITUTIONE INCLUSARUM*

Jocelyn Price

The anchoritic house holds the line between inner and outer, world and spirit, at its window. The imaginative fascination of this important boundary is testified to in the vigour with which it is invoked in treatises on the anchoritic life: it loses none of its force in, for instance, this fifteenth-century translation of Aelred's *De institutione inclusarum*:

> But many ther ben that knowe not ne charge not the profit of solitary liuyng, supposyng that it be ynow, oonly to shutte her body bitwene too walles, whan not only the thoughte rennith aboute besynes of the worlde, but also the tunge is occupied alday, either aboute tidynges, curiously enquering and sechinge after hem, or elles of her neighbores yuel name, by way of bakbityng, so that vnnethes now-a-dayes shaltow finde a solitary recluse, that either tofore the wyndowe shal sitte an olde womman fedynge hir with tales, or elles a new iangeler and teller of tidynges of that monke, or of that clerke, or of widowes dissolucion, or of maidens wantownes, of the whiche arisith lawghyng, scornynge and vnclene (f.178v) thoughtes slepynge or wakynge, so that atte last the recluse is fulfilled with lust and likynge, bakbitynge, sclaundre and hatrede and the tother with mete and drinke.[1]

A recluse's house could indeed become a kind of centre in village life: Meyr-Harting documents in vivid detail the case of St Wulfric of Haselbury, who served as arbitrator, administrator, adviser and sometimes banker to his community.[2] Cristina of Markyate is another well-known instance of an influential and sought-after recluse, whose spiritual commitment paradoxically evoked a flurry of worldly activity around her.[3] Jusserand long ago proposed the quoted passage's source in the *De institutione inclusarum* as evidence for one kind of historical situation in which fabliaux might have

---

[1] My transcription of this and other passages in MS Bodley 423 has happily been superseded by the appearance of *Aelred of Rievaulx's De Institutione Inclusarum*, edited by John Ayto and Alexandra Barratt, EETS 287 (London, 1984), which makes both the Vernon MS and the MS Bodley 423 translations of Aelred's Rule much more readily available. All quotations of both these translations are from this edition and will be referred to by page and line number in the text. For this passage, see p.l, ll.23–25.

[2] Henry Meyr-Harting, 'Functions of a Twelfth Century Recluse: Wulfric of Haselbury', *History*, 60 (1975), 337–52.

[3] See *The Life of Christina of Markyate*, edited by C.H.Talbot (Oxford, 1959).

192

arisen,[4] and Aelred's late twelfth-century treatise was certainly composed in an era beginning to see the rise of the great *entremetteuse* figures of fabliau such as Dames Trotula, Sirith, Auberée, as well as an increase in English interest in the reclusive life.[5]

Nevertheless, given that this fifteenth-century passage closely translates Aelred's late twelfth-century Latin,[6] it cannot be read simply in historical terms as, for instance, testimony to an observed decline in the standards of anchoritic houses. Indeed, a proverb quoted in *Ancrene Wisse* suggests that its subject matter was already a commonplace at the turn of the thirteenth-century: 'me seið i bisahe. From mulne 7 from chepinge. from smiððe 7 from ancre hus me tidinge bringeð',[7] and an epigrammatic passage in the late fourteenth-century *Book to a Mother* suggests that it remained proverbial rather than topical:

> Þerfore modir, ches þou Crist to þin Abbot. For he wol ӡeue þe no leue to ride ne to go out of þi cloister for recreacioun, and so be worse whannne þou comest hom þanne whanne þou wendest out; ne se uanitees, ne telle ne here idel tales, ne to speke ueine wordes, ne to haue lustes and likinges and worldli worschupes; *to be a good womman in o side of a wal, and in þat oper a schrewe …* (my italics)[8]

There is also an echo here of Cassian's theme that going out of the cloister is not just to fail to progress but actively to regress.[9] Other treatments of the important cell or cloister boundary occur: as Alexandra Barratt points out, the

[4] J.Jusserand, 'Les contes à rire et la vie des recluses au xiie siècle', *Romania*, 24 (1895), 122–28.

[5] For comment on some of these figures and their relation to the Wife of Bath and La Vieille, see William Mathew, 'The Wife of Bath and All Her Sect', *Viator*, 5 (1974), 413–43, and for a more general account of female managerial skills in the fabliaux see Lesley Johnson, 'Women on Top: Anti-Feminism in the Fabliau?', *MLR*, 78 (1983), 298–307. For an example of fabliau motifs enriching religious discourse see the interpolated passage in the late Middle English translation of Guigo's *Scala Claustralium*, 'A Ladder of Foure Ronges …' printed as Appendix B in *Deonise Hid Divinitee*, edited by Phyllis Hodgson, EETS 231 (London, 1955), pp.113–4, where God is presented as an enticing taverner (not unlike the youth of Watriquet de Couvin's fabliau, *Les iii dames de Paris*). The translation is discussed by Hodgson, '"A ladder of foure ronges by the whiche men mowe wele clyme to heuen." A Study of the Prose Style of a Middle English Translation', *MLR*, 44 (1949), 465–75, who comments (p.466), 'one cannot be certain whether these additions are in fact translation or original prose, but it is indisputable that some of the most memorable passages are to be found in them'. The *Scala Claustralium* is edited by E.Colledge and J.Walsh in Sources chrétiennes, 163 (Paris, 1970). On English recluses, see further R.M.Clay, *The Hermits and Anchorites of England* (London, 1914).

[6] See the edition by C.H.Talbot, 'The "De Institutis Inclusarum" of Ailred of Rievaulx', *Analecta Sacri Ordinis Cisterciensis*, 7 (1951), 167–217 (p. 177, l. 20 – p. 178, l. 10).

[7] *Ancrene Wisse, MS Corpus Christi College Cambridge 402*, edited by J. R. R. Tolkien, EETS 249 (London, 1962), f. 23a, p. 48. All quotations are from this edition and will henceforth be cited by folio and page number in the text.

[8] *Book to a Mother*, edited by A. J. McCarthy, Salzburg Studies in English Literature, Studies in the English Mystics 1 (Salzburg, 1981), p. 124, ll. 6–12.

[9] *Cassian, Conférences*, edited by E. Pichery, *Sources Chrétiennes*, 42, 54, 64 (Paris, 1955), VI xv pp. 239–40.

story of Dinah – Dinah, who 'egressa est . . . ut videret mulieres' (Gen. 34.1) and was herself seen, desired and raped – is an often-used exemplum of how 'the apparently trivial violation of physical enclosure entails disaster'.[10] Abelard in his Rule for Heloise's Paraclete uses the Dinah story and also Jeremiah 9.21 ('Quia ascendit mors per fenestras nostras,/ Ingressa est domos nostras') to warn that sin enters the soul through the window of the senses.[11]

In *Ancrene Wisse* itself, the boundary is concentrated on in several ways. Though Aelred is less closely followed than in the fifteenth-century English translation, his *anus garrula* turns up, in Part Two's discussion of 'þe heorte warde þurh þe fif wittes' (f .12a–b, p .29), as the 'ald cwene' whom, it is said, every anchoress must have 'to feden hire earen' (f .23a, p .48) as in Aelred's 'eam fabulis occupet, rumoribus ac detraccionibus pascat'.[12] The world coming with its feast for the senses to the anchoress's window is evoked in scornful verbal elaboration:

A meaðelilt þe meaðeleð hire alle þe talen of þe lond. a rikelot þe cakeleð al þ ha sið 7 here   (f .23a, p .48).

Ancrene Wisse also gives concentrated imagistic and psychological attention to the anchorhold's windows in Part One, a concentration recently illuminated by Georgianna's discussion of the progression of images from the windows themselves to King David's 'eye-window' to the leaping heart and Eve's fall as illustrative of the way in which 'looking, though seemingly innocuous and certainly passive enough, can abruptly become leaping in this tiny but concentrated spiritual landscape'.[13]

The power of the passage first quoted is then, rhetorical, a matter of effectively re-handling a *topos* rather than, necessarily, of social or historical observation. The passage's own metaphorical procedures enact the blurring of the demarcation and opposition that should exist between recluse and village gossip. In the structuring metaphors of exchange and ingestion, physical and spiritual become not only interchanged but worryingly mixed: the 'lust and likynge, bakbitynge, sclaundre and hatrede' with which the recluse is fed take on alarming corporeality, while the food she returns to the old woman is 'mete and drinke', not spiritual example. The recluse herself ingests 'tales' with which she is 'fulfilled', while the food which should be used simply to satisfy her own bare physical needs becomes the currency of a debased exchange with the world. These violations are disturbing because they un-fix and re-open the whole question of what, and in what way, the image of the enclosed recluse means. There are questions here not only for the recluse herself, but, as the continuing use of the *topos* in medieval transmission of anchoritic rules beyond their original audiences and to wider

[10] Alexandra Barratt, 'Anchoritic Aspects of *Ancrene Wisse*', *MAE*, 49 (1980), 32–56.

[11] T. P. McLaughlin, 'Abelard's Rule for Religious Women', *Medieval Studies*, 18 (1956), 241–92 (p. 255).

[12] Talbot, 'The "De Institutis . . ." ', p. 178, ll. 3–4 (future quotations will be referred to by page and line number in the text).

[13] Linda Georgianna, *The Solitary Self: Individuality in the Ancrene Wisse* (Cambridge, Mass. and London, 1981), p. 64.

publics over several centuries testifies, for medieval audiences, to say nothing of ourselves.

As the passage in question says, shutting one's body between two walls is not a straightforward or adequate basis for a reclusive life, even though it may be a condition of entry to it. Indeed, faced with the once-for-all enclosure in which, on occasion, the Office of the Dead is said over the recluse as she enters her cell for ever, the imagination rebels – how *could* anyone choose such a life? – and responds with vicarious curiosity about what, minute by minute, a recluse does. One ready imaginative short-cut says that as the official conditions of her life are obviously unendurable, she must corrupt them: hence the faintly prurient piquancy of the frequently-repeated recluse/*entremetteuse* opposition (sometimes, as later in this example, developed into 'ancresse selle' *versus* 'bordel hous' or, as in the Dinah story, into chaste enclosure *versus* rape). The imagination tests and probes the absoluteness of this boundary of enclosure, and flirts with the possibility of subverting it (hence Jusserand and Aelred agree, for different reasons, on the probability of fabliau matter arising here). The Outer Rule and Part One of *Ancrene Wisse* offer, in particularly clear form, some practical answers to the problem of what a recluse does: the ceaseless round of offices and devotions, instruction of servants, sewing and other manual work, blood-letting and other penitential practices clearly occupy much time and thought in the way of legitimate busy-ness for the recluse. To imagine why anyone should choose such a life however, both the recluse and other audiences for the treatises written for her require the disciplined exploration and articulation of inner space beyond the cell-boundary which Aelred and *Ancrene Wisse* offer in corrective development of the fabliau-like stylizations of the untutored imagination.

If the fascination of the recluse in her cell, as strong in its different way as that of the 'burde in the bour', is in part due to the way her existence seems the visible instituting of a boundary-line between flesh and spirit, it is also true that the recluse's own body continues to exist on the further side of that boundary. What account, then, is offered by these anchoritic treatises of the concept of the body in the recluse's existence? And what kind of demarcation is involved in the boundary-line of the cell with its window and its metaphoric capacity to represent the human body: where, so to speak are 'inner' and 'outer' and how absolute are they? (There is no reason to assume that medieval accounts of the sense of body-space and personal territory – of the location of inner and outer – will be the same as our own).[14]

[14] See, for example, Colin Morris, *The Discovery of the Individual 1050–1200*, Church History Outlines, 5 (London, 1972). Morris prefaces his study of developing medieval interest in the individual by quoting Auden's poem:

> Some thirty inches before my nose
> the frontier of my Person goes;
> and all the untilled air between
> is private *pagus* or demesne ...,

which, as Morris points out, evokes the un-medieval 'experience of individual identity ... familiar to most of us. We think of ourselves as people with frontiers, our personalities divided from each other as our bodies visibly are' (p. 1), whereas part of the interest of medieval notions of individuality for us must be precisely that they are not predicated as ours are.

Any complete dismissal of the body would of course be heretical to the incarnational theology of Christianity. Javelet's survey of pre-scholastic theoretical terminology abundantly demonstrates, in its sixth section 'Nature et corps, vestige de Dieu', how much early medieval thinkers are prepared to work with the idea of the body even if they are sometimes tempted to feel it as a nuisance and a hindrance.[15] Although the 'ressemblance de Dieu' is reserved by some thinkers (such as Gilbert of Thierry) as a capacity of 'l'homme intérieur', this does not mean that the body is 'en soi un poids ou une tentation' (p.234). There is also discussion of the extent to which the soul can be an 'exemplar exterioris hominis': Javelet points to Yves of Chartres' reflections on how, although the soul is not corporeal, 'dans les rêves elle se voit marcher, s'asseoir, aller ou voler ici et là' and that this 'ne se fait pas sans une certaine ressemblance avec le corps' (p.233, *PL* 161.969). For the pre-scholastics, Javelet proposes, 'il n'est pas de métaphysique ou de psychologie pure: l'être est inseré dans l'esprit' (not, as one might expect, 'l'esprit dans l'être', p.179) and he concludes that 'pour attendre la perfection il faut bien se connaître: il n'est donc pas de spiritualité authentique sans qu'il soit tenu compte de corps' (p.224). The *Speculum Inclusarum* written in England in the fourteenth century as readily includes a discussion of the heavenly glories of the body as of the soul. These include such gifts as refulgent shining (cf. Matt. 13.43 'iusti fulgebunt sicut sol'), as shown by Christ 'in corpore suo, quando transfiguravit se in monte et facies eius resplenduit sicut sol (Matt. 17.2)', and the *agilitas* which Christ showed in walking on the water and which will be restored, in resurrection, to the body (particularly the anchoritic one) which has endured restriction by being 'buried with Christ'. There will be such a bond of union between body and soul, says the *Speculum*, that the joy from the soul will flow uninterruptedly in the body: now we see these things in a glass darkly, but *then* 'clare videbimus et sencibiliter percepiemus'.[16] Though there may be a temptation to leave the idea of the body at the cell entrance, anchoritic rules do not and should not succumb to it.

The consonance of this theology with the imagistically rich practice of vernacular texts has been indicated in John Burrow's seminal article on the *Cloud of Unknowing*. The *Cloud* author, in Burrow's argument, shares a difficulty with the anchoritic writer in that 'even if we successfully stop thinking *about* created things, we will still go on thinking *with* them'.[17] Religious discourse is 'radically metaphorical' (p.286) and it is thus all the more crucial that physical and spiritual are seen to have their own integrity. In an ascetic treatise on negative mysticism we might expect the contemplative's concern with the problem of avoiding 'bodily conseite of a goostly thing': the equivalent concern with 'goostly conceite of a bodely thing' is more

---

[15] R. Javelet, *Image et ressemblance au douzième siècle: de saint Anselme à Alain de Lille*, 2 vols (Paris, 1967).

[16] *Speculum Inclusorum Auctore Anonymo Anglico Saeculi XIV*, edited by P. L. Oliger, *Lateranum*, 4 (Rome, 1938), 3–148 (pp. 132–34).

[17] J. A. Burrow, 'Fantasy and Language in *The Cloud of Unknowing*', *EC*, 27 (1977), 283–298 (p. 284).

surprising, but is necessarily and appropriately present (Burrow, p.284). Similarly, in locating anchoritic treatises' concern with the body, the appropriate starting point is their characteristic figurative procedures and their implications for how the recluse's continuing bodily existence is imagined.

A recluse's life, as the fifteenth-century translation from Aelred insists, must not have a story in or to it. The recluse must neither hear nor provide the material for a narrative, her life must have a structure but not a plot. In imagining and articulating this life, anchoritic rules do include exemplary narratives: Aelred uses both well-known figures and case-histories known to him and *Ancrene Wisse* turns the image of Christ the lover-knight of the soul into a miniature chivalrically-toned *exemplum*.[18] Nevertheless, the more characteristic rhetorical form for these treatises on the enclosed, physically stable and highly-interiorized reclusive form of the religious life is the analogy or *similitudo*, a form which enables the writer to 'think with created things' (Burrow, p.285) and to structure inner space without becoming a tale-teller. 'Similitudo' is in some ways an awkward term in that it has extra-rhetorical medieval meanings (Javelet, p.xxiii), in that analogy is a mode of thought as well as a specific rhetorical device, and in the fact that medieval terminology is not always fixed and *similitudo* and *exemplum* are on occasion used of much the same kind of rhetorical structure (*Ancrene Wisse*'s vernacular terms for its narrative of the lover-knight are 'a tale' *and* 'a wrihe forbisne' (f.105a, p.198) for that matter).[19] In general however, a distinction seems maintainable (and is usually maintained in medieval usage) between the exemplum's self-contained, plot-based narrative, inserted into discourse and used for exemplary purposes, and the narrative articulation of a continuous configuration of circumstances or particular images which constitutes the more intrinsically allegorical mode of the *similitudo*.

One early formal fixing of the *similitudo* in religious discourse which was in all likelihood known both to Aelred and the *Ancrene Wisse* author is the collection of Anselm of Canterbury's talk which became known to the middle ages as the *De similitudinibus*. The title *Liber de humanis moribus per similitudines* given the earlier recension of this work by Southern and Schmitt

---

18 Talbot, 'The "De Institutis . . ." ', p. 191 (St Agnes); p. 192, ch. 18 (the ascetic monk known to Aelred); p. 194, ch. 22 (the man known to Aelred). *Ancrene Wisse*'s lover-knight story is discussed by Dennis Rygiel, 'The Allegory of Christ the Lover-Knight in *Ancrene Wisse*: An Experiment in Stylistic Analysis', *Studies in Philology*, 73 (1976), 343–364.
19 In Anselm's *Liber de humanis moribus* (see below, p. 200 and note 20) no. 141 is called a '*Similitudo* inter divina alimentae et praecepta' while no. 142 is called an '*Exemplum* novi vasis semel imbuti' (italics mine) without there being an obvious reason for the distinction. Though the text was in all likelihood drafted by Anselm, Boso of Bec probably worked on it after his death and, as the editors point out, though 'all the manuscripts have *some* rubrics' there is 'almost no measure of agreement between them' (p. 8, see note 20 below). See also the discussion of 'L'"exemplum" dans le sermon' by Schmitt in Claude Brémond, Jacques Le Goff, Jean-Claude Schmitt, *L'"exemplum"*, Typologie des sources du moyen âge occidental, 40 (Turnhout, 1982), pp. 148–64.

in their edition[20] is more suggestive of its construction, which is, as they point out, that of 'a treatise and not a series of Dicta' (p.7): it is 'the first attempt at a systematic study of the psychology of the religious life' (p.4). In setting out psychological phenomena and their application in the religious life however, the book uses analogy to such vivid effect in its procedure as to have been most influential as a reservoir of useful *similitudines*.[21] The pregnant brevity of the second *similitudo* makes it a good example of Anselm's method:

> *Similitudo inter mulierem et voluntatem*
> Voluntas itaque illa, quae est instrumentum volendi, sic est inter deum et diabolum, quomodo mulier inter suum legitimum virum et aliquem adulterem. Vir ei praecipit, ut sibi soli coniungatur; adulter vero persuadet, ut et sibi copuletur. Si itaque se soli legitimo viro coniungat, legitima est et ipsa, filiosque legitimos generat. Si autem adultero se iunxerit, adultera est et ipsa, filiosque adulterinos parit ...
>
> (p.31)

For all its apparent simplicity, this *similitudo* uses effective 'grammatical rhyme' and sound-patternings ('praecipit ... persuadet', '... coniungat, legitima ... iunxerit, adultera ...', for instance, or the polyptoton of 'adultero ... adultera ... adulterinos'). In its content, a dynamic sense of process is quickly engendered in the move from verbal definition ('voluntas ... instrumentum volendi') to metaphysical positioning ('inter deum et diabolum') to a concretizing image-set, the relations between whose members structure both terms of the comparison. The imagistic content of the simile gains cumulative suasive power in its articulation and, as the initial image-set generates further members of itself which then appear to have been predictable, the analogy as a whole gains conviction and its subject matter greater memorability (literally, one might say, greater 're-member-ability').

Particularly notable use of the *similitudo* is made by Aelred in his *De institutione inclusarum*. It has been argued that this work separates spiritual and corporeal more rigidly and harshly than *Ancrene Wisse* (Georgianna, pp.46–50). The two rules are certainly very different, for all *Ancrene Wisse*'s use of *De institutione*,[22] but the clarity about literal and figurative uses of body and spirit which we could feel as harshness in Aelred's transitions between the two may express acceptance of both categories, rather than a rigid dualism. Certainly Aelred felt strongly that the 'outer' aspects of monastic rules could not be dismissed and, to rebuke a suggestion to this effect, wrote a short

[20] Edited by R.W.Southern and F.S.Schmitt, *Memorials of St Anselm*, Auctores britannici mediiaevi, I (London, 1969). The manuscripts of the treatise's second, expanded version (the *De similitudinibus*) suggest that it was not widely circulated before the thirteenth century: the earlier version, the *Liber de humanis moribus*, was quickly known in the West Midlands (see Southern and Schmitt, Introduction, pp.11–18).
[21] See R.W.Southern, *St Anselm and His Biographer* (Cambridge, 1963), pp.221–26 and the Introduction to the edition cited in note 20. J.E.Wells long ago drew attention to vernacular use of the treatise: see *A Manual of the Writings in Middle English* (New Haven and London, 1916), p.285, and see also p.274.
[22] Ayto and Barratt, pp.xxxviii–xlii.

treatise on the monastic life asserting the relation between outward observance and inner disposition.[23] Here in *De institutione*, his sense of the recluse's mental and physical life in his use of analogy suggests that he does not deal in simply reductive 'outer' and 'inner' dichotomies.

As might be expected, Aelred makes especially heavy use of analogy in the second stage of his Rule, as it moves from chastity to charity and considers the relation of the recluse's bodily condition to her spiritual fulfillment. Virginity is as gold, tempered in the furnace of the anchoritic cell (p.189, ll.21–4); the recluse is like a timid dove wisely haunting the clear river-waters in which the predatory shape of the hovering kite can be discerned when she studies the scriptures and is warned of the devil's approach (p.193, ll.6–11). Many of these images offer imaginative consolation for, or a perspective on, the restriction and sensory deprivation of the recluse's life: a Cistercian concern with external plainness is complemented by attention to the meditative inner eye. Thus, bidden to put away ornament as vanity, the recluse is invited instead to don a golde hemmed coat of the virtues:

> Sed illam te nolim quasi sub specie deuocionis sequi gloriam in picturis uel sculpturis, in pannis auium uel bestiarum, aut diuersorum (f.21) florum ymaginibus uariatis … Iungatur castitati humilitas, et nichil erit splendidius. Prudencie societur simplicitas, et nichil erit lucidius … In hac uarietate tue mentis oculos occupa … cui si fimbrias (f.21v) aureas addas, uestem polimitam in qua te sponsus cum summa delectacione conspiciat texuisti. Fimbria extrema pars, quasi finis est uestimenti. Finis autem precepti caritas est …   (p.195, 1.15 – p.196, 1.2)

The recluse, having abandoned external richness, can become a soul going to its bridegroom in a fair garment, finished and supremely adorned with charity. This image articulates a shaping aspiration, the recluse's reason for crossing the boundary between world and cell in the first place. But it is not adumbrating a once-for-all exchange of body for spirit and outer for inner: the recluse's interior condition should shape her attitude to her continuing external environment of the cell. Aelred now gives his most extended *similitudo* as a model for how the recluse should direct her corporeal eye[24] in the light of her inner vision:

---

[23] A.Wilmart, 'Un court traité d'Aelred sur l'étendue et le but de la profession monastique', *Revue d'Ascétique et de Mystique*, 23 (1947), 259–273; see also C.Dumont, 'L'équilibre humain de la vie Cistercienne, d'après le Bienheureux Ælred de Rievaulx', *Collectanea Ordinis Cisterciensium Reformatorum*, 18 (1956), 177–89, esp. p.178 ('Pour le Bienheureux Ælred, en effet, comme pour saint Bernard, ces deux pars [body and soul] de la vie monastique se tiennent comme les deux montants de l'échelle de l'humilité dont parle saint Benoit …') and p.185 (Aelred's belief in 'La béatitude dans notre corps aussi bien que dans notre âme' in the resurrection).

[24] Medieval theories of vision presuppose a closer connection between the nature of the perceived object and the resultant internal physiological processes than modern optics: see David Lindberg, *Theories of Vision from al-Kindi to Kepler* (London and Chicago, 1976); see also M.W.Bundy, *The Theory of Imagination in Classical and Mediaeval Thought*, University of Illinois Studies in Language and Literature XII (Illinois, 1927), esp. ch.9 and the discussion in ch.10 of Hugh of St Victor's *De unione corporis et spiritus*, *PL*, Vol.CLXXVII, col.285.

In hiis glorieris, in hiis [the ornamenting virtues of the gold-hemmed garment] delecteris, intus non foris, in ueris uirtutibus, non in picturis et ymaginibus. Panni linei candidi tuum illud ornent altare, qui castitatem suo candore commendent, et simplicitatem premonstrent. Cogita quo labore, quibus tunsionibus terrenum in quo creuit linum colorem exuerit, et ad talem candorem peruenerit, ut ex eo ornetur altare, Christi corpus ueletur. Cum terreno colore omnes nascimur, quoniam in iniquitatibus conceptus sum, et in peccatis meis concepit me mater mea. Primum igitur linum aquis immergitur, nos in aquis baptismatis Christo consepelimur. Ibi deletur iniquitas, sed necdum sanatur infirmitas. Aliquid candoris recepimus in peccatorum remissione, sed necdum plene terreno colore exuimur pro naturali que (f .22) restat corrupcione. Post aquas linum siccatur, quia neccesse est post aquas baptismatis corpus per abstinenciam maceratum illicitis humoribus uacuetur. Deinde linum malleis tunditur, et caro nostra multis temptacionibus fatigatur. Post hec linum ferreis aculeis discerpitur, ut deponat superflua, et nos discipline ungulis rasi, uix necessaria retinemus. Adhibetur post hec lino suauiorum stimulorum leuior purgacio, et nos uictis cum magno labore pessimis passionibus a leuioribus et cotidianis peccatis simplici confessione et satisfaccione mundamur. Iam tunc a nentibus linum in longum producitur, et nos in anteriora perseuerancie longanimitate extendimur. Porro ut ei perfectior accedat pulchritudo ignis adhibetur et aqua, et nobis transeundum est per ignem tribulacionis et aquam compunccionis, ut perueniamus ad refrigerium castitatis. Hec tibi oratorii tui ornamenta representent, non oculos tuos ineptis uarietatibus pascant   (p .196, ll .3–23).[25]

Where the non-literal fairness and brightness of virtues ornamented the soul's garment in the preceding metaphorical scheme, here the literal whiteness of the altar cloth signifies its traditional meaning of purity: not the *tabula rasa* purity of blankness and absence of colour, but the purity resulting from processes of purging and penance, as fulling removes colour and stain from flax. Here the semantic field of cloth-making re-structures the recipient field of human life under the aspect of penance. Not only does one lexical set produce a series of correspondences with another, but, as Gillian Evans has said of Anselm's *similitudines* 'the structural relation between the parts of the analogy is the same as that between parts of the argument'.[26] The simultaneous multiplication of terms for cloth-fulling and penitential development and their structural proportion encourage the prediction of similarities,

---

[25] Space here precludes quotations of the lively, expansive translation of this *similitudo* in the Vernon MS, but comparison of Aelred's Latin and the Vernon version is made in more detail by my student Jennifer Potts (in her forthcoming Liverpool Ph.D. thesis) in the introductory chapters on medieval and modern linguistic theories and early religious prose which preface her concordance to MS CCCC 402 of *Ancrene Wisse*.

[26] 'St Anselm's Analogies', *Vivarium*, 4 (1976), 81–93 (p .85).

the sense of coming upon them with recognition rather than receiving them as new information. As with Anselm, this cumulatively suasive effect is a major source of our cognitive pleasure and conviction of cogency in the *similitudo*. The processes of anticipation, recognition and confirmation are important, for the audience must be drawn sufficiently into the metaphoric logic to accept the conclusion that in the proper development of a human life penitential purgation is a necessary and continuous condition. For the recluse, above all, austerity and penance are not individual acts, or aberrations to be patiently endured: they are the condition of human life, ideas which properly inform it, just as the principle of acting on the substance of a raw material fashions that raw material to its proper end in cloth.

A plain white altar cloth is a permitted item of the limited anchoritic cell-furniture in stricter rules, though in general church vestments were of plain linen only when the surface was intended to be 'completely hidden by needlework', and silk was preferred for vestments embroidered, as they often were, 'cum ymaginibus Sanctae Mariae, et Johannis Baptistae et diversis animalibus' or with 'leonibus, serpentibus, volantibus aquilis, piscibus interjectis, cum punctis albis et nigris', and fringed 'cum aurifrigio'.[27] Recluses usually had their own separate altar furnishings and were forbidden to have custody of church plate or vestments,[28] though often the manual work of female recluses was embroidery of vestments for churches and churchmen (Christina of Markyate for instance made some famous mitres and sandals 'operis mirifici' which were sent to Adrian IV).[29] The actuality of this altar cloth is an important part of Aelred's argument. Present to the recluse's eye both before and after the fulling analogy, the cloth serves as the point of departure and return for a meditative process. Its plainness becomes heavily freighted with meaning: not only its whiteness, but its function (wrapping Christ's body) and its very composition and substance become more semantically weighty than any figurative surface of embroidery could be. The white cloth should now instantly summon, whenever the eye falls on it, this inner 'narrative' of purity, making plainness the chief ornament of the recluse's cell.

In the cogency with which this *similitudo* converts literal into spiritual meaning it is hardly to be outdone by such vivid and extensive analogies as Anselm's 'Similitudo inter cor humanum et molendinum' (no. 41) and its structural positioning is not without point either. Preceded by the ornamental figurative garment of virtues, it is immediately followed by encouragement to use the veritable representative power of the crucifix (a further actual furnishing of the cell, but one which requires no *similitudo* in order to signify) as a direct incitement to charity, and it is finally enclosed within a return to the wedding garment which ends in, or is fringed by charity, and which now becomes the starting point for a 'diuisio caritatis' (p.36, l.414). The

[27] A.G.I.Christie, *English Medieval Embroidery* (Oxford, 1938), pp.19, 40, 39.
[28] Meyr-Harting, 'Functions of a Twelfth Century Recluse ...', p.347.
[29] Christie, *Embroidery*, pp.1–2.

metaphoric schemes concerned with ornament and its meaning are thus in developmental, not fortuitous, contiguity. The recluse's acceptance of penitential austerity is a continuing daily process in the circumstances of her life (as summed up in the altar cloth's plainness) and is framed by her initial commitment to renouncing *gloria* in order to don the wedding garment of the *sponsa Christi*. These ideas have their counterparts in prescription in the 'outwarde lyuinge' as MS Bodley 423 calls the first part of the Rule (p.9, l.339): the recluse's external garment 'non sit de panno subtili uel precioso, sed mediocri nigro, ne uideatur colore uario affectare decorem' (p.118, ll.16–17). Here, in the recluse's 'ynner conuersacion' (p.9, l.340), ornament and its literal and figurative absence and presence is further explored in a mental landscape as vigorous as the framing definitions of space and lively interchanges of boundaries in an illuminated Romanesque initial. This account of the inner life of the recluse in part derives its vigour from a continuing recognition and use of the recluse's physical circumstances: Aelred is not prescribing a simply dualistic replacement of corporeal by spiritual life.

Though Aelred's Rule takes more subtle cognizance of the recluse's physical existence than might at first be thought, it is not *Ancrene Wisse*. The *Ancrene Wisse* author works with a physiological level of response to analogy, which, re-internalized, and exploited rather than suppressed in the conceptual apprehension of simile and metaphor, allows his reclusive audience still further dimensions of imagined bodily experience. In his analogies, the audience's co-operative prediction of correspondences is both drawn on and disrupted: more startling kinds of engagement are demanded by *Ancrene Wisse*'s readiness to exploit its analogies' unexpected or apparently inert elements.

Near the opening of Part Six on 'Penitence' a comparative triad is set out:

Þreo manere men of godes icorene liuieð on eorðe. Þe ane mahe beon to gode pilegrimes ieuenet. Þe oþreʳ to deade. Þe þridde to ihongede wið hare gode wil o iesuse rode. Þe forme beoð gode. þe oþre beoð betere. Þe þridde best of alle.

(f.94b, pp.177–8)

This encourages the audience to look for a relation between 'pilgrim', 'dead' and 'crucified' which will structurally replicate that of the grammatical degress of positive, comparative and superlative.[30] Since, by a basic orientational metaphor 'UP is GOOD',[31] the highest 'steire' (f.95a, p.180) of the superlative is felt to be furthest away from the analogy's audience. Certainly the first two degrees of comparison provide matter enough so that

[30] On grammatical metaphor, see John A.Alford, 'The Grammatical Metaphor: A Survey of Its Use in the Middle Ages', *Speculum*, 57 (1982), 728–60.
[31] G.Lakoff and M.Johnson, *Metaphors We Live By* (Chicago, 1980), pp.14–19.

the question of what the superlative might be or mean temporarily recedes. The paradox of death as a better mode of life 'on eorðe' involves a greater tension between the elements of the comparison than in the analogy of casual attachment to the world as pilgrimage, and the mental progression involved in following the triad enacts physical movement up the degrees of a stair.

The logic of the triad however, now demands a superlative, and a superlative for a comparative ('death') which, taken literally, is itself an absolute. Urged by much rhetorical prompting and preparation, the audience must now address itself to predicating this third, impossibly remote and highest degree of the triad:

Þis [death to the world] is an heh steire; ah ȝet is an herre. Ant hwa stod eauer þrín? Godd wat þe þe seide. Michi absit gloriari nisi in cruce domini mei iesu christi. per quam michi mundus crucifixus est 7 ego mundo. þis is þ ich seide þruppe (f.94a) Crist me schilde forte habben eani blisse i þis world; bute i iesu cristes rode mi lauerd. þurh hwam þe world is me unwurð; ant ich am unwurð híre as weari þe is ahonget. A lauerd hehe stod he þe spec o þisse wise. *ant þis is ancre steire*

(f.95b, p.180; italics mine)

As with Langland's Do-Best, the power of the superlative *retrospectively* to render distinctions of degree irrelevant is here fully exploited. Just as the relation of the superlative to the positive and the comparative is different from theirs to each other and transforms the previous structure of comparison, so the 'ancre steire' (that 'i na þing ne blissi ich me bute i godes rode. þ ich þolie nu wa 7 am itald unwurð as godd wes o rode', (f.95b, p.180) is not just less or more indifferent to pain and shame but can convert their meaning:

Þe pilgrim i þe worldes wei þah he ga forðward toward te hám of heouene; he sið 7 hereð unnet. 7 spekeð umbe hwile. wreaðeð him for weohes. 7 moni þing mei letten him of his Iurnee. Þe deade nis namare of scheome þen of menske. of heard. þen of nesche; for he ne feleð nowðer. 7 for þi ne ofearneð he nowðer wa; ne wunne. ah þe þe is o rode 7 haueð blisse þrof; he *wendeð scheome to menske; 7 wa ín to wunne.* 7 ofearneð for þi hure ouer hure

(f.95b, p.180; italics mine).

Moreover, the audience's position vis à vis the analogy is also fully exploited. Intuitively oriented to distance and difficulty in the superlative, the anchoress finds that she is already there, living within a difficult choice already made. It is as if the anchoress is pushed around by the analogy as her instinctive conceptual orientation towards it is reversed. *Ancrene Wisse*'s comparisons can act more violently on their audience than Aelred's, not only demanding cognitive and imaginative assent, but, in so far as conceptual re-direction is experienced as movement, offering a further dimension to the anchoress's experience of inner space and internalizing the physical movement denied her by her choice of stable enclosure.[32]

The immediately following sequence of images in *Ancrene Wisse* Part Six offers equally multi-dimensional uses of analogy. Pain and shame are the two sides of a ladder raised to heaven (f.96a, p.181). Like Langland's plant of peace (Passus I, ll.148–60), which from being light as a linden leaf and 'persaunt' as a needle-point grows by authentically disturbing development in its own metaphorical vehicle into the battering-ram which assaults hell,[33] this comparison is mobilised by the development of the ladder uprights into Elijah's chariot wheels, streaking firily up into heaven. The heat of these flaming wheels signifies all the pain flesh is heir to, the redness of their fire signifies shame (an explication which among other things prepares the way for later exploitation of the physiological reaction most immediately available when heat and redness are linked with shame – the blush that is to connect Christ's blood and the anchoress's penitential existence (f.96b, p.182). But – and here the semantic patterning of items in the analogy is daringly extended[34] – if we assent to the relation by which pain and shame may be structured through fire and redness, then we must also accept the relevance of a further property of the chariot wheels; they *are* wheels, they are *hweolinde*, they revolve as readily as shame and pain are *hwilende* – transitory (f.96a, p.181). We get here a linguistic paradigm of the way in which accepting fully the nature of the counter-intuitive experiences of pain and shame will turn out to be a way of dealing with them. This re-orientation is expressed in the conceptual equivalent of a physical right-about turn, as the new lexical item enters the analogy in a mode other than the already established relations and directions of its parallels. Once again analogy is exploited less as aesthetically and cognitively cogent patterning than as conceptually violent experience, in which it is not so much a matter of the audience's perceiving cognitive structures with an internal vision as of its being pushed and dragged through interior space.

Near the end of Part Six's discussion of penitence, the anchoresses' ability to interiorize pain and shame is presupposed as so developed that it can be imaged in the following terms:

[32] On the general internalization of the concept of *peregrinatio* and the increased value of enclosure as opposed to eremiticism, see J.Leclercq, 'Monachisme et pérégrination du ixᵉ au xiiᵉ siècle', *Studia Monastica*, 3 (1961), 33–52.

[33] See David Mills, 'The Role of the Dreamer in *Piers Plowman*', in *Critical Approaches to Piers Plowman*, edited by S.S.Hussey (London, 1969), pp.180–212 (p.201), where it is argued that the development here is by association and creates a series of partially adequate images, the inadequacy of any single one of which to convey the infinite is the point of the passage. *Ancrene Wisse*'s practice offers ways in which the extension of imagery can occur without entailing an enacted linguistc break-down or inadequacy.

[34] See Adrienne Lehrer, 'Structures of the Lexicon and Transfer of Meaning', *Lingua*, 45 (1978), 95–123, esp. p. 96: 'If there is a set of words that have semantic relations in a semantic field . . . and if one or more items pattern in another semantic field, then the other items in the first field are available for extension to the second semantic field. Perceived similarity is not necessary'. See further Eva Kittay and Adrienne Lehrer, 'Semantic Fields and the Structure of Metaphor', *Studies in Language*, 5 (1981), 31–63.

Al þ ich habbe iseid of flesches písunge: nis nawt for ow míne leoue sustren. þe oðerhwile þolieð mare þen ich walde. Ah is for sum þ schal rede þis inohreaðe: þe grapeð hire to softe. Noðeles ʒunge ímpen me bigurd wið þornes leste beastes freoten ham hwil ha beoð mearewe. ʒe beoð ʒunge impen iset i godes orchard. þornes beoð þe heardschipes þ ich habbe ispeken of. 7 ow is neoð þ ʒe beon biset wið ham abuten. þ te beast of helle hwen he snakereð toward ow forte biten on ow: hurte him o þe scharpschipe 7 schunche aʒeínwardes

(f .102b, p .193).

Thorns are grasped with pain and aversion: they are usually conceptualized as pointed towards us, intrusive into body-space. Here, the normal direction of apprehension is reversed: these thorns are grasped by their roots, the points turned outwards from the body in defense. Penance is not a martyring crown of thorns pressing into the skin, but a protective girdle turned outwards against the depredations of the serpentine devil who tempted Eve in God's first orchard. The conceptual reversal of thorns into a protective barrier sums up a reversal, worked for throughout this section, in the audience's conception of and affective response to, pain and shame. Comparable development of the sensorily counter-intuitive into the acceptable occurs in, for example, the images of the tearing of the flesh as the joyful irresponsibility of children with a rich father towards outer garments (f .98a, p .185); the desirability of closeness to the rebound of the blow to Christ which protects from the devil's cudgel (f .99a, p .187); and the imprint of the beloved on the mountains which is desirably heavy rather than light (f .103a, pp .193–4).

The author uses the anchoresses' corporeal existence as he uses their desires, fears, hopes and memories. The anchoress's continuing experience of inhabiting a body in space is drawn on, where Aelred's recluse is essentially imagined as immobile, using only her vision within the framing boundary of her cell. Aelred's use of the recluse's inner and outer vision within her cell is, as I have argued, imaginative and vigorous. It well exemplifies the value of analogy as a mode for illuminating the spiritual *via* correspondences with physical structures and processes, of using 'outer' to specify 'inner' and 'inner' to place 'outer'. With characteristic boldness and thoroughness, however, *Ancrene Wisse* develops still further a common heritage of linguistic structures and conceptual modes for the articulation of the demanding reclusive form of spiritual life. Its figurative language is not a-corporeal or anti-corporeal, but demands a physical and spatial engagement founded on the fact of physiological being as well as cognitive and emotional response.

If *Ancrene Wisse* reminds us that the body is one of the 'created things' (Burrow, p .284) with which the recluse goes on thinking and responding, it is also true that the concept of the body may, in these anchoritic treatises as in other medieval works, be delimited in wider ways than we first assume. Thus, for instance, preceding Aelred's analogy of the garment of the virtues in *De institutione*, there is a brief discussion of humility ('securum uirtutum omnium fundamentum', p .194, 1.24) and its corresponding vice, pride. Pride is divided into two kinds: 'in carnalem scilicet et spiritualem' and these are (not very illuminatingly) further explained:

> Carnalis superbia est de carnalis, spiritualis de spritualibus super-bire.
>
> (p.195, 1.1)

What does Aelred mean by 'bodily pride'? How can it occupy an equivalent category to all the obviously more numerous kinds of pride possible in the mental life? When Aelred goes on to subdivide bodily pride, it is obvious that his category includes more than physical pleasures and enjoyment of one's own body's looks or strength: bodily pride is of the two kinds, boasting and vain-glory ('iactanciam scilicet et uanitatem'), and

> Vanitatis est si ancilla Christi *intus in animo suo* glorietur se nobilibus ortam natalibus, si se diuiciis paupertatem pretulisse pro Christo (f.20v) delectetur, si se pauperibus et ignobilioribus preferre conetur, si se contempsisse diuitum nupcias quasi magnum aliquid admiretur
>
> (p.195, ll.2–6; italics mine).

MS Bodley 423 glosses 'carnalis superbia' as 'bostynge and veyn-glory of outwarde bodily thinges' (p.14, ll.533–4) and the Vernon MS warns the recluse against a 'fleshly delytyngge þat sche haþ forsake richesse of þe wordle' (p.33, 1.1). Aelred's bodily pride is wider than the individual's pleasure in her own corporeal being, and includes genetic vanity and genealogical inverted snobbery. It applies to ideas about, and uses of, the body and does not register a simple division into physical and spiritual.

Similarly, *Ancrene Wisse*'s treatment of pride, though it includes strong passages on the filth and weakness of the body ('Amid te menske of þi neb. þ is þe fehereste deal. bitweonen muðes smech. & neases smeal. ne berest tu as twa priue þurles? ...' f.775b, p.142), does so in exemplifying for *both* body and soul, the two things which are particularly appropriate for the humbling of each. Filth and weakness are the body's equivalent categories for sin and ignorance in the soul.

The body may be troublesome, but it is not a straightforward concept and cannot be simply dismissed any more than one's relation to it can simply cease in an anchoritic cell. We should be careful in reading medieval texts not to impose on them a harsher dualism than they in fact subscribe to. In her translation of *Ancrene Wisse* Mary Salu suggests that the text of a complicated passage in Part Three is in error, though with admirable care for presenting all the relevant information she allows the *lectio difficilior* to stand:

> Spearewe haueð ʒet acunde. þ is biheue ancre þah me hit heatie. þ is þe fallinde uuel. for muche neod is þ ancre of hali lif 7 of heh habbe fallinde uuel þ uuel ne segge ich nawt þ me swa nempneð: ah fallinde uuel ich

cleopie. licomes secnesse. oðer temptatiuns of flesches fondunges. hwer
þurh hire þunche þ ha falle duneward of hali hehnesse

(f.47a–b, p.91).

The sparrow has another characteristic which is becoming to an anchoress,
though it is generally unpopular, and that is the falling sickness. For there is
great need that an anchoress whose life is holy and exalted should have the
falling sickness; I do not mean the actual disease which is so called;[1] I am
giving the name 'falling sickness' to a disease of the body,[2] temptations of the
flesh by which she feels as though she were falling down from a height of
holiness.

1. Epilepsy
2. *Sic.* but perhaps an error for 'soul'.[35]

Not only do both Corpus Cristi College Cambridge 402 and MS Cotton
Cleopatra C. vi have the reading 'licomes' at the point of Salu's second
footnote but Dobson's Scribe D in MS Cotton has glossed the word as
'bodies' (gen. sg.).[36] It seems more likely that the *Ancrene Wisse* author has
an extended sense of bodily temptations (more like Aelred's than ours) which
he is specifically distinguishing from the particular disease, epilepsy, and that
the translation 'body' should indeed stand here.[37] As the author says, there
are, apart from epilepsy, many things that drag the body down, depress its
inhabitant and which can affect the interior life of the anchoress. Instead of
the instinctive confining of the body to the literal and forgettable which we
tend to bring to ascetic matters, the *Ancrene Wisse* author sees the body as
territory worthy of the complex and multifarious articulation of inner space
we many unwarily reserve for the spiritual. As he says:

Þah þe flesch beo ure fa.˙ hit is us iháten þ we halden hit up. wa we
moten don hit as hit is wel ofte wurðe.˙ ah nawt fordon mid alle. for hu
wac se hit eauer beo.˙ þenne is hit swa iculpet. 7 se feste ifeiet to ure
deorewurðe gast godes ahne furme.˙ þ we mahten sone slean þ an wið þ
oðer   (f.38a, p.73).

The recent work of Dahood and Ackerman has drawn attention to the
anchoresses' devotions in Part I of the Inner Rule, and not the least
extraordinary aspect of *Ancrene Wisse* is its care for the gestures and postures
of the anchoresses in their daily offices. Unusually among monastic and

---

[35] *The Ancrene Riwle*, translated by M.B.Salu (London, 1955), p.77.
[36] *The English Text of the Ancrene Riwle, Cotton Cleopatra C. vi*, edited by E.J.Dobson, EETS
267 (London, 1972), p.134, l.13, note 6.
[37] Bella Millett of Southampton University has suggested to me that one could also read 'licomes
secnesse. oðer temptatiuns of flesches fondunges' (f.47a, p.91) taking 'oðer' not (as Salu does)
as meaning 'in other words' but as 'or'. This would give the translation 'physical illness [ie. in
general] or temptations caused by the flesh [to which the soul succumbs, thus producing spiritual
illness]': a translation which makes better sense and which also suggests that 'licomes' is the
correct reading. (I am very grateful to Dr Millett for this and other helpful comments).

related rules, these are set out in full and precise detail.[38] The author's concern for bodily posture – his belief that stance and gesture need and deserve thought and ordering as they accompany, express or conduce to the anchoress's inner life – is also evident in other appropriate places in his Rule, as in the famous 'dog of hell' passage with its instructions to 'smit smeortliche adun þe cneon to þer eorðe. 7 breid up þe rode steaf. 7 sweng him o fowr half aȝeín helle dogge' (f.79a, p.150).

It is also worth remembering that, however subservient to the Inner Rule, the Outer Rule, with its practical and literal concern for the body, is equally present in *Ancrene Wisse*'s structure. Its position at the very end of the work demonstrates the priority of the Inner Rule, yet the final position is still a suprisingly climactic one for the Outer Rule. Where we might have expected the practical ordering of physical existence to be a preliminary to be got out of the way before consideration of the inner life can begin, *Ancrene Wisse* evidently positions this concern differently, as a mere but inevitable afterthought. The body is acknowledged in a regulated and proportionate way: dismissing it entirely cannot be the foundation of a continuing spiritual life.

We should guard against reading *Ancrene Wisse*'s concern for the corporeal and conceptual use of the body as evidence either for liberalizing impulses in what remains a very ascetic Rule, or as crudely dualistic. *Ancrene Wisse*'s articulation of the tensions and imaginative challenges of the cell's boundary-line is carried out within a theologically proportionate concern for body and soul. The resultant 'radically metaphorical' discourse could usefully expand the limits of empirical data available to the body of modern theory which sees metaphorical processes as linguistically central rather than deviant,[39] as it can expand our categories of 'inner' and 'outer'. In their accounts of medieval religious lives, anchoritic rules offer us potent imaginative and literary challenges.

[38] R.W.Ackerman, 'The Liturgical Day in *Ancrene Riwle*', *Speculum*, 53 (1978), 734–44; *Ancrene Riwle, Introduction and Part I*, edited and translated by R.W.Ackerman and Roger Dahood, Medieval and Renaissance Texts and Studies, 31 (Binghampton, New York, 1984).
[39] For a useful collection of modern theoretical studies see *Metaphor and Thought*, edited by Andrew Ortony (Cambridge, 1979).
[40] An earlier version of this paper was given in March 1984 in the Department of English Language, University of Edinburgh, whose members and students I thank for their hospitality. I am grateful to the British Academy for a grant with the help of which further work was done.

BOOKS OF COMFORT

Douglas Gray

Probably the most celebrated 'book of comfort' written in English is *A Dialogue of Comfort against Tribulation*, which was, as the rubric of the 1557 edition says, 'made in the yere of our lorde 1534, by syr Thomas More knyghte, while he was prysoner in the tower of London.' It is an extraordinary and a unique work, yet like other works of great originality it both uses and transforms traditions long in existence. Its most recent editors[1] remark that while it 'would seem to be closely related to the Christian tradition of comfort', it is 'different from all other comfort books both in the way in which it incorporates the classical *consolatio* and in its superior literary technique, which carries with it More's whole manner and mode of thought – the complexity of the dialogue form, the artistic structure and design, the various levels of audience address, and the strange, Menippean combination of merry tales and anecdotes side by side with the grim realities of mental and physical torture'. In their brief but valuable account of its literary background they distinguish two main lines of tradition, one, represented by the *De Consolatione Philosophiae* of Boethius, looking back to the ancient moral philosophers, and another which is fundamentally religious, and presents a Christian promise of eternal reward for men's sufferings on earth. 'Works of this sort' they say, 'were usually addressed to a popular audience and rarely rose above their doctrinal content. Their purpose was essentially didactic, and whatever literary distinction they achieved was derived primarily from interweaving orthodox themes and traditions, such as the imitation of Christ, the way of the cross, the *contemptus mundi*, and the *ars moriendi*.'[2] All this, no doubt, is in general true, but a student of medieval literature might wish to put forward two suggestions – firstly, that the 'philosophical' tradition is represented in great variety in the Middle Ages (and indeed in some cases can be seen blending with the 'religious' tradition), and, secondly, that the specifically religious books of comfort, even though they do not pretend to self-conscious literary artistry, are not entirely without art, or variety, or interest.

To sustain the first suggestion would require a long study. I shall simply list a few points and examples. To begin with, it is clear that Boethian influence is widespread, and fascinating in its diversity and ramifications. Nor were all the moral philosophers of antiquity forgotten: Seneca in particular is quoted in consolatory contexts. Works in similar vein by later writers are popular –

---

[1] *A Dialogue of Comfort against Tribulation*, edited by Louis L. Martz and Frank Manley, *Complete Works of Thomas More* (New Haven and London, 1963), XII (1976).
[2] Martz and Manley, p. cxviii. I have not been able to find a copy of Beach Langston's thesis on 'Tudor Books of Consolation', referred to in note 2.

Petrarch's *De Remediis Utriusque Fortunae* was widely read (and the fact that a section translated into fifteenth-century English is found in a manuscript containing contemplative and theological works suggests that it appealed to readers of 'religious' as well as 'philosophical' tastes).[3] Petrarch's version of Boccaccio's story of Griselda, Englished by Chaucer, perhaps owes some of its popularity to its 'consolatory' elements (it is no accident that at the end we are referred to the Epistle of St James, itself a little book of comfort against tribulation). Chaucer presents as one of his own offerings to his pilgrims a version of the *Livre de Mellibee*, based ultimately on the popular *Liber Consolationis et Consilii* of Albertano of Brescia. Even in More's day, Lord Berners was completing (1533) an English version of the *Golden Book of Marcus Aurelius*, another book which could be read as a general 'philosophical' book of comfort. And if one were to continue to search for 'consolatory elements' one could find them everywhere in medieval literature (in consolations in fictional narratives, for example for melancholy or despairing lovers, etc.). Nor was the tradition of the formal *consolatio* forgotten. Some of the consolatory topics or *solacia* of pagan antiquity (e.g. 'death is man's common lot' or 'nothing is to be gained by immoderate grief') were adapted by Christian writers, and can be found in such later works as *Pearl*.[4] What is very striking about the best 'consolations' in the vernacular is the highly individual way that grief and the mystery of suffering may be treated – as can be seen if we add to *Pearl* the *Book of the Duchess* or *Le Réconfort de Madame du Fresne*.[5] Of these earlier writers, More had certainly read Chaucer, and may well have been attracted by his combination of philosophical seriousness (we should think not only of his translation of Boethius but also of the questioning speeches he gives to his Palamon and to his Dorigen when they are weighed down with great tribulations) and merriness. It is tempting to think that Chaucer's strange, Menippean combinations of jokiness with grimness and with *solacia* in his account of Arcite's death or of 'earnest' and 'game' in the *Book of the Duchess* may have had some part in the formation of More's own technique in the *Dialogue*.

Consolatory elements are as ubiquitous in the area of specifically religious writing (we may find them, for instance, in Julian of Norwich or in Margery Kempe), and again, some of the most widely read religious books (such as the *Imitation of Christ*) can be used for consolation. However, my second suggestion, concerning those books designed expressly for 'comfort', can be illustrated in short space, though there are problems here too. A number of texts are not easily accessible. (Jolliffe's excellent check-list gives a good idea of the scope of the material.[6]) Most books and treatises of this kind are certainly aimed at a general audience, rather like their modern counterparts

[3] *A Dialogue between Reason and Adversity*, edited by F.N.M.Diekstra (Assen, 1968).
[4] See Ian Bishop, *Pearl in its Setting* (Oxford, 1968), pp.13–26.
[5] See the discussion in Erich Auerbach, *Mimesis*, translated by Willard Trask (Princeton, 1953), ch.10.
[6] P.S.Jolliffe, *A Check-List of Middle English Prose Writings of Spiritual Guidance*, Pontifical Institute of Medieval Studies, Subsidia Mediaevalia, 2 (Toronto, 1974), Section J.

which can be found in some numbers on the shelves of religious bookshops. One of the essential functions of religion in most ages has been to offer consolation in times of trouble. The lack of interest shown in the consolatory literature of the later Middle Ages (with the exception of the *Ars Moriendi*) has had the unfortunate result that the grimmer, more macabre aspects of the religion of that period have been sometimes grossly exaggerated.[7] However, the evidence clearly suggests that even if preachers tried sometimes to strike terror into their congregation's hearts by the pains of hell or the fear of death, confessors and counsellors at the beds of the sick and dying spoke of consolation, of fortitude and of hope.

Books of comfort intended for those suffering are usually simple and practical, and certainly without great literary pretension. A typical (and apparently popular) example which is now available in a good modern edition is *The Boke of Tribulacyon*, translated (perhaps in the late fourteenth century) from a French *Livre de tribulacion*, itself based on a Latin treatise probably of the thirteenth century. Its editor, Alexandra Barratt,[8] draws our attention to its very general nature. 'Tribulation' is taken in a wide sense, with the result that all readers could find their problems mirrored in the text. She also isolates very exactly the problem to which this kind of book addresses itself:

> ... human beings do not find suffering in itself intolerable; what they cannot bear is the fear that suffering is meaningless and has no purpose. The author ... tries to give an answer to the question, why do men and women suffer? In fact he provides not one, but twelve answers. His treatment may seem crude and unsatisfying to us, but let us at least give him credit for locating the problem.[9]

Like some other works in this genre it has a numerical pattern as its structure: the twelve 'services' which tribulation offers. As in many sermons, the matter of each is expounded through distinctions, and enlivened by vivid images. Thus the third 'service' is to 'purge' a man (a traditional topic): there are five 'manner of purgacions' – of the body (by medicine or by bleeding – and by bleeding either 'by veyne or by garsyng (cutting)'); of metals (by fire or by filing); of vines and trees; of grain (by the flail); of wine (by the presser). In general, the style is plain and workmanlike, but probably not many anthologists of religious prose would take an extract from it. This, however, would not always be the case with other works of the same type. My three

---

[7] On the *Ars Moriendi* see M.C.O'Connor, *The Art of Dying Well* (New York, 1942), and N.L.Beaty, *The Craft of Dying*, Yale Studies in English, 175 (New Haven and London, 1970). Interestingly, More, who showed in his earlier *Four Last Things* a remarkable skill in the 'macabre' style, eschewed it totally in his last book of comfort, whereas his friend Fisher makes use of it in his Tower work of consolation (*A spiritual consolacyon, written by Iohn Fyssher Bishop of Rochester, to his sister Elizabeth,* in *The English Works of John Fisher*, edited by J.E.B.Mayor, EETS e.s. 27 (London, 1876)).

[8] *The Book of Tribulation*, edited by Alexandra Barratt, Middle English Texts, 15 (Heidelberg, 1983).

[9] Barratt, p.31.

211

examples (of varying degrees of literary merit) come from the end of the period. They are chosen because they are almost totally unknown, and because they show the diverse traditions of consolatory devotion and of religious prose living on into More's own time.

Only two years before More's incarceration, Wynkyn de Worde produced an edition of *The Doctrynall of Dethe*, a work which he seems to have printed first c.1498.[10] The death-bed scene which prefaces it clearly indicates its type and purpose: it is a variant of the *Ars Moriendi*. It is to be used in the manner of the *Ars Moriendi*, as a preparation for death: 'this treatyse ... is to be redde afore a man or a woman whan it semeth that they be in the artycle (i.e. moment) of dethe' ...; '... rede this as it foloweth afore the seke persone.' If the sick person is not near to death, he should be read some 'holy matter'

> of þe love of our blessed lorde or of his great mercy/ or the commaundementes of god or some confessyonall/ that is to say/ some boke which techeth a man how he sholde confesse hym   (f.Bi).

The 'ideal' death-bed scene of the Middle Ages is evoked as the author continues

> Also se þt there be plente of holy water and þt it be ofttymes cast aboute þe house of the sycke persone. Also set in the syght of the syke a crucyfyx/ and also an ymage of our lady ... eyther in pycture or in carved werke ...   (f.Biᵛ)

Not surprisingly, the matter of this little book is totally traditional: 'a lytell payne in this lyfe avoydeth gret payne after this lyfe.' (f.Aiiᵛ) The arguments for patience and submission to God's will are put in the simplest theological setting: 'al sekenesse and payne cometh of synne for yf there had neuer ben synne there shold neuer haue ben no payne.' As in other 'arts of dying', there is great stress on the need for counsel against the temptations that will arise in extreme need. The devil, says the author, is likely to tempt steadfastness in faith; he will say, for instance, that Christ is not true God and man (f.Bii). Or he will tempt the sick person to despair (the contrary of which, hope, is encouraged by the example of sinners – including some saints, like St Peter – who were forgiven), to anger instead of patience ('the kyngdome of heuen sayth saynt Gregory is opened to suche as grutcheth not wt þe werkes of god' (f.Ei)), 'to vayne glorye agaynst perfyte mekenes' (f.Ciᵛ), or 'to haue the mynde occupyed with worldly thynges more than with goostly prouffyte of the soule.' (f.Cii) The intellectual level of the consolatory doctrine is simple, and popular: we might compare a remark made almost casually by the author as he advises the provision of a 'goostly physycyan' who 'can blessedly helpe to order the soule agaynst the departynge from the body' – for 'all the wele of the lyfe hangeth of that endyng. Yf it hath ben neuer so wretched a soule/ yf

---

[10] *STC* 6931–32. Quotations are taken from the 1532 edition.

þᵉ ende be good it shall be saued' (f .Ciiiᵛ) – with the discussion of last-minute repentence in More's book. The most interesting feature of the *Doctrynall* for a literary reader is the high level of its prose style, notably in the devotional passages and in the prayers which are provided at the end.

In the more general tradition of books of consolation is *The Boke of Comforte agaynste all Tribulacyons*, printed by Wynkyn de Worde c.1505 (the fact that it is printed also by Pynson, while not surprising in an age before copyright, may well be a testimony to the demand for this kind of material).[11] It seems to have been translated from French, which may explain some odd expressions ('fleynge the voluptees corporalles' (f .ciiᵛ), etc.) and some rather ponderous Latinate experiments ('. ... coronacyon of thornes/ bytter potacyon extencyon on the crosse/ denudacyon/ conclauacyon ...' (f .Biii) etc.), although sometimes these are successful in forming a more ample and rotund style. Not only is the title of the book similar to that of More's, but it is in the form of a dialogue between 'the poore synner' and 'the swete sauyour Jhesus hangynge on the crosse':

> The poore synner
> I am a poore myserable synner fallen in to þᵉ fylthes myseryes and infelycytees of synne in peryll & daunger to be dampned eternally yf þᵉ dethe take me in my synnes.
> The blessyd sauyour Jhesu answereth
> Leue leue this drede and so fere not þᵉ dethe eternall ne the greuous tormentes of helle ... For I am descended downe from the realme of god my fader full of joye & solace and of blessydnesse: and am come into this vayle of mysery and wretchednesse for to take and receyve intollerable dolour/ payn/ and pouerte/ both in my soule and in my body ... and for to redeme the pore synners & them to delyuer from eternall heuynesse/ & from the horryble paynes of helle/ & them for to brynge & to redeme in to the realme celestyall of god my fader/ where they shall fynde Joye incomprehensyble wᵗouten ende ...   (ff .Aii–Aiiᵛ)

There is obviously nothing like the conversational tone of Vincent and Anthony (nor would that be appropriate). Sadly even within the devotional limits of the scene it cannot be said that the possibilities of the dialogue framework are realized. In the next exchange, the 'poor sinner' launches into some quite unexceptionable penitential matter, ending: ... 'thou ... louest man as thyn owne selfe and nothynge hatest but the abhomynable and horryble synne whiche is infyxed in hym by contynuaunce ...', to which Christ responds, 'Truely my frende there is no thynge that I hate so moche as synne & cursed wyll . . .' (f. Aiiiᵛ–iv) There is much of this edifying agreement. A genuine question is provoked when Christ describes the pains of his passion in grim affective detail. There is a touch of real anguish in the 'poor sinner's' words:

[11] *STC* 3295–6. Quotations are taken from the Wynkyn de Worde edition.

O my swete sauyour and onely lorde Jhesu I knowe now that thy
passyon hath be the moste terryble and the moost dysesefull that euer
was Alas than what shall I do myserable synner and wretched creature/
whan my lorde god and sauyour hathe suffred soo moche for me/ where
shall I become what thynge for suche and so grete benefyte unto hym
shall I yelde ...

(ff .Aiv^v–Av)

The contemplation of Christ's passion is the centre of the book. Woodcuts
with scenes from the passion help the reader to visualize and 'image' the
sufferings. The author makes full use of the traditional images of devotional
literature – Christ as the 'very knyght the whiche hathe made the felde and
foughten valyauntly and borne awaye the vyctorye agaynste the greate and
myghty puyssaunt and auncyent enemye of mankynd the deuyll of helle'
(f .Av), or the fire of Christ's charity which can make the sinner's heart 'for to
be softe & to melte as þe waxe dothe before the fyre and as þe snowe doth by
the hete/ and feruour of the sonne.' (ff.Av^v–vi) The reader's mind is totally
(and deliberately) concentrated in what is in essence an affective meditation
on the passion. The tribulations which afflict men are mentioned almost in
passing – as when Christ remarks 'thynke that yf it were possyble that thou
myghtest deye a thousande dethes yet were it not for to be compared vnto the
paynes that I suffred for the ...' The clear implication is that the sufferings of
men are subsumed in and healed and 'answered' by the sufferings of
Christ.

Some of Christ's speeches have an impressive eloquence. One example is a
long passage in which he argues that his pains surpassed those of any other
martyrs. It begins with a 'pyteous exclamacyon' based on a verse which was a
favourite with devotional writers:

O vos omnes qui transitis per via*m* attendite. That is to saye. O all ye the
whiche passe by the waye beholde and consyder yf that there be ony
dolour comparable vnto my dolour/ as yf I wolde say. Nay/ there is none
suche. Now herken how ...

(ff .Bi–i^v)

His exposition is enlivened by an extended simile:

As a pylgryme the whiche hathe to passe necessaryly a peryllous passage
thynkynge nyght & daye howe he myght best escape it & auoyde the
daungers the whiche he fereth to fynd in his passage/ & thus hathe he no
maner of rest in hymselfe neyther daye nor nyghte/ vnto the tyme that
his pylgrymage and voyage be parfayte and ended in lyke wyse is it of
me ...

and by changes of rhythm, as

The sonne lost his lyght. The erthe dydde trymble. The stones dydde

214

cleue. The mou*n*taynes opened as yf they had taken compassyo*n* by clamours and lamentacyons of my shamefull deth and ryght dolorous passyon ...

The enormity of his suffering is emphasized by a quaint piece of devout physiology: his body 'was proporcyoned & complexyoned for to lyue without synne or more longly than lyued Adam and bycause of this so stronge complexyon the dethe vnto me was so horryble and so paynfull ...' (f.Bii^v) Christ's passion lasted throughout his 33 years. And this brings us back to the (much briefer) sufferings of the martyrs:

Myne apostle Bartylmewe was flayne the space of a daye. My frende Laurence was rosted the space of a nyght. And my spouse katheryn was tormented the space of an houre (f.Biv).

The conclusion is that the strait path of tribulation is the only way into Paradise: 'the ryche couetous man wyll not chastyse hymselfe in the worlde by penaunce/ & therefore is he tormented in helle withouten ende/ & the pore Lazar the which here suffred moche dolour is in joy perpetuall in paradyse' (ff.Bvi^v–Ci) (a text often used in these books). The point is reinforced visually by a small crucixion scene placed beside Christ's words: 'whan I hange on the tre of þ^e crosse I promysed not paradyse but onely to theym whiche ben crucyfyed on the crosse ...' The work ends with some thoughts on the Last Judgment, but with the reassurance that Christ's mercy is everpresent for the sinner that repents. The author clearly envisages his book as one to be of use to those still in the pilgrimage of life. Whoever reads it diligently, he says, and puts its doctine into practice, 'he shalbe enlumyned in his vnderstondynge & mynde. And shall perfytely knowe howe he sholde lyue in the worlde ...' (the reader is instructed to 'rede euery daye thre leues therof in sauoury*n*ge it wel' (f.Dii^v) – and if he fails in this to give three pennies for God's sake or say 'thre Pater noster/ with Aue maria'). The treatise is followed by 'the mater of the seuen mortall synnes and of the doughters or braunches of them/ & with theyr remedyes', the ten command-ments, five wits and seven sacraments, twelve articles of faith, and finally 'a ryght consolatory contemplacyon in fourme of a dyaloge' between Man and Reason.

Different again in its approach is a much more interesting, and – I think – totally neglected work, *The Rote or myrour of Consolacyon and Conforte*, printed by the remarkable Wynkyn de Worde in 1496 (again, three later editions extending to 1530 testify to its popularity)[12]. This 'lytell treatyse' (which runs to just over 100 pages of text) addresses itself directly to the task of providing comfort. It opens with a quotation from St Paul:

---

[12] *STC* 21334–37. Quotations are taken from the 1496 edition (I am grateful to the Dean and Chapter of Durham Cathedral for allowing me to consult this), except where it is incomplete (i.e. after f.Gi), where I have used the 1511 edition.

Per multas tribulaciones oportet introire in regnum dei. Thus sayth the apostle saynt Poule in the boke of actes and dedes/ that is to saye in englysshe. By many trybulacyons we must entre in to þᵉ kyngdome of god.   (f.Aiᵛ)

And it is quick to insist on the necessity of patient suffering: 'trybulacyon is bytter/ but the ende that hit bryngeth to is moost swete and delectable.' (f.Aii). It is not adversity itself which brings the reward of eternal joy, but adversity which is accepted with patience ('thus pacyence maketh trybulacyon profytable'). With patience comes meekness; the meek heart sets little store by temporal prosperity. And as the author expounds the question of why prosperity is granted to the wicked, he sets up a kind of dialogue with his reader:

Yf thou aske me wy our lorde wyll gyue these temporall goodes to suche as he knoweth þᵗ are wretched synners and vse them euyll. I answere. One cause is to shewe his parfyte and haboundant goodnesse whiche gyueth good thynges not only to suche as be good/ but also to suche as are euyll & wretched synners.   (f.Aiiᵛ)

God sends good things to evil men so that they may be moved the more to penitence when they see that they have offended so kind a lord, and he often sends tribulations to good folk who are not perfectly good, because they do not take tribulations thankfully. The conclusion is stated in a patterned form (much favoured by this author): 'thus by his ky(n)denesse[13] he bryngeth euyll folke to penaunce/ and by his sharpnesse he bryngeth good folk to pacyence.' (f.Aiii) Conversely, he sometimes gives prosperity to good men and women to nourish them in his love and sends tribulations to the evil to make them fear him: 'and thus the good folke he bryngeth to loue by worldely prosperyte. And euyll folke he bryngeth to drede by aduersyte.'

It will already be evident that this is more carefully and more elegantly written than our previous examples. The writer likes a nicely balanced phrase with discreet alliteration:

Wherfore these faythfull soules have more fere than fauoure/ more payn than plesure in grete possessyon of worldely goodes/ they are not inflate ne exalte in themself by pryde in prosperyte ...   (f.Aiiii)

And he can produce a resounding period:

Also suche as he seeth that sholde be blynde[d][14] with temporal prosperyte/ he sendeth theym the temporall aduersyte/ bycause that they sholde lytell make of this lyfe where as they suffre so grete trybulacyon/ and make moche of that lyfe wherby they shall receyue the

13 *Text* kydenesse, *corrected in 1511.*
14 *Text* blyndeth, *corrected in 1511.*

grete prosperyte of that flourynge felicyte that neuer shal fade by aduersyte/ but euer be alyke fresshe without ende in eternyte.

(f .Av)

Almost everywhere we find a confident and clear sense of style:

There is noo temporall payne that ony crysten soule suffreth in this lyfe but they deserve hit well and moche more both for offences that they doo in themselfe and also ayenst theyr neyghbours. There is noo man neyther noo woman the whiche lyueth soo Innocently and soo vertuousely in this lyfe/ but many tymes they offcnde doynge not after ryght and reason/ but after the euyll desyre of theyr flesshe.

(f .Avi)

In the manner of earlier devotional treatises points are emphasized by homely and traditional similitudes. Pain may be the same, but those who suffer it are not – 'lyke as in one fyre golde glystereth and the grene blocke smoketh/ and vnder one fleyle the whete is purged and the chaf is broken/ so one maner of payne or trybulacyon purgeth the pacyent/ and fyleth and destroyeth the vnpacyent.' (f .Av^v) Just as no man will desire a bitter drink unless he expects some benefit from it, when he will drink it be it never so bitter, so it is with a sinful soul and a sharp draught of tribulation. Also in the manner of some earlier treatises is the constant good sense and moderation: 'Trybulacyon for hit selfe is not to be desyred but for the profyte that groweth therof & for the specyall helpe that the soule hath therby' (f .Avii), etc.

The organisation of this work, like that of *The Boke of Tribulacyon*, is numerical: twenty 'fruits' which come from 'tribulation well taken' are enumerated and expounded (the later ones usually more briefly), and sometimes there is a numerical set of distinctions within each one (the third consolation is 'in purgynge of the soule fro synne and wretchednesse' and the treatment of this follows exactly the pattern of that in the *Boke of Tribulacyon* or its antecedents). But it is presented with great verve and liveliness. The writer constantly imagines possible objections from his reader – 'thou wylte saye peraduenture …' – and the objections are rational and cogent. The imagined reader is much less of a 'stooge' than the 'poor sinner' of the previous example. He objects, for instance, that tribulation has lessened his sense of God's presence, not increased it. He complains that consolation comes very slowly:

But peraduenture thou complaynest & sayest. Syr hit is longe or this consolacyon cometh. A this is the complaynte of louers/ what thynge so euer hit is that is gretely beloue[d][15] the deferrynge therof is paynfull.

(f .Biiii)

---

[15] *Text* belouet, *corrected in 1511*.

The author pays some attention to the structure of the argument, sometimes bringing his sections to a forceful conclusion, as in the ending of the first 'fruit':

> ... troubles of this worlde/ sekenes & payne are frendes to the soule for they drawe hit from synne. Wherfore yf thou hate thy frendes and loue thyn enemyes thou seest what Jeopardy þ^{u} standest in/ wherfore saye welcome my frende trybulacyon/ and fy of erthely Joye. (f.Bv^{v})

There is a flow of homely images. Tribulations are the 'herberers' who prepare a lodging for the soul in heaven, (f.Biii^{v}) an idea later developed in a distinctly 'merry' form in a little picture of souls finding their earthly tavern shut and having to wait for the opening of their heavenly one:

> ... be not mysmade yf thou abyde a whyle at the tauerne dore afore it be opened to the for the lenger thou abydest at the dore knockynge the more thou shalt haue whan it is brought to the suffre thy thurst to waxe for the more delectable the wyne shal be to the ... (f.Fiv)

The rod of correction brings the soul to wisdom: just as the young child is easily moved 'to haue the eyen fro the booke and wantenly to loke aboute the walles & rather to pycke strawes and to clatter to his felawes than to lerne the lesson ... but whan the mayster ly[f]teth[16] the rodde to stryke hym than he loketh vp to hym & say[th][17] he wyll amende & is sory þ^{t} he laboured not better his lesson', so the frail soul looks down to earthly things, but repents 'whan the grete mayster almyghty god ly[f]teth[18] the rodde of trybulacyon.' (f.Cvi) Tribulation is like the goldsmith's hammer which makes metal stretch 'on longe'; it makes the heart stretch so that it becomes a fit vessel to receive the benefits of God's grace – and the idea is repeated and developed: 'Be not as an olde broken panne whiche whan the werker stryketh it breketh & maketh many mo holes than were before ...' (f. Eviii) A wicked heart is like a common minstrel (and might almost qualify for a part in *I Pagliacci*):

> ... as it is comonly sayd. A clene herte a Joyfull herte. And sorowfull may that herte be that is lykened to a comon mynstrel or a Joguler whiche is more in other me*n*nes houses than in his owne. And whan he syngeth & maketh moost myrthe in other mennes houses than soone after he is moost sorowe[ful][19] in his owne house. (f.Diiii^{v})

Common or proverbial sayings enliven the style – 'and to do one shrewde tourne for an other', 'he dare not ones sette out his fote at the dore', (f.Diiii) 'setteth not by after the comon spekynge as we saye/ this man knoweth not me

[16] *Text* lysteth, *corrected in 1511.*
[17] *Text* sayd, *corrected in 1530.*
[18] *Text* lysteth, *corrected in 1511.*
[19] *Text* sorowe. *1511* sorowe ful.

whan he taketh lytel kepe of me' (f.Fv^v) – yet it is often at its best when it is based on a scriptural verse:

> Ubi thesaurus tuus ubi cor tuu*m* Loke where that thynge is that þ^u louest ther is thyn herte. Thus the herte of the couetous man is with his golde and syluer. The herte of the lecherous man is with the persone there he hath moost flesshely pleasure to. The herte of the proude man is there he hath moost reuerence & with his fresshe clothes ...
>
> (f.Diiii)

The doctrine is, of course, totally traditional ('pylgremage goynge' appears as an approved activity alongside 'almesse dede doynge' and 'redynge of good bokes of vertue'). Self knowledge is important, as is patience (exemplary sufferers include Job, Jonah and Lazarus – 'for as many sores and Infyrmytees as Lazarus had in his bodye as many mouthes he had cryenge to god' (f.Giiii)). The service of God makes absolute demands:

> These whiche ordeyne them moost specyally to kepe ther hertes and lytell sett by those thynges whiche worldely folke moost desyre are called foles in this worlde but they are called wyse of god ...
>
> (f.Dvii)

and the 'life of man upon the earth standeth in battle and knighthood'. Earthly joy is always mingled with sorrow. There is one passage on the pains of hell, but it is quickly turned into a praise of the joy which will reward the virtuous sufferers. In hell, lords and ladies will weep for their apparel and their beauty, every craftsman for the misusing of his craft, merchants for their 'penyworthes'. But those who provide for their souls while still on earth are heavenly merchants

> the whiche ordeyne theyr labours of this lyfe to bye the heuenly Joyes and than they shal see the grete penyworthes passynge all the estymacyons of all the erthely creatures the whiche they shall receyue of the handes of almyghty god in those grete Joyes of endlesse blysse.
>
> (f.Evi)

As he develops the idea, the author repeats the words 'joy', 'joyful' again and again:

> And now yf ye take these lytell paynes Joyfully ye shall go lyghtly awaye and hastly to þ^t Joyfull Inherytau*n*ce and moost blyssed feloushyp there it shal not be possyble to suffre ony payne/ thy payne shall be lesser in comparyson to these Joyes than the leded cou*n*ters are whiche lye in the cou*n*te in comparyson to the grete so*m*mes þ^t they lye fore ...
>
> (f.Evi^v)

Douglas Gray

until the last phrase of the section: 'and purchesse to you eternyte of Joye'.

We take leave of this book with an extended passage on man's journey to heaven which shows its style and its spirit at their best:

The fyfthe consolacyon in tyme of trybulacyon is to remembre how þᵘ art made therby hastely to spede the in the waye to heuen/ & to the blyssed presence of thy lorde god. For as it is sayd before. Euery payne cometh of god/ wherfore euery payne is ryghtwysse. And euery synne is vnryghtwysse wherfore as many trybulacyons & payns as þᵘ hast as many messengers þᵘ hast sent fro heuen to spede þᵉ thedᵉʳ lyke as a man whiche in þᵉ flouryng tyme of somer goynge thorugh a felde ful of fayre floures & a swete medowe oftyme wyl gydᵉʳ of the floures & for the swetnes & solacyous abydynge in þᵗ place he wyl syt or laye hym downe/ & somtyme falle on slepe/ & so þᵉ nyght comethe vpon hym afore he haue ende(d)²⁰ his Journey/ And þᵉ man whiche laboureth in the foule waye the wynter tyde he fyndeth no place to reste in to he come to the ende of his Journey & [þᵗ]²¹ maketh hym to haste faste þᵗ he may come to an ende of his labour. Lyke wyse the folke whiche are in the plesaunt pro[s]peryte²² of this lyfe/ they are so occupyed with gaderynge thynges of plesure as rychesses/ flesshely delectacyons/ honours & dygnytees þᵗ they forgete ther Jorneye whether they are bounde out of this worlde For here they seke reste in the plesure of this lyfe in maner as ther were none other felycyte ordeyned for man/ & here they lye slepyⁿge in synne & wretchednesse to þᵉ nyght of deth come vpon hyⁿ/ & than they are taken with the deuyls of helle/ & neuer come to see god in his glorye whiche sholde haue ben þᵉ ende of her pylgremage. But suche as be in the wynter waye of aduersyte ful of grete blastᵉʳˢ of temptacyons in þᵉ soule/ ful of sharpe thornes of paynes & bodely sekenes/ ful of grete flodes of worldly trybulacyon these folke haste hyⁿ/ for in ther waye they fynde but bytternesse & therfore they haste hym that they may come to reste hyⁿ swetly at þᵉ ende of ther Journey after theyr sore labour. For þᵉ bytternesse of trybulacyon taketh fro the herte al false plesure of this worlde/ & so it maketh the good soules whiche our lorde vtterly & specyally loueth to spede hem to hym/ & wyl not suffre hem to reste hem & abyde in the waye/ the thynges whiche he calleth the to by trybulacyon pacyently takeⁿ are so grete/ so precyous/ so perdurable/ & euerlastyngly abydynge that he wyl not þᵗ þᵘ shalt make taryenge in the lytell thynges whiche shal slyp & vanysshe awaye.   (ff .Ei–ii)

²⁰ *Text* endeth, *corrected in 1530.*
²¹ *Text* yet.
²² *Text* pros-/speryte (*divided at end of line*), *corrected in 1530.*

220

Even in such an excellent work as the *Rote* we find only hints and premonitions of More's masterpiece. But it can be said firmly that these 'books of comfort' are interesting and sometimes accomplished examples of an attractive type of medieval devotional literature, which shows no sign of tiredness or decay.

'THE DIALOGES OF CREATURES MORALYSED': A SIXTEENTH-CENTURY MEDIEVAL BOOK OF ETHICS

Gregory Kratzmann

In recent years there has been a renewal of interest in Gabriel Harvey, the sixteenth-century Cambridge academic, controversialist and bibliophile, the friend of Spenser and the antagonist of Nashe. Virginia Stern's study of Harvey's library – which includes works by such illustrious moderns as Castiglione, Machiavelli, and Peter Ramus, as well as an impressive array of classical authors – does much to confirm C.S.Lewis's view of Harvey as 'a modern, concerned with period, with being contemporary, anxious to follow the change of times'.[1] He was not a modest man, at least in his claims to knowledge. In his copy of Domenichi's *Facetie, motti, et burle*, Harvey observes in Latin of his persona Eudromus that life is 'multitechnical and multipragmatic', and that some books must be disdained as being 'matters of grammar, philology, imaginary and superfluous things'. Eudromus-Harvey must care 'only for energetic, distinguished matters of superior forcefulness ... the pure choice of the greatest'.[2] It is all too easy to mock, as Nashe did, the pomposity of the autodidact Huddleduddle; Harvey's scholarship, evidenced by his marginalia and other writings, was formidable, his interest in the new worlds of learning admirable.

A recent addition to knowledge of Harvey's library and his habits as an annotator is *The Dialogues of Creatures Moralysed* (STC 6815; Nijhoff-Kronenberg *Nederlandsche Bibliographie* 2774). Harvey's copy of the book belongs to the University of Queensland Library, and its existence was first drawn to my attention by George Russell, who many years ago had noticed Harvey's signature with its date of March 1577 and the accompanying motto 'Arte, non Marte'. No attempt will be made here to describe in detail Harvey's annotations.[3] The purpose of this essay is, rather, to provide a brief account of the ancestry and some of the characteristics of the text, in the hope of bringing the book to the attention of students of medieval and renaissance prose. Like the three prose 'books of comfort' printed by Wynkyn de Worde, discussed by Douglas Gray elsewhere in this volume, *The Dialoges of Creatures Moralysed* has been virtually ignored by modern commentators.

---

[1] *Gabriel Harvey: His Life, Marginalia, and Library* (Oxford, 1979). Lewis comments on Harvey in his *English Literature in the Sixteenth Century* (Oxford, 1954), pp.350–54.

[2] Stern, p.184.

[3] See my 'An addition to the library of Gabriel Harvey: *The Dialogues of Creatures Moralysed*', *Notes and Queries*, 29 (v) (October, 1982), 413–15. Dr Elizabeth Gee and I have recently completed an edition of the *Dialogues*. There is no modern edition of the work, which was produced in a limited edition by John Haslewood for Robert Triphook (London, 1816). The inaccuracies of this old edition are repeated in a modern American limited edition from the Allen Press, Kentfield, California (1967).

One possible reason for the neglect is that the work is in prose; another, that it is a translation. (Although there can be no objection to saving from oblivion mediocre vernacular verse, it is regrettable that vernacular prose, which is generally of superior merit, should have suffered such neglect.) Perhaps an equally valid explanation of the inadequate state of knowledge of early sixteenth-century prose is that so much of it defies our notions of period: most readers are singularly incurious about the strong survival into the age of More and Tyndale of the taste for medieval books, whether for edification, amusement, or some combination of the two. After examining H. S. Bennett's lists of the publications of Wynkyn de Worde and of translations into English printed before 1560 we can be in no doubt about the prevailing conservatism of English book-buyers.[4] E .Ph .Goldschmidt's astringent remarks about the medievalism of so many books printed in the sixteenth century deserve to be quoted in full:

> An analysis of the published output of the printers, whom we must assume knew something of the demands of the reading public, clearly demonstrates that a great proportion of the surviving writings of the Middle Ages were not only known but in current use and circulation continuously till about 1600 ... The full eclipse and total oblivion of the 'monkish' literature of the 'Dark Ages' does not set in till the seventeenth century and the 'Age of Reason'. It is because *we* view the Middle Ages from the other side of that 'Ice Age' that we look upon these writings as texts to be brought forth from oblivion.[5]

The *Dialogus creaturarum moralizatus* was already two centuries old by 1530, the approximate date of its translation into English. The identity of the translator is unknown, although it may have been Laurence Andrewe, who is known to have translated other books for Jan van Doesborch of Antwerp, the printer most likely to have been responsible for the English version. The attribution to van Doesborch rests mainly on the evidence of woodcuts, initials and other ornaments, although the type itself is not known to have been used elsewhere by this printer.[6] This book contains no printer's name, device, or date. The English translation is the last known edition of the work: there are at least sixteen earlier editions, most of them of the Latin text, the remainder being translations into Dutch and French. The authorship of the *Dialogus creaturarum moralizatus* (or as it is sometimes known, the *Liber contemptus sublimitatis*) is open to conjecture, but the work may have been written by the Milanese scholar and physician Mayno de Mayneri, who died

---

[4] *English Books and Readers, 1475–1557* (Cambridge, 1952), pp .241–319.
[5] *Medieval Texts and their First Appearance in Print* (The Bibliographical Society, London, 1943), pp .23–24.
[6] See the information provided in the Nijhoff-Kronenberg *Nederlandsche Bibliographie*, Vol .2, pp .276–77. The revised Short Title Catalogue follows this attribution rather than the original STC attribution to the press of Martin de Keyser.

about 1364.[7] There are at least nine extant manuscripts, but it is difficult to know how wide the work's currency was in the fourteenth and fifteenth centuries since there are few indications of influence upon other books. The *Dialogus creaturarum moralizatus* became widely known after the advent of printing, however, due mainly to the enterprise of the Netherlandish printer Gheraert Leeu, who has justly been described as 'the most original printer in the Low Countries in the fifteenth century.'[8] The *editio princeps* came from Leeu's press in Gouda in 1480 as an illustrated folio, and he was to print at least four other Latin editions before 1492, as well as two translations into Dutch and one into French. All of his books use the same woodcuts, one for each *dialogus* or chapter. Other continental printers were quick to follow where Leeu had led: Latin texts came from presses in Cologne, Stockholm, Geneva, Lyons and Paris, and there were several translations into French. The popularity of the *Dialogus* in the later fifteenth century is reflected not only in the number of editions, but also by the significant fact that it was the first book to be printed in Sweden. In this respect its status is comparable with that of *The Canterbury Tales*, which recent research has shown to be the first substantial book printed in England by Caxton.[9] (It seems unlikely that Snell or Caxton would have speculated upon books for which there was not a safe market.)

The Preface to Leeu's first edition (and repeated in all subsequent Latin printed texts) leaves little room for doubt about at least one area of the book's potential market. The writer, who is almost certainly not the author of the work, since the manuscripts have a shorter prologue with a rather different emphasis, argues for the use of fictions drawn from the phenomena of the natural world, and cites the authority of Christ for the use of parables:

> Salvator enim noster omnium praedicatorum perfecta forma fabulis, palaestinorum more usus est, ut rerum similitudine ad viam veritatis homines perduceret. Auctor ergo libri praesentis jocundo modo morales doctrinas in exterminium vitiorum et virtutum promotionem introducit.[10]

The earlier part of the preface had touched upon the need to accommodate the weariness of listeners, and now it turns more insistently towards

[7] The only substantial study of the authorship and manuscripts of the *DCM* is that by Pio Rajna, 'Intorno al cosiddetto Dialogus Creaturarum ed al suo autore', in *Giornale storico della letteratura italiana*, vols 3, 4, 10 and 11 (1884–88).
[8] W. and L.Hellinga, *The Fifteenth-Century Printing Types of the Low Countries* (Amsterdam, 1966), vol.1, p.72.
   A good account of Leeu's career is provided by M.E.Kronenberg, *Een der eerste noord-nederlandse drukkers: Gerard Leeu, Gouda, 1477–1484* (Gouda, 1956). For a brief account in English see G.Duff, *A Century of the English Book Trade* (The Bibliographical Society, London, 1905).
[9] L.Hellinga, *Caxton in Focus: the Beginning of Printing in England* (The British Library, London, 1982), pp.81–82.
[10] Quotations are from J.C.Th.Graesse, *Die beiden ältesten lateinischen Fabelbücher des Mittelalters* (Tübingen, 1880), which I have checked against Leeu's 1491 edition.

justification of fiction as recreation, preparing the mind for more serious concerns:

> Utilis est ergo praesens liber praedicatoribus et aliis quibusque intelligentibus contra fatigationem animalem, ut per delectationem jocundae materiae aliqualiter intermissa intentione ad insistendum rationis studio simplicium animi ad altiora trahuntur.

The emphasis here upon the needs of preachers for sermon material which is at once edifying and appealing is heightened by the explanation of the book's second index, one arranged according to moral topics:

> Secunda tabula alphabetico ordine generaliter singulas materias virtu- tum et vitiorum ad mores componendos et corrigendos predicatorem et inquirentem docet, quo sint quaeque loco reperiendae, quae scilicet cuilibet narrationi sibi in processu sermonum convenire possunt.

(In her discussion of arrangement and classification in sermon exemplum books, Janet Coleman notes that the *Dialogus* has indexes which are among the 'most evolved and useful' in works of this kind.[11]) Although it is unlikely that Leeu and other printers saw the market for their book as an exclusively clerical one, it is evident that the work has strong affinities with the genre of the sermon-exemplum handbook. Whether it was compiled as such by its fourteenth-century author is not altogether certain, but in structure and style it has much in common with known exemplum books; the exempla of Jacques de Vitry, for example, and those of Étienne de Bourbon, Nicole Bozon, John Bromyard and others.[12] The *Dialogues* of Gregory and the *Vitae patrum* of Jerome provided authority for the form, but it is not until the new emphasis given to preaching in the thirteenth and fourteenth centuries (associated with the Franciscans and the Dominicans) that the efflorescence of the exemplum and of compilations of exempla began.

The reasons for the popularity in sermons of various kinds of narrative from saint's life to fabliau are not difficult to understand: Jacques de Vitry's 'Multi enim incitantur exemplis, qui non moventur praeceptis' differs only in the spirit of its utterance from the Pardoner's 'For lewed peple loven tales olde,/ Swiche thynges kan they wel reporte and holde'. The most popular of all exemplum collections, if we are to judge from the frequency with which it is quoted in sermons and in other collections, was the *Gesta romanorum*. The *Gesta* may not have been originally compiled as a sermon manual, but as T.F.Crane observes, it reveals 'a distinct tendency in that direction'.[13]

---

[11] *Medieval Readers and Writers: English Literature in History, 1350–1400* (London, 1981), p. 175.
[12] Reliable and comprehensive accounts of the exemplum tradition are provided by T. F. Crane, *The Exempla of Jacques de Vitry* (The Folk-Lore Society, London, 1878: Kraus Reprint, 1967), and by J. A. Mosher, *The Exemplum in the Early Religious and Didactic Literature of England* (New York, 1911).
[13] *The Exempla of Jacques de Vitry*, p. lxxxv.

Gheraert Leeu appears to have recognized that the *Gesta* was a similar kind of book to the *Dialogus*: he issued an editon of the *Gesta* only a few weeks after the first edition of the *Dialogus*, and in the following year he produced translations of both into Dutch. He may well have decided to specialize in prints of the *Dialogus* because the *Gesta* was already being printed in several towns in the Netherlands and in Germany. Another factor to be considered here is that the *Dialogus* offers greater scope for variety in woodcut illustration: Leeu's illustrations of creatures show an effective balance between bold outline and naturalistic detail, and it is not surprising that they were so often used and so frequently copied. There was a good market in England for both books. Goldschmidt observes that 'from a survey of the geographical distribution of the earliest editions we can conclude that the market for the *Gesta romanorum* was primarily in England, and in the second line in the Netherlands and north-western Germany'.[14] L. and W.Hellinga conclude that since the early provenance of all eight surviving copies of Leeu's third Latin edition is English, 'at least a substantial part of this edition was sold wholesale to England'.[15]

It is not surprising that the English translation of the *Dialogus*, made more than half a century after Leeu's first edition, should also have been printed in Antwerp, since its presses had come to supply a high proportion of books for sale in England, written in both Latin and English. Leeu himself pioneered the export of books from Antwerp to England; after the death of Caxton in 1491, Leeu moved quickly to reprint three of Caxton's titles, and to supply at least one new book in English.[16] Jan van Doesborch was an enterprising supplier of English books: about one-third of the fifty or so titles he produced before 1530 are English, grammars, devotional works, pratical manuals, a natural history, and a number of romances and popular tales.[17] This variety, with its balance towards fiction and an accompanying interest in illustration, suggests that van Doesborch was a printer who had much in common with Leeu. Although the English translation follows the Latin original very closely, it would appear to have been directed towards a more general readership than its predecessors. Two significant changes have been made in the preliminary matter of the book. The first is the considerable reduction of the preface: it is less than half the length of the original, and it concludes rather abruptly before the point at which in the Latin the example of Christ is given. Thus there is no reference to preachers and preaching. What this implies about the nature of the projected audience is strengthened by the omission from the English translation of the second alphabetical index of moral topics, nearly 280 of them, running from Abstinentia to Ypocrisis. Even though one must

---

[14] *Medieval Texts and their First Appearance in Print*, p.10.
[15] 'Caxton in the Low Countries', *Journal of the Printing Historical Society*, 11 (1976–7), 30.
[16] See Frederick Avis, 'England's Use of Antwerp Printers, 1500–1540', *Gutenburg Jahrbuch* (1973), 234–40.
[17] The best, although now somewhat dated, account of van Doesborch's books is that of Robert Proctor, *Jan van Doesborgh, Printer at Antwerp* (The Bibliographical Society, London, 1894).

regard with caution Rastell's claim that by 1527 'the unyversall people of this realm had great plesure and gave themself greatly to the redyng of the vulgare Englyssh tonge', it is clear that the expansion of literacy and the consequent demand for books had made it possible for a printer to look with confidence beyond a clerical market for a book of this kind. Comparison can be made with the popularity of works such as Mirk's *Festial* and the *Golden Legend*, both of which would half a century before have been read by a predominantly clerical audience. Wynkyn de Worde printed Mirk's book nine times between 1493 and 1532, and the *Golden Legend* seven times between 1493 and 1527. Yet although the printer or whoever had commissioned the English translation of the *Dialogus creaturarum moralizatus* had in mind a lay readership, he chose to omit from the preface not only allusions to preaching, but also the spirited defence of *jocunditas* which is so conspicuous in the Latin preface. The emphasis of the English preface falls squarely on 'holsome erudicyon' and the amendment of life. Consistent with this is the insertion at the conclusion of some chapters of a little sentence of moral comment which is not present in the original: e.g., 'And therfor pryde is to be reprouyd' (1), 'And therfor all transitorye and worldely worshyppe is lytell worth' (82).

Like its original, *The Dialoges of Creatures Moralysed* contains, after the preliminary material, 122 chapters, each of which is headed 'Dialogo', although strictly speaking, the dialogue or confrontation occupies only the first part of each chapter. The dialogue itself consists of an encounter (usually a contention, and usually in direct speech) between two objects or creatures, concluding with a summarizing *sententia* in couplet form; in the second part, various aspects of the 'moralitee' are elaborated by means of quotations from and allusion to a wide variety of authorities (among which the Bible and patristic writings are prominent), and notably by the accumulation of further exempla. It is in the first part of each chapter that the most original material is to be found. The author appears to have invented the fables upon which the dialogues are centred, whereas the second parts almost invariably contain material drawn from well-known narrative sources such as the *Vitae patrum*, the *Gesta romanorum* and the *Facta et dicta memorabilia* of Valerius Maximus. Since *The Dialoges of Creatures Moralysed* is so little-known, a complete chapter is reproduced here in order to illustrate some of the work's characteristics of thought and style. 'Of rewe and of venymows bestis' is Dialogue 26.

In the boke of De Virtutibus Erbarum it is wryttyn: Rewe amonge all othir vertuys that she hath, in especyall this ys oon, that if she be takyn in drinke or in mete she meruelously preuaylythe agayne venyme and agayne al maner of venymows bytynges or styngynges if she be brosid or stampyd with garlyke, salte and nottis. And so for this greate vertewe that she hath agayne venyme, all venymows bestis came togider to her and sayd: 'We pray the, departe owte of compenye and medle not betwene vs and mankynde, for we intende in all owre mynde for to sowe owre venyme amonge men and for to destroye them, for the which cawse they pursewe vs and slee vs.' To whom rewe answerde and sayde:

'Yower wordes be wycked and myscheuows. Of yowe it is wryttyn in the Psalter, Psalmo XIII: The venyme of aspys is vndir theyre tongis. Ye cursyd serpentis, why be ye aboute to destroy man whom God hath created and made to be lorde of all thinge? And forasmoch as ye saye that I haue grace and vertewe agayne yowe and also agayne yowr venyme, fro this tyme forthwarde the grace of God shall not be voyde in me. But his grace shall euer dwell in me, for I shall euyr aplye me to be contrarye vnto yowe and vnto yower badde disposycyon, and resyste yowe that ye shall not fulfyll yowre euyll intent.' And also she sayde these wordes:

> 'Gode people owith euyr to preuayle
> Agayn synfull that wold them assayle.'

Evyn thus shuld rulers doo, and wyselye euyr resiste to bad folkys and to saye naye to them and to punyssh them. For Seneca sayth: He noyeth goode folkys that sparyth the bad. For sothly a iuge owithe not to spare malefactowris, for a iuge correctynge not the synfull committith to synne, as sayth Seneca. Wherfore Ambrose sayth: When indulgence and fauour is shewyd to the vnworthye, many othir be prouokyd to synne therbye. As Valery rehersith in his V. boke, of oon callyd Bruto, the whiche was first consull of Romaynes, the whiche comaundid his owne sonnys when they were brought before hym syttynge in jugement to be sore betyn with roddis and aftyr that to be behedid, for by cawse they intendid to reduce the lordshyppe of Tarquynye which he had expulsyd. For he had leuyr to be withowte chyldryn then to lacke to doo dewe punyshment. A semblable shewith Saynt Augustyn, V. de Ci. Dei, that a sertayn emperower of Rome comaundid vppon payne of deth that no man shuld fight agayn the fowwarde of his ennemyes. And his owne sonne which was oftyn prouokyd of them onys faught with them manly and defendid the contray and put them to the worse. But all that notwithstandynge his fader comawndid hym to dethe for brekinge of his comawndment. And therfor rightwysnes is euyr to be kept and obserued.

The introductory account of the curative properties of rue reflects a clear indebtedness to the tradition of the herbal. There is nothing very unusual in the presence of information about natural history in a sermon exemplum, just as there is usually no clear division between physical description and moral reflection in works which belong to the genres of the encyclopaedia, the etymology, the bestiary, and the lapidary. G.R.Owst's study of English sermon material contains several such illustrations from the natural world, in terms which reflect acquaintance with such scientific works as Isidore's *Etymologiae* and Bartholomaeus Anglicus's *De proprietatibus rerum*.[18] Many of the plant, bird and animal dialogues provide quite detailed accounts of

---

[18] *Literature and Pulpit in Medieval England* (Oxford, 1933; 2nd rev. ed., Oxford, 1961, repr. 1966), pp.190–200.

physical properties and etymology; frequently, the noun is accorded a status equal to that of the object it signifies. In the chapter quoted above, the dialogue between rue and her antagonists is quite skilfully developed from the connection long established in herbal tradition between rue and 'venymows bytynges or styngynges'. Here, the herb is firmly characterized as the vessel of Grace, which prevails against the subversive force of evil. It is interesting to compare this exemplum with the chapter in Bozon's *Contes moralisés* which begins with a similar account of the herb's medicinal properties (both are derived from Book VII of Bartholomaeus Anglicus):

> Si homme seit poyné de serpente ou mors de chien, prenge ruwe et des aux e seel e le noel dez noyz, et de ces quatre chosez face un confeccioun e la beyve od vyn, si trovera garison. Auxint vous di especialment, si homme seit entoche par mortiel pecché par le deable, prenge ruwe, qe signifie contricion, e des aux qe enchace venym, ceo est verreie confession, e du seel q'est penance solom descrescion, e le noel de noiz, qe signifie la douceour de la passion Jhesu Crist, par qi vertue home ert sauvee, si la prenge od vyn de bon devocion ...[19]

The difference between the two treatments of this *remedium* lies in the greater literalism of *The Dialoges of Creatures Moralysed*; underlying the dialogue is the symbolic opposition of good and evil, God and Satan, but the moralization is essentially literal in its emphasis upon virtuous conduct. The application in Bozon's account, on the other hand, is much more insistently allegorical, in that it assigns a precise signification to each element of the literal remedy: thus, the serpent comes to signify the devil; the rue, contrition; the water, confession, and so on. Although Bozon also uses stories in a fairly literal way (as in the *narratio* of the woman of Rome which is appended to this moralized herbal remedy), he shows an exegete's fascination with the connections that can be established between letter and spirit, phenomenon and concept. By contrast, the author of the *Dialogus creaturarum moralizatus*, here and elsewhere in the book, shows a remarkable lack of interest in explicit allegorization. In only two chapters, Dialogues 32 and 70, does the second part begin by explicating literal elements of the preceding fable ('The rosyer betokenithe the worlde', 'The crowe signifieth the deuyll'), while a few others contain allegorical material incorporated from sources (36, 39, 102).

In the second part of the chapter quoted above, the moral of the fictional dialogue is applied to practical moral conduct and to the articulation of an ideal of civic virtue. The admonition addressed to rulers is typical of the applications to various estates with which the second part often begins. Others, for example, address regular clergy ('So it is sure to a relygyows man to continewe and abyde in his cloystre'; 15), and merchants (who 'shulde take hede hereto and not to be desirows of hasty wynnynges'; 99). In many chapters the author represents himself as the voice of the community ('Evyn

[19] *Les Contes Moralisés de Nicole Bozon*, edited by Lucy Toulmin Smith and Paul Meyer (Paris, 1889; Johnson reprint, 1968), pp. 107–8.

so it is conuenyent for vs to do when we haue a good ruler'; 3). The appeal, in the second part of 'Of rewe and venymows bestis', to *sententiae* from the writings of Seneca and Ambrose is equally characteristic of the didactic method. So too is the iterative, non-organic approach to structure that is illustrated by the two short 'Roman' narratives at the end of the chapter. These reinforce the moralisation about the need for rulers to be impartial, applying the theme to an ideal of righteous civic conduct on the part of parents. (The mutual obligations of parents and children is a common theme in the *Dialoges*.) The final sentence of moral comment is the translator's only addition; elsewhere, the translation is faithful to the letter of the original, and the occasional syntactic lapse is probably the result of a too-scrupulous adherence to the Latin word order.

Although it contains a number of exempla which extol the way of solitude and spiritual contemplation, *The Dialoges of Creatures Moralysed* embodies a morality which places high value on civic virtue and social harmony. Its tropology has a firm basis in the tradition of the cardinal virtues, as it addresses itself to that great late medieval question posed so memorably in Chaucer's account of the Monk: 'How shal the world be served?' The emphasis which the preface to the Latin printed editions places upon the need for teaching to accommodate the common desire for recreation is manifested in the vein of comedy which runs through the work. This can be seen, for example, in a number of stories drawn from the anti-feminist tradition (Dialogues 30 and 78), and in the engagingly colloquial dramatic language of some of the dialogue sequences. In Dialogue 23, for example, the lock indignantly repudiates the intrusion of the key: 'Dayly thow entrist in to my bowellys and tournyst my stomak vppe and downe. Cece of thy greef and trowble me no more, or ellys I shall caste the awaye or make the crokyd'. Dialogue 58 concludes with an amusingly concise account of the reply given to a man who asks another how he has come to fall into a pit: 'I praye the inquyre not how I fell inne, but assaye rather be what meanys thow canste helpe to gete me owte'.

Unlike most other collections of sermon exempla, the *Dialogus creaturarum moralizatus* is not structured on the basis of either an alphabetical ordering by moral topics or by what Welter calls an 'ordre logique': such orders include the cardinal virtues (*Speculum sapientiae*); the gifts of the Holy Spirit (Étienne de Bourbon's *Tractatus de diversis materiis predicabilibus*); the seven deadly sins (William of Wadington's *Manuel des pechez*).[20] The 122 chapters of the work are arranged, instead, by groupings according to subject matter, although there are no formal headings or *distinctiones* in the printed texts. All but the final two dialogues – 'Of man and woman' and 'Of lyfe and deth' – are arranged in multiples of twelve: 1–12 concern planets, stars and the elements; 13–24, precious stones and metals; 25–36, herbs and trees; 37–48, fish and reptiles; 49–84, birds and bees; 85–120, beasts. The numerical ordering of the material suggests that the author may have been following a

---

[20] J.Th.Welter, *L'exemplum dans la littérature réligieuse et didactique du moyen âge* (Paris, 1927), p.212.

simple numerological scheme based, for example, on the Days of Creation. (It may be relevant to note that a contemporary exemplum collection, the *Scala celi* by the Dominican Johannes Junior, also contains 122 chapters.)[21] Not surprisingly, the sections on birds and beasts each contain three times as many dialogues as the preceding sections (12 × 3): these allow full play for the development of that congruence between animal and human appearance and behaviour which is fundamental to the popularity of the Aesopic fable.

The long dialogue entitled 'Of the hare that was a lawyer' (105) epitomizes in both content and form the kind of moral teaching which the work as a whole promotes. The tale, which has a strongly secular milieu, tells of the hare's successful attempt to convince the lion-king of his worthiness to hold public office. This he does by recording his judgement of a number of instances of civil conflict, in the form of a series of proverbial couplets of precisely the same kind as those which separate the two parts of each chapter. The lepine wisdom is predictable and pragmatic, paying respect to learning rather than strength, patience rather than rebellion, self-protection rather than gestures of principle. The second part of the chapter supports this advocacy of applied morality by its Ciceronian definition of the 'philosofir', who is to be 'a serchar of the mynde, which drawith owte vicis by the rote and purgith them, and makith redy the sowlys to bringe forth goode frute'. The University of Queensland copy of *The Dialoges of Creatures Moralysed* is annotated quite heavily by at least two sixteenth-century hands, and on many of its pages there are written proverbial comments which have been abstracted from the couplet moralizations: for example, 'Clime not abooue thy estate' (A2v); 'Auoyde strife and discorde' (B2r); 'All is not gowld that glisterith' (L4v). There are also marginal glosses which draw the reader's attention to moral topics, and a variety of Latin *sententiae*. At least some of these were written by Gabriel Harvey: for example, there can be no doubt that the 'Nota' which occurs every few pages, like the brackets around the couplet moralizations, are his, since they correspond to his practices as an annotator of other books. Notations of this kind occur throughout Dialogue 105, and Harvey's endorsement of the hare's wisdom is indicated quite explicitly by his characteristic diacritical mark for legal material, 'J. C.' *Jurisconsultus*) with the note *Media via in dubiis*. Diacritics pertaining to medical and rhetorical matter occur on other pages. Harvey's obvious attraction to *The Dialoges of Creatures Moralysed* as a storehouse of practical moral knowledge is eloquent testimony to a continuing interest in the commonplace ethical wisdom of the early fourteenth century, whatever Harvey may have said about Eudromus. The English translation was not printed again in its entirety until early in the nineteenth century, no doubt because of changes in the climate of religious belief, although in 1556 the London printer Robert Wyer brought out the first seven dialogues as a pamphlet, with the prefatory comment 'By these dialogues a man maye take

[21] See Crane, pp .lxxxvi–lxxxix.

to hym selfe good counsayle' (STC 6816). Towards the end of the sixteenth century Thomas Lodge was to plunder *The Dialoges of Creatures Moralysed* in an apparent attempt to enliven his otherwise rather dull prose treatise *Catharos Diogenes in his Singularity.*

AN ENGLISH LATE MEDIEVAL CLERIC
AND ITALIAN THOUGHT:
THE CASE OF JOHN COLET, DEAN OF ST PAUL'S
(1467–1519)

J.B.Trapp

John Colet is an enigma, a contradiction. His piety, at the same time fervent and rigid, which made him such a faithful servant of the Church, was so critical of mere observance in religion as to give the view of him as a Reformer *avant la lettre* a colour of truth. Though he helped to shape the more forward-looking, more learned and suppler piety of Erasmus, his attitudes were firmly rooted in medieval thought. He faces both ways.

To examine the implications of these sweeping statements would need a book. What is offered here is no more than a brief interim account of Colet's intellectual contacts with Italy. It is intended as a modest contribution to understanding a mind and heart which were as open and generous as they were impetuous and striving in their attempt to understand how the fire of love could best work to the amendment of life.

According to Erasmus, John was the eldest child, and the only one to survive infancy of twenty-two, equally divided between sons and daughters, born to Henry Colet, Mercer, later Sir Henry and twice Mayor of London, and Christian his wife.[1] He surely went to school in London, whence he passed in due course to the university. His University may have been Oxford – but the registers for the period are lost. In the surviving Cambridge registers, on the other hand, a John Colet appears at just the right moment. Given the record of Colet's father as a benefactor in the Cambridge grace–books, and given the strong East Anglian connexions of Christian Colet, née Knevet, it may well be that John's early university days were passed at Cambridge.[2] There Henry VI had been a principal benefactor. Though both Gloucester and Tiptoft had made gifts, and William Grey had

---

I am grateful to John B.Gleason, Jill Kraye and the late D.P.Walker for help and correction; they are not, however, responsible for my incapacities.

[1] Erasmus, Letter to Justus (Jodocus) Jonas, 13 June 1521, in *Opus epistolarum Des. Erasmi Roterodami*, edited by P.S.Allen, 4 (Oxford, 1922), no.1211, pp.507–27 (which I refer to as 'Allen'); translated by J.H.Lupton in *Erasmus' Lives of Vitrier and Colet* (London, 1883), pp.19–47. Lupton's own *Life of Colet* (London, 1887), is still standard. For a summary but up-to-date account see J.B.Trapp, in *Contemporaries of Erasmus*, edited by P.Bietenholz, 1 (Toronto, 1985), pp.324–28.
[2] W.Robert Godfrey, 'John Colet of Cambridge', *Archiv für Reformationsgeschichte*, 65 (1974), 6–18.

233

been bishop of Ely, Italian humanism had a weaker presence, to say the least, than at Oxford. Roberto Weiss has put together the handful of evidences of Cantabrigian humanist interest in the form of books and manuscripts in the libraries, notably of King's College.[3] About 1478, it is true, Lorenzo Traversagni da Savona settled in Cambridge, he of the *Nova rhetorica*, and Caius Auberinus in the 1480s. There was the Platonist John Doget, Provost of King's, and there was the commentary on Plato's *Phaedo*, dependent on Bruni's Latin and making use of Pier Candido Decembrio, which he completed between 1473 and 1486. Doget had studied law at Padua and Bologna, learned also to write a sort of Italian hand, and returned to Cambridge to take up his interests as a theologian and a pluralist. He 'approached the *Phaedo* from the standpoint of Christian piety rather than rational speculation',[4] his work as a commentator chiefly directed by the Hermetic and Neoplatonic writings and the wish to enlist Plato among the apologists of Christianity. A good deal of remaking would be required to make this cloak fit Colet, who was an original thinker of a peculiarly English kind, but it is – I suppose – just possible that Colet's impulse to Platonism owed something to Doget. Certainly Doget and the young Colet share a preoccupation with etymology. Doget quotes Plotinus from St Augustine. Colet owed much to the same Father. Doget used Ficino's version of the Hermetic *Pimander*, which Colet knew. If Doget was not a humanist in the strict sense, nor was Colet. If – as Weiss suggests – 'the main interest of Doget's commentary is his handling of antique materials with scholastic methods towards the fulfilment of a scholastic ideal' then his conclusion is just: 'he embodied that compromise between medieval and modern learning which was typical of the earlier stages of English humanism'.[5] There is much in that conclusion that is applicable also to what might be called second-phase English humanism, the humanism of England before Erasmus, Colet included. Nevertheless, Colet stands out among fellow-countrymen of his generation at least as strongly as did Grocyn and Linacre, born a decade or more previous to him, and as Thomas More, ten years his junior, was later to do.

Whether Colet began his university career in Cambridge or in Oxford and spent his seven years in logicals and philosophicals at Magdalen College – there is no Colet in the College books – it was to Oxford that he returned from his travels in France and Italy in about 1496 and began to make his reputation as a lecturer-preacher-commentator. We do not know why he embarked on such a journey, or exactly when. As we have seen, he had models in either Cambridge or Oxford, though more of them in Oxford. He travelled, says Erasmus, like a merchant looking for fine goods.[6] In Rome by March 1493, he was still there, or there again, in May of that year.[7] Then we

---

[3] Roberto Weiss, *Humanism in England during the Fifteenth Century*, third edition (Oxford, 1967), pp.160–7.
[4] Weiss, p.166.
[5] Weiss, p.167.
[6] Allen, p.508; *Lives of Vitrier and Colet*, p.21.
[7] George B.Parks, *The English Traveler to Italy*, 1 (Stanford, Calif. and Rome, 1954), pp.357–82, 466–7.

lose sight of him until the end of 1495, when he was in Paris on his way home. He may well have spent time in Paris on the way out also, and he studied at Orleans, though it is not clear when. That is what we know. By the time Colet left England, William Grocyn was back in Oxford, after three years in Italy, during which he had met and studied with Poliziano and Chalcondylas in Florence, possibly in company with Linacre, and with the future Leo X. Linacre himself probably did not return to Oxford until some time before 1499. It is at least possible that he and Colet were simultaneously in Rome. These two may well have told Colet, if he needed telling, of Florentine luminaries such as Ficino, Pico della Mirandola and Savonarola, as well as those with whom they had been in closer contact.

More than a century ago, J.H.Lupton pointed out Colet's substantial acquaintance with the works of Ficino, as attested by considerable quotations from his *Theologia Platonica*,[8] his translation of Plotinus[9] and his *Epistolae*.[10] He also showed that Colet was familiar with the *Heptaplus* and the *Apologia* of Pico.[11] Moreover, he established that the translation of another Neo-platonic authority – the pseudo-Dionysius, at that time held to be both the disciple of St Paul and 'Platonicorum primus' – which Colet knew and used was the then new Latin version made by Ambrogio Traversari.[12] Almost a century after Lupton, it was demonstrated that the volume that Colet read was almost certainly a copy of the edition published by Jacques Lefèvre d'Etaples in 1499.[13] Embedded in Colet's *Treatise on the Hierarchies*, as Lupton was able to show, was a long verbatim quotation from Ficino's *Epistolae*. In the early 1950s the late N. R. Ker discovered in the library of All Souls College in Oxford the very volume of Ficino's *Epistolae* once owned by Colet and copiously annotated by him, in a hand so cursive as often to be illegible – a hand which certainly owes something to one or perhaps both of the hands we now know as Roman and Italic. This edition was printed at Venice in 1495.[14]

At this point it will be as well to acknowledge a handicap which afflicts the would-be interpreter of Colet. With the exception of his sermon to Convocation, delivered in 1510 and printed in Latin almost at once, none of

[8] Colet, *Lectures on Romans*, edited by J.H.Lupton (London, 1873), pp.29–32; id., *Exposition of I Corinthians*, edited by J.H.Lupton (London, 1874), p.140 (cf. p.130).
[9] *Lectures on Romans*, pp.16–17.
[10] Colet, *Two Treatises on the Hierarchies of Dionysius*, edited by J.H.Lupton (London, 1869), p.xviii. The passage quoted by Colet is on fols LIr–LIIIr of Ficino's *Epistolae* (Venice, 1495). John Gleason reminds me of Colet's strictures on Italian womanish outcry at funerals (*Ecclesiastical Hierarchy*, ed. cit., p.138).
[11] Edited by J.H.Lupton (London, 1876), pp.xxiii–xxiv, 10–11; *Lectures on Romans*, p.27 (*Heptaplus*); *Exposition of I Corinthians*, pp.138–9; *Exposition of Romans*, p.95; *Treatises on the Hierarchies*, pp.109–112 (*Apologia*).
[12] *Treatises on the Hierarchies*, p.18.
[13] Review by Eugene F.Rice Jr., of Sears Jayne (see n.14), in *Renaissance News*, 17 (1964), 108–9.
[14] These annotations have been edited and translated, with a long introduction, by Sears Jayne, *John Colet and Marsilio Ficino* (London, 1963). I draw heavily on this book, which I refer to as 'Jayne'.

Colet's works were printed in his lifetime. Everything else lay in manuscript for the best part of five centuries, until Lupton published the entire corpus in five volumes between 1867 and 1876. In the manuscripts there are cancellations, additions and annotations in the hand of Colet and another. Lupton incorporates them into his texts. It is usually and, in my view correctly, assumed that the writings of Colet to which his manuscripts bear witness were composed in Oxford between about 1496, when he returned to England and (at latest) 1505, when he finally left Oxford for London and the Deanery of St Paul's. When they were put into the format which I have described as the 'collected edition' is unclear. It is not likely to have been before 1505 and is certainly before 1517. When the annotations and changes were made is uncertain.[15]

For the present, at least, there is nothing for it but to use Lupton's texts, assuming both that they represent, broadly speaking, Colet's attitudes and his reading as they were in the late 1490s and the very early years of the sixteenth century, and that it was in these years that Italian influence on Colet was at its strongest. It looks as if that influence was most directly and interestingly exerted by the two great Florentines Ficino and Pico. There is little or no sign of Savonarola, perhaps surprisingly. The friar's popularity in England seems to come a little later, and then most frequently in the rather conventional form of his *Meditations* on the 30th and the 50th Psalms, written while he was in custody and at the point of death. Wynkyn de Worde printed one of these in Latin in 1500 as well as an English translation in the 1530s. Some time after 1517 the *Meditations* were written out, in Latin, for the influential cleric Christopher Urswick (?1448–1522), as well as for others at an indeterminate date, by the one-eyed Brabantine scribe Pieter Meghen, who is documented in England from 1503 to 1540, spending his last ten years as Writer of the King's Books to Henry VIII.[16] It may well be that Meghen owed his appointment to the influence of Duwes, the royal librarian. Duwes had had a part a few years before in bringing the Horenbouts and with them a totally new dimension in book illumination and in portrait-miniature painting into England.

One of Urswick's chief concerns was the maintenance of the liberties of the Church. He was something of a text-pusher among the important and influential. In choice hand-written copies he circulated the tract by Celso Maffei of Verona known as the *Dissuasoria* – it was later to be translated, in

---

[15] I am greatly indebted to Lupton's works. For a preliminary, tentative and sometimes mistaken account of the problems presented by Colet's manuscripts, see my 'John Colet, his Manuscripts and the ps-Dionysius', in *Classical Influences on European Culture 1500–1700* edited by R.R.Bolgar (Cambridge, 1976), pp.205–21.

[16] Trapp, 'Pieter Meghen, 1466/7–1540, Scribe and Courier', *Erasmus in English*, 11 (1981–2), 28–35; id., 'Pieter Meghen, yet Again', in *Manuscripts in the Fifty Years after the Invention of Printing*, edited by J.B.Trapp (London, 1983), pp.23–28. Andrew J.Brown, 'The Date of Erasmus' Latin Translation of the New Testament', *Transactions of the Cambridge Bibliographical Society*, 8, 4 (1984), pp.351–380, has recently shown that the Erasmus text was added by Meghen to the manuscripts of the New Testament owned by Colet at some time in the 1520s, after Colet's death. I am greatly indebted to Mr Brown for allowing me to see his article in typescript.

Elizabeth's reign, by Everard Digby – with its arguments in favour of the maintenance of church endowments and revenues and against laymen's appropriations of them. He also circulated other medieval favourites such as the pseudo-Ambrosian sermon on the episcopal dignity, a sort of *speculum episcoporum* adjuring prelates drunken, litigious and grasping to mend their ways by apostolic example and give in turn the example to the laity lest they be sucked into the same whirlpool of wrongdoing.[17]

Urswick was in many respects the antithesis of Colet: affluent, like Colet, he was not so by inheritance; he was more of a pluralist and holder of office; an opportunist and something of a status-quo-ite; a clerical administrator and an ambassador; a strong churchman; a man of genuine piety but without Colet's incandescence, without Colet's single-mindedness; importantly, like Colet however, a favourer and patron of Erasmus.[18]

Contacts between Urswick and Colet were close enough for Colet to have got hold of a book or books for Urswick in Rome in 1493.[19] Had he passed through Florence on that journey and met Ficino, or Pico? There is no word of it in his extant correspondence, or the correspondence of the others. Chronologically, it is possible: Pico lived until 1494, and Ficino survived Colet's departure from Italy by several years. Given, however, that Colet owned or at least read books by both as soon as he returned to England, at the latest, would he not have sought their authors out? This is not the view of Sears Jayne, who edited the marginalia in the All Souls volume some twenty years ago (Jayne, p .20). According to him, the two letters from the master that Colet copied on to the flyleaves of the volume – together with his own awkward and unsyntactical attempt at a complimentary letter that would turn Ficino's compliment back upon himself – indicate that the two never saw each other face to face. To me, the testimony is not so sure. The All Souls volume gives indisputable evidence, on the other hand, of a thorough absorption by Colet of Ficino's doctrine, from the most convenient available source. The *Epistolae* are brief statements of Ficino's views on important matters, and they represent him at his most accessible. There is no letter to Colet in the printed volume, but the proud recipient had copied with his own hand the words that he has received in response to his question about the relation between intellect and love (Jayne, pp .82–3).

Intellect, Ficino tells Colet, is primary, inward-looking, purer, clearer, truer; it is pure and refined will; it produces love, which is secondary, born of intellect, outward-looking, more mixed, denser, thicker, and is, in fact, crude and unrefined intellect. Being more appetitive, it precedes understanding, as fire heats before it illuminates, that is to say before it makes incandescent. I

---

[17] Trapp, 'Pieter Meghen, yet Again', pp .25–6.
[18] A .B .Emden, *Biographical Register of the University of Oxford to 1500*, 3 vols (Oxford, 1957–9), pp .1935–6; *Biographical Register of the University of Cambridge to 1500* (Oxford, 1963), pp .605–6, 685; and the summary account in *Contemporaries of Erasmus*, edited by P .Bietenholz (Toronto, forthcoming).
[19] Wallace K .Ferguson, 'An unpublished Letter of John Colet', *American Historical Review*, 34 (1934), 696–9.

have elsewhere suggested that Colet's doubts about the order in which to place the elements of the Pauline triad of faith, hope, charity were continuous and unresolved during his Oxford period, to which belong almost every word of his that we have extant; and that his Platonism, whether derived from pseudo-Dionysius or from Ficino, had much to do with his doubts.[20] I have also complained elsewhere of how difficult it is to characterize what Colet was taking from Ficino as he read.[21] To say, with Professor Jayne, that Colett is a voluntarist and Ficino an intellectualist, is to get it roughly right, I believe (Jayne, p.55). Colet was no philosopher and mistrusted the erected wit at least as much as he mistrusted the infected will. Many of the notes are mere *aides-mémoire*, sometimes in the midst of a moralized summary of a moralizing passage in Ficino. The letter of Ficino's expounding the principle that 'The only refuge in the midst of evils is the *summum bonum*', for example, clearly struck a responsive chord in Colet. He annotates it copiously. Whatever the life one lives – active, contemplative, voluptuous – he remarks, human life is a mere play, a tragedy. However we look at happiness and think it consists in power, wisdom or pleasure, we can see in the end that all these things are misery. All that contemplatives learn when they seek to understand the whole by means of its parts, is doubt and confusion. Solomon calls human wisdom full of labour and grief, Paul calls it foolishness before God, Isaiah vanity. We are blind, we wander in darkness. To act is to court suffering, to seek power is to be abased, to seek pleasure is to fall into pain, wisdom is foolishness. We must find power, pleasure, wisdom in God, putting our trust only in Him, who is the only truth and the only singleness and the only stability; let us not be distracted by the multiplicity of the world to lose our hope of unity. 'The light of God accompanies this desire as light accompanies a flame, and it shines most brightly where the flame burns hottest. Love is the flame of the good and God true love and charity, true light which is faith and true good which is hope; he is a kindly light, a shining good (Jayne, pp.118–20). Elsewhere in the volume, on a flyleaf, Colet notes the application of this to I Corinthians (Jayne, p.131).

The ideas are all in Ficino, and in that sequence – yet somehow, when they have passed through the mind and pen of Colet they have become more heavily weighted with moral force – they have become precepts, from having been statements.

Of Colet's notes on Ficino there are other things to be said. One finds, throughout, a characteristic preoccupation with the stages of ascent to union with God, of purification, illumination and perfection (Jayne, pp.60–65, 70–75, 104–9). Sometimes Colet embarks on long passages of semi-independent speculation; sometimes he will write a prayer to the Virgin in a margin (Jayne, p.103); sometimes he will gloss a word. 'Palinode', for example, used by Ficino in passing in his text, is given the sort of elaborate definition that suggests Colet had had to look it up in the *Cornucopia* of

---

[20] Trapp, 'John Colet and the Hierarchies of the ps-Dionysius', *Studies in Church History*, 18 (1982), 146–7.
[21] Ibid., p.148.

Perotti, for example (Jayne, p. 114).[22] Twice he copies out Ficino's list of the nine orders of angels (Jayne, pp. 108–9). Why? Surely he knew these without reminding himself? Sometimes he gives us a sort of autobiographical glimpse. There are many in our time, says Ficino, lovers of dignity rather than of learning – *philopompi* not *philosophi* – who too proudly profess a great knowledge of Aristotle's meaning, when they have hardly read any Aristotle and know no Greek. When they speak in public among children, they seem to the uninstructed to know a great deal. Question them in private and in an instructed way, and you will find that they are ignorant of physics, more ignorant of mathematics and most ignorant of metaphysics. 'Philopompi' writes Colet in the margin; and then, as it were after a pause for reflection, 'Cambridge men' (Jayne, p .98). Is this facile, joky opposition? Does it reflect disillusion with his early training at that university among Thomists and Scotists? Can one know whether, in closely paraphrasing a passage of Ficino's on the worthlessness of astrologers' pronouncements, Colet is as it were greeting a new notion? Or is he merely noting (as so often we do) approval of an opinion which corresponds to his own: 'The pronouncements of astrologers, based on the influence of the stars, are false and worthless in themselves. They are also the cause of pernicious error. They deprive God of His omnipotence by asserting that all events necessarily occur as they do because the stars compel them. If all is the result of influence from these stars, which are inferior to God, what becomes of God's supreme providence and his absolute and self-sufficient authority?' (Jayne, p .117). More interesting, perhaps, is the table of planets and their attributed qualities on the title page: holiness-strictness-piety directed to God – Saturn; wisdom-kindness-piety directed towards one's neighbour – Jupiter (Jayne, p .86). Or the list of lawgivers – something akin to the *prisci theologi*, beginning with Moses and passing through Osiris, Zoroaster, Zalmoxis, to Mahomet and Plato; with Jupiter-God and Mercury-angel correspondences for good measure (Jayne, p .88). Or the divine madness – for Colet the divine madness applied to the happiness of the soul in the presence of God (Jayne, p .89). He goes on to meditate on heavenly love and heavenly beauty and their relation to earthly varieties; to note that all faculties of the soul are employed in listening to the music of the spheres, that poets are inspired to imitation of the divine harmony, that the muses have a part in it all, and the sirens; that Orpheus is a theologian and Virgil a Platonist; that the pre-Christian philosophers are delivered from hell; that we must make beautiful objects to remind ourselves always of the divine beauty; that we must look on the body not in order to love it, but in order to remind ourselves of the ineffable beauty of the divine; that Plato concealed the divinity of his wisdom in obscure and repellent dress, so that the stupid reader would pass it by without understanding; that we must advance by stages from ordinary, worldly virtue to the ideal virtue which is divine; that this process cannot be shared by the *plebs*, the *plebs* being an animal like a polyp, in that it is an animal with many legs and no head; that souls are divine and live impiously only because of the clogging and

---

[22] For Colet and Perotti, see below, pp. 244–6.

contamination of the earth in which they are obliged to live; that one must seek to fly from evils, because one cannot eliminate them; that man is a stupid and wretched being; that morning dreams are most efficacious for prophecy; that love is the beginning of the law (Jayne, pp.89–99). A passage is noted with resonances in several of Colet's Commentaries – Romans XII. 9, for example (Abhor that which is evil; cleave to that which is good), or I Corinthians: 'Avoid multiplicity, confusion and tumult; seek simplicity, tranquillity and peace' – good Neo-Platonic doctrine (Jayne, p.99). Avoid the crowded way, and seek the by-paths. Cultivate memory of the good. Seek learning, because this will give you a good and strong intellect and a stable will, whence good actions, and the habit of such. Speculation will bring wisdom, the knowledge of God, whence worship, whence the habit of worship. For a guide to life, learn to reason; for another get experience; for another, learn about both the past and the present; live the life of the mind, and learn to despise the body – but do not be misled into disrespect for yourself. The Augustinian triad: love of God, love of neighbour and love of self, a favourite formulation of Colet's and of Erasmus's, was perhaps reinforced by this passage: certainly we find it being worked over more than once in Colet's annotations in this volume of the *Epistolae* (Jayne, pp.130–1). What is happiness, and how rulers and philosophers have defined it; the elements; bodily form; a brief compendium of the Platonic theology – a long, painstaking, even slightly fumbling summary, this (Jayne, pp.105–6). Then, as one would expect from Colet's devotion to St Paul, the most fully annotated letter of all on the *De raptu Pauli ad tertium caelum* (II Cor. XII. 2–4); (Jayne, pp.105–6). Though a substantial quotation from this is embedded in Colet's *Abstract* of the *Ecclesiastical Hierarchy* of the pseudo-Dionysius, the section on God and the cherubim, that particular passage is not marked.[23] The impiety of wishing to get to heaven by our own efforts is stressed: the dross of earth holds down the soul and it must be raised; by faith and hope you may ascend to charity (Jayne, p.107). Love, as St Paul says, is the superior way to heaven, being the way of the seraphim, who are the closest to God: the cherubim, who seek him by knowledge, come below them: and the will is contented only in God. Knowledge, intellect, can enjoy God and the good in a finite way; love in an infinite. Light is a topic much canvassed by Ficino: its composition, as pure light and coloured; and the fact of its being visible only when it strikes an object. Beyond the shadow of the body one sees God face to face, clearly; within it, one can see God only in a glass darkly. It is light that we must strive for, and the imitation of Christ; good custom will help us to this. God is a sun, according to the Orphic comparison, though we must beware of worshipping the sun as if it were the creator – just as (as we have seen) we must not ascribe too much power to the planets (Jayne, pp.113–7). We must also remember, however, that it is possible to write a book on the sun and on light without impiety; and we must remember that Platonists worship both their god and the *anima mundi* by contemplation alone: both are supra-corporeal (Jayne, p.123). The world

---

[23] Ed. Lupton, pp.106–111; see also *Exposition of I Corinthians*, p.177.

soul sustains the world body with which it is united. What is within the world soul gets light and life from it. Midway between body and soul are the spirits or demons, good and evil, composite of both soul and attenuated body. These the Christians call angels and the pagans demons; between them the world is divided, and everything derives part of its character from these spirits, including the characters of men. In thick, incrassated bodies, the life infused by the world soul becomes gross and reckless – this applies both to demons and men – and the demons represent themselves to men as good, not evil, gods to be worshipped; they compel men to evil. Angels, however, strive to purify us even by dreams, and 'the saintly man, his soul divine and dedicated to God, pure and holy, united to a body chaste and pure' and therefore impervious to demons is not so much as troubled by them (Jayne, pp .123–4). The demons act by sensory effluences which flow into bodies: the demons of gluttony, for example, are attracted by meat and enter it, so that it is made demonic and will infect the man who gulps it down. The demons feed on odours, too, in their incorporeal parts, cooking odours especially. If we allow ourselves to be attracted by so much as the smell of food, we are liable to taint: so the philosophers tell us to abstain. Theologians ought to beware of warm, steaming dishes; if they are not obliged to *faire maigre*, they will do better so. Keep out of restaurants and pagan temples alike – and avoid the smell of cooking and of sacrifice – and so present to God a pure and unperturbed mind and – Colet and Ficino himself might well have added – your body a living sacrifice (Jayne, p .125). Ficino on demons was clearly of interest for Colet in the context of I Corinthians X. 20: 'But I say, that the things which the Gentiles sacrifice they sacrifice to devils and not to God; and I would not that ye should have fellowship with devils'. What Colet says of this passage in his Commentary, however, bears little relation to Ficino's precise characterization: he is more directly concerned with the spiritual meat and drink that are the subject of Paul's chapter, with the worship of devils – which he says is the real point at issue – than with precisely how these devils or demons operate. He sets his explanation in a historical frame. Paul's continuous topic is the correction of the Corinthians, who thought that they could eat idol-meats with idolators, indulge habit and pleasure and still remain Christians. The fact is that *fratres dominici* and *gentes demoniae* cannot and must not mix. Colet extends the simile of the table, though I see little if any trace of Ficino's *Epistolae* there. True Christians, says Colet, ought only to feast at a table where Christ is the food. Though the Old Testament was a table, according to David as expounded by St Paul (Romans XI. 9), its dishes are covered and sealed. Those of the New Testament are open. The point is made visually in the manuscript of Colet on I Corinthians in Emmanuel College Cambridge, where there is a little marginal drawing of open and covered dishes.

'At other tables,' says Colet, 'even the books of Christian authors, in which there is nothing that savours of Christ, nothing that does not savour of the Devil ... no Christian, certainly, ought to seat himself ... As the grass grows, so grow the cattle. A man's growth also is consistent with his food ... If anyone says, and it is often said, that the reading of pagan authors is an aid to the correct understanding of Scripture, let him rather think that reliance on them is an obstacle ... For, doing thus, you mistrust the power which is available to you of understanding the Scriptures by grace alone, and prayer, and by the help of Christ and of faith ... Those books alone should be read ... in which Christ may be feasted upon ... others are a mere table of devils'.[24]

In his commentary on Romans VI and the following chapters Colet makes further use of the demonic passages, especially, for example, in the long exposition of Romans XII.[25] There Paul, having shown how God's righteousness is revealed by bringing men into a new order of life in the Spirit and giving them the power to live righteously, turns to show how regenerate man ought to behave. There is much of the pseudo-Dionysius in this chapter, as Lupton long ago pointed out; and there is a generic debt to Pico, as he also pointed out; but there is an even greater debt to Ficino's *Epistolae*.[26] Colet's extended passage on the intermediary spirits at Romans XII is a good example of the way he turns to his own exhortatory purposes what he reads.

Others of Marsilio Ficino's works were laid under contribution by Colet. If, as Erasmus says, he had read his Plato and his Plotinus,[27] he would surely have read them in Ficino's translations, printed in 1484 and 1492 respectively – whether or not he had seen the *Phaedo* in Bruni's version, or Doget's commentary. This can be no more than conjecture. There is a substantial passage from Ficino's *Theologia Platonica*, first printed in 1482, in the Commentary on Romans VIII. 35: 'Who shall separate us from the love of Christ ...?' as well as other reminiscences. Here Colet paraphrases freely, as usual: The two most excellent objects of a man's most excellent actions through the most excellent parts of his soul, are the knowledge and the love of God. But the intellect is too feeble to know; man is capable only of loving, which he can achieve only by despising and neglecting all else. Knowledge puffeth up, but charity edifieth. God is more pleased to be loved and worshipped, than surveyed and understood. Knowledge of God – such as that, in Colet's opinion, pretended to by the scholastics, defining and delimiting – may be used amiss sometimes, love never. Love is infinitely more agreeable than knowledge to the lover as well as the loved; trying to know God puts too much strain on the feeble human intellect. 'So much I have said', he goes on, 'about the excellence of love according to Marsilio; but I have in general used my own words as I felt inclined, and my own style. I would not dream of saying that my expression is better or clearer than his. There cannot be anything better than Ficino's way of writing philosophy. My

---

[24] *Exposition of I Corinthians*, pp. 109–110; cf. Ps-Dionysius, *Epistolae*, IX, 1.
[25] *Lectures on Romans*, pp. 58–92. As noted below (p. 247), Colet wrote more than one commentary on Romans. In my text I refer to them indifferently as 'Commentary on Romans'; in the footnotes I cite Lupton's edition of the extended commentary on Romans I–V as *Exposition of Romans*, and the commentary on the whole Epistle as *Lectures on Romans*.
[26] *Lectures on Romans*, pp. xxix–xxxv.
[27] *Lives of Vitrier and Colet*, p. 21.

way allows me to take the opportunity of putting in whatever I wanted as I wrote and turning it to my own purpose'.[28]

Ficino takes his examples from Plato and Plotinus in order to forward an epistemological analysis of love and intellect – the mystery that Colet asks him to explain, we remember – as speculative faculties by which the soul may obtain a knowledge of God. Colet converts this into a moral argument in favour of love, changing Plato and Plotinus to Paul (Jayne, p.50). I do not see that this is necessarily to come down on the side of the active as against the contemplative life: the power of love is after all one of the great tenets of the mystics. It is, however, a natural derivation from the late nominalist sort of theology which also produced Luther, and it implies a strong conviction of the abjectness of man and the power of grace.

Again and again in the All Souls volume, Colet translates Ficino's classical ideas and expressions into moral, Christian terms. If, says Ficino, Juno will not help us – i.e. in Christian terms Martha-*vita activa* – let us turn to Minerva – i.e. to Mary-*vita contemplativa*, sprung from the head of Jupiter. Wisdom is to be sought from wisdom: so Socrates tells us. Colet turns this, so that moral goodness and a right valuation of learning become the objects: we are to seek our aid from Christ, and imitate Solomon in desiring wisdom only so as to distinguish good from evil (Jayne, p.116). On another occasion, Colet sweeps Socrates out of Ficino's condemnation of the judgment of the common people: his instances of faulty estimation are the Jews' view that Christ was insane, and Herod Agrippa II's that Paul was similarly afflicted (Jayne, p.117). There are other points at which Colet seems merely to be noting what Ficino says. In Colet's only extended discussion of law, for example, there is scarcely a trace of Ficinian influence. On Romans II. 11–29: 'For there is no respect of persons with God. For as many as have sinned without law shall also perish without law; and as many as have sinned in the law shall be judged by the law', Colet takes law in its divine sense.[29] For him, faith was superior to law, and the new law to the old; true law and the will of God were identical; and law was to be divided into law of nature, of obedience, and of grace (Adam, Moses, Christ). What Ficino has to say in the *Epistolae* is that all the great law-givers have thought of law as dependent on divine authority and that law is natural, divine and human. He allegorizes the parts of a perfect lawyer's body: his soul corresponds to worship of God, his spirit to regard for the law, his brain to clarity of judgment, his eyes and tongue to learning, his breast to a retentive memory, his heart to a right will, his feet to perseverance, and his entire person to equity (Jayne, p.98). Perhaps Colet's interest in this last passage can be explained by his exposition of Romans V. 21, where he bursts out: 'How I wish that the ministers of ecclesiastical affairs, and those so-disant interpreters of canon law would realize that their administration of the law for Christ's people is in vain without grace'.[30] It is not that Colet needed Ficino to tell him that law was human, natural and

---

[28] *Lectures on Romans*, pp.29–32.
[29] *Exposition of Romans*, pp.75ff.
[30] *Exposition of Romans*, p.162.

divine. Nor is there any close connection between what he is saying here and Ficino, nothing in Ficino of Colet on how those ecclesiastical lawyers thrust in the knife to punish, and drain away the golden blood of the laity. There are other authorities lurking in the background, not least of them – as Lupton pointed out long ago – Cicero himself, in the characterization of these legal adepts, reciters of formulas, watchers for syllables.[31]

As I have suggested above, Colet often absorbs ideas, by means of jotted summaries; but does not use them. An even more striking example is the treatment of marriage, which Ficino defended and Colet, in despite of St Paul, rejected. Both Colet and Ficino were themselves celibate. Colet merely notes from Ficino that marriage conforms to the law of nature and produces children; that Socrates learned moral discipline from his wife; that Venus and the Muses mix; that wedlock is a social bond (Jayne, p.115).

Though Colet was anxious to get at exactly what Ficino was saying, it is often difficult to show positive influence on Colet from Ficino's *Epistolae* because so many of Colet's ideas can have come from a variety of sources. St Augustine could have given him help with sun-imagery, say, and a justification for thinking of Plato in a Christian context, and there was the pseudo-Dionysius. There was also Cicero. Colet's notion of emanation from sphere to sphere, in the *Letters to Radulphus on the Mosaic account of the Creation*, the essence of neo-Platonism, was mediated to him not by Plotinus, or the pseudo-Dionysius, or even Pico, from whom he took so much for that work, but by Cicero.[32] It seem possible that Erasmus, in implying Colet's direct knowledge of the works of Plato and Plotinus, was using the licence of the elogium. He may also have been doing so, as we shall see, in the case of Origen.[33] Certainly, he was right to remark on Colet's almost exclusive taste for sacred authors.

If we speak of Colet's first acquaintance with the work of a contemporary Italian Platonist, however, we may be speaking of Pico rather than of Ficino: Colet knew and relied on both the *Heptaplus* and the *Apologia*.[34] If we are looking for his first contact with an Italian author, we shall find it – as far as concrete evidence goes – in an Italian who was in close contact with the first generation of English pupils of Guarino of Verona. Niccolò Perotti, who had been taken up by William Grey, later Bishop of Ely, and had gone to Rome in Grey's considerable suite of scholars and scribes, made his mark with, among other things, a Latin grammar and the *Cornucopia*. The *Cornucopia* began life as a concordance to Martial and ended it as a Latin etymological dictionary, later much used by other dictionary-makers and improvers of vernaculars. It was the basis of the dictionary of Calepino, which in turn was the basis of Sir Thomas Elyot's Latin-English dictionary of the 1540s, and some of Elyot's enrichments of English in the 1530s. It is possible that Colet as a boy used Perotti's grammar, which was popular in England until the

---

[31] *Exposition of Romans*, p.163.
[32] *De natura deorum*, I.15; see *Letters to Radulphus*, p.18.
[33] Below, p.250.
[34] Below, pp.248–51.

mid-sixteenth century, though losing ground in the 1490s to that of Sulpizio. Thomas More praised Sulpizio above all, but also recommended Perotti. There was a special edition of Perotti in 1486, issued from Antwerp for the English market.[35]

So far, I have been speaking as if Colet had written only one commentary on Romans. In fact he wrote two – or three, according to one's method of counting. One was a painstaking exposition of the first five chapters. The other passes rapidly over the first five chapters and then, at considerably greater length, expounds chapters VI–XI and then XII–XVI, in terms of their historical situation and their spiritual message, in the Platonizing way that is familiar from the *Exposition of I Corinthians*[36] The commentary on Romans I–V may well have been written first: at all events we have it in fair copy. Its explicatory method, on the whole, stays closer to the text, is more traditional, with explanation following hard on the heels of quotation. There is little Platonism, though influence is discernible from Pico, and there is more etymologizing, for example. The commentary on Romans VI–XVI looks rather at the Epistle as a whole, in historical context, as the message of Paul the Platonist. It includes a paraphrase of Ficino's Plotinus, actually naming him, in dealing with the sway of the animal part of man over man's present state.[37] Incidentally, he does not go as far as Ficino, who not only has the inner man complaining of the outer but compares the animal part of man to Eve, formed out of Adam when he was asleep and off guard. Colet deals with the imperfections of the animal part only. A little later, too, he quotes the *Theologia Platonica* at length.[38]

In the *Commentary on Romans I–V*, Colet will pass from what is almost transcript of Perotti to denunciation. Thus, expounding Romans III. 31: 'Do we then make void the law through faith? God forbid. Yea we establish the law', he writes of how the old law is advanced, completed, perfected by Christ. Jesus, he says, 'Vetus testamentum Dei illustravit suo novo perfectiori; non diripuit testamentum, sed stabilivit ...' Then we have a definition of a man's last will and testament – 'a just decision about what we should wish to have done after our death' – that is to say a perfecting by some good man of what we have been forced to leave incomplete by death. The definition comes from Perotti, in all likelihood. Colet continues:

Not unconnected, I think, with this matter is that of the probate of wills, as now practised by officers of the church, more for their own base gain, than for the real examination of the wills [a frequent complaint against the church]. Their duty is to weigh carefully, as though in the scales of charity, the wills of the sons of the church, to consider every single provision therein contained; to add, diminish and alter, as reason and

35 Constance Blackwell, 'Niccolò Perotti in England: John Anwykyll, Bernard André, John Colet and Luis Vives', *Res publica litterarum*, 5 (1982), 13–28, gives other instances.
36 E.g., *Exposition of I Corinthians*, p. 138.
37 *Lectures on Romans*, pp. 16–17.
38 Ibid., pp. 28–32.

the balance of charity demand; and not to account them ratified and established until they are brought to the measure and rule of charity by the Bishop – who has in his hands, by the grace of God, the power to do so.

Then Colet goes on to pun and play with the concept of the will as a legal document and the will of every Christian, which should be to subject himself to the will of God and his ministers. He quotes the *Decretum*, and Augustine from the *Decretum* – and he breaks into extempore prayer to the Virgin, as he does in his annotations of Ficino.[39]

At Romans IV. 13–14: 'For if they which are of the law be heirs, faith is made void and the promise made of none effect', *abolere* is the verb used in the Vulgate. Colet expatiates by way of Perotti's definition, which insists on the utter blotting out, so that not even odour remains.[40]

Perhaps the most remarkable example of this kind of etymologizing comes at Romans II. 25 and again at IV. 15. It concerns the words *praevaricator* and *praevaricatio*. Colet is, as it were, circling round the question of inward belief and outward observance embodied in Paul's proposition that 'circumcision verily profiteth, if thou keep the law'. If there is transgression, circumcision is reduced to a mere observance. 'Si autem praevaricator legis sis, circumcisio tua praeputium est – thy circumcision is made uncircumcision'. Colet explains *praevaricator* as transgressor, and goes on:

> Now varicate, or prevaricate, is a term derived from the large, swollen, distorted varicose veins that some people have on their legs. Curing these is dangerous and physicians are accustomed to transgress them, that is to pass them by. So prevaricate means transgress. Jurists use the word in another sense – i.e. to mean someone who changes sides and aids an adversary's case by betraying his own, or conceals evidence.

Justinian is a possible source for the legal use of the term, but the derivation and the similitude are both in Perotti – and Colet almost certainly took them from him. Whether one can call this a dependence on Italian thought is a moot point. Valla, it is true, gives the same information about the etymology of *praevaricator*, but Colet, as far as we know, knew Valla only via Erasmus. Erasmus, incidentally, in his new translation of the Epistles, uses *transgressor* for the Vulgate *praevaricator*.[41]

Colet's obligation to another great Italian – Pico della Mirandola – is most pronounced in the unfinished *Letters to Radulphus on the Mosaic Account of the Creation*, a work heavily in debt to Pico's *Heptaplus* of 1489, first published in 1490. Pico left his mark also on the Commentary on Romans VIII, where Colet is talking of the emollient action of the Spirit, in the form

[39] *Exposition of Romans*, pp.109–113.
[40] Ibid., p.143.
[41] *Exposition of Romans*, pp.81–2, 144–5; cf. Valla, *Elegantiae*, VI.50.

of a paraphrase of the proem to Book VII of the *Heptaplus*.[42] This particular book of Pico's work is not used by Colet for his fragmentary treatise on the Creation itself. In his earlier *Exposition of Romans I–V* the beginning of his treatment of Romans III ('What advantage then hath the Jew?'), and in his Abstract of the *Hierarchies*, Colet allows the Jews the advantage not only of the Law in its five books, but also the hidden and true explanation of the Law, and its spiritual meaning. This is supported by a long quotation from Pico's *Apologia*. The passage is re-used in summary in the later *Commentary on Romans*. A Pichian valuation of *Hebraica veritas*, and of the Kabbalah is implied.[43]

Given that Colet had carefully read at least two works of Pico's, it seems likely that he used the *Opera Omnia* of 1496 or 1498 rather than individual editions. That he ignores others such as the *Oratio de hominis dignitate* and the *Conclusiones* themselves may perhaps be explained by the uncongenial optimism of the one concerning the human condition and the overweening intellectual challenge of the other.

It is in the *Letters to Radulphus* that Colet draws most explicitly, extensively and particularly on Pico. How he came on the *Heptaplus*, Pico's sevenfold explanation of the seven days of creation, we do not know. His adaptation of it removes three of Pico's categories. Pico begins with a justification of the allegorical method in line with the practice of Moses, who is said to have found it necessary to accommodate himself to the weaker intellects of the Jews of succeeding ages, and in line with the parables of the New Testament, where a similar process operates. Then comes an account of the successive days of creation of the world, taking the world in its widest sense. First there is the super-celestial, angelic, intellectual world; then the celestial; and then our sublunary world. Anything that exists in any of these must have a corresponding existence in all, though its form may be different. Thus the element of fire, as we know it here on earth, corresponds to the sun of the celestial world; and to the fire of seraphic intelligence in the super-celestial world. Since man is the microcosm, the fourth world, the Biblical account embraces his creation also. As the natural heaven and earth are connected by light, the soul and body of man are connected by spirit. The fifth and sixth worlds are the first four treated as to difference and similarity, and the seventh is the sabbatical, by which all is referred to Christ. Colet removes the final three dimensions and makes four worlds only – of which none is the little world of man, though he expressly states elsewhere in the *Letters* that man is a microcosm.[44] His four are the divine world, which is stable, immoveable, eternal; the angelic which, though eternal is moveable; the celestial which, though also eternal, is sensible; and the earthly, which is both sensible and corruptible.[45]

---

[42] *Lectures on Romans*, p.27.
[43] *Exposition of Romans*, pp.95ff.; *Lectures on Romans*, pp.5–6; *Treatises on the Hierarchies*, pp.109–112; cf. Pico della Mirandola, *Opera* (Basel, 1557), pp.175–8.
[44] *Letters to Radulphus*, p.22.
[45] Ibid., p.10.

In his second letter, Colet names the *Heptaplus*.[46] He also laments his lack of Hebrew, as he was later to lament his lack of Greek. He follows Pico in his characterization of Moses as concealing the higher truths that he was telling and as adapting his surface meaning to the intellectual weakness of those for whom he was writing. Moses is seen as the wise and considerate law-giver, imparting religious knowledge to a barbarous people.[47] Colet calls Moses a poet, citing Origen as his source.[48] It may be that he was drawing in this instance on the *Contra Celsum*, either at first hand or having been told of it by Erasmus. Two other citations of Origen very likely come through Pico or at least show Pico's influence. At Romans III.2: 'Unto them (sc. the Jews) were committed the oracles of God', Colet comments: 'And by this is meant (as Origen would have it) not only the literal law, but also the spiritual interpretations, derived from Moses through a succession of seventy wise men ...'[49] In the Treatise on the *Hierarchies* he cites the same verse from Romans and speaks of 'that explanation and spiritual sense of the whole literal Law, which Moses, as we have said, received from God' as being 'what we call the anagogic sense ... which is the loftier and more divine ...'[50] In each case, Colet identifies this view with Origen and adds that the spiritual sense is known as 'the science of the Kabbalah, or reception'. Origen makes no such identification. Pico is surely the intermediary.

Erasmus's obituary letter for Colet in 1521 specifically mentions Origen as one of the Fathers to whom Colet was especially attracted.[51] There is no doubt of his importance for Erasmus himself. Before the *editio princeps* in Latin of Origen's works in 1512, however, two works only would have been accessible to the Greekless Colet. The *De principiis* existed only in the free Latin version made by Rufinus in late Antiquity. The *Contra Celsum*, which we have seen may have been known to Colet, had been translated by Cristoforo Persona and first published in 1481. Since Pico and Ficino both knew Origen, and Erasmus's Greek in the 1490s was not yet of the standard he attained later, it seems to me highly probable that Colet got most, if not all, his acquaintance with the Greek Father from Pico.[52] It is significant that the name

[46] Ibid.
[47] Ibid.
[48] Ibid., p .27.
[49] *Exposition of Romans*, pp .95–6; cf. *Lectures on Romans*, pp .5–6.
[50] *Treatises on the Hierarchies*, p .112.
[51] *Lives of Vitrier and Colet*, p .22.
[52] On Origen and Judaism, see N .R .M .de Lange, *Origen and the Jews* (Cambridge, 1976); for Origen in the fifteenth and sixteenth centuries, N .Schär, *Das Nachleben des Origenes im Zeitalter des Humanismus* (Basel and Stuttgart, 1979), esp. – for Colet – pp .232, 246–9, 299; and D .P .Walker, 'Origène en France au début du XVIe siècle', *Colloque de Strasbourg 1957* (Paris, 1959), pp .101–119. For Erasmus and Origen, especially in his Paraphrase of and Annotations on Romans (1517ff.), see A .Godin, 'Fonction d'Origène dans la pratique exégétique d'Erasme: Les Annotations sur l'Épître aux Romains', *Histoire de l'exégèse au XVIe siècle*, edited by O .Fatio and P .Fraenkel (Geneva, 1978), pp .17–44; and now Erasmus, *Paraphrases on Romans and Galatians*, edited by R .D .Sider, trans. and annotated by John B .Payne, Albert Rabil Jr., and Warren S .Smith Jr., *Collected Works of Erasmus*, 42 (Toronto, 1984), passim.

Kabbalah is attached to the spiritual explanations by Colet, but not by Origen. Colet's respect for Kabbalah at this time looks like the young respect of intellectual discovery. In 1517 he exclaims to Erasmus, à propos Reuchlin's 'cabbalistic and Pythagorical' speculations, that the imitation of Christ is a more acceptable road to holiness.[53]

Like Pico, Colet takes the first five verses of Genesis as an epitome; and the first exercise of divine power comes with the union of form and matter. This was common doctrine: direct borrowing need not be implied. The first day is divine eternity, universal now: the Augustinian notion of creation not in time but together with time. The second day is eternal time. The waters above the firmament and the waters under the firmament are separated from each other by heaven: the angels are the waters above. Colet here expressly cites Pico,[54] though the notion does not originate with him, but with Origen, continued by Augustine; it becomes standard. Pico, Colet points out, placed the heavenly world midway between the angelic and the earthly. From Pico Colet may also have taken the notion that the plants were created before the stars in order to protect men from a belief that plant growth was astrologically determined.[55]

Of the Hermetic philosophy there are a number of echoes, at least, in Colet. They surely come through Ficino's translation. The *Pimander* must lie behind Colet's characterization of man as *genitura mundi* in the *Letters to Radulphus* and the notion of man as a compound of the universe in his Commentary on I Corinthians.[56]

There remains the question of Italian humanist influence on Colet as an educationist. The debt exists, but it is a debt with a difference, owed to Erasmus and the Erasmian modification of the Italian humanist programme. In Erasmus's own *De ratione studii*, published just as St Paul's School was founded,[57] the debt to Italy is perhaps clearer than it was in the mind of Colet – at least as far as the statutes of the school are concerned. The statutes that Colet wrote for the School, re-founded and newly built to his specifications between 1508 and 1512, reflect – it seems to me – his lifelong dilemma concerning pagan learning and the Italian Renaissance valuation of it. In spite of the disobliging story that Erasmus tells of Colet's mistaking the purpose of the second book of the *Antibarbari* – he was deceived in taking its rhetorical dispraise of pagan literature for sincere deprecation[58] – there can be no doubt of his wish to take advantage of the improvements in knowledge of the classics initiated by Italian humanism. He had a good knowledge of the philosophical works – at least – of Cicero. On the other hand, he had an almost Dominician fear of the impact of pagan thought on tender minds. In

---

[53] Allen, 2 (Oxford, 1910), no.593, p.599; *Collected Works of Erasmus*, 4 (Toronto, 1978), p.398.b
[54] *Letters to Radulphus*, p.12.
[55] Ibid., pp.10–11.
[56] *Letters to Radulphus*, p.22; *Exposition of I Corinthians*, p.133.
[57] See now *Collected Works of Erasmus*, 23–24: *Literary and Educational Writings*, edited by Craig R.Thompson (Toronto, 1978).
[58] *Collected Works of Erasmus*, ed. cit., 23 (1978), pp.8–9.

famous and passionate words his statutes inveigh against 'all barbary all corrupcion all laten adulterate which ignorant blynde folis brought into this worlde and with the same hath distayned and poysenyd the olde laten spech and the varay Romayne tong which in the tyme of Tully and Salust and Virgill and Terence was vsid, whiche also seint Jerome and seint ambrose and seint Austen and many hooly doctors lernyd in theyr tymes. I say that ffylthynesse and all such abusyon which the later blynde worlde brought in which more ratheyr may be callid blotterature thenne litterature I vtterly abbanysh and Exclude oute of this scole'.[59] To equate the Fathers with the pagan classics as guides to good Latin usage is standard Italian humanist practice. Colet appears here to be making no distinction between pagan and Christian in prescribing the reading of 'suych auctours that hathe with wisdome joyned the pure chaste eloquence'. Just previously to these words, however, he had stated his purpose in founding the school and given a list of specific set books:

> my entent is by thys scole specially to incresse knowlege and worshipping of god and oure lorde Crist Jesu and good Cristen lyff and maners in the Children And for that entent I will the Chyldren lerne ffirst aboue all the Cathechyzon in English and after the accidence that I made ... and thanne Institutum Christiani homines [sic] which that lernyd Erasmus made at my request and the boke called Copia of the same Erasmus And thenne other auctours Christian as lactancius prudentius and proba and sedulius and Juvencus and Baptista Mantua-nus ...[60]

In all these authors pagan content and pagan language has been disinfected by specifically Christian use. Colet's idea of chasteness of Latin usage is very far from that of the professional humanist. If it can be said with some truth that Colet's foundation of St Paul's School, with its emphasis on Greek as well as on Latin, marks the establishment of the Vallan-Erasmian idea of education in England, it must be said also that the statutes, at least, have more of Erasmus in them than of Valla, and more still of Colet himself. It remains true, nevertheless, that without the Italian contribution to his make-up, whether it came at first, second or third hand, Colet would not have required, and still less rewarded, the considerable effort of study. No Englishman of his time, or of a good time after, grappled so hard or so earnestly with the Florentine Platonists. This is the index of a striving, earnest, struggling character, seeking its own version of *pietas litterata*. The contribution of France to his intellectual and spiritual make-up, and especially the contribution of Lefèvre d'Étaples, has yet to be fully explored.[61] When that is done, we shall have a better chance of seeing Colet whole.

---

[59] Lupton, *Life of Colet* (London, 1887), pp. 279–80.

[60] Ibid.

[61] Andrew Brown tells me that the text of the Pauline Epistles written out by Meghen in British Library Royal MS 1.D.XI–XV is that of Lefèvre. If it was transcribed from a printed book, as seems virtually certain, it must have been written in 1512 or later. On palaeographical grounds (Brown, art. cit. n. 16 above) it cannot be later than 1517.